A
HISTORY
OF THE
PHILIPPINES

A
HISTORY
OF THE
PHILIPPINES

From Indios Bravos to Filipinos

Luis H. Francia

THE OVERLOOK PRESS
New York

First published in hardcover in the United States in 2010 by

The Overlook Press, Peter Mayer Publishers, Inc.
141 Wooster Street
New York, NY 10012
www.overlookpress.com

Cataloging-in-Publication Data is available from the Library of Congress

Book design and type formatting by Bernard Schleifer
Manufactured in the United States of America
ISBN 978-1-59020-285-2
FIRST EDITION
1 3 5 7 9 10 8 6 4 2

To Filipinos Everywhere

CONTENTS

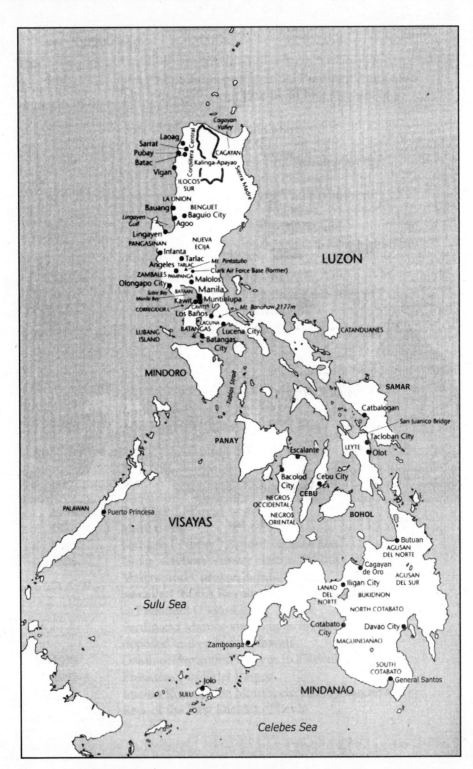

Laoag
Sarrat
Pubay
Batac
Vigan

Cagayan
Valley

Cordillera Central

CAGAYAN

Kalinga-Apayao

ILOCOS
SUR

Sierra Madre

LA UNION

Bauang
Baguio City
Agoo
Lingayen

BENGUET

LUZON

*Lingayen
Gulf*

PANGASINAN

NUEVA
ECIJA

Infanta

Tarlac   *Mt. Pinatubo*
Angeles   TARLAC
ZAMBALES PAMPANGA Clark Air Force Base (former)
Olongapo City Malolos
BATAAN Manila
Subic Bay
Manila Bay Kawit Muntinlupa
CAVITE   *Mt. Banahaw 2177m*
CORREGIDOR I.
Los Baños
LAGUNA
BATANGAS Lucena City
LUBANG
ISLAND Batangas
City

MINDORO

CATANDUANES

SAMAR

Catbalogan

San Juanico Bridge

Tacloban City
Olot

Tablas Strait

LEYTE

PANAY

Escalante

Bacolod
City

Cebu City

CEBU

NEGROS
OCCIDENTAL

BOHOL

NEGROS
ORIENTAL

PALAWAN   Puerto Princesa

VISAYAS

Butuan
AGUSAN
DEL NORTE

Cagayan
de Oro

AGUSAN
DEL SUR

Sulu Sea

LANAO
DEL
NORTE

Iligan City

BUKIDNON

NORTH COTABATO

Cotabato
City

Davao City

MAGUINDANAO

Zamboanga

SOUTH
COTABATO

Jolo

General Santos

SULU

MINDANAO

Celebes Sea

THE PHILIPPINES

INTRODUCTION

N O COUNTRY IS AN ISLAND, THOUGH THE COUNTRY THAT IS THE subject of this book, the Philippines, claims as its territory more than 7,000 islands. On the eastern edge of insular Southeast Asia, these islands stretch for more than 1,150 miles, bookended in the north by Taiwan and in the south by Indonesia and Brunei. The mighty Pacific Ocean interposes itself between the archipelago and North and South America on the other side of the globe, with Hawai'i at roughly midpoint. To the west the South China Sea links the Philippines to continental Southeast Asian countries, among them Vietnam, Malaysia, and Thailand.

As a republic, it is barely more than six decades old, gaining emancipation from U.S. colonial rule in 1946, less than a year after Japan surrendered and brought the Pacific War to a halt. From 1946 to 1950, even as the United States and the Soviet Union were defining the world through the prism of the Cold War and their competing ideologies, the colonial order in Asia was disintegrating. India and Pakistan sprung into bloody being, twins separated at birth in 1947. Two years later, in 1949, the world took notice of yet another quarrelsome pair: Mao Tse-tung and his Communist army, having defeated the Nationalists under Chiang Kai-shek, lay the foundation of the People's Republic of China—and indirectly, of the Republic of China in Taiwan, Chiang having fled across the straits in defeat. At the end of the same year, the Dutch recognized Indonesia as a sovereign nation.

Gaining independence, while exhilarating, was no panacea for a Southeast Asian archipelago that had continuously been occupied by a foreign power since 1565. Along with the metaphysical thrill, and challenge, of managing one's own destiny, one still had to pay bills (as well as pass them). There were hungry mouths to feed, an economy and infrastructure to build and rebuild, and institutions of governance to be either revamped or set up. The devastation wrought by World War II made recovery an excruciatingly difficult task. The fact that a triumphalist United States imposed certain inequitable conditions as a sine qua non of independence rendered establishing bona fide sovereignty an even harder challenge. What the great Indonesian writer Pramoedya Ananta Toer, in his *Child of All Nations*, said bears repeating: "As to defining what is colonial, isn't it just the conditions insisted upon by a victorious nation over the defeated nation so that the latter may give the victor sustenance—conditions that are made possible by the sharpness and might of weapons?"

Nevertheless, the Philippine republic could now choose its own path. The odyssey to that point had been long and hard and violent. Though founded in 1898, the republic had seen its flowering delayed because of two wars: the Spanish-American War, which the United States won handily; and the subsequent 1899 Philippine-American War, when the revolutionary government under General Emilio Aguinaldo refused to accept its role as booty for the Americans. It was a brutal conflict that lasted a decade and resulted in U.S. occupation for half a century. And while 1946 signaled the birth of a nation, one of the first to take its place in the ranks of post-colonial states, the Philippines was indelibly marked by the DNA of colonialism. How could it be otherwise? Embedded and incarnated endlessly over the course of four hundred years, what and who had been strangers from foreign shores—to slightly alter Ronald Takaki's memorable phrase—had metamorphosed into the familiar. The country's very name encapsulates its colonial history. The Anglicized "Philippines" or the Spanish "Filipinas" is forever a reminder that this Southeast Asian archipelago was so named in 1543 by Ruy López de Villalobos in honor of the sixteenth century Spanish crown prince who would in 1556 become King Felipe II.

There have been ill-fated attempts to toss out the Hispanic appellation and adopt a new one. The nineteenth-century revolutionary General Artemio Ricarte once proposed naming the country the Rizaline Islands, after its foremost national hero, José Rizal (with Filipinos henceforth to be known as Rizalinos). In 1978, during martial law, Ferdinand Marcos half-heartedly tried through the *Batasan Pambansa*, or National Assembly, to rename the nation "*Maharlika*," a Tagalog word meaning nobility—part of his skewed notion of aristocratic lineage and dressed-up history. (One foreign writer, eager to believe the exotic Orientalist bit fed to him by some clever jokers, wrote that it was a glorified term for the penis.) Neither name gained much traction; Filipinos of all ideological stripes, most of whom bore and continue to bear Hispanic names, were simply too used to the moniker to seriously consider changing it. Besides, whether one acknowledged it or not, by overstaying its welcome, Spain provoked the formation of a nationalist consciousness. Just as the name New York recalls its partly English provenance (replacing the Dutch Nieuw Amsterdam), so too does Las Islas Filipinas reflect the partly Hispanic roots of Filipino nationhood.

This book is a modest endeavor to introduce the reader with little or no knowledge of this Southeast Asian country to the realities that have marked the journey of becoming Filipino, from pre-colonial times to the first decade of the second millennium. No attempt at a definitive history is being made here; a mission impossible, at any rate. And let me be the first to acknowledge that this is an incomplete history, as every history must be. Significant new archaeological finds may and will probably be made; new interpretations will be offered, as well they should be. For what is past never stays put and lives on in us; it is, according to the late Filipino historian Renato Constantino, a "continuing past," illuminating the present just as surely as light from a distant star. Nevertheless I believe that this book summarizes clearly and concisely the different forces that have, for better or worse, transformed an archipelago into a republic, and imparted to its inhabitants a notion, however imperfect, of a nation.

Who were the Indios Bravos? Brilliant nineteenth-century polymath, doctor, bon vivant, and writer José Rizal and his friends gave themselves the name, half in jest and half in all seriousness, after having watched a Wild West show in Paris in 1889. *Indio*, of course, was the disparaging term the Spanish used for the indigenous populations in their colonies. Rizal and these other expatriate *ilustrados*, or the enlightened ones, as they were referred to, admired both the excellent horsemanship and the dignity of the Native American performers—and recognized in them kindred spirits. They were indeed brave Indians, their peculiar status in the world mirroring somewhat that of the Filipinos themselves, who were highly critical of the Spanish colonial regime in Manila and who in Madrid and Barcelona advocated far-reaching reforms at the same time that they professed loyalty to Mother Spain. By appropriating the term meant to put them in their place, Los Indios Bravos were signaling the Spanish their intent to take charge of their own destiny. It was a highly symbolic act, representing a paradigmatic shift in the burgeoning nationalist consciousness.

In addition, the term resonates for me, personally. I first heard the term when I barely had any inkling of the richness, complexity, and contradictions of the history behind it. Los Indios Bravos was a café my late oldest brother Henry and sister-in-law Beatriz Romualdez, along with some writer friends, opened in the 1960s in the then-genteel district of Malate, once a suburb of old Manila. The café interior was a conscious effort to re-create a proper nineteenth-century literary salon, or *tertulia*, though this being the 1960s, the zeitgeist could hardly be called genteel. Café Los Indios Bravos was filled with bohemians; argumentative students, myself included, flush with radical ideas if not with cash, aiming to remake the world, or simply being on the make; writers of every stripe; dowagers hoping for a Roman spring; American and European expatriates; and fashionistas. We all trooped to Los Indios Bravos; in a sense we were Indios Bravos ourselves, not just intensely aware of but embodying the legacies of the Spanish and the North Americans, in our lives and ways of thinking, even in our blood—to be wrestled with, confronted, transformed, but not eliminated. Only the besotted romantic could ever believe that the imprint of four centuries of foreign presence could be cleansed by the waters of some imaginary pre-colonial river Jordan. For better or worse, the adaptability of the modern Filipino can be traced to the age-old commingling of the foreign and the familiar, resulting in a decidedly mestizo culture.

As did Andrés Bonifacio, Macario Sakay, and other working-class stalwarts of the 1896 Revolution against Spain (who wrestled with the same issues as the *ilustrados* but with a pronounced urgency given that they were in a more precarious position physically, socially, and financially), Rizal and his peers foreshadowed the existential dilemma of the contemporary Filipino/a who must grapple with divided loyalties and with a central government, no longer Spanish (nor American) but made up of fellow citizens, whose policies and actuations are often at odds with the well-being of the electorate.

In a very basic sense, these islanders who dared to cast themselves as separate from Spain also viewed themselves as bound together not simply by their opposition to colonial rule but by their affinities for one another, artificial as these affinities might have seemed. They may not necessarily have expressed themselves in this manner but their approach to history was, I believe, as an inventive but necessary fiction. Those who have assailed and continue to assail the concept of a collective identity based on a construct cobbled together from myriad loyalties, languages, and geographic boundaries are right to do so. Yet their very insistence only proves that veracity can be crippling and lead paradoxically to an intellectual and spiritual cul de sac. Even when regimented by logic, facts sans imagination remain limp and bloodless. But the *idea* of a nation can inspirit dry facts by creating space for a transcendent imagination. And what is colonialism finally but the denial of space—geographic, political, and psychological—for the collective imagination of a people?

The gap between the colonial governors—the target of reformist zeal and revolutionary ire—and the governed, objects of colonial desire, still exists, still yawns dangerously. Spanish rule served as the centripetal force that yoked together three clusters of islands: Luzon, Visayas, and Mindanao. Without it, these islands may have gone their separate ways as independent states or been subsumed in part or in toto by a neighboring nation such as Indonesia or Malaysia. Colonialism then, in its various facets, its effects and aftereffects, including indigenous resistance, is the book's main focus. Even the condition of the Muslim, the *Moro* or Moor, a reluctant, some would say second-class, member of the Philippine polity, has been shaped almost as much by colonialism's permanent legacy as by Islam: the Christianization of the islands, coming some seventy odd years after Ferdinand and Isabella, *Los Reyes Catolicos*, had in 1492 reclaimed Granada and finally driven out the Moors from Al-Andalus, the urbane and tolerant (more so than the Catholic monarchs) kingdom that ruled the southern part of the Iberian peninsula for seven hundred years. The reunification of the different Spanish kingdoms unforgivingly cast the Moor as the unassimilable Other. And so was he assigned that role in Spain's only Asian colony, particularly in Mindanao. While church and state are formally separate in today's republic, the reality is that the former still wields considerable power not too far off from the dominant role it once exercised for more than three centuries in the islands, Catholic crucifixes in a mostly minareted sea. So intertwined with the state was the Spanish colonial church that the late Filipino diplomat-cum-writer León María Guerrero—a modern-day ilustrado himself—could open *The First Filipino*, his 1961 biography of Rizal, with a somewhat exaggerated but fairly accurate summation: "The Spanish history of the Philippines begins and ends with the friar."

Out of the five centuries the book spans, from the sixteenth to the first decade of the twenty-first century, nearly four hundred years saw three foreign powers separately at the helm: Spain, the United States, and Japan (this last for barely more than three years). For all the cultural, racial, and political differences among the three, they exhibited the same attitude towards the indigenous population: couched in official rhetoric, the natives were to be saved from themselves—whether through Spanish Catholicism or U.S. democracy or Japanese asceticism; unofficially, the Indios constituted a resource to be cultivated, exploited, made use of, particularly in the extraction of bounty from islands rich in natural resources.

The Indios who were to be "bettered" didn't exactly roll over and play along. They resisted individually or collectively. They moved out of population centers into the thickly forested interior, or to the mountains. They often took up arms against their would-be exploiters. Until the 1896 Revolution, however, rebellions were local and easily quelled, with some notable exceptions. On the other hand, one of the characteristics of any colonial occupation has been the collaboration of certain of the colonized with the colonizer, positing themselves as mediators. They almost always came from the chiefly class. Their role, after all, was to deal with outside forces—a role that often turned out to be materially rewarding and thus prone to corruption.

One reason, perhaps, that the contemporary body politic survives and even flourishes, in spite of the many shortcomings of the state, is that its members have become so habituated over the centuries of dealing with governments they couldn't quite trust, that they have come to rely on informal networks, on their respective clans and local patronage, rather than on public institutions. There has always been a tradeoff between the national leadership, whether colonial or post-colonial, and local leaders, with the latter acting as go-betweens between the former and their own constituents. The blessings of the state, thus, have almost always flowed down through the calculated beneficence of individual but powerful clan leaders, going back all the way to when the *datus* or chiefs ruled over the *barangay*, the pre-Hispanic foundational social and political unit whose borders were coterminous with that of the clan. With its roots therefore in pre-colonial times, the political sphere has almost always been overwhelmed by the personal.

Aside from the first chapter, which looks at what life in the pre-Hispanic archipelago may have been like, the initial half of this book deals with both the formal Spanish and U.S. colonial periods, including the World War II occupation by the Japanese Imperial Army. The other half examines a post-World War II, post-colonial Philippines, ending in 2009, with national elections slated to take place in May of 2010. My intent was to construct a historical narrative that would be more than just a notation of events, signal dates, and relevant personages; that would serve as a useful guide in understanding what it is we see when we cast our eyes on that uniquely situated and multifaceted republic and simultaneously push against what surrounds the Filipino in the diaspora: the anonymity and oblivion against which there is, as Kierkegaard wrote, "no weapon so dangerous as the art of remembering." To all those for whom remembering remains a vital, even courageous, act, I offer *A History of the Philippines: From Indios Bravos to Filipinos.*

In the writing of this book, I was immensely aided by the critical and peerless eye of Vicente Rafael, as well as, for certain sections, by Andrew Hsiao and Allan Isaac. My older brother Joseph H. Francia, an economist and college professor, helped me understand some basic truths about the Philippine economy. My wife Midori Yamamura provided, as always, much-needed encouragement and sustenance while my editor Juliet Grames, who first proposed the idea of the book, carried out the role of General Reader conscientiously. The Asian/Pacific/American Institute at New York University helped fund a research trip to Manila. To them all, my heartfelt thanks, *mil gracias, domo arigato, maraming salamat.* Whatever shortcomings the book may have are to be attributed solely to me.

—LUIS H. FRANCIA
New York City

A
HISTORY
OF THE
PHILIPPINES

1. THE ISLANDS BEFORE THE CROSS: PRE-1521

"Hail! In the Saka-year 822 [900 C.E.], in the month of March-April, according to the astronomer, the 4th day of the dark half of the moon, on Monday, At that time, Lady Angkatan, together with her relative, Bukah, the child of His Honor Namwran, was given, as a special favor, a document of full acquittal by the chief and commander of Tundun, the former Leader of Pailah, Jayadewa, to the effect that His Honor Namwran through the Honorable Scribe, was totally cleared of a debt to the amount of 1 kati and 8 suwarna, in the presence of His Honor, the Leader of Puliran, Kasumuran; His Honor, the Leader of Pailah, namely Ganasakti,; and His Honor, the Leader of Binwagan, Bisruta. And His Honor Namwran with his whole family on orders of the Chief of Dewata representing the Chief of Mdang, because of his loyalty as a subject of the Chief, therefore all descendants of His Honor Namwran have been cleared of the whole debt that His Honor owed the Chief of Dewata. This document is issued in case there is someone, whosoever, some time in the future who will state that the debt is not yet acquitted of His Honor . . ."

> —The Laguna Copperplate Inscription, translated by Antoon Postma, quoted in E.P. Pataññe, *The Philippines in the Sixth to the Sixteenth Centuries*

THE FULL STORY BEHIND THE LAGUNA COPPERPLATE INSCRIPTION (LCI) may never be known. Discovered in 1989 buried in a riverbank in Laguna Province, south of Manila, the LCI was drawn up in 900 C.E., the equivalent of the Sanskrit calendar date inscribed on it—more than five hundred years before the *barangay* (village or settlement) of Maynila turned into a Muslim community, and more than six centuries before the Europeans first learned of the archipelago's existence. The inscription—the oldest known document of pre-Hispanic times in the Philippine archipelago—is vital to understanding how people in the islands, at least in certain parts, lived and what kind of society or societies they might have constructed.

The LCI writing bears remarkable similarities to the ancient Kawi script of Indonesia. Analyses by experts in both ancient Philippine and Indonesian scripts reveal a language that contained not only Sanskrit but also old Javanese, old Malay, and old Tagalog words. It antedates *baybayin*, the native script in use when the Spanish came calling in the sixteenth century, one that, with variations in alphabet according to the region, essentially consisted of twenty letters. The LCI script, no longer extant, lingered on in the baybayin's formative influences such as Sanskrit and Arabic. With the advent of the Spanish, and the intervention primarily of the friars, the Castilian alphabet replaced the native scripts, but those communities in the interior that managed to steer clear of Spanish rule and the new faith kept their old systems of writing. A form of baybayin can still be seen, for instance, in the script of the Hanunoo Mangyan of Mindoro Island, off the southwestern coast of Luzon, a tribe that continues to inscribe on bamboo a form of its poetry known as the *ambahan*, with seven-syllable lines meant primarily to be chanted.

The copperplate mentions place names that still exist in latter-day Bulacan, a province abutting the northern edge of Tondo, another ancient settlement that faced Maynila across the Pasig River delta. More significantly, it persuasively attests to the Hindu influence of the Sumatra-based Srivijaya empire, which had spread beyond the central part of the Philippine archipelago—and to which the colonists had affixed the name "Visayas"—to the strategically located barangays of Tondo and Maynila, where the river empties out onto a magnificent bay and the South China Sea. Through the two barangays, which would have controlled river traffic, some form of Hindu influence would have spread to other areas in Luzon where the Tagalogs (the principal tribe of Tondo and Maynila) were also dominant. Indeed, modern-day Tagalog possesses words that are Sanskrit in origin: *budhi* (conscience), *mukha* (face), *guro* (teacher), *tala* (star), *dukha* (needy), *diwata* (muse, goddess), among them.

Perhaps most tellingly, the LCI indicates the crucial role that slavery played in barangay pre-colonial life. Lady Angkatan, Bukah, son of Namwran, and members of their immediate family were almost certainly debt slaves, and this document would have given them a tremendous sense of relief. We will never know whether Lady Angkatan was Namwran's widow, aunt, mother, or sister; nor what the Honorable Namwran did to acquit the family of this debt. Had he distinguished himself in battle, giving up his life for the sake of his chief? Or was it Bukah who bore arms bravely? It seems clear that this was a seemingly well-born family that through misfortune or Namwran's misguided business dealings found itself unable to pay back a substantial loan.

Now, they could hold their heads high once more. In a sense, they were fortunate to have been indebted to the paramount chief of their clan. It would have been worse had they been abducted by their clan enemies or by tattooed raiders from the Visayas, the cluster of islands in the archipelago's center, whom the Spanish called *pintados*, or painted ones. The number and intricacy of a Visayan warrior's tattoos signaled to friend and foe alike his strength and abilities as a warrior. More than land or goods, slaves were a sure sign of one's wealth and status, especially slaves captured in raiding parties on other barangays. As war booty, not only were they tangible proof of a datu's leadership and martial prowess (more so than homegrown, as it were, slaves), they were more likely to be treated as disposable property, sometimes put to death when the master moved on to the next world.

Another basis of slavery was as punishment for crimes. These included bearing false witness against someone; the transgression of taboo customs, such as, according to the sixteenth-century account of the Jesuit Pedro Chirino, "failure to preserve silence for the dead" or "happening to pass in front of a chief who was bathing"; murder; adultery; or failing to do one's duty (during war, for instance) when the chief, or datu, asked for it. Such crimes could be forgiven if the transgressor could pay the proper fee of goods or gold to the aggrieved party.

Colonial rule under the Spanish, which lasted for 333 years, from 1565 to 1898, eliminated certain aspects of barangay life, such as slavery, though modern-day critics might assert that slavery persists in disguised forms in today's highly inequitable society; introduced Christianity and Western concepts such as bureaucratic state rule and private property; and modified, if not strengthened, some features of pre-colonial ways of living, e.g., the melding of the private and public spheres of life.

In the archipelago, the Iberians had come upon different societies, at once static and dynamic, with well-defined frameworks within which the world made sense. To the Spanish, of course, infected with an overbearing sense of racial superiority and entitlement, the native way of life was savage and therefore had to be supplanted with the European notion of civilization. The conquistador Miguel de Legazpi, who led the 1565 expedition that successfully brought most of the islands under the dominion of the Spanish Crown, after grudgingly noting that the island men treated and loved their wives well, summed up rather succinctly what he and most of his compatriots really thought: "They are all barbarians and have no manners or politeness."

What kind of archipelagic societies did the Spanish first encounter? What were the various island communities like before the advent of the West? How did the pre-Hispanic Filipinos relate to the rest of Southeast Asia? To draw a portrait, which must of necessity be forever incomplete since history is a never-ending process of revisions and counter-revisions, one needs to begin with geography, for geography helps shape destiny. It is a major element in determining how history and hierarchy in the islands evolved.

The archipelago known today as the Republic of the Philippines lies on the northeastern rim of Southeast Asia, a necklace of 7,107 isles strung from north to south over 1,152 miles, situated between the vast and mighty Pacific Ocean to the east and the gentler, lesser South China Sea to the west. The islands cover a total area of 115,831 square miles, roughly the same size as Italy. Only 2,773 of the islands bear names, with elongated Luzon in the north the largest, and Mindanao to the south the next in size. These two islands constitute two-thirds of the country's land mass. Between them are the Visayan Islands, consisting mainly of Samar, Leyte, Cebu, Negros, Bohol, and Panay. The western edge of the country is taken up by the mini-archipelago of Palawan Province, made up of the island of Palawan and 1,700 satellite isles.

This semi-tropical island chain has only two—but very distinct—seasons: dry and wet. The northern and eastern regions lie within the typhoon belt: areas directly affected by storms that come raging out of the Pacific during the latter half of the year. On the average, typhoons maul the eastern Visayas and Luzon twenty times annually, at one time prompting a frustrated lawmaker to propose a bill outlawing them. In the Cordilleras of Northern Luzon the weather can be downright chilly, when winds from as far north as Siberia, along with migratory birds, travel south. With the typhoons breaking against the eastern flanks of mountain ranges, there is less of a pronounced dry season on the Pacific side. Hence, more people and businesses reside in the western part of the country, rendering the west more industrialized and economically developed.

Island geography owes much of its ruggedness to being part of the Pacific Rim of Fire, a line of volcanic formations that extend, in the northern hemisphere, from Alaska and the Aleutian Islands to Japan, the Philippines, and Indonesia. The Philippines contains thirty-seven volcanoes, the majority thankfully dormant, though one volcano blowing its top is always a reminder that others could follow suit. Such was the case with Mt. Pinatubo which, six hundred years after its last awakening, erupted in 1991 with such ferocity over five days that gaseous plumes ascended to as high up as twenty-four miles and spewed out seven cubic kilometers of ash and rock—the worst such eruption in the country's history and possibly of the twentieth century. On the other hand, volcanic deposits are one reason the land is fertile, generating life where once it buried it.

East of the archipelago, off the coast of northeastern Luzon south to Halmahera Island in Indonesia, the Philippine Deep, also known as the Mindanao Trench, stretches for close to a thousand miles, measuring roughly nineteen miles across. At its deepest it extends 34,850 feet below sea level—deeper than Mt. Everest is tall. The Philippine Deep rests on the Eurasian and Philippine Sea tectonic plates, which constantly shift and grind against each other.

As an entity that gained political independence only in 1946, the nation is quite young, a little more than six decades old. Geologically, however, it is a different story. Large swaths of Luzon and Mindanao are more than 25 million years old, while the age of the rest of the country varies, from 100,000 to 10 million years old. During the late Pleistocene era, some islands were linked to the Asian mainland; among these were Palawan, Mindoro, and Panay. Palawan, having once been part of Borneo, has flora and fauna not found in the rest of the country. Evolution and the formation of a rather isolated archipelago has resulted in an astonishing biodiversity over a landmass of 30 million hectares, or 66 million acres, with a number of endemic species, e.g., 70 percent of its reptiles and 44 percent of its avian creatures are not to be found anywhere else.

However, the rate of population growth is quite high. In 2008, with a population of 90 million, it was 2 percent a year, in large part due to an exceedingly influential and conservative Catholic hierarchy that rails against government-sponsored family planning. (In contrast, the 2008 rate for the United States was less than 1 percent.) This, along with a depressed economy, has resulted, perhaps most critically, in an environment continually under siege. Many species have a tenuous hold on life, as they require primary-forest habitats. Such is the case with the Philippine Eagle, more popularly known as the monkey-eating eagle—a large and magnificent avian predator with a wingspan of nearly seven feet. A pair needs approximately twenty-five to fifty square miles of forest to sustain themselves and to propagate.

AS WE WERE: PRE-COLONIAL BARANGAY SOCIETY

It was long held as common wisdom that populations in the archipelago were the result of migrations that took place in neat, successive waves, between 30,000 B.C.E. and 200 B.C.E.—the last wave composed of Malays from the south who had more advanced forms of metallurgy and crafts, such as the weaving of cloth and the manufacture of glass ornaments. This theory's biggest proponent was the late American anthropologist H. Otley Beyer, at one time head of the anthropology department at the University of the Philippines, who based his conclusions on pioneering fieldwork done from the 1920s to the early 1940s.

While the artifacts recovered from the field were indeed valuable, his theory has since fallen out of favor. According to linguists, various languages were already being spoken throughout the archipelago thousands of years ago. Too, archaeological evidence reveals that trade was flourishing in the region in the first millennium B.C.E., probably even earlier—both pointing to the fact that groups of people of different origins came and stayed or went, sometimes in larger numbers, sometimes in smaller, but never so methodically as envisioned in Beyer's grand theory.

There seem to have been at least two discrete movements of people that, over time, dispersed through insular Southeast Asia: the Australoids, characterized by dark pigmentation, and the Austronesians, or brown-skinned peoples, who started to arrive about six millennia ago, from the south via Borneo and Indonesia, and the north from southern China and Taiwan. Later migrations included people from Champa, a Hinduized kingdom of seafarers and traders in southern and central Vietnam that flourished from the seventh century to the fifteenth century C.E.

It wasn't just one way, apparently. The eminent archaeologist Wilhelm G. Solheim II adds another layer to this diffusion when he suggests that the cultures of the natives of Southeast Asia, whom he calls Nusantao, and their descendants, had their beginnings in, or at the very least were influenced by, maritime-oriented tribes of insular Southeast Asia, dating to 5000 B.C.E. or even earlier. Islanders came and went, as did the coastal dwellers of mainland eastern Asia, the twain meeting—and mating—repeatedly over the course of millennia.

According to Solheim, long-distance seafaring vessels known as *balangay* and outfitted with innovative bamboo outriggers may have been devised about 4000 B.C.E., initiating major outmigrations by water. The buoyant outriggers helped balance the shallow-draft vessel while at the same time enabling it to navigate smoothly and speedily over the water—a feature remarked upon in later accounts of European navigators used to bulkier and slower ships. The larger ones, equipped with sails, could be used in war as well, with rowers on each side. These war vessels, known variously as *karakoas* and *prahus*, had platforms above the outriggers upon which as many as a hundred warriors could stand.

By the third millennium B.C.E., these migrations had resulted in settlements in both the Indonesian and Philippine archipelagos. By the second millennium B.C.E., they had gone as far west as Madagascar, off the eastern coast of Africa. Human settlements known as *barangays*, after the outriggered boats, were thus firmly in place in the Philippines well before the Spanish arrived, with a number of larger barangays trading with foreign ships that plied Southeast Asian waters.

While archaeological evidence attests to human presence in the archipelago as far back as 250,000 years ago, the earliest known human settlements were in caves on the southern reaches of long, dagger-shaped Palawan Island. Evidence suggests that the caves were continuously inhabited from 50,000 years ago, during the Pleistocene Age, until 9,000 B.C.E.—one vanguard of the seafaring peoples who formed the main matrix of contemporary populations. Known as the Tabon Caves and set into ocean-facing cliffs, they would have afforded a clear view of waterborne visitors and provided easy access to the waters themselves. Possibly the oldest *Homo sapiens* fossil in Southeast Asia, nicknamed the Tabon Man, was unearthed here, carbon-dated to 47,000 years ago. But the Tabon Man was more than one individual, the finds including a skullcap, jawbones, teeth, and bone fragments, with one tibia being the oldest fossil. The Tabon Man appears to have had Negritoid characteristics—strengthening the argument that the islands were originally inhabited by the Australoids, ancestors of the modern-day Negritos, otherwise known as the Agta, Aeta, or Ati. Food gatherers and hunters, the Tabon men and women, devising necessary strategies of survival, progressed from basic flake tools to instruments such as adzes and axes.

Like the Tabon Cave dwellers, most of the islanders lived by or close to water, whether ocean, river, or lake—sources of abundant food. Water was obviously the only transportation route to other islands, and these dwellers by the water engaged in brisk trade not just with nearby isles, but with ports as disparate as those on the southern coast of China and the Straits of Malacca. Larger population centers sprung up due to trade and, in some areas, most notably in Mindanao, the insistent call of Islam. But there were no fiercely ambitious warlords, no Tokugawa or Genghis Khan, who set out to unify many fiefdoms. Until the Spanish appeared on the horizon, no nation-state existed, only a far-flung collection of islands untroubled by the notion of a center.

Trade

The archipelago formed the outer edges of an established trade circle, one that extended from the Persian Gulf in the Middle East to Southern China, thus encompassing Southeast Asia. It was at its most active from the seventh to the ninth century C.E., and antedated European invasion in the sixteenth century. Chinese records from 671 contain references to Persian ships. Later accounts, including Japanese ones, mention not just the Persians but Indians and Malays as well, all trading at Canton. By 851, this trade route was well-established, with ships making calls at India's Malabar Coast, the Nicobar Islands, the Malay Peninsula, passing through the Straits of Malacca, with more calls at Cambodia and Vietnam, before heading to Canton. According to historian Janet Abu-Lughod, in her book *Before European Hegemony*, "The easternmost circuit was Chinese 'space,' the sea that joined the east coast of Indochina and the northern shore of Java with the great ports of South China being under the hegemony of the Sung and Yuan navies. This . . . was the domain par excellence of what scholars have called the tribute trade."

Of the pre-colonial Philippine ports that formed part of this trading world, Butuan was one of the most active, probably the center of trade and commerce in the islands during the eleventh century. Situated on the northwestern coast of Mindanao by the Agusan River, Butuan was a putative city-state by October 1003, the first pre-Hispanic Philippine barangay known to formally deal with Imperial China when it sent two envoys by the names of Lihiyan and Jiaminan (the names suggest Sinicization) to Beijing, to recognize the Divine Son of Heaven as undisputed sovereign, and, not coincidentally, to petition for the right to trade. The Butuan traders likely would have brought tropical hardwoods, beeswax, cinnamon, civet cats, cowry shells, abaca, and gold. Some of these would have been gifts for the royal court. Butuan also traded with the kingdom of Champa. Between 900 and 1200 C.E., in addition to Butuan, the Champa established trading outposts in Sulu. By the fifteenth century, 400 to 500 junks from Cambodia, Champa, and southern China were visiting the islands annually.

Yet, while situated strategically between the Persian Gulf and China, thus ensuing their value as transit points, Southeast Asian pre-colonial entrepots were not the region's dominant players. They acted mostly as sources for raw materials, or as transshipment centers, of which the most valuable was the port of Malacca. (Malacca was also a major slave market, where slave raiders brought their human cargo, abducted from various coastal towns in Southeast Asia, to be sold to customers as varied as merchants looking for laborers and ship captains wanting to supplement their crews.) It had four harbormasters for ships originating from as near as Sumatra and Java, as far west as Persia, and as far north as the Ryu Kyu Islands and China. Commercial traffic along the Straits of Malacca thus helped shape the burgeoning global trade, especially during the thirteenth and fourteenth centuries.

According to William Henry Scott, in *Barangay: Sixteenth Century Philippine Culture and Society*, "It was in Malacca that Europeans"—specifically, the Portuguese—"first met Filipinos," a decade before the Spanish expedition led by the Portuguese navigator Ferdinand Magellan came across the archipelago in 1521. These pre-Hispanic Filipinos were called "Luzones," from the island whence they had come. The Luzones were known not only as merchants and traders but also as fierce mercenaries active in various military campaigns in the region, employed, for instance, by the Achenese and the Burmese kings, or crewing on pirate ships. West of Malacca, on the coast, was a community of 500 Tagalogs, while in Malacca itself, according to Scott, "they had their own shops and included a number of prominent businessmen."

The Portuguese took over Malacca in 1511, with Magellan as part of the conquering force. It was in Malacca that he purchased a young Malay slave he had christened Enrique, who would prove to be an invaluable asset when, ten years later, the Spanish exploratory fleet Magellan headed came across the islands later to be called the Philippines. It is therefore not unreasonable to assume that even before 1521, Magellan and the Portuguese knew of the Philippine archipelago, east and northeast of the Malay Peninsula.

The region was rich in natural resources, from minerals to spices to forest and maritime products, and this, coupled with rising demand from countries outside the region, ensured an almost perfect fit among supplier, manufacturer, and consumer. In short, as Abu-Lughod points out, Malacca was ideally located as a comprador site, just as Hong Kong and Singapore are now. In this trade world, the Chinese were active, if not dominant, players. At one time the Middle Kingdom commanded an enormous fleet—the so-called Treasure Fleet, under the command of a seven-foot-tall eunuch, Cheng Ho. On its initial voyage in 1405, the fleet was made up of 27,800 men and 1,500 vessels, dwarfing any of the European fleets then. The Chinese had as their sole aim forging trade relations with their Asian neighbors. On several voyages, the Chinese fleet sailed to Africa and the Persian Gulf, and points between, setting up a trading network that built on previous outposts. Unlike the European expansionists later on, the Middle Kingdom had no imperialist ambitions, disdaining to rule over the non-Chinese, whom they dismissed as barbarians—except for the Koreans, the Japanese, and the Annamese.

The dynamics of this trade system underwent a drastic change, however, when the Chinese shut down their ports to foreign ships, essentially abandoning their trading network and mothballing the kingdom's powerful navy in the fifteenth century, during the Ming Dynasty. Until then, no one nation had attempted to dominate the Asian trade. The sea-lanes were remarkably free, for the most part, from armed conflict and thus relatively peaceful. The withdrawal of China's powerful fleets resulted in a vacuum the Portuguese gladly filled in the early sixteenth century. The Portuguese and, later, other European powers, were thus accidental beneficiaries of the Middle Kingdom's hermetic move. By the mid sixteenth century Spanish and Portuguese galleons and warships, along with pirates (who still plague the Straits today), prowled the shipping lanes without any challenge from the Chinese navy.

Transactions with the Philippine archipelago, while profitable, did not constitute major business for foreign traders, as the islands were on the eastern edge of the trade routes. But international commerce was extensive enough to generate a vital inter-island trade that relied as much on foreign goods coming in—from, for instance, China, Borneo, and Champa—as on local products. From China came porcelain, finished silk, musk, stoneware, incense, artillery, and tin. Brass, steel blades, and woven mats were brought from Borneo, batik from Java, and precious stones from countries such as Burma. In exchange, foreign traders could purchase in a transshipping port like Cebu—smack in the middle of the archipelago—such items as pearls, beeswax, tortoise shell, animal skins, cotton, and civet cats.

The coastal dwellers traded as well with the hunter/gatherers who lived in the interior and in the highlands, bartering, for instance, salt for honey, and cloth for beeswax—forest products that could be retailed to foreign traders. (At times, lowlander and highlander were at each other's throats, but never so habitually or bitterly as to prevent trading.) That water played a central role in the lives of the islanders can be further gleaned from the names of both places and tribes. For instance, Mindanao has its etymological roots in *danao*, referring to a body of water. The same is true of Lanao, Maranao, and Maguindanao. Tausug, the name of the major ethnic tribe in the Sulu archipelago, means "people of the current," with "Tau" a variant of "tao" or person. Tagalog, the name of the ethnic group predominant in Central Luzon and parts of Southern Luzon, means literally "from the river," or *Taga-ilog*. And the city of Manila, located in the Tagalog region, is a shortened form of the original *Maynila*, "place of water lilies." Similar aquatic correlations attend other place names, such as the province of Pampanga ("site of river banks") in Luzon and, in Mindanao, the Agusan River, with "agusan" meaning "where the water flows," rendering the English name linguistically redundant.

Whether coastal, riverine, or hinterland, the different communities developed ways of living that—influenced by fertile soil, infrequent harsh weather, and a uniform ecology—were quite similar. As the Philippine historian Onofre D. Corpuz observed, "The generally benign tropical climate and the largely uniform flora and fauna favored similarities, not differences." However, reflecting island geography, precolonial Philippine society was not an unbroken, homogenous entity. It is therefore more accurate to speak of "societies," though there were enough similarities among these to indicate common origins and an archipelago-wide interaction, from north to south, from west to east. Interestingly, according to William Henry Scott in *Barangay*, the similarities "also suggest that lowland Filipinos in the sixteenth century had more in common with highland minorities in the twentieth than with their own Christian descendants"—an indication of how the intervening centuries of Christian colonization of the lowlanders widened the heretofore inconsequential gap between them and the highlanders.

Hierarchy

Native societies, as the Spanish found them, were, like Caesar's Gaul, divided into three parts: the ruling elite, their peers and followers, and slaves. (It must be kept in mind that most descriptions and judgments of a pre-colonial Philippines are mainly derived from Spanish accounts, with all that that implies in terms of a priori notions stemming from the observers' own Christian and European backgrounds.) The social structures that existed in both the Visayas and Luzon were remarkably similar, consisting of the *datus* and the *maginoo* at the top, the *timawa* and *maharlika* in the middle, and, occupying the bottom rungs, the *alipin*.

The smallest politico-social unit was the barangay, which, as has been noted, originally referred to the seagoing vessel on which a family or clan traveled. Usage of the term for land-based settlements indicated that the settlers favored a location by a body of water, be it river, lake, or ocean. Most barangays were small, consisting of only thirty to one hundred houses, with from one hundred to five hundred persons. Off the trade routes but still on the coast were even smaller settlements, probably no more than eight to ten houses. Still, there were some giant barangays. Maynila, for instance, had two thousand inhabitants at the time of Spanish conquest, while Cebu and the sultanates in Sulu and Mindanao were comparable in size, if not larger. But these bigger barangays were the exceptions rather than the rule.

A datu headed the barangay, with each barangay more or less self-contained, though there were occasionally alliances among various barangays. There were no formal allegiances beyond the barangay, except in the Muslim settlements to the south. Relations within the barangay were largely influenced by kinship ties on both parents' sides and by economic status. Members of the original barangay, having traveled on the same boat, would have been part of the same clan. Blood ties were thus of the utmost importance, for they guaranteed fealty to the barangay. Alliances between two chiefs of different barangays would often be sealed through a blood compact, where each would drink wine mingled with the other's blood—or suck the blood directly from a cut made on the arm of the other. Simulating blood ties, the rite was called *sandugo* (or "one blood"). To the Spanish, this barangay ritual must have been an eerie reminder of the Eucharist, the Christian sacrament based on a belief in transubstantion, the conversion of bread and wine into Christ's body and blood, communicants becoming one with the Divine, one reason that the Spanish may have taken readily to this ritual.

Hence, the barangay was essentially an extended family, a gathering of a particular clan. Well into the mid-eighteenth century, with the

Spanish long entrenched, people forced to resettle into new towns (due to the colonial policy known as *reducción*) still referred to themselves as *kabangka*—from the "same boat," *bangka* being another word for boat. One's position within the barangay was affected less by birthright (though the position of datu could be inherited) than by acknowledged prowess both in leadership and in providing for the survival of the barangay—roughly identical to one's worth in keeping the boat ship-shape. There were then no claims to a divine imprimatur or special access to the heavens, no boasts about having a hotline to God. In any case, such claims to otherworldly connections would have been the province of the local shaman and seer, the *katolonan* in the Tagalog regions, and *babaylan* in the Visayas, who could be male (even a cross-dressing one) or female but was more often than not the latter.

Since the barangay was not a political state as we know it, the datu could be more properly thought of as the head of a social unit, the paterfamilias, if you will. Consequently, a datu's authority rested as much on his abilities in combat, especially raids that resulted in the capture of slaves, as on his wealth, the strength and depth of his followers, and his lineage. Thus, a datu could be oppressive or generous, broad-minded or narrow in outlook in the way he governed and adjudicated disputes within the barangay. He was expected to be his followers' champion in battle. (With the Tagalogs, the class to which the datu belonged was that of the *maginoo*, or his peers, a term that could refer to either sex.) Members of a barangay reciprocated by contributing labor, such as helping to harvest his crops, and paying tribute for his household's maintenance.

The datu's followers were the freemen, either the *timawa* or the *maharlika*—the distinction being made on the basis of service rendered to the datu. The timawa rendered theirs primarily in non-military ways, though they could bear arms if they so desired. The maharlika, on the other hand, functioned roughly as knights did for a king. To think of these freemen as commoners would be misleading, however. In a self-contained society that was the barangay, the timawa and the maharlika had a close relationship with the datu, albeit in varying degrees. In essence, they made up his court: close by at his feasts, alongside him in battle, whether on the field or in a ship, acting as his emissaries, etc.

Since a settlement and its social structure arose out of barangay conditions, relations among the three groups were more fluid than can be accommodated by the idea of "class," though there were societal divisions of labor, to be sure. But even such hierarchical relations could be and were often radically altered. A datu could be deposed, a maharlika reduced to dependence, and a debt-slave become free if he or she paid off his/her debts—or if, as in the case of the fortunate Namwran, those debts were forgiven.

The barangay social order being an extension of the family, the notion of private ownership of land was irrelevant. It made no sense to claim particular tracts permanently, given there was so much land available. Hence, individuals would not have thought of acquiring land, though they had the right of usufruct if they had cultivated a particular parcel. Every member of the barangay was a shareholder theoretically and could derive profit from land use. The datu, however, representing the apex of communal society, was instrumental in determining how such lands would be used. One could thus utilize the land but not hold title to it—the idea of "title," of course, not coming into play. With fixed-site agriculture and fishing primarily for livelihood, barangay economies were tailored mostly to meet the barangay's needs, and for possible barter with other barangays.

As in any family or clan, the stress was on shared labor, whether this was in farming, say, or house building. The practice of *bayanihan* (literally, communal solidarity) in today's evolving, not to mention disappearing, rural society can be traced to this tradition of shared labor. Producers owned their means of production, and any surplus from a bountiful harvest was stored against a rainy day or for barter, rather than for purely speculative purposes. In a word, the archipelagic barangay was not only pre-colonial but also pre-capitalist. Probably the most spectacular and awe-inspiring instance of enduring bayanihan are the rice terraces of Northern Luzon, high up in the Cordillera Mountain Range. In continuous use since they were built two millennia ago by the Ifugao (one of several tribes based in the Cordilleras), these magnificent embankments were carved out of stubborn and treacherous mountainsides. Organizing the labor, building up the paddies, and devising the placement of rocks and irrigation canals were daunting challenges that required a tight, cohesive, and efficient social structure.

Made up of kinship ties, the barangay did not constitute a system independent from its inhabitants—it had no existence as a legal fiction, unlike a modern-day township. Thus, a barangay had no public buildings for government or community affairs, no castles or town halls. The datu's residence would have been the largest building and the center of the barangay. The idea of what passed for "public" was really the private world writ larger. (However, the highlander tribes in Northern Luzon, or Igorot, as they are collectively known, had and still have what is known as the *dap-ay*, an open-air community space, like a table in the round, where the elders gather to discuss pressing issues.)

Nonetheless, some barangays developed supra-barangay affinities, such as the Muslim sultanates. The earliest one, the Sultanate of Sulu, established in the fifteenth century, a century before the advent of the Spanish, arose in Jolo in the Sulu archipelago, southwest of Mindanao and in close proximity to Borneo and the Indonesian archipelago. The second, later sultanate emerged in Maguindanao, with tradition holding that a certain Sharif Muhammad Kabungsuwan moved north to Mindanao from Malacca, after the Portuguese took over that port city in 1511.

Three other large barangays were the aforementioned Butuan in northwestern Mindanao; the principal Visayan trading port of Cebu, in the center of the islands; and Maynila in Luzon. By the sixteenth century, however, Butuan had declined as a trading center. Maynila, which the Spanish would make the seat of power in the islands in the late sixteenth century and shorten its name to "Manila," constituted the preeminent settlement in Luzon, since it, with links to Muslim communities in Mindanao and Borneo, had a higher stage of political development. Its burgeoning status as a sultanate was however forever disrupted when the Spanish razed Maynila in 1571, forcing the ruling datu and his people to flee. The year after, the Spanish started to erect the Walled City of Intramuros on the ashes of what could have been the Sultanate of Maynila.

As noted, pre-colonial society was also marked by slavery, which, while it had several gradations, fell generally under two types of *alipin*: those who had their own houses and tended their own fields, and those who dwelt with their master. The former were known as *namamahay* (literally, one who keeps house), while the latter were referred to as *sagigilid* (literally, on the edge or periphery, i.e., living in the master's household but of marginal status). The namamahay had more freedom than the sagigilid, and were practically freemen when not called upon to serve the master—which was not too often. In contrast, the sagigilid, usually unmarried and being part of their master's household, were expected to render service on a daily basis. They also faced the possibility of being sold. But even they could eat at the same table as their master and had the prospect of moving up the social rung either through marriage—including marriage into the master's family—or, if they earned enough, through buying their freedom.

The most common cause of slavery was the inability to pay a debt, and the debtor had to remain in servitude, or his family (remember Namwran?) if the debtor had in the meantime passed away, until the debt was repaid with interest. Since barangays at heart were kin-based, the hardships and conditions of bondage were relatively benign, compared, say, to the horrific conditions that African slaves endured when trafficked by Europeans to their colonies.

Slaves, however, who were captured in battle or in raids on other barangays, being outside the clan, faced other potentially grim fates. They could be candidates for human sacrifice when the occasion demanded it, such as the death of a powerful datu. In his *Relación de Las Islas Filipinas* (*Account of the Philippine Islands*), published in 1604, a detailed and subjective portrait of sixteenth-century mores among the indigenous people, the Spanish Jesuit Pedro Chirino observed "it was easy to increase the number of slaves. Consequently, they used to have, and still have, a very large number of slaves, which among them is the greatest of riches." He also wrote, "In former times, they would not let them depart to the other world alone, but gave male and female slaves to accompany the dead. These slaves, having first eaten a hearty meal, were then immediately killed, that they might go with the dead man. It once happened that they buried with a chief a vessel manned by many rowers, who were to serve him in his voyages to the other world."

Nevertheless, social status in native society appeared to be quite fluid, malleable due to the possibilities of upward mobility through reducing one's indebtedness and correspondingly increasing one's social prestige. The idea of an immutable hierarchy, as in the Hindu caste system, was notably absent. According to historian Vicente Rafael, in his *Contracting Colonialism*, "Village society owed its apparent mobility to the displaceability of obligations. Status reflected indebtedness, not the person. . . . Indeed, the possibility of shifting

from one rank to another—as evidenced by the fine gradations of servitude—bespoke the tendency to dissociate status from person."

PEOPLE TRAVEL AND SO DO IDEAS

Ports by nature are interactive sites, as true millennia ago as it is now.
Merchants, seamen, travelers, and emissaries from various culture
zones not only traded goods but stories and ideas as well. Along with
commerce, ideas made their way between the Mediterranean and the
Middle East and the South China Sea, a globalization anticipating that
of contemporary times. Traders, in short, brought themselves and not
just their goods. They were individuals with specific worldviews and
beliefs that often were new to a port. Thus, Islam migrated via the
Indian Ocean into Indonesia and the Malay Peninsula in just such a
manner. However, this mix of religious, social, political, and cultural
elements resists facile categorizing that would have the flow of influences only one way, from the "greater" to the "lesser," as Abu-Lughod
points out.

The long unquestioned assumption has been that China and India
were major influences on Southeast Asia, whose smaller states or communities were perceived as beneficiaries of supposedly more sophisticated continental cultures. But the reality was, as it is now, more complex
than that. Interactions among different cultural agents were more lay-
ered and diverse than is conventionally presented. In fact, according to
Solheim, archaeological excavations in Thailand indicate that domesti-
cation of plants there began as early as 10,000 B.C.E. The excavations
turned up an imprint of a grain of rice carbon dated to about 3,500
B.C.E., a thousand years before its presence was detected in India or
China. According to Solheim, Thai metallurgy began in about 4,000
B.C.E., and fine quality bronze was already being produced by the third
millennium, some 500 years before it was found in India and 1,000
years before China.

Because of the development of the long-distance outrigger boats,
trading in the Indian Ocean and South China Sea was underway by the
first millennium B.C.E., enabling the two-way flow, as much from the
lesser to the greater as vice versa. Nevertheless, while Southeast Asia
was a more interactive player in cultural matters than is usually envisioned, by the first millennium C.E., it was subject to major influences

such as Buddhism and Hinduism, coming from China and India. In the tenth and eleventh centuries, with new powers in Asia coming to the fore—e.g., the Cholas, the Khmers, and the Burmese—diverse sets of relationships came about among realms that were not yet politically or culturally unified entities. And by the late thirteenth century, the Srivijaya empire had declined even as the Java-based kingdom of Majapahit was gaining power and Islam was taking root in Indonesia and the Malay Peninsula, shouldering aside the Hindu influence of the Srivijaya— though it has remained firmly rooted in the kingdom of Bali.

The influence of the Srivijaya empire extended to parts of the Philippine archipelago, with Srivijaya colonists, as pointed out earlier, implanting the distinctive name of "Visayas" on its central cluster of islands. By the end of the eighth century, the empire included all of the Malay Peninsula, a large portion of Sumatra, parts of Siam, and central Java. It had four substates—Bandjarmasin, Sukadara, Southern Sarawak, and Brunei. From Bandjarmasin settlers went to Sulu and west-central Visayas; the Borneans sailed to Panay, Palawan, Mindoro, and southern Luzon. Very likely the Laguna Copperplate Inscription is the cultural residue of such migration.

Spanish documents from the sixteenth century record the existence of diverse crafts, such as shipbuilding—an absolute must in the archipelago—metallurgy, pottery, and weaving. They noted native weapons of the time as including the *lantaka* (bronze cannons that were often mounted on swivels), lances and daggers tipped with iron, as well as bronze culverins. Metallurgy had long been practiced in the islands, along with dry agriculture, weaving, boat-building, and the construction of elevated lightweight houses with thatched roofs.

In Palawan, the Manunggul Cave—part of the Tabon Cave complex—yielded iron objects and the extraordinary Manunggul Jar, described by the late American anthropologist Robert Fox as "perhaps unrivalled in Southeast Asia," when compared to artifacts of the same era, providing "a clear example of a cultural link between the archaeological past and the ethnographic present." This remarkable burial jar is made of clay with finely incised motifs, and dates to the late Neolithic period, or about 710 B.C.E. The jar's cover depicts two figures on a boat, a rower ferrying the dead person to the next realm, with its implicit belief in the soul and the afterlife. This type of jar was most likely introduced by the Hakka migrating from southern China's Fukien region.

Metallurgy was also evidenced in fine goldsmithing, with gold jewelry and ornaments widespread throughout the archipelago, an indication of the mineral's abundance. The Spanish noted the delicacy and high degree of craftsmanship of gold work in the islands, particularly in the Visayas and in certain parts of Mindanao. Fervent capitalists, they complained that the mines were being worked only as needed and never at their maximum. The observant Chirino writes, "The islands are numerous and thickly inhabited by a people who, though not rich, were accustomed to wear cotton and silk garments, and gold pieces (not merely of thin plate) and brooches to fasten them; and rich necklaces, pendants, earrings, finger-rings, ankle rings, for the neck, ears, hands, and feet—the men as well as the women. They even used to, and do yet, insert gold between their teeth as an ornament." Earlier, in 1521, the Venetian chronicler of the Magellan expedition that had come across the archipelago, Antonio Pigafetta, had noted the existence in some of the islands of "mines of gold, which is found by digging from the earth large pieces as large as walnuts and eggs."

Discoveries in the 1970s in Surigao, northeastern Mindanao, of more than a thousand gold artifacts dating to the tenth to thirteenth centuries C.E., reflect sophisticated artistry and unusual craftsmanship. Acknowledging outside influences, experts on the subject nonetheless have concluded that pre-colonial Philippine techniques and motifs were unique to the islands. Among other items the cache included golden sashes, earrings, diadems, funerary masks, body ornaments, and ritual containers. One piece is particularly impressive: a gold halter of nearly four kilograms, quite possibly representing the Sacred Thread, a mark of the Brahmin caste in Hinduism. The halter and other objects with similar motifs clearly reflect Hindu influences—cultural reverberations from the Srivijaya empire—underscoring the presence of yet another layer in the archipelago's diverse and complex pre-Hispanic culture.

LIFE, LANGUAGE, AND LOVE

Being home to a diverse array of ethnicities, the islands possess close to 170 languages and dialects, with many on the verge of extinction. Nevertheless, the Austronesian language tree is the dominant source of the Philippines' eight major tongues—Cebuano, Tagalog, Hiligaynon,

Waray, Ilocano, Pangasinan, Bicolano, and Kapampangan. Evidence indicates that Austronesian languages came to the Philippine archipelago earlier than they did, say, to the Malay Peninsula. By the sixteenth century, today's languages were well established, evolving from their Austronesian roots to their distinct formations as a result of the conditions peculiar to the islands. Tagalog, the lingua franca of historic Manila, capital of colonial times (both of Spain and the United States), forms the basis of the national language, Pilipino—much to the dismay of Cebuano speakers who outnumber native Tagalog speakers, and who remind anyone who listens that Cebu was where the Spanish first set up a settlement.

In terms of script, at least ten syllabaries are known to have been used in pre-colonial Philippines, though literacy was not widespread, even if a number of Spanish accounts like Chirino's say so. Tagalog script probably influenced the development of writing among the Visayans, whose pre-1565 culture stressed singing and chanting, relying on oral history for the transmission of tradition. Such practices occasioned socializing, and reinforced a barangay's joie de vivre—antedating by several hundred years that contemporary and widely popular and communal form, the karaoke songfest.

In Maynila, its datus wrote in the Kawi script, which seems to have disappeared by the time of Spanish conquest. They now wrote in a Malay or Arabic script called *baybayin*, as mentioned earlier, since they corresponded with the Sultan of Borneo—an indication of Islamic conversion up north, not only in Maynila but in other areas such as Batangas in the southern Tagalog region. Historian Corpuz believes that "the presence of writing and the making of written laws in the Manila area placed Manila ahead of other native communities in political development at the time of the Spanish contact, with the exception only of the Sulu and Maguindanao areas."

Unlike the sudden impact of the Spanish, extra-insular cultural influences seeped in gradually, with none of the intensity of other cultural encounters elsewhere in Southeast Asia, where Buddhism and Hinduism led the charge. Not surprising, as the more than 7,000 islands were on the northeastern edge of Southeast Asia. As noted earlier, pre-Hispanic Filipinos proved to be as peripatetic as anyone else, with small settlements in Malacca, Brunei, and Timor. They even fought as mercenaries in the employ of the Burmese kingdom.

Given the abundance of and easy access to water, and the warm climate, the islanders were attentive to matters of personal hygiene, especially to bathing—impressing both Pigafetta and Chirino. Chirino wrote admiringly:

> Both men and women swim like fishes, even from childhood, and have no need of bridges to pass over rivers. They bathe themselves at all hours, for cleanliness and recreation; and the women after childbirth do not refrain from the bath, and children just born are bathed in the rivers and springs of cold water. When leaving the bath, they anoint the head with ajonjoli [i.e., oil of sesame] mixed with civet. . . . Through modesty, they bathe with their bodies drawn up and almost in a sitting posture, taking the greatest care not to be seen, although no one may be near to see them *[except perhaps for the odd priest]*. The most general hour for bathing is at the setting of the sun, because at that time they have finished their labors, and bathe in the river to rest and refresh themselves; on the way, they usually carry some vessel for bearing water to use in their domestic duties.

Visayans used citrus in laundering their garments, for the pleasant odor it imparted. They were fastidious, Scott notes, in their personal hygiene, using swabs to clean their ears and "vegetable husk for cleaning and polishing the teeth."

Unlike Legazpi, Chirino was impressed by the civility, courteousness, and upbringing of the Tagalogs, particularly in the use of the third person when addressing someone. Chirino was less taken by the Visayans, who "are more rustic and less civil in manners, just as their language is harsher and less polished." On the other hand, Pigafetta commends the Visayans for their hospitality, graciousness, love of feasting, and music. It could very well have been a matter of individual temperament—Pigafetta more attuned to worldliness than the priest—or Chirino having a bad day in his interaction with the Visayans. Not surprisingly, both Pigafetta and the good Jesuit noted the relaxed attitude towards sex, especially among the women. The pious cleric disapproved heartily of island hedonism. He believed that the devil had convinced women that their salvation was in the hands of men, "that a woman, whether married or single, could not be saved, who did not have some lover. . . . Consequently, virginity was not recognized or esteemed among them; rather, women considered it as a misfortune and humiliation. Married women, moreover, were not constrained by honor to remain faithful to their husbands, although the latter would resent the adultery, and hold it as just cause for repudiating the wife."

Pigafetta, no stranger to his shipmates' earlier bacchanals in South America, gave a more detailed, at times, clinical, description of the islanders' sexual mores, leading one to infer that, being a scrupulous observer, he had witnessed Cebuanos in actual coitus and perhaps he had availed himself of the charms of the unmarried nubile women, whose beauty he remarked on: "These girls were very beautiful, and almost white and tall as ours. They were naked, except that from the waist to the knees they wore a garment . . . covering their nature." Sexual pleasure, it seemed, was seen as a mutual goal—women were as important as men in this regard—rather than simply for the gratification of male desire and the propagation of the species.

To that end, to please their partners, according to Pigafetta, men "have their penis pierced from one side to the other near the head, with a gold or tin bolt as large as a goose quill. . . . Some have what resembles a spur, with points upon the ends; others are like the head of a cart nail." He goes on: "When the men wish to have communication with their women, the latter themselves take the penis not in the regular way and commence very gently to introduce it, with the spur on top first, and then the other part. When it is inside, it takes its regular position; and thus the penis always stays inside until it gets soft, for otherwise they could not pull it out." Two lovers could thus remain locked in passion for hours, even a whole day.

In this context, virginity was neither prized nor desirable, and polygamy was accepted—both of which practices the zealously Catholic Spanish attempted to and did for the most part wipe out. To the macho Spanish, a sexually independent woman was intolerable. One account described island women as "generally depraved . . . given to abominable lustful habits." The fact that female desire was given equal weight profoundly disturbed the repressed and repressive Spanish patriarchs. Gender equality was evident in a language such as Tagalog with its nongendered nominative pronouns and in the prevalent creation myth that had man and woman as emerging from bamboo at the same time, both fully formed. In contrast to the biblical story of the creation of Adam and Eve, this one held the implicit promise of nonsexist gender treatment, as manifest in the sexual attitudes that titillated and shocked the Europeans. Variations on the creation myth included both sexes arising from green coconuts, or as the result of an argument between primeval sky and water.

The Tagalogs, Visayans, and the Igorots expressed belief in a supreme deity, as of course did the Muslims in the south. To the Tagalogs this god was known as Bathala May Kapal ("Bathala" is likely derived from the Sanskrit word for noble lord, *Batthara*); to the Visayans, Laon; and to the Igorots, Kabunian. They also believed in lesser deities, such as those ruling over seas and rivers. The crocodile, once plentiful in the archipelago's waterways, was revered, with offerings tossed on the water to placate its ravenous appetite.

The Visayans termed the lower-ranked powers *diwata* (from the Sanskrit *deva*), among them Magwayen, who ferried the dead to the afterlife; Makabosog, a Bacchus-like deity who inspired humans to prodigious bouts of eating and drinking; and a mischievous trio of expert poisoners— Naginid, Arapayan, and Makbarubak. Inhabiting the netherworld were frightful creatures such as the *aswang*, flesh eaters, and the *manananggal*, literally a fly-by-night ghoul that would leave half of its body in a secret place, while the other, upper half would move through the dark sky in search of a victim, preferably the fetus of an expectant mother, which it would then suck out, with its long, needle-like tongue.

Acting as intermediary between this world and the unseen one was the *babaylan* (*katalonan* to the Tagalogs, *mumbaki* to the highlanders of Luzon). This individual could be of either sex but was more often female, though the male babaylan were known for cross-dressing. The babaylan's most common function was a diviner of fate. In a public ritual common to both lowlander and highlander, a sacrificial swine, preferably reddish in color, was killed by a quick, unerring thrust to its heart by the babaylan/katolonan/mumbaki who had gone into a trance. The pig's entrails would be read, then consumed, with certain parts reserved for the seer.

As a medium for spirits and practitioner of sacred rites, the babaylan occupied an important, and lucrative, position in the barangay. S/he acted also as medicine wo/man, midwife, dispenser of herbs and potions that healed the physical wounds, or of charms and incantations if a person's illness, or bad fortune, were thought to be the result of a hex put upon him or her—possibly by another babaylan more attuned to black than white magic.

As with the Spanish and their Southeast Asian neighbors, the pre-Hispanic populations believed in an afterlife, recognized the existence of invisible spirits, and feared demons, all of which were thought to significantly affect their lives. Many of their beliefs were animistic, attributing supernatural power to elements of Nature. One basis for their sense of the otherworldly was the need to honor and respect their ancestors, whom they would sometimes elevate to deity status. Thus, they reverenced stones, the wind, headlands of water, and trees. To cut down an old tree, for example, was considered a sacrilege. Or to fail to ask permission to pass in front of an ant mound in a field was tantamount to inviting retribution (usually in the form of a mischievous trick) from the mound's resident spirit, to which the Spanish word *duende* was affixed, though the meaning was closer to that of leprechaun than of creative spirit. Often, beside a house, would be a much smaller one, that contained some tools and handicrafts but was also dedicated to an *anito*, or a local deity—similar to the shrines for the *penates,* household gods of the Romans, and the spirit houses of the Thais. The Ifugao carved wooden icons they called the *bulul,* a guardian deity of indeterminate sex that stood guard over their warehouses of rice and was even thought to increase the supply of stored grain.

As exemplified by the Manunggul Jar, shuffling off this mortal coil meant a journey of the spirit to the next realm. Upon a person's death, the corpse was prepared in different ways in anticipation of its voyage. In the Tagalog regions, the body was decorated and dressed in finery. In the highlands of northern Luzon, depending on the tribe, burial rites ranged from the placement of coffins in the vaulted ceilings of caves to mummification. In one region, the corpse was cleaned, dressed, set upright on and bound to a chair as members of the clan gathered around to mourn the person's demise. There was no cemetery as such, and the dead could be buried in the ground underneath the house, usually elevated on hardwood posts, or in the fields.

On occasion, with the death of someone of high status, such as a datu, slaves captured in raids were interred as well. The manner of death may have differed—sometimes speared to death while tied to

crosses, sometimes crushed by a boat that would roll over their pros-
trate bodies—but the intent was the same: for the dead slaves to accompany the master on the new voyage, as they had when he was among
the living.

The soul or spirit of the deceased person wandered in another
realm but could return, in which case those left behind made preparations to welcome that spirit. In a practical vein, the family would try to
put that spirit to use in divining what the future might hold and otherwise putting in a good word, or intervening, to assure the bestowal of
good, and the avoidance of ill, fortune. At the wake, if the family could
afford it, professional mourners would sing songs, eulogizing the
deceased and relating, according to Chirino, "the fabulous genealogies
and vain deeds of their gods."

THE CRESCENT BEFORE THE CROSS

Islam predated the arrival of Christianity by at least a century and a
half. Towards the end of the fourteenth century, Muslim missionaries
from the by then mostly Islamicized Malaysia and Indonesia brought
the word of the Messenger concerning Allah to the southern
Philippines, even reaching Palawan, Mindoro, and the east coast of
Luzon, notably Maynila. With *ulamas*, or Muslim communities, taking root, two large sultanates were subsequently established: in Sulu
in the fifteenth century, under Sharif ul-Hashim, and in Maguindanao,
near Cotabato City in the early sixteenth century, under Sharif
Muhammad Kabungsuan, who had left Malacca for Maguindanao.
Thence, Islam spread to Maranao territory (around Lake Danao),
inexplicably skipped the Visayas for the most part, and sailed north to
Mindoro Island and Maynila and Batangas in Luzon, and west to
southern Palawan.

Converted indigenous tribes such as the Tausug, Maranaoans, and
Maguindanaoans could look to the older ulamas farther south.
Certainly there were other outside influences, mainly from China and
India, and their legacies can be seen in such diverse areas as language,
art, cuisine, and kinship groupings, but Islam acted as a catalyst for
intra-settlement alliances and the beginnings of a civil state. This fea-
ture, which distinguished the Muslim communities from the non-
Muslim ones, proved essential in resisting Spanish efforts at colonizing

southern Mindanao. Writing in 1603 to the Spanish king of the para-mount Muslim datus of Mindanao—Umpi, Silonga, Buycan, and Rajaniora—Don Pedro de Acuña noted, "They have usually dissensions and controversies among themselves, for he who has the most people and wealth seeks to be more esteemed than the others. But against the Spaniards and their other enemies, they confederate and unite, and ordi-narily Silonga has the most power."

The sultanate had a centralized government similar to Islamic states in Borneo and Indonesia. Its head, the sultan, was owed alle-giance by other datus. Though the latter governed their own followers, they occupied a subordinate position vis à vis the sultan, who alone could declare war, engage in dealings with other states, and otherwise decide on matters affecting the sultanate as a whole.

The highly ceremonial courts in both Sulu and Maguindanao had Arabic speakers, religious scholars, and gentry with distinguished line-ages. Clearly Muslim, still, these courts didn't completely disavow pre-Islamic practices. As Scott puts it in *Barangay*, "Maguindanao ruled over a great many pagan people, and even the celebrated [Sultan] Kudarat was reported to have sacrificed three of his household slaves during a terrifying volcanic eruption."

With Islamicized communities spread strategically through the archipelago, from Luzon in the north, Sulu and Maguindanao in the south, and Palawan in the west, a persuasive argument can be and has been made that the archipelago would have evolved towards an Islamic state or states, either as an independent nation, or part, say, of Indonesia or Malaysia, were it not for the Iberians. Spanish colonization meant the displacement of the crescent by the cross in most of the country.

THE CHINESE AND OTHER MINORITIES

As early at least as the tenth century, Chinese traders were regular visi-tors to the islands, going by the first mention of a Philippine island—Ma-Yi, current-day Mindoro—in extant Chinese records, which list 985, 1372, 1406, and 1410, as years of contact with the islands. Place names, such as Ma-Yi, Min-to-liang, Su-lu, and Lu-sung, indicate recur-ring visits, with small Han communities springing up. In his accounts from the thirteenth century, Chao Ju-Kua, China's Superintendent of Sea Trade from 1277 to 1287, referred to Ma-Yi (here taken to indicate the Philippine archipelago), San-hsii (the Visayas) and Lin-hsing (Luzon). Imports from Southeast Asia, including from the Philippines, included cotton, yellow wax, coconuts, onions and woven mats.

But the steady and continuing influx of the Chinese in larger numbers began only in earnest with the colonization of the archipelago by the Spanish, who needed the crafts and skills of Chinese artisans. To the Chinese traders—most if not all of whom were from the southern China coastal provinces such as Fujian, Amoy, and Guangdong—this meant a link to yet another trading network as well as access to sought-after Mexican silver, brought by the Spanish from Mexico. Both silver and new markets were accessible because of the profitable galleon trade between Manila and Acapulco, the transshipment point to Spain and the rest of Europe. (The galleon trade will be discussed in the next chapter.)

The very nature of the archipelago, with more water than land, meant the existence of numerous tribal groups, other than the dominant ones—the Tagalogs, the Kapampangans, the Ilocanos, the Bicolanos, the Cebuanos, and other Visayans. Now known as cultural minorities, some sixty of them were and are to be found, still, throughout the country. Due to remoteness or effective resistance, they had limited contact with the Spanish. The Muslims of Mindanao, alert against Spanish encroachment, were themselves composed mostly of three distinct tribes: the Maranaoans, the Maguindanaoans, and the Taosug, Islam being the religious glue that bound them, albeit loosely but never too loosely as to prevent unity (most of the time, anyway) against the Iberian foe. Other cultural minorities in Mindanao, especially those in the southern regions, such as the boat-dwelling Badjao, the Sama Laut, and the Yakan, were subject to pressure to convert to Islam. And for the most part they did. Tribes such as the T'Boli, the Mandaya, the Manobo, and the Bagobo, because they lived in the highlands, never converted wholesale to Islam.

In Mindoro Island, off the western coast of Luzon, live the Mangyan in the rugged, mountainous interior, whose Hanunoo branch was mentioned earlier in connection with the use of baybayin, the pre-Hispanic script. Scattered along the western coast of Luzon, especially in its mountainous interior, and found on some Visayan islands, are the Negritos (whom the Spanish also referred to as *Negrillos*). Also known as Agta, Aeta, Ita, Ati, they are shorter than the average Filipino, of dark pigmentation and curly hair, and are related to the Australian Aborigines. There is an ongoing debate as to when they established themselves in the archipelago, but their presence is believed to be older than that of the Austronesian migrations. They are thought to have used land bridges 30,000 years ago, most likely through the isthmus that once connected Palawan Island and Borneo.

In the highlands of northern Luzon—the Cordilleras—live the previously mentioned Igorot tribes, *Igorot* meaning "peoples of the mountain." Among these are the Kalinga, the Bontoc, the Kankanay, the Ibaloi, and the Ifugao—the last named the builders of the magnificent rice terraces. Famed for their martial skills, bravery, and codes of honor and retribution (including headhunting), the Igorots were too high up, too fierce, and the Spanish too sparse in number, for the few attempts at spreading the Gospel to succeed. Only under United States colonial rule in the early twentieth century would Christianity gain a foothold in the mountains.

2. EXPEDITIONS, ENTRENCHMENT, AND SPANISH COLONIAL RULE, 1521-1862

"The method which they pursued was consistent with the practice of those nations in forming a friendship—a method not altogether their own, as it was a custom among the most ancient heathen peoples, mention of which we find in serious authors. Those who made peace in the name of the rest, and established the pacts of perpetual friendship, pricked and wounded their own arms; the Indian sucking the blood of the Spaniard, and the Spaniard that of the Indian. In this wise they became as if of the same blood, and were closer than brothers. These are called sandugo, *which means 'consanguineous,' or 'of the same blood.'"*

—Pedro Chirino, S.J., *Relación de las Islas Filipinas,* 1604

I N 1517, AN INTREPID AND BATTLE-TESTED THIRTY-NINE-YEAR-OLD Portuguese navigator by the name of Ferdinand Magellan, out of favor with the crotchety Portuguese King Manuel, crossed the border into Spain and convinced its young, adventurous seventeen-year-old Hapsburg monarch, Charles, to finance an ambitious undertaking: He, Magellan, would discover a new route to the fabled Spice Islands by sailing west across the Atlantic, to South America, from where he could then sail to the desired destination without running afoul of his countrymen, Spain's fiercest rivals.

Magellan assured the Spanish court that his voyage would observe the line of demarcation Pope Alexander VI had drawn, essentially dividing the planet between Catholic Spain and Catholic Portugal. Established on June 7, 1494, the demarcation was one hundred leagues west of the Azores and Cape Verde: All lands west were marked for Spain; east, for Portugal. However, if land in either half was already ruled by a Christian sovereign, it was to be left alone. Everything else was up for grabs. A simple enough agreement, yet the papal bull was constantly challenged to suit the agenda either of the Portuguese or the Spanish. This interminable wrangling led to modifications through the 1506 Treaty of Tordesillas (a small town in northern Spain). The line was moved 370 miles west of Cape Verde, approximately in the middle of the Atlantic.

The papal blessing provided Spain and Portugal with theological cover for their voyages of conquest and the brutal but profitable undertaking of land expropriation and exploitation of indigenous peoples, otherwise known as colonization. Through the conquistadors and the civil and religious personnel that followed in lockstep, Rome extended its reach wherever these two European countries planted their flags—a perfect combination of economic enterprise, worldly power, and religious zeal.

Magellan's voyage was financed officially by the Casa de Contratacíon in Seville. If the venture succeeded, it would guarantee much needed revenue for the Spanish treasury. On August 10, 1519, the flagship *Trinidad*, the *Victoria, San Antonio, Concepcíon, Santiago*, and 260 men under the command of Magellan slipped their berths at Seville and sailed down the Rio Guadalquivir and into the Atlantic. Accompanying the voyage was Antonio Pigafetta, a young and healthy Venetian nobleman eager for adventure, whose journals of the expedition constitute the main source of what we know today about this precedent-setting expedition.

After an epic voyage filled with extraordinary adventures, hardships, maritime disasters, and a mutiny that nearly succeeded, the fleet, reduced to three, discovered the straits, now bearing Magellan's name, that lead to the Pacific Ocean—so christened by Magellan as his expedition happened upon that great body of water, when the storm season hadn't yet begun. Entering the vast and calm ocean, the ships tacked their way across for more than three months without being able to reprovision—causing untold hardships and deaths—before sighting the Marianas (present-day Guam) on March 6, 1521. Magellan and his men named it Isla de Ladrones (Isle of Thieves), for the inhabitants' light-fingered proclivities, though the inhabitants, forebears of latter-day Chamorros, had been generous with their food. (This could have simply been a case of cultural misunderstanding: what the Europeans considered theft, the islanders thought of as sharing.) In punishment, Magellan ordered his men to burn some of the natives' homes, killing seven men as a result. According to Pigafetta's account, crew members who were ill asked that the entrails of a dead man be brought to them, "for immediately they would be healed"—a request that suggests pre-Christian beliefs coexisting with Christian ones onboard.

Magellan and his men pushed on and, on March 16, 1521, came across Homonhon, an isle off the Pacific-facing coast of Samar, a much larger island in the archipelago yet to be named the Philippines. The ships had sailed into the eastern flank of the Visayas, the archipelago's central region. That day being the feast day of a saint, Magellan christened the islands aptly enough the Archipelago of San Lazaro, as the fortuitous landfall meant a revival of their lives, if not their fortunes. The Visayans, whom the Iberians subsequently referred to as *pintados*, for the elaborate tattoos that marked them, proved hospitable. From Homonhon the expedition proceeded to the island of Limasawa south of Samar. There several large boats approached the ships, boats that Pigafetta noted were called *balang-hai* and that on the average measured approximately eighteen meters long.

Pigafetta, whose journals provide a fascinating, first-hand account of this historic voyage, loved to make lists, and in one, he enumerated words from the language of the islanders—words that are used to this day. In another, he itemized products and domestic animals he had come across, among them: rice, ginger, oranges, lemons, sugar cane, garlic, honey, bananas, corn, millet, citrus, wax, goats, chickens, dogs, cats, and pigs. In addition, there were cinnamon, pepper, nutmeg—all valuable spices—as well as, and more importantly, gold. He noted the practice of betel-nut chewing and cockfighting—both common in Southeast Asia. But of all the tropical produce that Pigafetta got to know, it was the coconut that so enchanted him he deemed it the near-perfect food. He was convinced two trees could sustain a family of ten for a hundred years.

On Easter Sunday, in a portent of impending Christianity, the priest accompanying the expedition celebrated mass on Limasawa. Thence, guided by Limasawa's datu (a lesser-ranked ally of the datu of Butuan, the much larger port in Mindanao, further south), the ships proceeded to the busy port city of Cebu, arriving on April 7. Acting as the translator and interpreter was Magellan's Christianized Malayan slave, Enrique de Malacca—Malacca being the port and slave market where Magellan had bought him. Malacca was Southeast Asia's principal entrepot, a vital transshipping port in the trade routes that extended on one end from the Mediterranean to southern China, at the other. Enrique may not necessarily have been from Malacca, or from the Moluccas. The young man, as it turned out, not only looked like these pre-colonial Filipinos, he also spoke their tongue. He may very well have been from the central part of the archipelago. And indeed, if he were, this slave (whom Magellan in his will decreed be set free upon his death) would therefore have been the first known individual to have completed a circuit of the Earth *before* Sebastian Elcano and the few survivors of the Magellan expedition returned to Sevilla in 1522.

Cebu was ruled by Rajah Humabon. After a short period of

unease between the pragmatic native king and the imperious navigator—the former had initially demanded tribute from the latter, as was
traditionally expected from ships bringing goods—the two sides settled
into what presumably was an amicable relationship. It helped that a
Muslim trader from Siam, knowing something about the rather brutal
history of conquistadors, had advised Humabon to come to some sort
of accommodation with Magellan. Consequently, Rajah Humabon
agreed to an alliance with Spain, wherein the rajah not only acknowledged Spanish sovereignty but also converted to the Catholic faith,
along with his principal consort and his subjects. Humabon was baptized Carlos, after the Spanish monarch, and Humabon's queen, Juana,
after Carlos's mother, Juana la Loca (Joanna the Mad, so named for
her mental instability and her bizarre, fetishistic desire to keep the
corpse of her husband Philip the Handsome close by her).

Newly converted, Humabon complained to Magellan about a petty
ruler from nearby Mactan Island—across the straits from Cebu—by the
name of LapuLapu who would not bow to either the cross or the Spanish
crown. Given the highly decentralized nature of Southeast Asian chiefdoms and competition for trade, Humabon may very well have enlisted
the unsuspecting Magellan in a strategy to get rid of his rival. Despite the
sage advice of his officers, who rightfully pointed out that they had no
business interfering in local affairs, and, more importantly, feared losing
all their hard-earned gains, Magellan decided to teach LapuLapu a lesson, with only sixty men—all volunteers—in three long boats, and in the
process impress his native ally no end. Magellan had by now been infected with evangelical zeal, his head full of grandiose notions of lording it
over the archipelago. Being viceroy of the islands would have made him
and his family unbelievably rich and vindicated his defection to the
Spanish court.

Humabon offered Magellan a contingent of his warriors, but
Magellan disdained the offer, boasting that one of his men, clad in body
armor, was worth a hundred of the enemy. He had earlier arranged a
display showing his armored men repelling blows. Besides, his ships'
cannon were larger and more powerful than the *lantakas*, or artillery, of
the enemy. It was an empty boast: as dawn broke on April 27, 1521,
Magellan and his armed party of sixty waded ashore on Mactan and
there engaged LapuLapu and his men. Outnumbered and outmaneuvered—LapuLapu had tricked his enemies into coming in at low tide, so

the Spanish ships were anchored too far out for their cannon to be effective—the tough, forty-one-year-old Magellan paid for his adventurism with his life, cut down on the beach as his companions, their ranks depleted, fled to the longboats. Pigafetta, who had fought that day, mourned Magellan's death, calling him "our mirror, our light, our comfort, and our true guide."

The aftermath of the battle was bloody as well. Enrique, wounded at the battle on Mactan, had been humiliated by Duarte Barbosa, now one of the two leaders of the expedition (the other being João Serrão), who refused to give him his freedom, as promised in Magellan's will. Enrique convinced Humabon to invite the officers and crew to a banquet. There, in a scene worthy of Shakespeare, Humabon's guards slaughtered twenty-six of them, including Barbosa. Humabon was willing to have Serrão ransomed for the gifts the rajah had given Magellan, but João Carvalho, who had escaped the massacre and assumed command, refused. Serrão, according to Pigafetta, "prayed God that at the day of judgment he would demand his soul of his friend João Carvalho."

The survivors sailed off in the three ships, but scuttled one off the waters of Bohol Island, leaving only the *Victoria* and the *Trinidad*. And only the *Victoria*, of the original five, completed the circumnavigation of the globe, limping into Sanlúcar de Barrameda in 1522, three years after the expedition set out. Just eighteen of the original complement of 260 men survived. With Sebastian Elcano as the pilot, the crew was said to have been the first to circumnavigate the globe. But the slave Enrique de Malacca may have beaten them to the punch. The voyage had ended disastrously for Magellan and all the hardy souls who perished on that mind-blowing trip, but it prepared the way for four other Spanish expeditions.

AFTER MAGELLAN, THE DELUGE

The first post-Magellanic expedition was headed by Francisco García Jofre de Loaísa, with Elcano as his second-in-command. Seven ships and 450 men set off in 1525 from Coruña, Spain. Unfortunately, it was a voyage marked, even more than Magellan's, by disaster. By the time it had navigated its way through the Straits of Magellan, only two vessels were left. Subsequently, Loaísa and Elcano died within a few days of each other. Two more successors perished. The last, Hernando de la

Torre, steered the ships to Mindanao and thence to the Moluccas, where the crew was imprisoned by the Portuguese. Few survived, only eight returning to Spain in 1536, including Andrés de Urdaneta, who would return with the Legazpi expedition.

As directed and organized by Hernán Cortés, famed conqueror of the Aztec empire, the second expedition of three ships and 110 men, under the command of Alvaro de Saavedra, departed Mexico in 1527—the first Spanish voyage to Asia launched from the New World. Saavedra bore a royal letter for the ruler of Cebu, apologizing for Magellan's conduct and at the same time seeking to ransom any Spanish prisoners the good rajah might be holding. But only one ship reached Mindanao. Unable to locate Cebu, Saavedra sailed to Tidore in the Moluccas, where, meeting the remnants of the Loaísa expedition, he and his men were taken captive by the Portuguese. Released, he set sail for Mexico, but died at sea.

In the meantime, under the Treaty of Zaragoza of 1529—yet another renegotiation of the line of demarcation—Madrid gave up its claims to the Moluccas in return for 350,000 ducats from the Portuguese. Being west of this demarcation, the Philippines was theoretically within the ambit of Portugal, but Spanish attempts to colonize the archipelago did not cease, nor did Portuguese harassment of the Spanish, until it became clear that the Spanish had successfully colonized the islands.

The third expedition, made up of six ships and 300 men, set sail from Navidad, Mexico, on November 1, 1542, under Ruy López de Villalobos. After landfall in Palau and the Carolinas, the expedition arrived at the east coast of Mindanao in 1543. In Sarangani, the men started a colony, but lack of food forced them to sail to Tidore, where, not surprisingly, the Portuguese held them captive, and where Villalobos expired, attended to by the brilliant Jesuit missionary and future saint, Francis Xavier, later to head to Japan, thence to China, on pioneering evangelical missions. It was the Villalobos expedition that christened the islands Filipinas, after Felipe, the son of Charles I.

The final and most successful expedition was commanded by Miguel López de Legazpi, a Spanish Basque conquistador who had arrived in Mexico in 1530 and prospered. By the time of the Legazpi voyage, Crown Prince Felipe, or Philip II, had grown up and now occupied the Spanish throne. A zealous Catholic and partisan of Mary, Queen of

Scots, claimant to England's throne, he detested the English Protestant Queen Elizabeth. In 1588, Philip assembled a mighty fleet of warships, known simply as the Spanish Armada, consisting of 130 ships, with 8,000 sailors and 18,000 soldiers. Its purpose was to invade England, but Philip's much-vaunted armada was humiliated by the British navy in a series of engagements. The royal treasury had incurred tremendous expenses in assembling the Armada, and new sources of revenue, such as the Philippines promised, would be invaluable.

Legazpi's mission, as all the previous ones, was to secure a base in Southeast Asia and thence establish a route back to Mexico, so that precious cargo could be transported sans interference from the Portuguese. As with the other would-be conquistadors, Legazpi would be richly rewarded with money, trade concessions, and land. In the agreement between the Spanish monarch and the conquistadores, the Crown reserved certain rights in the colonies while the latter enjoyed the spoils of conquest. Thus, the desire for riches and prestige furnished powerful incentives for the men who undertook such dangerous expeditions, as they did for the royal court.

Legazpi's expedition left Navidad on November 21, 1564. Urdaneta, now a member of the Augustinian order, was coaxed out of retirement from a monastery in Mexico to pilot successfully the fleet to Cebu. (On board were six other members of the Augustinian Order, the first to undertake the Christianization of the islands.) Urdaneta then returned to Mexico in 1565, charting the route to be used in the galleon trade between Manila and Mexico that would be the new colony's financial lifeline for two centuries. Other key members of the Legazpi expedition were Martín De Goiti, Legazpi's grandson Juan de Salcedo, and Miguel de Loarca, who was to write *Relación de las Islas Filipinas*, a detailed account of his stay in the Philippines. Legazpi and his men began a sustained and ultimately successful effort to colonize the islands, with the Spanish Basque becoming the first governor general of this latest addition to the Spanish Empire.

Guided by Spanish colonial experience in both Americas and decrees from Madrid, Legazpi, as well as his successors, devised and enacted certain measures for the pacification and administrative control of the archipelago and to strengthen and protect Spanish sovereignty from enemies within and without. The colonial apparatus set in place was intended primarily to facilitate the exploitation, rather than the progressive development, of the islands for the benefit of the Crown and, in the process, enrich those who had claimed and ruled the territory on behalf of the monarch. From the outset the indigenous population was viewed through the prism of racism and a deeply held sense of cultural superiority. Unfortunately, having to deal with an inferior race was the cost of doing business.

Legazpi, like Magellan, initially based himself in Cebu, which the Spanish christened *Santissimo Nombre de Jesus* or the Most Holy Name of Jesus after a statue of the Santo Niño, or Holy Infant, a gift from Magellan to Rajah Humabon's Queen Juana, was found by a soldier in a hut. Harassed by the Portuguese, who believed that the islands fell within their side of the demarcation, Legazpi moved to nearby and more easily defended Panay Island. Seeking, as Magellan did, to strengthen his alliance with local datus, Legazpi entered into a blood compact in March 1565 with two chiefs of Bohol Island, Datu Sikatuna and Datu Sigala. It was a move precipitated by the fact that two years earlier, in 1563, according to Legazpi's account of the voyage, the Portuguese had, under the guise of friendship, plundered Bohol. The datus and their followers were therefore understandably wary of these strangers who resembled the Portuguese.

Hearing of a larger settlement up north blessed with an excellent bay, on the island of Luzon, Legazpi sent an exploratory mission, under the command of Goiti and De Salcedo. That settlement was Maynila, at the mouth of the Pasig River, its ruler Rajah Suleiman. Maynila was a large, fortified port, with cannons forged in foundries right by Suleiman's royal compound. The Pasig was an important artery leading to the lush lands east and south of Maynila, as well as to the country's largest freshwater lake, later named Laguna de Bay, and passage upriver required tribute paid to Maynila's ruler. Prior to 1565, Muslim port communities had already established themselves north of Mindanao, in Mindoro, and in Luzon, principally in the Maynila region and in what is now the province of Pampanga. The datus in Maynila and Tondo (across the river) were converts to the Muslim faith. Loarca noted that the river delta inhabitants were *Moros*—the Spanish word for "Moors," or Muslims—and that they had the art of writing, indicative of the fact that pre-Hispanic Maynilans possessed not only their own script, but were aware of Bornean and Arabic writing.

The Goiti mission made overtures to Rajah Suleiman, but suspicious of the Spanish, the rajah rejected these, and inevitably fighting broke out. Goiti emerged triumphant and Maynila was burned to the ground. On the departure of the Spanish for Panay, however, Suleiman and his men returned to rebuild the port. The next year, 1571, the Spanish returned, this time with Legazpi himself in command of a larger force that included twenty-seven boats (most supplied by the Visayans), 280 Spaniards, and a contingent of pintados, or Visayan warriors. Rather than yield, Suleiman ordered Maynila razed once more. Later on Suleiman would assemble a coalition of like-minded datus from barangays in nearby Bulacan and Pampanga, but the native force was decisively defeated. With Suleiman's defeat, on June 3, 1572, Maynila was designated the seat of Spanish power in the islands, its name streamlined to Manila.

Strategically located and fronting a magnificent bay with a natural, deep-water harbor, Manila was granted a royal charter, which described it as the "distinguished and ever loyal city of Manila." Inhabitants of the new city were to be limited to Spaniards. In the process of this gentrification-cum-segregation, the native residents—disparagingly called "Indios"—were forced to resettle elsewhere. Manila was to become the capital of the newest colony, made up of Luzon, Visayas, and parts of Mindanao. While the colony was formally named "El Nuevo Reyno de Castilla," most preferred the easier-to-say Filipinas, and that is what stuck.

Acquiring its own coat-of-arms, Manila was planned as a European-type city, with a grid of streets and a main plaza, around which were to be the cathedral and various important public edifices. Sites were designated for monasteries, schools, and hospitals, as well as for a fort (the extant Fort Santiago), which would have its own smaller plaza. By 1603, formidable stone walls and a moat encircled the city, hence the name of Intramuros. By then there were approximately 600 houses within, while another 600 houses were located without. One estimate of the archipelago's population at the time put it at close to a million—a low-population density (Sumatra alone had a population of 2,400,000). Probable causes of this were the agricultural labor expected of women, abortion, disease, and warfare.

With Manila now in Spanish hands, and with smaller Spanish settlements in Cebu and Panay, Legazpi turned to the business of expanding and consolidating Spanish sovereignty. His intrepid grandson Juan

De Salcedo headed an expeditionary force that traveled as far south as the Bicol Peninsula, along the way winning some 26,000 Tagalogs over to the Spanish Crown, invariably by persuading their local datus that it was in their interest to be allies rather than foes. In Paracale, Bicol, they came across what every conquistador dreams of: gold mines. Subsequently, Legazpi ordered De Salcedo north, where, with the aid of Rajah Lakandula, ruler of Tondo and uncle of the impetuous Suleiman, he was no less successful, putting down resistance in the provinces of Zambales, Pangasinan, and the Ilocos region. During his sojourn in the tribal lands of the Ilocanos, Villa Fernandina (named in honor of Fernando, eldest son of Philip II) was founded. It is now the city of Vigan, capital of the province of Ilocos Sur.

Though harried by the Portuguese, perhaps the greatest threat to early Spanish dominion came from the seagoing Chinese warlord Limahong, who appeared off Manila in late 1574, commanding a flotilla of sixty-two warships, 2,000 warriors, and as many seamen, along with artisans, farmers, and women. By this time, Legazpi had died of a heart attack, succeeded by Guido de Lavezares. Confident that he could overwhelm the Spanish, Limahong sent an attack force of 600 men, commanded by his Japanese lieutenant with the Sinicized name of Sioco. Working their way from the city's southern environs, Sioco and his men laid waste to the towns in their path, among them Malate, now a neighborhood of modern Manila. In this initial encounter, Martín Goiti was killed, but his and his men's stubborn resistance gained time for Manila's defenders. The Chinese force assaulted Manila but were repulsed by the garrison there.

De Salcedo, who had in the meantime marched south from Vigan— or Villa Fernandina, which he had been granted as an *encomienda* or district over which an appointed Spaniard ruled—arrived to take over the defense of the city just before Limahong himself, still confident of victory, landed with the bulk of his men. Complicating matters was a revolt threatened by Rajah Lakandula and Rajah Suleiman, as the conflict with Limahong loomed. The two rulers felt their prerogatives as chiefs were being ignored by the Spanish. De Salcedo won them over by promises of reforms and concessions. Together with his Filipino allies, de Salcedo and the battle-tested Spanish soldiers beat Limahong's army back to their ships. The Chinese warlord sailed up the northwestern coast to Pangasinan, perhaps thinking to settle there, but Salcedo and his by now larger force pursued and destroyed the Chinese fleet, though Limahong escaped.

The Spanish weren't the only ones desirous of seeing the corsair dead. The Chinese imperial government had sent over a high-ranking official in 1575 to request the repatriation of Limahong, though that was no longer possible. But the Spanish, under the direction of Governor General de Lavezares used the occasion to send a delegation to China, to establish friendly relations and trade. Indeed, Beijing sent over an emissary in 1576, to conclude a commercial treaty, and immigration from the Middle Kingdom was encouraged as a source of skilled and cheap labor.

While friendly relations with China ensured that the Iberians didn't need to worry about threats from Beijing, Chinese immigration would periodically contribute to rising tensions between the Spanish settlers and the growing numbers of Chinese laborers and artisans. There were attempts to restrict the influx to no avail. In 1603, the Crown decreed that no more than 3,000 Sangleys (from the Chinese phrase for traders) be allowed to live in the colony, proposing that ships from China be sent back "full of people. In this way they can be removed and the country cleared of them, with more gentleness and kind treatment, as has already been done with many of them."

The tensions would sometimes lead to armed uprisings and the inevitable bloodbaths that followed. Governor Arandia in 1578 might have foreseen this when he attempted to supplant the Chinese with mestizos and a larger influx of Spanish. But Spain was too far, and China too near, for this to succeed. And the Chinese émigrés, with a presence then as now throughout Southeast Asia, had excellent survival as well as artisanal and trading skills to flourish in an environment that was to them far more conducive to growth than in China. By the end of the sixteenth century, more than 20,000 Chinese resided in the Parian district, just outside the walls of Intramuros, outnumbering the Spanish. The rapid growth of the Chinese immigrant community made the Spanish uneasy, and when a Chinese mission arrived in Manila in 1603, desirous of obtaining gold, the suspicions of the Spanish civil authorities were easily aroused. They instituted precautionary measures that in turn inflamed the resident Chinese, who decided, under the leadership of Juan Bautista de Vera, a Chinese convert to Catholicism, to strike the first blow. Their assault on Intramuros was repulsed, however, and the rebels fled to the mountains of Laguna and Batangas, where they were defeated by the Spanish forces—a combination of Spaniards, Filipinos, and even some Japanese. About 23,000 Chinese were killed as a result.

There were other revolts by the Chinese, for in spite of restrictive measures against their immigration, their numbers increased steadily. In 1639, in the town of Calamba, not far south of Manila, they took up arms against the local authorities and succeeded in destroying and plundering more than twenty towns before the rebels were defeated. In 1662, following the example of Limahong almost a century earlier, Koxinga, a Chinese warlord who had conquered Formosa, threatened to invade Manila unless the Spanish paid him tribute. The Spanish refused, to no consequence. The Chinese threat to the Spanish would be mainly from within, but the tensions would diminish as the Han immigrant communities set down roots even as they expanded.

In addition to the Chinese, the Japanese also had small communities in the islands, for, as the Chinese, though not as numerous, the Japanese had been a presence even before the arrival of the Spaniards. There were Japanese communities in a neighborhood of Manila (present-day Paco) as well as in Bulacan, and in what was to become known as La Union, a coastal province up north. Salcedo had run-ins with Japanese ships off the coast of Pangasinan in 1572, and in 1583, a Spanish captain engaged the Japanese by the mouth of the Cagayan River.

In 1591, Toyotomi Hideyoshi, unifier and shogun of Japan, demanded tribute and homage, but military expeditions in Korea the next year, through which he hoped to conquer China and, later, his death, forestalled any planned invasion. Iyeyasu Tokugawa, the succeeding shogun, worried by the threat that Christianization might undermine his rule, closed off the island nation to the *gaijin*, and proceeded to ban Christianity and prosecute, to the point of executions, those who had converted. Some Japanese Christians sought and were given asylum in Manila, among them some lords such as Takayama Ukon.

SEVENTEENTH CENTURY: SETTLEMENTS THROUGHOUT THE ARCHIPELAGO

By the beginning of the seventeenth century, largely through the foundational and level-headed leadership of Legazpi, the sword arms of de Salcedo and Goiti, alliances with regional datus, and the missions established by hardy friars, the Spanish exercised sovereignty, even if only in rudimentary form, in Luzon (except for the mountainous regions up north and the eastern coast) and in much of the Visayas. By no means did this mean the disappearance of threats from without or within. All throughout Spanish rule, such threats existed, from small- and large-scale revolts, foreign invasions, harassment out at sea, and the ever-present threat from the Muslim south. The Protestant Dutch constituted the most serious threat to Spanish hegemony. Dutch warships threatened Manila and its surrounding settlements at least on three occasions, between 1600 and 1647, but each time were repulsed by the Spanish and their Filipino conscripts.

Early on, there was some discussion as to whether it was worth keeping the islands. Legazpi, writing to the King in 1569, was convinced that the islands were worth holding onto, that "if the land is settled and peopled by Spaniards we shall be able to get plenty of gold, pearls, and other valuable articles. . . . [T]hus partly through commerce and partly through the articles of commerce, the settlers will increase the wealth of the land in a short time." Madrid finally decided to stay put, persuaded as well by the friars that the archipelago could be a base for missionary forays to mainland Asia, and by its own ambition of extending its empire throughout the East. Indeed, from time to time, Spanish ships sailed out of the islands on exploratory expeditions or to do battle in defense of their colony. Until the eighteenth century, the Philippines served mainly as a military outpost, subsidized by grants from Nueva España, or Mexico, the galleon trade, and tribute from the indigenous population.

The new colony was ruled by the Spanish king, of course, but through the viceroyalty of Mexico. The archipelago's Governor and Captain General was to be the King's representative in the islands, enforcer of the *Patronato Real* (Royal Patronage) and overseer of the King's interests. The Patronato Real was essentially a Crown policy that set rules for the presence and behavior of the Catholic Church in the colonies, guaranteeing that this would be under the supervision of the throne and of the particular colonial government. In effect, the clergy became part of the government, bringing about a union of church and state. As it turned out, this marriage proved to be more felicitous for the former than for the latter.

As a reward for his success in driving away the infidel Moors towards the end of the fifteenth century, the Catholic King Ferdinand had asked for and received from the pope the right of patronato real over all churches to be established in the territory of the *reconquista*. This was exactly what the Crown wanted, and Ferdinand skillfully maneuvered thereafter to secure from the papacy extensions of his patronato to all his overseas dominions on the ground that evangelizing the heathen, or Indios, was the same as recovering Granada for Christendom.

Evangelical work in the new territory thus came under royal supervision. Since the colony was to be administered from Mexico, Rome had no direct contact with the clergy in the new lands. The Spanish monarch also had veto power over the promulgation of papal bulls and exercised through his viceroys close supervision over ecclesiastics in his dominions. The Crown energetically used this prerogative, thus precipitating constant conflicts between, on one hand, Madrid and its servants, and, on the other, Rome and its men of the cloth. The Patronato Real was the primary instrument by which Spain could recruit the Church, as a complement to its rising commercial ventures. To speak of the Church in the Philippines during the Spanish regime was thus to speak of the Spanish clergy and the Spanish empire, each serving the ends of the other.

Even though spreading Christianity and converting the natives to the faith was the primary justification for the Spanish presence, the king as patron of the Church in the Philippines had the authority to determine the limits of the mission territories and approve the assignment of missionaries. He also had the duty to protect them as well as provide for their support. In addition to being representatives of Rome, the friars were in effect salaried employees of the Spanish court.

The supreme authority in the administration of the colonies would lie in the hands of the Council of the Indies, created by Ferdinand and reorganized by Charles in 1524. On behalf of the throne, the Council enacted laws and decrees to govern the colonies—the compilation of which came to be known as *Leyes de Indias*. As with other Spanish colonies, Las Islas Filipinas was to have the *Real Audiencia*, a legislative-judicial body. There would be a full panoply of civil servants while a separate set of officials managed the Spanish king's personal estate in Las Filipinas. In sum, this Asian colony was to be governed in a manner similar to Spain's colonies in the Americas.

Encomiendas and Tributes

One mechanism by which control was exercised was through the *encomienda*. An encomienda was not a land grant, but rather a system—adapted in all the Spanish colonies—under which an *encomendero* (the term comes from the Spanish *encomendar* or "to entrust") was charged with a number of natives living within a specific geographic area whom he was supposed to instruct in the Catholic faith and the Castilian tongue. Natives living within the encomienda were deemed subject to Spanish sovereignty, with the encomendero taking on the role of petty king. He had the power to collect tribute, basically a tax, and to expect unpaid labor, or *corvée*, from the inhabitants of the encomienda. The tribute furnished the revenue for such expenses as those of the missionaries imparting Christian doctrine and running the encomienda. It provided the encomendero and his family with their means of living. The encomienda was usually the reward for military men who had participated in the conquest and could be inherited for two, sometimes three, generations. After the limit had been reached, the land, or more accurately, control over it, reverted to the Crown. The movement of the natives was regulated to ensure a steady supply of labor and the systematic and prompt collection of the tribute.

The encomendero was charged with ensuring the well-being of the Filipinos, a duty that included a good Christian education. Unfortunately, the battle-tested encomenderos treated the natives more like delinquent military units than a community of human beings, abusing them by exacting both tribute and labor. The encomienda system also gave the encomenderos a pretext for seizing land from barangay inhabitants. The system was finally abolished in 1720, though in the mid-nineteenth century, there still existed eleven encomiendas.

The encomienda was an important tool in the early stages of Spanish colonization, rewarding those who had served the Spanish throne well. (Such was the case with Miguel de Loarca, an early chronicler of the Spanish conquest and member of the Legazpi expedition, given an encomienda on Panay island.) While the encomienda encompassed native settlements, it was not to be confused with a hacienda. The latter meant that ownership of the land resided with an individual, and those working the land were his tenants. He could dispose of the land freely, and his family inherited the land. In contrast, ownership of land within an encomienda remained with individuals and their families. Upon the death of a landowner, rights to the land passed on to his or her heirs. In the absence of heirs, ownership of the land passed to the barangay or town, which could then utilize that property to help pay for the town's tributes.

The encomenderos enjoyed their privileges fully but barely fulfilled their obligations. To them, Filipinos were little more than a resource to be exploited. Far from the administrative reach of Spain and even of Mexico, and with the colonial state apparatus stretched thinly, an encomendero was and usually did act like a petty tyrant. He invariably demanded that the Indios in his encomienda serve him and, if he didn't get what he wanted, would punish them. According to the friar Martín de Rada's account, "We have gone everywhere with the mailed hand; and we have required the people to be friends, and then to give us tribute. At times war has been declared against them, because they did not give as much as was demanded." De Rada characterized the tribute demands as "excessive" and reported that the encomenderos "maintain stocks, in which they keep as prisoners the chiefs . . . who do not supply the amount of tribute."

Tribute was exacted from males between the ages of nineteen and sixty. Payment of tribute from slaves owned by the native nobility was required as well. If the slave was a sagigilid, then his or her master paid the tribute. A namamahay, on the other hand, living apart from the master, had to shoulder the tribute. (These conditions applied as well to the Spanish who did have slaves, though later they were forbidden to acquire them.) The encomendero kept a quarter of the tribute, a quarter, went to the friars, and the balance to the colonial government. In turn, the encomendero maintained peace and order, helped the missionaries in their apostolic work and ensured the encomienda's readiness to come to the defense of the colony, should this be required.

In addition, the local population was obliged to render a certain amount of personal service to the Spanish, whether to the encomendero, the *gobernadorcillo* ("little governor" essentially the town mayor), or the parish priest. Men between the ages of sixteen and sixty were expected to donate their labor, known as *polos y servicios*, for forty days each year to so-called community projects. These services ranged from servant work and the supply of foodstuffs to shipbuilding and military service, which in turn could be anything from crewing on a warship to working in artillery units. The exaction of forced labor—especially in the felling of trees and the building of ships—that continually disrupted livelihoods (such as working on one's land), would be a constant irritant to the subject populace and perpetual incitement to rebellion.

By the time of Legazpi's death of a heart attack in 1572, he had assigned 143 encomiendas to his men. Guido de Lavezares, his successor, not only assigned new encomiendas but reassigned those that fell vacant, thus disregarding explicit orders that such vacancies revert to the Crown. Once an encomienda did fall under the jurisdiction of the Crown, it was looked after by an *alcalde mayor*, who collected the tributes and answered only to Manila.

Such were the abuses and cruel exactions from the encomenderos, and later from the various government officials who would take over their functions, that the local populations wound up impoverished and degraded—conditions they now had to endure regularly and so very different from the lives they had led prior to Spanish rule. In many instances, the conditions approached those of slavery, leading friars to complain—though, as the friars themselves grew to be very much a part of the colonial establishment, these diminished as their own abusive behavior increased. By mid-seventeenth century, as more and more administrative positions were taken over by the civil government, the number of private encomiendas dwindled with the corresponding increase in Crown lands.

Keeping the Filipinos in Line

Combining the exactions of tribute and physical labor with the imperative of gaining converts to the Catholic faith demanded a framework for control. In practical terms, this meant integrating the original barangay into such a framework. Given how few the Spaniards were, and how much larger the native population, how was this to be accomplished? Part of the answer lay in resettlement, or *reducción*, wherein a large number of barangays lost their autonomy and were consolidated to form pueblos, the agglomeration of which, in turn, constituted the provinces of the new dispensation.

In Spain's South American colonies, resettlement was implemented jointly by church and state. In the Philippines friars shouldered the lion's share of the burden. It was only natural that there would be opposition to the resettlement program, for it meant whole villages being uprooted from areas where they had their fields and lived for generations. A number of techniques were employed by the clergy, and by the civil authorities as well, to convince the reluctant native to move, such as gifts of housing within the reducciónes. Barangay chiefs were given titles and awarded honors. Too, the theatricality of church rites—from the saying of Mass to the administering of the sacraments—seemed to have been another attraction. Otherwise, backed by soldiers, the friars resorted to threats.

Quite often, aware of the power of the friars, inhabitants of barangays would elect resettlement under the charge of the religious to secure protection from the oppression and cruelty of the encomenderos. Some sort of compromise allowed those still reluctant to move into the reducción itself to live in nearby areas, giving rise to the *poblacíon* (town) and barrio (outlying district) system which continues to this day. The church in each poblacíon symbolized the power of the colonial state as much as the *municipio*, or town hall, the seat of civil authority, and served as the focal point of the cultural and social life of the town.

Similar to that of Intramuros, the layout of each pueblo centered on a town plaza, around which were situated the church-convent, the municipio, and *la escuela* or schoolhouse, embodying the hierarchy in colonial society. Naturally, the homes of the town's more prominent citizens—members of the *principalia*, or power-holders—were located at or near the plaza, a nod to their importance. As go-betweens for both the colonizer and the native population, the principalia identified and were identified with those above them, their increasing wealth creating a gap separating them from the rest of their countrymen and leading to a class structure more pronounced than in pre-colonial days. More often than not, these officials were drawn from the ranks of the pre-Hispanic elite—ensuring the survival of a significant portion of the old ruling class. It was lucrative for former datus to be believers not only in the faith of the church but in that of the Spanish state as well.

The highest position open to the Filipino was that of *gobernadorcillo*, the equivalent of town mayor. He was the colonial state's point man, as it were, collecting tributes and mobilizing labor for government projects. Any shortfall he had to shoulder, otherwise he could be fined or, worse, imprisoned. The advantage of course was that the system could be gamed so that the position provided the official a steady and relatively easy means of making money.

The new settlement pattern was partly determined by the notion that every resident live *abajo de las campanas,* "under the bells," or within hearing distance of the church. Being able to hear the bells meant being able duly and faithfully to attend mass, and respond to a call to arms should the need arise. More importantly, it placed a majority of the town's inhabitants within the immediate orbit of the cleric, ensuring that the people had to be in a Spanish friar's *doctrina,* or mission station, for their instruction in the faith. There were those who, desiring not to live too close to the town center, moved to the surrounding barrios where they straddled two worlds, that of their traditional ways and that of the colonizer and learned early on how to move easily between two cultures, in effect creating a third space. They lived in subordinate villages or barrios and in even smaller communities called *sitios.* There was a practical reason for this: many resisted moving far from their fields. The clergy adapted by constructing chapels in the larger villages and making periodic visits to say mass and teach the catechism, which practice came to be known as *visita.*

Native life under the colonial regime acquired a complexity not heretofore known. Each colonized Filipino was expected to live in a pueblo for purposes of civil government; be part of a doctrina, for religious instruction; and of an encomienda for the exaction of tribute, produce, and labor.

THE FRIARS AND THE CIVIL STATE: WHO REIGNED AND WHO RULED?

An ongoing debate, and at times open conflict, during the Spanish colonial period, was between the religious orders and the civil administration. Underlying the debate was the question of who was truly sovereign in the archipelago, the Vatican or Madrid? It was clear from the Patronato Real that the Spanish monarch held sovereign sway over all matters pertaining to the conditions in the colony, be these in the secular or the spiritual realm, including oversight of the appointment of religious personnel to the distant colony. On the ground, however, it was a far different story as to who held actual power, at least as far as the local populace was concerned.

The distance from Madrid meant relatively few lay peninsular Spaniards made it to Southeast Asia. The *peninsulares* (as they were called) were augmented by Mexican Spaniards, but the aggregate still wasn't sufficient. Hence, the religious did double duty, as spiritual and material administrators, wherever they had set up missions and, later, in parishes under their control. The subsequent increase in prestige and material wealth of the friars led to power struggles with the colonial establishment. Invariably, the priests would claim the authority of the papacy to justify their position and resist the authority of the archbishop who nominally had jurisdiction over parishes. One of the early instances of the two spheres conflicting was in the case of encomenderos, who were mostly ex-military men. As noted, the encomienda system was rife with abuse. The friars complained of such abuses—which included the encomenderos' withholding the friars' fair share of the tributes—to the colonial government and to the King.

The discord between the encomenderos and the friars was really about power: Who was to be the guardian over the lives of the encomienda's inhabitants, whose labor and property, after all, served as the source of both their revenues? But friar complaints were often seen as self-serving. In the late sixteenth century, one governor general, Gómez Pérez Dasmariñas, for example, felt the friars were using the alleged abuses to highlight what they believed to be their own superior qualifications. The not-so-hidden rifts between the civil and religious worlds could be traced to the question undergirding Spanish presence on the islands: What was the moral and legal basis of their sovereignty over the populace? The arguments propounded basically rested on the rationale that colonial presence was a mutually beneficial and legitimate compact between the Filipinos and the Spanish overlords. The Spanish king promised them even-handed administration, protection from their enemies, and religious education. It was as though individual pacts between the datus and the Spanish—the ones between Rajah Humabon and Magellan, and Sikatuna and Legazpi, being the prototypes—held true for all of the islands. In effect, the population was being asked to believe that their subjugation was really their liberation.

In sum, Spanish colonial Philippines, though less than a perfect union of Church and State, could be "viewed either as a civilizing Church or a missionary State," as the late, twentieth-century Filipino Jesuit historian Horacio de la Costa put it.

With so many fresh souls to be harvested—one could say the colony formed a kind of spiritual Spice Islands for missionaries—priests were in demand for this faraway outpost of the Spanish empire. At the outset, those assigned to Las Islas Filipinas were experienced and genuinely committed to the spiritual goals of a missionary life. The first Bishop of Manila, the Dominican Domingo de Salazar, convened a council of clerics in 1582. Through his urging the council declared that sovereignty and adjudication "by natural right belong to the Indios and neither the King nor the Pope can take it away from them. . . . the Indios are as free in their lands as the Spaniards are in theirs, and their liberty is not taken away by the King or by the Gospel."

Such noble sentiments, being resolutely anti-colonial, were easily and subsequently disregarded, as the trappings of power came to fit the friar as comfortably as they did the civilian administrator. The economic and social privileges granted to them by the king gradually resulted in the lowering of standards, intellectually and morally. The very real possibility of getting materially rich made priesthood in the Philippines a lucrative proposition; God's calling the cover under which Mamon could be served eagerly and faithfully. The early years of hardship and asceticism gave way to pampered living.

Thus, for instance, by 1698, the Manila archbishop, on his visitation to certain parishes in Laguna, where friars acted as parish priests, had to forbid the exaction of fees from the parishioners for the performance of the sacraments. Charging a fee to hear a confession was not uncommon (anticipating, perhaps, the fees charged by modern-day psychiatrists). For Holy Communion to be administered to the dying, instead of the priest making a house call, the family was obliged to carry the individual to the church. Otherwise the family would have to pay a fee. In his book *The Roots of the Filipino Nation*, Onofre D. Corpuz remarks that "this had been the practice of the Spanish friars and curates since the early days of Hispanic Christianity in Filipinas. Previous orders prohibiting this practice . . . were ignored." Exorbitant fees effectively made the poor even poorer. In addition, the friars charged parishioners for supplying them with religious items such as rosaries and required them to provide both personal services and food—often, with a surplus that the good friar could then sell for profit. Nor was concubinage uncommon, leading to the popular albeit exaggerated observation that most Filipinos today have some friar blood in their veins.

Geographical distance and consequent isolation rendered consistent supervision difficult. And relying on the friars for administrative tasks, normally the province of civil servants, frequently resulted in their spiritual calling too often taking a back seat.

There were friars who stuck to their spiritual calling, of course, but absolute power corrupts absolutely. With their economic power, indispensable role in civil administration, and spiritual authority often wielded with the threat of excommunication, the friars succeeded in marrying their avowedly spiritual goals to the less pristine pursuit of material gain—with the latter assuming a more prominent role than would be seemly for the demands of a spiritual life. In this the friar was aided by the principalia, who had vested interests in the status quo; the inroads Catholicism had made into indigenous culture; and the availability of armed force should the Indios prove to be too restless under the strict rod. This unusual combination of power and prerogative made the friar the principal figure in each community and the Church the de facto dominant institution in the country.

A major reason for the ensuing corruption of the friars was land, now a commodity subjected to individual ownership, a concept the Spanish had introduced to the islands. Being in charge of parishes (normally reserved for the secular clergy, or diocesan priests who did not, unlike the friar, belong to any religious order and were therefore under the direct supervision of the diocesan bishop), the friar orders could own lands for their support. In time, the clergy replaced the encomenderos, whose arbitrary and exploitative practices they used to denounce. How did the men of the cloth acquire lands? By royal bequest; donations; inheritances from the pious desirous, no doubt, of assuring themselves a place in heaven; through the outright purchase of property from the locals with the money the friars had gained from church fees, from trade, or from the produce of lands earned through forced labor; and from foreclosures, the tenant farmer unable to pay the money he had borrowed, most likely from the friars themselves, and thus forced to give up the land he had pledged as collateral.

The principalia, agents of the Spanish colonial apparatus, also took advantage of the privatization of property, disregarding the tradition of communally held land. Land was previously seen principally as a source of food for consumption and barter and not an index of wealth. The principalia were able to acquire individual and legal titles to land, with the resident tillers now as tenant farmers—a new and disempowering status. During the seventeenth century the process of transferring more land to fewer people grew apace, so that by 1800 the provincial hierarchy, heavily dependent on agriculture, was made up of the estate-owning friar orders, the land-owning principalia, and the local popu-lace—the latter consisting mainly of tenant farmers and agricultural laborers.

Those working the friar lands—whether simple tenant farmers or *inquilinos*, natives who had the means to sublet their leases to tenant farmers—had no recourse when their rents were raised almost every year. When accepting rent in kind, the friars determined the value of the goods, naturally below market rates, since they were powerful enough to fix the prices at which produce was to be bought and sold. Aside from their investments in land, the orders were actively engaged in the com-mercial life of the country. Through benevolent associations known as *obras pias*, which in effect acted like commercial banks, they invested in various commercial enterprises. Parishes were thus run like the colonial state that engulfed it: a seemingly endless source of profit that could be justified, and was, by the earthly demands of their, the friars', spiritual mission. Building the road to heaven didn't, after all, come cheap.

Since pacification rested mainly on the indigenous embrace of Catholicism, the religious played an inordinate role in maintaining Spanish power in most communities. Moreover, in so many of the barangays, no other Spaniard existed but the good friar, the only sym-bol of colonial authority.

Governors often complained of clerical abuses and appealed to Madrid to keep the clerics in line. A number of them took steps to curb the clerics' power but their efforts were for the most part successfully rebuffed. Perhaps the most extreme reaction to an activist governor was in 1719, when Governor General Fernando Bustamante—a military commander of high rank and the first such to be appointed governor general of the Philippines—was slain by a mob led by friars, who stormed the palace, overpowered the guard, and knifed the governor and his son to death. The governor had apparently found out that the friars had borrowed heavily from the government and from the obras pias. Bustamante demanded repayment of the loans and, to assert his authority, had the archbishop imprisoned on charges of having conspired against the government.

In another, earlier clash between the civil and religious spheres that ended bizarrely, Governor General Sebastián Hurtado de Corcuera, Spanish governor of the Philippines from 1635-1644, exiled Archbishop

Hernando Guerrero to Mariveles, a remote town across the bay. The cause for this humiliation? The prelate, along with most of the clergy, was enraged when the governor had a Spanish artilleryman by the name of Francisco de Nava dragged out of the San Augustin Church in Intramuros even though he had claimed sanctuary. Nava had knifed his female ex-slave to death in front of the church for refusing to marry him. He was tried, found guilty of murder, and hanged at the gallows erected right across from the church. To the clergy, particularly the Augustinians, this was a brazen insult. The archbishop had religious rites and services suspended.

Once Hurtado stepped down, the clergy (except for the Jesuits, who thought Hurtado had justifiable cause to ignore the right of sanctuary) insisted he be brought to court and punished. And so he was, found guilty and imprisoned for five years before finally being freed by royal order. It is said that as part of his sentence he was compelled to stand at the doors of churches, clad in the drab attire of a penitent, holding a lighted taper and a rope around his neck.

It wasn't as though the civil authorities themselves were models of democratic behavior and restraint. They were no less exploitative. For instance, the Guardia Civil, the nineteenth-century successor to local militias and essentially a police force found in major towns and villages, was much feared by the local populace for their often arbitrary and abusive behavior, as were petty town officials. In effect, extracting the most profit out of the colony turned into a fierce albeit unofficial competition between two rival spheres.

DEVELOPMENT OF THE ISLAND ECONOMY

Galleon Trade

The galleon trade, the foundations for which had been laid by Andrés de Urdaneta's successful return voyage to Mexico in 1565, involved the highly profitable shipment of goods from Manila—goods that for the most part came from China—to Acapulco. The voyage from Manila took four months, with the ships including in their cargo spices, ivory, porcelain, lacquerware, and processed silk. The goods were then trans-shipped overland to Veracruz, where they were loaded onto ships bound for Spain. Payment was in Mexican silver, so the galleon returning from Acapulco would be laden with the highly prized metal, along with provisions and passengers bound for the islands, providing a tempting target for privateers roaming the Pacific.

This trade was monopolized by Spaniards in Manila—and even then, only a select group that included the governor general, members of the Royal Audiencia, and the religious orders. Mexican silver helped sustain the colonial enterprise and was highly valued in China. Very little Philippine produce or products were shipped out, hence the galleon trade did little to spur domestic manufacture. Precisely because the galleon trade was profitable, the Spanish colonists paid scant attention to developing either the agricultural or manufacturing industry.

The lucrative Manila-Acapulco run led merchants in Spain, particularly in Cádiz and Sevilla, to petition the Crown to limit the number of ships that could ply the trade route. Hence, starting in 1593, only two ships a year were permitted to sail between Manila and Acapulco. Exports from Manila were limited to P250,000[*] worth of goods (later increased to P500,000). Mexican goods brought back were not supposed to exceed double the value of the exports. The profits from the galleon trade made Manila a prosperous city, evident in the construction of solid buildings and outer walls and the availability of luxury goods for those who could afford them. By 1650 the population of the Walled City and its surroundings was approximately 42,000. Most of the Spaniards in the islands were concentrated in Intramuros, while a thriving Chinese community occupied the Parian district, which lay just outside the city walls. As an indication of continuing Spanish distrust of the Chinese, on the thick walls of Intramuros facing the Parian were cannon trained on the district, in case its residents suddenly got restless.

But the galleons carried more than goods, bringing letters and decrees to and from Spain and Mexico, as well as new species of crops, such as maize, avocado, tomato, cacao, and sweet potato. (The word for the latter is *kamote* in Tagalog, *camotli* in Nahuatl.) And of course human cargo: officials, clerics, soldiers, etc. Inevitably, these commercial and administrative links between Mexico and Las Islas Filipinas had a cultural impact. A tangible symbol of those days and one of the most venerated icons in Philippine Christianity is the Black Nazarene, ensconced in a shrine at Quiapo Church in the heart of Manila. Carved by a Mexican craftsman and brought to the colony

---

[*] P for peso, the currency then, as now, of the country.

during the seventeenth century, the Nazarene is the object of daily ven-
eration by countless worshippers, an adoration that reaches its climax
every January 9, when it is paraded through the surrounding districts,
pulled by men and only by men, amidst sweaty, swaying throngs of
believers who attempt to wipe their handkerchiefs on the icon in the
hopes that its miraculous power will somehow be transmitted.

The trade between Mexico and the Philippines meant small colonies
of Filipinos taking up residence in the New World, and likewise, Mexicans
staying on in the Philippines. Probably the earliest settlement of Filipinos
in the New World was made up of crew members who jumped ship when
the galleons docked at Acapulco, the earliest know instance being in 1618,
when seventy-four Filipinos stayed on. Filipino sailors were to settle elsewhere in the Mexican state of Guerrero and even in the bayous near New
Orleans. These Louisiana Filipino expatriates were thereafter referred to as
the Manilamen. The earliest recorded settlement in the United States was
circa 1850, when St. Malo, a small fishing and shrimping village of
Filipinos, as well some Chinese and Native Americans, grew on the out-
skirts of New Orleans. (In 1883 the Anglo-Greek immigrant Lafcadio
Hearn wrote a feature on the village for *Harper's Weekly*, and described its
inhabitants as a "swarthy population of Orientals—Malay fishermen who
speak the Spanish creole of the Philippines as well as their own Tagal and
perpetuate in Louisiana the Catholic traditions of the Indies." In 1890
Hearn moved to Japan as a correspondent. There he married, took on the
Japanese name of Koizumi Yakumo, and acquired a reputation as a popu-
larizer of traditional Japanese culture.)

Essential to the way the island economy took shape were the
Chinese, already living, as we have seen, in the archipelago, albeit in
small numbers, when the Spanish arrived. Their numbers grew, however, once the Spanish had settled in and exerted control over the
islands. The presence of the Europeans and the galleon trade meant an
expansion of commerce—with Manila as the transshipping port—and
the acquisition of the much-valued Mexican silver. Spanish presence
also meant the demand for the services of Chinese artisans. Gradually,
the influx of traders and artisans, mostly from the southern coastal
provinces like Fujian, Amoy, and Guangdong, caused the resident
communities of Chinese to expand.

Relying on the profitable galleon trade and the prerogatives of
colonial government (especially the polos y servicios) to lead privileged

and often luxurious lives, the Spanish left the retail trade and the crafts to the Chinese who came to dominate both. Thus was laid the foundation by which the Chinese assumed a prominence, if not dominance, in the economy that continues to the present.

Soon ubiquitous in the rural areas, the Chinese merchants acted as intermediaries between the cash system and the product-oriented native economy. And so Chinese retailers and tradesmen had an enormous impact on the colony's economic life, distributing Chinese goods to Philippine villages and selling local products to the Spaniards. In this way, too, the Chinese dispersed through the archipelago, to as far south as Muslim Jolo, seat of the Sulu Sultanate.

Consequently, the Philippine economy developed three distinct tiers: that of the Spanish, that of the Chinese, and that of the natives— corresponding to the existence of three distinct cultural communities. Intermarriage did occur frequently between the Chinese and the locals, so that by the late eighteenth century, enough Chinese mestizos existed as to be classified separately by the government. (In addition, to ease the suspicions of the Spanish, many Chinese converted to Catholicism.)

The existence of these distinct economies would invariably be affected by the country gradually opening up to global markets, especially by the middle of the eighteenth century (a globalization that moved along on cultural and political axes as well as economic ones). Driven by an entrepreneurial spirit, and with an informal network already in place, the Chinese more than the colonizing Spanish assumed a larger and more vital role in the economic development of the country, the Chinese being the middleman, buyer, and often the supplier in the numerous towns and villages upended the pre-conquest economic patterns of the Filipinos. Especially in the retail trade, the Chinese rose to preeminent positions.

For all that, government regulations were antiquated, the product of a vanished era. Some attempts at the close of the eighteenth century were made to institute far-reaching economic reforms that would have helped the colony metamorphose into more than just an outpost of a declining empire and source of raw materials. By then, the colony's population stood at a million and a half, with the bishoprics of Manila and Cebu consisting each of 500,000 inhabitants. Governor José de Basco y Vargas (1778-1787) formed the Sociedad Económica de Amigos del País, to regularize agricultural enterprises and improve methods and techniques. He established a monopoly on tobacco in 1782, beginning in

Nueva Ecija, Cagayan Valley, and Marinduque. The monopoly proved to be highly profitable, but these profits were siphoned off due to corruption. Later, the monopoly was expanded to include the Ilocos region.

Taking advantage of the monopoly, a minor Spanish nobleman, Marqués de Comillas, founded the Compañia General de Tabaco de Filipinas, popularly and still known as Tabacalera, one of the oldest tobacco leaf dealers in the world. The company essentially took over the tobacco factories the Spanish had set up in the archipelago, controlling the export of tobacco to Spain. Tabacalera soon expanded into sugar, copra, shipping, and liquor.

Basco also established a branch of the Royal Company of the Philippines, which had been founded in Spain in 1785 and loosely patterned after the British East India Company. The company aimed to regulate commerce between the mother country, Spain, and Asia, by way of the Cape of Good Hope, and to bring goods directly from China to Manila, without being bound by the schedule of Chinese junks. The company also hoped to spur domestic manufacturing through the exploitation of natural resources. An attempt to compete with textiles from Bengal and Coromandel, however, resulted in heavy losses. And by 1790, the company had yet to establish trade relations directly with India, China, or Japan, relying as before on middlemen in Manila. As much as an agent of change that it may have been, the Company's privileges were revoked, and by 1834 the agency was abolished. It had proven to be a complete failure, crippled by consistently bad management and excessive speculation.

The colonial government declared Manila to be a free and open port in 1789 for a limited time and made permanent in 1805. In 1796, the first American merchant ship docked in Manila. By 1814, Manila had a vibrant community of foreign merchants. (In the Visayas, the ports of Iloilo and Cebu were declared open to foreign trade in 1855 and 1865 respectively, resulting in the local economies expanding and a corresponding increase in the ranks of the petit bourgeoisie.) Even so, the foreign merchants could only trade in Asian goods and were not allowed to participate in the trade between the colony and Spain. Easily circumvented, these restrictions were gradually lifted. With that, more than two centuries of isolation ended. This opening up to the West, for it was the West that most avidly desired it, took place more or less at the same time other Asian ports were opening up: in China, Japan, and Siam (present-day Thailand).

The opening up of Manila meant that the once-sleepy port was now booming. Trading ships from Europe and North America made regular calls. The city's population grew to approximately 150,000 by the middle of the nineteenth century. Migrants from nearby provinces flocked to the city for jobs as well as for higher education and cultural enrichment—the typical lures of any developing urban center. It accelerated the opening of the rest of the country while foreign investment and capital stimulated the local agriculture industry.

This was especially true in the sugar, abaca, and copra industries. Technological improvements, the rising demand for these products in international markets, and the subsidies provided by foreign traders and importers led to dramatic increases in yields for these crops. They had become prime commodities globally, though naturally subject to the vagaries of the marketplace.

Sugar was a prime illustration. Until the mid-nineteenth century, sugar was a bit player in the Philippine economy. But with Iloilo as an open port in 1855, the sugar industry took off on Negros Island, across Guimaras Straits, its soil perfect for sugar cultivation. The island population increased dramatically, from 30,000 in 1850 to 320,000 by 1893, as land was cleared for sugar plantations and towns were built and infrastructure put into place. The introduction of steam-powered mills in 1860 by British merchants, much more entrepreneurial than the Spanish, caused a 600-fold increase in output, from 200 tons in 1850 to 120,000 tons in 1893. Similar increases in sugar production took place in Central Luzon as well.

By the close of the nineteenth century and well into the twentieth, sugar constituted a major source of export earnings. The abundance of sugar meant the production of rum, of which sugar is the most important raw material. In 1860, a trading partnership and steamship company founded a few years earlier by a Spanish family, the Elizaldes, built the Tanduay distillery in Manila that to this day produces its signature rum. But while sugar provided the sweet life for a few landed families, it in turn caused dislocation and bitter misery for peasants deprived of their land. The late nineteenth-century agrarian upheaval caused by large-scale *azucareras* (sugar refineries) created a class of seasonal farm laborers called *sacadas,* who migrated to different plantations during the harvest season to work for abysmal wages while enduring degrading living conditions. (In the twenty-first century, not much has changed. The sacada is still there and so is the exploitation.)

The liberalization of trade resulted in a relatively more diverse financial system. Up to then, local businessmen and farmers were subject to usurious loans, complicated by the fact that the domestic financial institutions were usually beholden to the friar orders. With foreign trading companies and their financial backers on the scene, local entrepreneurs could turn to them for less onerous terms.

The first bank founded by a Filipino was the Rodriguez Bank, circa 1831. Francisco Rodriguez was quite a wealthy man living in Manila when in 1823 he was wrongly accused of being involved in a local conspiracy spearheaded by three Mexican-born Spanish army officers in the islands. These officers were accused of harboring rebellious motives, due both to Mexico's new status as an independent nation and the fact that the newly appointed governor of the archipelago, Juan Antonio Martínez (1822-1825), had in 1822 brought with him several officers from the continent whom he favored, bypassing the more senior officers already in the colony, among them the three conspirators. The conspiracy was found out, two officers were deported, and the third, Andrés Novales, was reassigned to Mindanao. After a short time, however, Novales rallied 800 disgruntled soldiers to his side and led a mutiny, which was quickly put down and Novales executed. The Novales Mutiny as it was termed was the first attempted coup d'etat during Spanish colonial rule in the islands, although one that sprung from narrow grievances rather than any newfound sense of nationalism.

Implicated in the Novales affair along with several other civilians, Rodriguez was sent to Cádiz in 1825 as a political prisoner. He managed to escape and fled to London, from where he waged an unsuccessful campaign to convince his friends and relatives to plead his innocence before the civil authorities in Manila. Unable to gain access to his riches, he became destitute and undoubtedly would have died penniless and heartbroken had he not been taken in and cared for by Quakers in London, with whom he lived for five years.

Not surprisingly, Rodriguez became a Quaker as well as a British subject. By then, the Spanish government pardoned all those involved in the uprising. Rodriguez returned to Manila, where he established the Rodriguez Bank, to assist foreign traders, primarily American and British, in their dealings with Filipinos and in direct competition with

Spanish financiers. Mindful of the difference between how he had been treated by the Spanish and the British, Rodriguez wore his Quaker outfit much to the delight of the children on the streets who ran after and jeered him, and the consternation of former friends, relatives, and especially the local friars. The religious establishment tried to have him expelled, but his British citizenship afforded him the protection he needed. Upon his death, he bequeathed his fortune to the Queen of England, for the benefit of the widows and orphans of British soldiers killed in the Crimean War. His relatives challenged the legitimacy of the will and initially won their suit. On appeal by the British government, however, the Supreme Court in Madrid reversed the decision by the lower court. The bank was shut down, and Rodriguez's fortune was eventually paid out to the British. The Quaker had had his revenge.

Other financial institutions that arose were the Obras Pias and the Banco Español-Filipino. In 1841, all but four confraternities—with their origins in the late sixteenth century, run by the religious orders and meant to extend financial assistance to Spaniards—were dissolved, presumably to increase their efficiency in light of the lower interest rates offered by foreign bankers, trading interests who were only too willing to extend loans to local farmers. The latter had been customarily denied recourse to funds reserved for the Spanish or would be charged usurious rates by the friars.

In a pattern that remains to this day, tenant farmers on the huge landed estates of the friar orders borrowed money at exorbitant rates in order to work the land and harvest the crops. It was a system almost guaranteed to keep a tenant farmer perpetually in debt, as market prices for their crops were invariably controlled either by middlemen who had ties to the friar orders, or by the friars themselves. The foreign merchants provided an alternative which native entrepreneurs eagerly took advantage of.

The remaining four confraternities were ordered by Governor General Antonio de Urbiztondo (1850-1853) to amalgamate in 1851 and become Obras Pias. The next year Governor Urbiztondo authorized the founding of the Banco Español-Filipino, which handled the more lucrative aspects of banking, including the right to issue bank notes—previously, Mexican currency had been used—thereby becoming the de facto government bank of the colony. Realizing that favoring Spanish merchants over

Filipinos deprived them of a potentially larger market, Banco Español-Filipino adopted the more liberal practices of its foreign competitors. In 1912, in keeping with the new colonial dispensation, the bank renamed itself as the Bank of the Philippine Islands, a venerable institution that continues to this day.

Despite its awareness of the need to keep up with modern business and trading practices, the government in Manila dragged its feet in instituting needed reforms. Partly in response to pressure applied by traders, a Tribunal of Commerce was established in 1834, later transformed in 1835 into the Chamber of Commerce, which was charged with impartially adjudicating disputes within the business community. But like other colonial institutions, it was just as susceptible to influence peddling as any other agency, and rarely accomplished anything worthy of note.

Such bureaucratic hurdles discouraged foreign traders from investing in the Philippines, with many lured to trade in China, which, mainly controlled by the British, had more liberal laws. With a decline in trade, the Manila government turned to Sinibaldo de Mas, an adventurer, poet, and the person believed to have introduced photography to the Philippines—he had brought the first daguerreotype camera to the islands. Charged with studying business conditions within the islands, de Mas came out with his *Informe Sobre el Estado de las Filipinas en 1842* (*On the Conditions of the Philippines in 1842*). Clearly against a protectionist policy he advocated that ports in addition to Manila should be opened, the tobacco monopoly be terminated, and immigration should be encouraged. He compared the Philippines with another Spanish colony, Cuba, and demonstrated convincingly how that Caribbean island, with a smaller population, had trade contracts worth $27 million, while the Philippines, with four times more inhabitants and a bigger physical and agricultural base, only took in about $5 million annually. When the reforms he had suggested were adopted and began to take effect, trade improved, with the Americans and the British becoming preeminent.

NATIVE RESISTANCE: MERCENARIES, CONSCRIPTS, AND REBELS

The Filipinos as colonial subjects bore most of the burden of a rule that theoretically was meant to benefit them. They were thus on the frontlines, whether on expeditionary trips to Borneo and the Moluccas, or fighting the

Dutch and the English on the high seas, or providing most of the labor on the galleons that plied the Manila-Acapulco route. In the early seventeenth century the Christianized Filipinos fought their non-Christian brothers in campaigns against Mindanao and Jolo, as well as putting down, often savagely, Chinese uprisings.

The earliest revolt came shortly after the Spanish had made Manila the seat of their still-shaky state, at a time when Limahong was threatening to destroy the city. As described earlier, Rajahs Lakandula and Suleiman (rulers respectively of Tondo and Maynila) felt their prerogatives had been slighted by the Spanish, but De Salcedo appeased them enough so that the two rulers added their forces to the corps of Manila's defenders. Limahong was thus defeated.

The imposition of colonial rule was rarely, if ever, smooth, with the indigenous populations in many communities resisting the curtailment of their traditional customs and liberties. Additionally, the obligation to pay tribute and render personal services—wartime duty, the building of ships, etc.—seriously limited their efforts to earn a living, necessary in the first place to pay the tribute, creating a vicious circle that seemed impossible to break. In the main, the locals were seen as another natural resource to be exploited, whether this was to increase the tally of souls saved, which the industrious friars kept tabs on, or to provide for a Spaniard's living. (The understandable reluctance of the indigenous folk to fulfill the demands of corvée would engender stereotypical portrayals of the Filipino as being naturally indolent—another reason advanced for the upliftment provided by colonial rule.) Abolition of the tribute and corvée were the main demands echoed by almost all uprisings throughout Spanish colonization.

From 1574 to the close of the seventeenth century, the Spanish colonial state had to put out fires of varying intensity, while dealing with external threats from rival European powers. Between 1574 and 1661, there were at least eight significant revolts. We have noted resistance offered by Suleiman and Lakandula. A decade later, in 1584, Agustin de Legazpi, a Christianized prominent citizen of Tondo, the ancient town that abutted Manila, organized a clandestine separatist movement—the first instance in the Spanish colonial period, and forerunner of the revolutionary movement that would erupt three hundred years later. Even with arms smuggled in by a sympathetic Japanese sea captain, the conspiracy was foiled, and de Legazpi and seven others were executed, including Magat Salamat, datu of Tondo. Fifteen others were deported to Mexico.

Uprisings occurred in various regions of the islands, indicating widespread dissatisfaction with Spanish colonial rule. Simultaneous though uncoordinated revolts by Bankaw in Leyte and Tamblot in Bohol in 1621 were to protest the imposition of a new faith, each leader wanting a restoration of traditional beliefs and practices. The very fact of their non-Christian appellations indicated either a refusal to be baptized or a discarding of their baptismal names. From 1649 to 1661, failed uprisings occurred in Samar, Pangasinan, Pampanga, and the Ilocos region. With no alliances beyond the particular barangay involved, these revolts were easily and bloodily suppressed.

During the first half of the seventeenth century, wars against the Dutch and military expeditions against the Muslims in the south strained the material and human resources of the Spanish colonists. As a result, abuses on the part of colonial officials, if not condoned, were overlooked for pragmatic reasons. In turn, such abuses generated resistance that took various forms depending on how organized a settlement was.

Dagohoy's Republic

The longest uprising during the Spanish colonial period took place on Bohol and was led by a *cabeza de barangay*, or barangay chief, Francisco Dagohoy. From 1744 to 1829—an astounding eighty-four years—Dagohoy and his followers numbering in the thousands lived in self-sufficient farming communities they had built in the mountainous interior of the island, for all intents and purposes declaring independence from Spanish sovereignty.

By all accounts an upstanding citizen who had until 1744 recognized the authority of both the church and the state, Dagohoy was incensed when the Jesuit curate of the town of Inabanga, Fr. Gaspar Morales, refused Dagohoy's brother, Sagarino, a Catholic burial. Sagarino, working for the town as a policeman, had been killed in an encounter with a fugitive, a former Christian turned apostate—a crime in those days. The Jesuit's reason for denying Sagarino a Christian burial was that his death had been occasioned by a duel, which the church forbade.

Understandably this refusal didn't sit well with Dagohoy, who, sworn to revenge, killed Fr. Morales. Another Jesuit curate in a nearby town was killed as well. Dagohoy led three thousand Boholanos to quit their pueblos and join him in setting up communities in the mountains. Dagohoy's following swelled to as many as twenty thousand over the years. Clearly, refusal of a Christian burial to his brother was the last straw, and emblematic of longer held grievances, the main one being the dreaded corvée. The charismatic Dagohoy would not have had such a large following had the rebels not already harbored their own festering resentments.

While Dagohoy and his followers observed the rites of Catholicism, such as baptism, and remained steadfast Catholics— though apparently without the services of ordained curates—they also emphasized the traditions of *bayanihan*, thereby eliminating tribute and forced labor. Best of all, the oppressive representatives and symbols of Spanish rule—the ubiquitous padre, the local militia, and the petty town officials—were absent. Life was so much better now for Dagohoy and his followers. In effect, they had become what the Spanish termed *remontados*—literally, "those who remount," i.e., take to their horses and leave the Spanish-controlled barangays, or people who had chosen to live outside the jurisdiction of the colonial state. Hampering the Spanish authorities' campaign to subdue the rebels were the well-entrenched positions and fortifications the latter had erected in their mountain lairs. Additionally, sympathizers provided them both supplies and information regarding possible Spanish attacks.

In the meantime, the Seven Years' War (1756 to 1763) had broken out in Europe. A global conflict that involved not only Europe but the New World (where it was known as the French and Indian War), Asia, and Africa, it was a battle between two colonial powers, France and England, with France losing most of its North American possessions as a consequence. With the Bourbon-descended Charles III of Spain allied with France, in 1759, a British military expedition organized by the British East India Company sailed to Manila from India. The invasion took the defenders of Intramuros completely by surprise, leading to an easy takeover in late 1762. Having to organize resistance outside of Manila, especially in northern Luzon, the Spanish and Filipino loyalist forces led by Simón de Anda, had their hands full. Dagohoy could wait.

By then, Britain was in the vanguard of the industrial revolution, its far-flung empire grown muscular and a source of tremendous wealth. The Bourbon-controlled Spanish empire, in contrast, was flaccid, in decline, and its speedy defeat by the British symbolized the latter's ascendant hegemony.

After the conclusion of the Seven Years' War, the British withdrew, and the Spanish flag flew once more over Intramuros. Unsuccessful attempts were made either to negotiate with or to subdue Dagohoy and his followers. In 1827, a force of 2,200 native and Spanish troops was sent against them, and again in 1828, but these campaigns failed. But by August 31, 1829, the Spanish had crushed the rebellion, taking a year of repeated assaults to do so. By then, Dagohoy had been dead, though no record survives of when and how he died. Three thousand Boholanos's escaped to other islands, 395 died in battle, 19,420 surrendered, and 98 were exiled. Only in Muslim Mindanao was resistance to Spanish rule longer than the Boholanos' eighty-five years, a rebellion that lasted through the tenure of twenty Spanish governors general.

The Silang Revolt

In northern Luzon, the local populations in Pangasinan and Ilocos took advantage of the turmoil brought about by the British invasion to advocate violently for reforms and try to shake off Spanish repression. The Pangasinan revolt began in late 1762 and was headed by Juan de la Cruz Palaris. It was put down in March of 1764, and its principal leaders executed. The more notable uprising was north of Pangasinan, in the Ilocos region, at that time made up of La Union, Abra, Ilocos Sur, and Ilocos Norte. The revolt was headed by thirty-two-year-old Diego Silang, a member of the principalia, who, orphaned at an early age, had been brought up by a parish priest in Vigan. He married a well-to-do widow and happened to be in Manila awaiting the arrival of a galleon from Mexico when the British occupied the city.

With the British takeover shattering the myth of Spanish invincibility, and encouraged by the uprising in Pangasinan—though no effort seemed to have been made towards joining forces—Silang and aggrieved Ilocanos demanded the elimination of the polos y servicios, and the expulsion of Spanish mestizos. A mini-civil war erupted between those agitating for reforms and those loyal to the Spanish. Silang gained the upper hand in the southern part of the region. Prior to this revolt, Silang had already been in the vanguard of protesting, in Vigan, against the abuses of the governor (the *alcalde mayor*) and demanding the dismissal of some local officials.

His demands, unacceptable though they were to the Spaniards, were nevertheless reformist rather than radical. Seeking the protection of the British as well as to trade with them, Silang sent communiqués to the British in Manila, and the latter responded by appointing him Sargente Mayor, Alcalde Mayor, and Captain in the War for his British Majesty. Though it was doubtful the British meant more than to flatter Silang, the latter, who seemed to have messianic tendencies, would have welcomed such titles. He declared Christ to be the Captain General, with him as second-in-command. Making Vigan his capital, he abolished tribute and forced labor, expelled the Spanish, and confiscated the wealth of the church.

But Silang's triumph was momentary. With the encouragement and blessing of both the local bishop and the Manila ecclesiastical authorities, Silang was assassinated by a Spanish mestizo, Miguel Vicos. Silang's widow, Gabriela, along with his uncle, Nicolas Cariño, took over, seeking refuge in the mountains and directing the uprising for another four months. But the northern region remained loyal and, with reinforcements from the outside, defeated the anti-Spanish forces. In late 1763, Gabriela and ninety others were captured and hanged.

Resistance in Religious Garb

Four years after the departure of the Redcoats, the Jesuits were expelled by royal decree in 1768, forcing them to abandon 114 missions and some schools. The Jesuits had arrived in the Philippines in 1581 and were assigned the Diocese of Cebu, which encompassed parts of northwestern Mindanao. They also took over a seminary in Manila, which became the Colegio de San José, the first college in the islands. (Twenty years later, in 1611, the Dominicans founded present-day University of Santo Tomás, the Catholic University of the Philippines, an institution older than Harvard, which was founded in 1636.) Their expulsion came about because the monarchical governments in France, Portugal, and Spain had grown wary of the Jesuits' education of the colonized, which was interpreted as empowering them, and therefore undermining colonial rule.

The Archbishop of Manila at the time, Sancho Santa Justa, had ordained Filipino seminarians assigned to these parishes, speeding along the Filipinization of the clergy—an unwelcome development as far as the Spanish friars were concerned. At the same time, the friars were opposed to or exceedingly reluctant to grant diocesan visitations, the normal prerogative of the archdiocesan bishop when it came to secular clergy. Since the orders already had their own superiors, the friars resented this additional layer of authority. Besides, it could lead to a further secularization of the parishes—and a diminution of friar power. In the Philippines, this was more significantly a racial matter, since the friars were peninsulares, or clergy born in Spain, while the secular clergy were *insulares*, or Philippine-born priests. By rejecting the right of visitation, the friars were indirectly repudiating royal oversight, as it was the Crown that determined appointments to bishoprics, and the bishops determined who staffed the parishes. Both issues—the appointment of native clerics to parishes and regulatory power from outside their friar estates—highlighted how these religious groups jealously guarded their hard-earned (and highly lucrative) preeminent role in the everyday lives of the Filipinos. Theoretically subordinate to the Crown, the friar estates in fact often held more power than the colonial regime. By the late eighteenth century it was all but impossible to remove Spanish friars as parish priests. In 1804 they came under the jurisdiction of a vicar-general based, not in Rome, but in Spain—adding another layer of insulation from the civil government and from the local diocesan bishop.

The Jesuits were allowed back in 1859, as authorized by a decree of Queen Isabella II. Re-accommodating them created a domino effect. The Recollects, who had replaced the Jesuits originally, asked the government for parishes in Cavite, across the bay from Manila. They as well as the Dominicans were assigned parishes in 1862, at the expense of native-born clergy who held these aforementioned posts. In this manner, Antipolo, a site of pilgrimage and one of the richest parishes in the country, was taken out of the hands of the insulares and entrusted to the peninsulares.

The native clergy rightly saw this as a government strategy to severely circumscribe their role. By then, the only colonies remaining in the once-great Spanish Empire were Cuba, Puerto Rico, the Philippines, and the Marianas. Given that Mexican creoles of Filipino descent had fought in the populist army headed by a priest, Fr. Miguel Hildalgo, who launched the war of independence against Spain in 1810, the colonial authorities were determined that the virus of nationalism would not be spread by sympathetic native priests. In fact, just before the British invaded the islands in 1762, there had been a Manila-born secular priest, Don Miguel Lino de Ezpeleta, who, having become the Archbishop of Cebu, went on to claim the See of Manila and the governor generalship—both positions having been vacant simultaneously —to the dismay of the Real Audiencia. When that august body asked the good archbishop for his authority, Ezpeleta pointed to the troops he had summoned to surround the building where they were meeting. Nevertheless, when the replacement Manuel Rojo arrived from Spain, Ezpeleta stepped aside after an intense period of negotiations. Ezpeleta was the first and last Filipino governor general under Spanish rule.

Secular clergy, under the leadership of native-born Fr. Pedro Pelaez, spoke out against their unjust displacement. They raised funds to send an emissary to Madrid to plead their case, and Fr. Pelaez wrote two tracts in defense of the native clergy. A vigorous and articulate champion, the priest sadly perished, buried under the ruins of the Manila Cathedral as it was flattened by the earthquake of 1863. The denouement in this struggle of the native clergy to be accorded equal rights would come barely a decade later, in the aftermath of the 1872 Cavite Mutiny, its principal actor Fr. José Burgos, who had replaced Pelaez as canon of the cathedral.

By the close of the eighteeenth century, the Catholic faith was firmly entrenched, the result of two-and-a-half centuries of assiduous proselytizing by the missionaries and the secular clergy. This did not mean, however, that these articles of faith brought over from Europe had completely supplanted pre-conquest beliefs and practices. In his *Estadismo de las Islas Filipinas (The Condition of the Philippine Islands)* Fr. Joaquín Martínez de Zúñiga, an Augustinian who served as parish priest in the islands just before the start of the nineteenth century, noted the persistence of what the Catholic Church dismissed as "superstitions." These included the continuing use of ritualistic practices in the burial of the dead and in dealing with their spirits; and the reliance, still, on amulets, or *anting-anting* to ward off demonic spirits and phantasmagoric creatures such as the Tikbalang, a monster that took various guises, and the Patianak, a mischievous figure that victimized pregnant women.

The locals, according to Zúñiga, still clung to old beliefs in animist spirits, or *nonos*. Their attitudes implied a healthy respect for nature and the environment. Thus, "when they wish to pluck any flower or fruit, they ask permission of the genius or *nono* to pluck it. When they traverse any field, river, creek, big trees, groves, and other places, they ask for the good favor of the nonos. When they are obliged to cut any tree, they ask pardon of the nonos, and excuse themselves to those things by saying, among other things, that the Padre ordered them to do it, and that it was not in their own purpose to fail in their respect to the genii, etc."

Zúñiga also noted the flourishing of the *nayon*, or barrio, outside the main population areas, where small groups of inhabitants had enough to sustain themselves sans extravagance, lived in a spirit of cooperation and harmony (*bayanihan*), and usually had a village elder to shape communal policies and adjudicate conflicts. In the nayon, life was a hybrid, an amalgam of traditional and Hispanicized mores. Its inhabitant was liberated from the insistent dogma of the priest and the church, free to construct a syncretic, personalized belief system. It was a rebellion, sans violence, sans fanfare, neither accepting colonial rule completely nor rejecting it outright.

A modern counterpart to the colonial nayon can be found in peaceful, agrarian, religious communities living on the slopes of Mt. Banahaw, in the southern Tagalog region not too far from Manila and considered to be a sacred mountain. There, combining elements of Christianity and folklore, the deification of local heroes, particularly José Rizal (whose life will be examined in the next chapter), and the recentering of the female as a spiritual force, homegrown cults live amicably side by side, free of the proselytizing and dogmatic fever of the larger, organized religions.

THE CRESCENT AGAINST THE CROSS

While the spread of Islam throughout the archipelago was halted by the arrival of the Spanish, they were unable to dominate most of Muslim Mindanao until the last two decades of the nineteenth century, and only then as an occupation force. The situation was the reverse of that in Spain. Islam was an older presence in Southeast Asia, with Christianity the new kid on the block. On the Iberian peninsula, it was of course the exact opposite. The Moors had conquered most of Spain and held on to the peninsula for 700 years, until they were finally driven out by the Catholic monarchs, Ferdinand and Isabella, with the reconquest of the last Moorish stronghold, Granada, in 1492. By melding religious zeal with nationalistic fervor, Ferdinand and Isabella had created a powerful and heady quasi-ideology. After the *Reconquista*, zealotry was the order of the day, spurring the Spaniards to both colonize and Christianize South and Central America and islands in the Caribbean and in Southeast Asia. The most telling manifestation of that zealotry was the Spanish Inquisition, promulgated by Ferdinand and Isabella, who used Catholicism as an instrument of national solidarity, forcing the conversion of Jews, for instance, to Christianity and otherwise expelling non-believers and persecuting and even putting to death alleged heretics. Its most infamous advocate was Tomás de Torquemada, who was appointed Inquisitor General in 1483, held the post for fifteen years, and is believed to have had 2,000 people put to death for alleged crimes against the faith.

Because of Islam, different ethnolinguistic groups in Mindanao and Sulu, mainly the Maranao, Tausug, and Maguindanao, had the most developed social organization. With more pronounced social stratifications, economic and religious contacts with fellow Muslims in Southeast Asia, and the ability to forge alliances, Muslim Mindanao could and did offer stronger, more organized, and determined resistance to Spanish claims to their territory.

Had Legazpi not appeared on the horizon, or even if he did but later on—say, at the beginning of the seventeenth century—most of the archipelago might very well have already come under the Crescent, whether as an independent state, a conglomeration of sultanates, or incorporated into either Indonesia or Malaysia.

The fact that the Muslims resisted Spanish domination is a source of pride for modern-day Filipino nationalists, though the notion then of defending a Philippine nation-state was inconceivable. Still, the Muslim raids on Luzon and the Visayas can be viewed, at the same time that the Spanish portrayed them as piratical, as both retaliation and resistance to colonialism. But there were other factors that contributed to their freedom from Spanish rule. For one thing, Manila and Luzon were front and center the focus of Spanish attention. For another, the Spaniards had to fend off threats from rival powers such as the Dutch and the

Portuguese (and later the British), as well as putting down uprisings in the areas under their control, hobbling their efforts to assemble a large enough force to dominate the Muslims.

Commercial interests were another factor in the intense rivalry between the Spanish and the Muslim Filipinos, particularly those of the Sulu Sultanate. With China, defeated by Great Britain in 1842 at the conclusion of the First Opium War, being forced to open up to Western trade, the sultanate developed into a vital trading center due to its strategic location and rich natural resources—the fortuitous combination of which made the sultanate a powerful player in the region. Jolo, the capital of Sulu, traded with various Asian ports, including Bengal, Canton, Macao, Manila, Borneo, and Singapore. Between 1768 and 1848 the sultanate enjoyed an ascendancy that Manila simultaneously resented and utilized for its own commercial interests. Such goods from Jolo as pearls, tortoise shell, shark's fin, bird's nest, cinnamon, rattan, ebony, cocoa, and cinnamon—produce of the sea and the forests—were prized by English traders due to the demand in China for such products.

The rise to power of the Taosug (the dominant ethnic group in Sulu) in turn meant their importation of weapons, rice, Chinese ceramics and earthenware, silk clothing, tobacco, wine, glassware, and even opium from India. Luxury goods reinforced elite status and were used to induce loyalty as well as for bride purchases. Sulu's control of the regional trade—in what the historian James Francis Warren described as the "Sulu Zone"—enabled the sultanate not only to hold on to its sovereignty but assert its regional dominance until the closing decades of the nineteenth century, when, Warren writes, "the Spanish naval campaigns of the 1870s and the large-scale immigration of Straits Chinese provided the formula for the economic and political collapse of the Sulu trading sphere."

The Sultanate's primacy rested a great deal on its slave raiding traditions, traditions that had always been a feature of the chiefly kingdoms in the archipelago but now intensified in the case of the sultanate with the need for more manpower, whether in the fields, seas, or in the port, where educated slaves would handle the books and manage the local elites' business affairs—in the process, a number of them amassing considerable wealth and essentially living as freemen. In this system trade and slavery formed a circle: trade created considerable wealth and power while slavery provided the necessary labor to keep the machinery of trade well oiled. Thus, as trade expanded, so did slave raiding expeditions.

Sponsored by the sultanates of both Cotabato and Sulu (with Jolo as the focal point), the raids bedeviled the rest of the archipelago, especially the Visayan Islands, and the coastal towns of northeastern Mindanao and southern Luzon. The economic and social costs were enormous, ranging from depopulated villages to the disruption of interisland shipping, particularly in the Visayas. Some of the slave-raiding fleets were enormous, consisting of forty to fifty fortified prahus (similar to the outrigger boat but with a heavier and deeper hull), around 2,500 to 3,000 fighters (mostly Moros from the Maranao or Cotabato region, and the Balangigi isles), and cannon. Slaves were trafficked to Dutch and Bornean ports as well as to Jolo. Captives could be ransomed, with a captured Spanish friar at the top of the list: he commanded the royal sum of 2,000 pesos, while an ordinary European fetched only 300 pesos and a male Filipino slave a measly thirty to fifty pesos.

There were periodic military campaigns waged against the Moros, but victory by arms was rarely followed by sustained occupation on the ground. The gains were thus temporary. For instance, even though a Spanish contingent that included Christian Filipinos assaulted Jolo in 1578 and defeated its sultan, he and his followers were able to rebuild once the Spanish withdrew. From then on, Muslim raids on coastal towns in the Visayas took on a punitive as well as acquisitive character. Later, in 1635, to help defend against such raids the Spanish erected a fortified settlement, Zamboanga, in northwestern Mindanao, where today Fort del Pilar still stands.

With Zamboanga as his base, Governor Corcuera headed a full-scale expedition against the Moros in February 1637. His force of 760 Spaniards and thousands of Christian Filipinos captured Lanao and, the following year, took Jolo after a protracted siege of three and a half months. Convinced that he had broken Muslim power, Corcuera returned to Manila in May 1638 where he was hailed as a conqueror.

In truth, for most of the Spanish colonial era, the Moros were never subjugated even in the light of such defeats. They would regroup, and the cycle of conflict would begin anew, essentially affirming the status quo, except for short-lived treaties between the sultanates and the

Spanish regime. The Spanish were too few, and faced too many threats from elsewhere. Instead they relied on a network of forts, watchtowers, and warships to guard against Muslim depredations. Watchtowers were often strategically located right by the town church so that bells could be rung in warning should Muslim prahus be sighted. There were watchtowers as far north as Laoag and Aparri in northern Luzon, but none on the eastern flanks of the archipelago, though the Pacific side did have occasional patrols.

By 1848 the Spanish had grown weary of English encroachment on its southern territories—or what it considered its territories, though the Muslims would have violently disagreed. Mistrust of their perennial rivals was only heightened in 1849 with a treaty of commerce and friendship between Sultan Mohammed Fadl of Sulu and the British government. This time, Manila decided to cripple the Sultanate's base. Under Governor General Antonio Urbiztondo and with fortified Zamboanga as its launching pad, a flotilla of steam gunboats as well as sailing ships, close to 3,000 soldiers, and nearly a thousand Filipino conscripts, set out for Jolo in 1851.

Fighting was fierce but not prolonged. The steam gunboats made short work of the Moro prahus. In the end, the sultan and his datus retreated into the island's rugged interior. Shortly thereafter, a treaty was struck, wherein Sultan Fadl acknowledged Spain's hegemony, agreed to severe restrictions on foreign trade, and allowed a Spanish naval presence in Jolo, to interdict foreign vessels and prevent or minimize the importation of weapons. But the treaty was doomed, since neither side really observed its provisos. Urbiztondo had failed to establish a garrison in the capital. Hence, the sultanate continued to trade as before.

Only in 1875 did the situation change, when the Spanish colonial government launched a much larger war fleet: nine thousand soldiers (a majority of whom were Filipinos), eleven transport ships, and twenty-two gunboats. In late February, the Spanish flattened Jolo and destroyed nearby Taosug strongholds in the following weeks. This time, a Spanish occupation force remained, erecting forts and rebuilding Jolo, as a European-style city complete with a wall. It was only in 1899 that the Spanish departed, giving way to the new plantation owners: the United States of America.

The fact that Christianized natives were regularly employed in the campaigns against the Moros, who were considered beyond the pale, did little to endear them to the latter. Not surprisingly, they subsequently viewed each other with mutual suspicion. Despite racial and cultural ties, each to each was the Other: foreign and hostile—an animosity that persists to this day and complicates efforts to negotiate a lasting peace on both sides of the religious and cultural divide.

3. FROM INDIO TO FILIPINO: EMERGENCE OF A NATION, 1863-1898

"[Padre Damaso] got up and in Tagalog said very ominously, 'When you come to see me it should not be in borrowed clothes, which is not for you.' . . . He went into his quarters and slammed the door, even though I wanted to stop him. What could I do? I barely have my salary. To get it I have to remain in the priest's good offices and make a trip to the head of the province, what could I do against him, the town's main moral, political, and civil authority, supported by his order, feared by the government, rich, powerful, consulted, listened to, believed, heeded everywhere by everyone? If he insults me I have to hold my tongue. If I answer back, he'll throw me out and my career will be over. How will that help education? On the contrary everyone will side with the priest, they'll insult me, they'll call me vain, proud, preening, a bad Christian, vulgar, and even anti-Spanish and a subversive. They don't expect knowledge or enthusiasm from a schoolmaster. They just want resignation, humility, inertia."

—José Rizal, *Noli Me Tangere* (trans. H. Augenbraum)

MORE THAN ANY OTHER FILIPINO SUBJECT TO SPANISH COLONIAL rule, the medical doctor, brilliant polymath, and writer José Rizal, in his incendiary 1887 novel *Noli Me Tangere*, exposed the state of the archipelago as it was during the waning decades of Spanish hegemony. The voice of the town schoolteacher lamenting his predicament to the protagonist Crisostomo Ibarra echoed eerily the voice of the politicized Indios who, though acutely aware of the need for changes in their society, felt powerless to work for these, blocked by the reactionary character of the dominant figure of the time, the friar; the narrow strictures of education; and a civil administration indifferent at best and mindlessly cruel at worst. (The sequel to the *Noli*, *El Filbusterismo*, or *The Subversive*, followed in 1891. Even darker in its appraisal of the colonial regime, the *Fili*, as it was commonly referred to, confirmed Rizal's pariah status in the eyes of the Spanish overseers.)

In the book, the rich Ibarra, recently returned from studies and travels in Europe, personified the *ilustrados*, "enlightened ones," who like Rizal and his peers were scions of the rising haute bourgeoisie and therefore had the means to go abroad to seek either further education, political exile, or simply a better life. For the most part, the ilustrados chose Madrid or Barcelona, with some opting to live in Paris. The Europe of *fin de siècle* nineteenth century had long been steeped in the ideas of the Enlightenment, the zeitgeist heady with the promise of liberty and equality, with its emphasis on individual rights, the centrality of reason, and the repudiation of oligarchy, whether in the realm of civil government or religious authority. Perhaps the most violent (and contradictory) manifestation of the Enlightenment's impact on the *Ancien Régime* was the French Revolution of 1789. European capitals provided the hothouse intellectual atmosphere that young, intellectually curious Filipinos lacked in Manila.

The opening up of the colony to international trade at the start of the nineteenth century resulted in a burgeoning middle class, which in turn meant the sons of these upwardly mobile families could be sent to colleges and universities both in Manila and Europe—an indispensable factor in the development of a national and nationalist consciousness. Principally through the actions and writings of the ilustrados, the currents of reform reached Las Islas Filipinas, so that the islands were inevitably affected by radical political and social changes in Europe. Change may have boarded a slow boat to Manila, but it was coming.

Spanish society had already undergone fundamental changes by the time the ilustrados arrived in Europe. The Southeast Asian colony was on the margins of the Spanish empire, distant enough so that these changes did not resonate instantly or as powerfully as might have been otherwise expected. Nevertheless, political and social alterations in Spain were bound to have an effect on the far-away archipelago. The combination of the Enlightenment with the upheavals brought about by the French Revolution contributed to the spread of liberal ideas in Spain. Specifically, the Napoleonic Wars of 1803 to 1815, continent-wide conflicts that pitted the armies of Napoleon against a varying cast of opponents, further accelerated change and the decline of the old order. The French invasion and occupation of Spain led to the Spanish War of Independence (1808-1814). Spanish resistance to the Napoleonic invasion, assisted by the British surreptitiously, brought about the temporary ascendancy of the Spanish liberals who produced the Cádiz Constitution of 1812, which extended democratic rights not only to Spaniards but also to all non-Spanish subjects of Madrid. Additionally, reflecting the prevalent liberal spirit, the Cádiz Constitution set limits on the monarchy.

The Cortes, or Spanish Parliament, was revived and now allowed for a representative from each colony, including the Philippines. The first representative for the archipelago was Ventura de los Reyes, who served from 1810 to 1813. The unheralded de los Reyes was one of the signatories of the Cádiz Constitution, promulgated in March of 1812, but proclaimed in Manila only a year after, in 1813. The constitution affirmed human and political rights. De los Reyes was also instrumental in curtailing the galleon trade, much to the relief of Spanish merchants who had always resented the galleon trade for cutting into their own import businesses. The dissolution of the Manila-Acapulco run freed up trade with other countries and liberalized the conditions under which entrepreneurs operated. Strictly speaking, however, Philippine representation in the Cortes was misleading, as the representatives were of Spanish descent, and indigenous Filipinos had no say in determining who was to "represent" them.

The upheavals in Spain had more immediate repercussions in her Latin American colonies, where she was heavily invested. With the Napoleonic Wars weakening an already vulnerable Spanish empire, the Creoles in the New World colonies set to the task of freeing themselves from colonial rule. Realizing their economic interests conflicted with those of Spain, the Creoles led national liberation movements, which resulted in the dissolution of most of the Spanish empire by 1820.

In 1814, however, the monarchy was restored, with Ferdinand VII reigning, and the liberal provisions of the Cortes revoked. In 1815 there were violent reactions in the archipelago to this revocation. News of the Cádiz constitution had reached the islands only in 1813, so its revocation after a little more than a year was viewed with suspicion by the indigenous population, who felt that the principalia arbitrarily and capriciously determined how the laws were to be interpreted and enforced.

By 1820, there was yet another swing towards Republicanism: the constitutional period was brought back, and Ferdinand exiled. At the same time, direct mail service was established between Spain and the Philippines. The Cortes, revived yet again, approved certain measures specific to the Philippines. Trade was further liberalized, so that products and goods manufactured in the islands were now considered "national," and thus entitled to the privileges and immunities the law bestowed on Spanish goods. These steps were undertaken essentially to stimulate native entrepreneurship.

With the declaration of Mexico's independence from Spain in 1821, Manila ceased to be administratively ruled from Mexico. It now had to be governed directly from far-away Spain, though the opening of the Suez Canal in 1869 was to shorten the distance considerably, bringing travel time down to five weeks, from the previous three to four months.

Another swing to the right in Madrid occurred in 1823, when Ferdinand was restored to absolute power by the French, wielding it until his death in 1833. Predictably, the king revoked the constitution, abolished the Cortes, and invalidated its legislative work. By the time of Ferdinand's restoration, only Cuba, Puerto Rico, the Philippines, and the Marianas remained Spanish colonies. Subsequent to Ferdinand's death, the question of succession proved destabilizing, leading to the Carlist

Wars. Essentially a long-running civil war between those who moved to uphold monarchism and tradition and those who favored the continuation of Enlightenment legacies of secularism and a republican form of government, the wars spanned more than four decades, from 1833 to 1876 (though the Civil War that erupted in 1936, between Republican forces and General Franco and the Falangists can be seen as the endpoint of this conflict).

Once more, the Cortes was revived, but this time with limited powers. Queen Cristina, Regent of Spain, ordered it to craft a new constitution. The result: the Constitution of 1837, which established a parliamentary form of government. However, in a blow to the rights of colonies, their right to representation was abolished. Its restoration was one of the goals which the ilustrados would demand.

EDUCATION AND THE SPREAD OF IDEAS

As the expatriate Indio community in Spain began to grow, there were attempts to improve the education system archipelago-wide, following an 1839 royal decree. Indeed, a marine school was established in Manila in 1840, its aim to graduate trained pilots for ships sailing to mainland Asia, Europe, or North America. However, while there were primary schools in towns and villages, these were handicapped by inadequate facilities and the lack of trained teachers. Moreover, local schools were under the control of the local friar, as they had been since the start of the colonial period. More than anything else, the friar was keen to see his young charges learn their catechism by heart, and not in encouraging their faculties of independent thinking.

For most of Spanish colonial rule, very little legislation existed that dealt with schooling; it was left to the religious orders to introduce a systematic method of primary education. At the outset of colonial rule in the late sixteenth century, the Augustinians—the first religious order in the colony—instructed its parishes to set up schools throughout the archipelago. In 1634 and 1636, archbishops and bishops were asked by Philip IV to educate the indigenous people. Towards the end of the seventeenth century, the Crown decreed that primary instruction should be free, and in 1792, Charles III suggested that schools should be supervised by civil authorities, an implicit recognition that education was mainly if not totally handled by the religious. Government legislation never established a detailed, consistent plan on educational methods for primary schools, even though royal orders placed emphasis on education, particularly with regard to the construction of buildings, the recruitment of divinity teachers, and the teaching of Spanish.

However, with the Educational Decree of 1863, the home government required the establishment of schools and the availability of free primary instruction for children between the ages of seven and twelve. This inevitably improved the system that heretofore privileged only the peninsulares and the native wealthy. One of the goals was for the young to learn Castilian. At any one time, only a small percentage of the subject population—estimated at between 5 to 10 percent—was fluent in Spanish, and this decree was meant to increase that percentage. But the goal that superseded everything else was still the imparting of Christian doctrine, morality, and what was termed "sacred history"—basically a study of the Bible—to be directed by the parish priest. (Not surprisingly, the first book printed in the colony, in 1593, was the *Doctrina Christiana en Lengua Española y Tagalog*, or the *Christian Catechism in Spanish and Tagalog*.)

The 1863 decree meant the government taking charge of higher education; official recognition of educational institutions established by the religious orders; a determination of teacher qualifications; and a pay scale. In turn, the religious orders gave up some higher-education tasks and focused on free primary, compulsory education for all children of both sexes. After the Maura decree of 1893, schools became free from inspection by the parish priests and thereafter became the responsibility of the local governments. By 1898, the last year of Spanish rule, one reliable estimate put the number of state schools at 2,143, excluding private and religious schools. The educational system in the colony may have developed in fits and starts, but by the time of the American takeover, there was enough of an infrastructure in place for American educators to implement an island-wide public-school system.

Having been at it for nearly three centuries, the religious orders had shaped the landscape of higher education in the country by founding colleges and universities. Among these is the oldest educational institution in the country, the University of San Carlos, established by the Spanish Jesuits in Cebu in 1595 but now run by the Society of the Divine Word order. All other noteworthy schools were founded in Manila: Colegio de San José (1603), founded by the Jesuits; University of Santo Tomás (1611) and the College of San Juan de Letrán (1620), both established by the Dominicans; and La Concordia College, founded exclusively for women by the Daughters of Charity in 1868. Outside of these universities, seminaries run by the religious offered secondary education to lay students.

The 1863 decree also established a normal school for teachers in Manila, to be under the direction of the Jesuits, who having been expelled in 1768, had been allowed to return to the colony in 1859. (That same year, the Jesuits took over the Escuela Municipal de Manila, which in 1865 was raised to the status of a college, the Ateneo Municipal de Manila, now the private Ateneo de Manila university, the third-oldest university in the country.) The normal school was to serve as an educational center for God-fearing and obedient potential teachers. Again, at the top of the list of intended goals was the imparting of religion, morals, and sacred history. The unremitting emphasis on religious tutelage allowed Catholicism to be deeply entrenched, often at the expense of the secular pursuit of knowledge.

As educational reforms began to take effect, however sporadically, the number of journals and newspapers increased. There were seventy-four during the last three decades of the nineteenth century. Among the better known were *La Opiníon, Manila Alegre, El Comercio, El Correo, El Católico Filipino*, and *Diario de Manila*. A majority of the publications were in Spanish, and some were bilingual—an indication not only of the spread of literacy but of news, however modified by the powers that be, outside of Manila. All had to contend with a board of censors that had been set up in 1856, made up of four appointees by the governor and four appointees by the archbishop of Manila, forever on the lookout for articles that might impugn either the state or the church—or both.

As imperfect as it was, the educational system heading into the latter half of the nineteenth century, along with economic and social changes brought about by the opening up of the colony to international trade, did turn out an intelligentsia, among them the ilustrados, the sons of upwardly mobile mestizo and indio families who had grown critical of colonial rule, and were at the forefront of the reformist movement that came to be known as the Propaganda Movement. But laying the ground for the political awakening of their generation were upheavals in the country's religious ranks.

SECULARIZATION AND THE CATACLYSM OF 1872

Presaging the concerted demands for Filipinization of parishes, as well as the revolutionary brotherhood, the Katipunan, which would spring up in 1892, a devout Indio peasant by the name of Apolinario de la Cruz, having had his application to join a friar order in Manila rejected in 1839, returned to the southern Tagalog provinces and formed the Cofradía de San José, or Confraternity of St. Joseph. De la Cruz (known in the Confraternity as Hermano, or Brother, Pule) was clearly a charismatic leader, for the lay religious brotherhood soon attracted numerous adherents, whose contributions enabled the Cofradía to sponsor regular masses for its followers, and even fiestas. The authorities, both civil and religious, viewed the confraternity with skepticism and deep suspicion. The church hierarchy refused to recognize its activities as legitimate, and its members were routinely harassed.

Institutional disdain and contempt led de la Cruz and the Cofradía to assert themselves as an independent group, claiming to have divine support and refusing anyone but full-blooded natives membership. Mestizos could be accepted but only with de la Cruz's express consent. At times his followers would proclaim de la Cruz as "King of the Tagalogs"—a clear reference to Christ being heralded as the King of the Jews. Inevitably the state, acting on requests by the friars, acted to suppress what was seen as a potentially explosive insurgent movement by sending troops to the Cofradía's stronghold in Tayabas, now Quezon, Province. Though initially successful in repulsing the attacks, Pule and his confraternity were defeated. At the age of twenty-seven, the would-be priest and his aide, called Purgatorio, were executed along with 200 other members of the Cofradía. De la Cruz's body was dismembered, his severed head stuck on a pole placed by the roadside in a manner reminiscent of the deaths of Christian martyrs at the hands of the Romans.

The Cofradía's clamor for change in the way religious groups were constituted was clearly emblematic of the groundswell of dissatisfaction with colonial rule and of the push for equal rights. Hence, the Filipinization of the clergy was not simply a religious issue but one in which broader social and economic issues came into play. Being that the Catholic Church and its priests (particularly the Spanish friars) represented the apex of Philippine colonial society, priesthood was viewed by many of the more ambitious natives as a sure means of social and even material advancement.

The Jesuits' return in 1859 revived the issue of Filipinization. Their earlier, forced departure in 1768 resulted in vacant curacies, especially in northern Mindanao. With not enough Spanish clergy to go around, these had gone to Filipino secular priests. Now, there was an order to transfer curacies in the Bishopric of Manila from native clergy to the Spanish religious orders, to accommodate those displaced by the returning Jesuits. The order to vacate what they had administered capably for more than ninety years embittered many of the seculars. (They had to give up, for instance, one of the wealthiest parishes in the colony, that of Antipolo, not far from Manila, and the archipelago's most famous pilgrimage site devoted to the Blessed Virgin Mary, Our Lady of the Voyage.) The official reasons, they felt, disparaged their abilities and cast aspersions on their character. These feelings would persist and lead many secular native priests later on to adopt nationalist causes. A breakdown in 1870 showed that out of a total of 792 parishes, 611 were administered by regular priests, i.e., belonging to the Orders, and 181 by secular priests, almost all of whom were Filipino.

At the same time, political turmoil continued in Spain. The Spanish revolution of 1868 resulted in the formation of yet another liberal, democratic form of government. The next year, 1869, the same year the Suez Canal was opened, the Cortes approved a new constitution, which established a limited monarchy; recognized individual freedom of expression, association, domicile, and worship; legalized civil marriages; and introduced the jury system. A wealthy liberal, Carlos María de la Torre, was sent over to the colony as the new governor general. Once installed, de la Torre banned flogging in the military, lifted restrictions on the press, public demonstrations, and the formation of associations aimed at reform, etc. The governor displayed his intentions for a more democratic dispensation by having creoles and mestizos at the Palace and proposing toasts to "Liberty!"

He took the unusual step of pardoning a group of dissidents in nearby Cavite province, who had been involved in agrarian disputes with local landowners. He had these same dissidents form a police force. De la Torre also went on walks in Intramuros sans the traditional armed escort in their fancy uniforms. Not surprisingly, such behavior scandalized the long-time Spanish expatriates and clergy, who feared this display of liberalism would only encourage the lowly natives to become uppity and entertain ideas of a free society. Naturally the rising bourgeoisie—native and mestizo alike—hailed him.

Unfortunately for this budding reform movement, Amadeo of Savoy was installed as king, and the leftward shift in Spain was arrested. De la Torre was recalled in 1871, and replaced by a right-winger Rafael de Izquierdo, who promptly restored the restrictions, and viewed with suspicion those who had supported de la Torre's policies. More tellingly, he also withdrew the exemption from tribute and forced labor (the *polos y servicios*) that the workers at the Cavite arsenal, the artillery barracks and engineer corps of Fort San Felipe—just across the bay from Intramuros—had enjoyed since 1740. The abolition of these privileges caused the men in the fort to mutiny on January 20, 1872.

Though seven Spanish officers were killed, the mini-revolt, never more than a brushfire, was quickly suppressed over a period of two days, but the incident was viewed as more than just a violent act of insubordination. Here was an opportunity to get rid of Filipino secular priests who had championed the Filipinization of the clergy—an insistent demand seen at the forefront of incipient nationalism. This demand had grown to include not only the native clerics but Creoles and Spanish mestizos as well. Among those swept into the net of suspected subversives were figures of social standing and three secular priests: Mariano Gómez, curate of the nearby town of Bacoor, Cavite; Jacinto Zamora, parish priest of Marikina Town, a suburb north of Manila; and José Burgos, a curate at the prestigious Manila Cathedral.

Of the three, the most well-known was Fr. Burgos, one of the most vocal and influential champions of the Filipino secular clergy and who had made his views known to de la Torre. Born in 1837, he was at the age of thirty already a doctor of theology and canon law, and the Synodal Examiner of the country's preeminent See—the Cathedral of Manila. He was also an expert swordsman and knew how to box. Tireless in his advocacy of Filipinizing the parishes and in defense of his fellow Filipino priests, in 1869 Burgos penned "To the Spanish People." Reading this eloquent essay, one can see why the Spanish friars detested him. He rebutted the baseless charges levied against the secular priests by *La Verdad*, or *The Truth*, a newspaper that clearly favored the entrenched Spanish clergy. He cited the main charge: " '. . . the Filipino who dedicates himself to the sacred office of the priesthood is wont to carry out faithfully and well the mechanical detail of church work but he never attains to the point of excelling in anything connected with the solemn priestly functions.'" Burgos highlighted the friars' refusal to obey royal decrees, especially that of 1863, commanding them to teach Spanish to their constituents. "So resolutely do the friars carry their intentions to its undue lengths that they come to abhor in their parish the native who speaks Spanish."

He described the friars as "sand in the cog wheels of the country's civilization" who "endeavor to keep the poor natives in a state of ignorance and boorishness"—the better to maintain both their influence and affluence. To forestall charges of treason, of being a *filibustero*, or subversive, he highlighted the secular priests' services in the past, declared that their abilities were equal to the best of the friars, and reiterated above all how loyal the secular clergy was to Mother Spain. If only the motherland would open her eyes and see, she would recognize instantly the great injustice that was being perpetuated.

He accused the friar orders of being in "possession of great riches and profitable estate incomes which they do their best to keep away from the eyes of the government," riches that were "now unhappily available at all times and is too often put to ill use, in the indulgence of pleasure, in the transgression of the law, in the corruption of justice and in the infliction of harm to their fellowmen." Strong, provocative words. In essence, Burgos had written a withering critique of not just the Spanish friars but colonialism itself, for colonial rule had prospered precisely because it condoned the friars' methods.

Confrontation with the friars was inevitable, though things would not come to a head for two more decades. Spain justified her presence in the islands—indeed throughout her empire—based on the evangelical belief in Catholicism's superiority and the imperative to spread it. Even though this religion brought over from Spain had sunk its roots deep in Philippine soil, the different localized resistance movements that rose out of deep despair, with the well of native forbearance running dry, had no choice but to see the friar as the main obstacle to freedom and, since the friar too was key to local economic development, material progress. Catholic theology was acceptable, but its Iberian herald was increasingly unwelcome.

In a mock trial, and implicated by one mutineer, the clerics were promptly found guilty of plotting to overthrow the regime. Significantly, Archbishop Martínez of Manila refused to defrock them, an implicit endorsement of their professed innocence, as well as a pointed rebuke of the friar orders, who continually resisted the diocesan bishop's right to visitation—a mechanism provided by the Patronato Real, through which oversight by the Royal Crown was exercised. On February 17, 1872, a month after the failed mutiny, Gómez, Burgos, and Zamora were publicly executed at the Luneta by means of the garrote, an iron collar bound around the condemned's neck and then twisted until the neck is broken. Burgos, the last to be killed, shouted out his declaration of innocence, to which one of the attending friars is said to have chillingly remarked, "So was Jesus." Ironically, the mutineer who had implicated the trio in the hopes of being pardoned or at least spared the death penalty, a man by the name of Saldua, was garroted as well.

Others were imprisoned and twenty-two others, including nine native priests, were banished to the Marianas Islands. A few of the banished laymen managed to make their way to Europe, among them Joaquin Pardo de Tavera and Antonio Regidor, who, along with other Filipino émigrés, formed the nucleus of an expatriate community that the later generation of Filipino upper-middle class intellectuals would join. That the trials were patently unfair is clear in the rebuke the Supreme Military Council in Madrid (the highest military tribunal) delivered to the colonial government in Manila, stating that its conduct was a violation of the law, and warning against a repeat. No punishment was decreed, however, for such a violation.

The Cavite Mutiny anticipated a much larger one when, on September 2 of the same year, close to 1,200 laborers in the same Cavite shipyards, according to Benedict Anderson in *Under Three Flags*, "went on the first recorded strike in Philippine history. Numerous people were arrested and interrogated but the regime failed to find an arrestable mastermind and eventually all were released." The peaceable strike was to protest the suspension of their privileges—the very same cause that sparked the brief armed insurrection.

There was a practical side to the stirrings of nationalism. Their widening economic interests made the colonized more aware of and sensitive to antiquated and unfair colonial policies, abetted by systemic racism and the denial of freedoms. This blatant oppression of liberal creoles, mestizos, and native clerics, though at other times strange bedfellows, resulted in a common cause being taken up. The drive to Filipinize the parishes was easily subsumed into the larger context of widespread discontent and the desire for substantial reforms. The fact that three men of the cloth had been killed in cold blood by the colonial state absolved would-be rebels from being castigated as anti-Catholic. No longer; they could be seen as anti-exploitation and even anti-Spanish but not as heretics. After all, they had priests on their side. Their souls were therefore not at risk of being damned, as the friars often warned those whom they deemed insufficiently subservient.

The 1872 Gomburza Affair, as it came to be known, planted the seeds of nationalist awakening in and politicized the younger generation, already exposed to Enlightenment ideas. In less than a decade, beginning in 1880, the Propaganda Movement would coalesce when Marcelo H. del Pilar, Graciano Lopez Jaena, and José Rizal—with other like-minded and older compatriots who had sought refuge in Europe earlier—systematically advocated for reforms. The Propagandists gave voice and shape to the growing aspirations of not just their social class but of the lower classes who, as always, felt most keenly the boot of social and economic oppression. In the end, though the Propaganda Movement failed to attain its objectives, it did lead to a heightened consciousness among various social classes, culminating in the 1896 Revolution against Spain. (One indication of how the martyrdom of the three clerics still resonated more than two decades later was the use of "Gomburza" as a password among the revolutionaries.)

The Chinese Mestizos

Even as a nationalist consciousness was emerging, fuelled by ilustrado aims and the unruly dreams of a restless populace grown both tired and testy due to habitual Spanish repression, the Chinese community was itself undergoing changes as many of its members, assimilating into native society, came to play an increasingly crucial role in the colonial economy. One way to assimilate was to convert to Catholicism, and adopt a Christian name. By 1755, Chinese mestizos—usually the offspring of a Chinese father and native mother—came to dominate rice trading, supplying Manila with much of its needs. They therefore acquired farm lands or leased from the religious estates. In turn, the Chinese mestizos, either as owners or *inquilinos* (lessees), allowed *kasamas* or sharecroppers to till the soil, in exchange for half of the harvest.

A vast majority of the tenant farmers had once owned their small farms but, failing to acquire titles to the land they and their families had worked for generations, lost them. A law passed in 1894 was particularly disastrous: landowners were given only one year in which to secure titles. A great number of small landowners, especially in the rural areas, were unaware of the new law. Not surprisingly, not much effort was made to spread news of this legislation. To their dismay their plots were suddenly incorporated in the titles secured by big landowners. Towards the end of the nineteenth century, at least 400,000 persons found themselves in this predicament, unable to avoid the humbling status of tenancy.

From the amassing of lands came the haciendas. The hacienda was an outgrowth of the new system that emphasized the cultivation of cash crops. Though modern in its orientation towards capitalism, management was decidedly feudal in the way overseers treated the tenant farmers and itinerant laborers who showed up every harvest—an exploitative system that continues today. While it is true that debt slavery and sharecropping existed even in the pre-Hispanic period, it is just as true that under the Spanish these exploitative aspects were not only exacerbated but institutionalized as well. One of the biggest was the Hacienda Luisita, totaling close to 16,000 acres and encompassing lands in several towns in what is now Tarlac Province. Originally deeded as a royal grant to the Tabacalera Company in 1880, it was eventually acquired by the Chinese mestizo family, the Cojuangcos, who have since figured as a political and social dynasty nationwide (the successor to president-turned-dictator Ferdinand Marcos in 1986 was a member of the Cojuangco clan: Corazon Cojuangco Aquino).

As inquilinos—Rizal's father was one—many Chinese mestizos grew wealthy, and along with their wealth and accumulated land, became vested in the ongoing development of the economy. They competed with alcalde mayors or provincial governors, the religious orders, and the ethnically pure Chinese in positioning themselves economically. Along with their new economic power, the Chinese mestizos acquired social status, facilitating assimilation and participation as part of the non-Spanish elite of society. In the emergence of a Filipino nation, this elite—a mixture of Chinese mestizos, Creoles, and the rising native middle and upper classes—played a crucial role. In effect, they constituted the new principalia. Inevitably, their ever-increasing desire for economic expansion, equated with a freer marketplace, kept bumping against the narrow, monopolistic policies of the old regime. Combined with the burgeoning sense of nationalism and the centuries-old resentments of the indios, the restlessness of the economic elite proved to be an explosive factor.

Out of these volatile elements emerged a tangible sense of being a Filipino and the notion of a nation-state to which such Filipinos might belong—an "imagined community," to use Benedict Anderson's apt phrase. The term "Filipino" was originally applied only to Creoles— Spaniards born in the Philippines. The Spaniards who had come over from the motherland didn't care for the designation, preferring instead the term "Peninsulares," implying a snobbish hierarchy. Anyone outside these two categories was simply an Indio—the term originally used by Columbus for the natives of the Caribbean, which he mistook for the Indies, or Spice Islands, of Asia. However, due to economic progress and a growing sense of a common cultural Hispanicized background that cut across ethnic boundaries, the Creoles, the mestizos (both Chinese and Spanish), and the educated natives came to view themselves as "Filipinos." The ilustrados were at the forefront of extending the term to all local inhabitants of Las Islas Filipinas—except for the Muslims, or Moros, who had never identified with the Christian majority and indeed resisted the incursions of the colonial state.

THE PROPAGANDA MOVEMENT

In Spain, in the meantime, political changes continued apace. In 1871 Amadeo, son of King Victor Emmanuel of Italy, was offered and accepted the job of King of Spain but proved unable to rule effectively. Shortly after an assassination attempt on his queen, he stepped down in February of 1873. After two years of political turbulence, Alfonso, son of the previously deposed Queen Isabella, gained the Spanish throne, his reign, from 1875 to 1885, a period of relative calm. The Cortes was revived and passed a new constitution in 1876. While Cuba and Puerto Rico were once again given representation, the Philippines was not; the Asian colony was to be governed by a set of special laws.

Thus, political changes and upheavals in Spain would be followed inevitably by shakeups in the Philippines, which had become a dumping ground for largely unqualified followers and favorites of well-connected patrons in the motherland. Such changes were superficial and frequent, as can be gauged by the fact that from 1850 to 1898, twenty-four governors general served in the Philippines, for an average term of two years. *Plus ça change, plus c'est le meme chose*: The purported changes only meant more of the same, with the colonial system plagued by corruption and systemic abuse. Real and abiding power lay in the hands of the civil administrators, especially the governor general, who had essentially dictatorial powers, and of the friar orders. They usually ignored, or interpreted narrowly, decrees from Madrid that they didn't like. Thus, the injunction to teach Spanish archipelago-wide to the Indios was observed haphazardly by the religious, who controlled education in the islands. Compounding the situation were the unabashedly racist views held by the Spanish officials, who tended to be domineering, contemptuous, and often physically abusive towards the Indio.

This was especially true at the local level, none more abusive than the Guardia Civil, notorious for manhandling villagers who may not have displayed the proper attitude of obeisance (like doffing their *salakots*, or native hats, promptly). Rizal's mother herself was forced to trek fifty kilometers from Calamba to the provincial capital Santa Cruz, where she was kept in jail on charges, never proven, by the mayor in collusion with the head of the local Guardia Civil. She had been falsely implicated as an accomplice in a purported plot, never proven, by her half-brother to poison his wife. In 1880, two years before he set sail for Europe, the son himself felt literally the heavy hand of authority. In a letter Rizal wrote of "being mauled and wounded one dark night by the Guardia Civil, for having passed by a statue and failing to salute it. The statue turned out to be the lieutenant commander of the detachment." Rizal attempted to report this injustice to Primo de Rivera, the governor general at the time, but was unable to see him.

While therefore gains had been made in trade and commerce (though still at the neglect of the industrial sector, which was in an embryonic state), and while infrastructure and communications had improved, no comparable gains had been made in the arena of personal and political freedoms. The gap between material progress and civil liberties was one the intellectuals and visionaries fervently sought to close.

The Propaganda Movement, an outgrowth of the 1872 Mutiny, was a crusade carried out clandestinely in Manila and openly in Spain by scions from the expanding ranks of the native bourgeoisie. This movement, while directly a result of the killings of the three martyr priests, can be traced further back, according to the writer Nick Joaquin, to the waning years of the eighteenth century. A number of Creole writers in the colony espoused the ideas of the Enlightenment and the French Revolution. They were anti-clerical and pushed for the same reforms the ilustrados would lobby towards the end of the nineteenth century. In particular, Luis Rodríguez Varela was the writer who, in Joaquin's words, "can most truly be called the precursor of Philippine nationalism." Varela called himself "El Conde Filipino" or the Filipino Count, and was the first to describe himself as a Filipino in print. (It is true the Creoles were described as "Filipinos" by the peninsular Spanish but the Creoles themselves until Varela preferred to be called "Spaniards.") He wrote several books that advocated social change and the liberalizing of education to include free instruction for the poor. He was also critical of the economic power wielded by foreign elements, notably the Chinese, and indirectly of the peninsulares as well. He was thereafter viewed with suspicion, marked as a man who would undermine the ruling order. He was expelled from the colony in February of 1823.

The aim of the Propagandists was to put pressure on the Spanish government by spotlighting for the Spanish public the injustices and backwardness of Spanish rule in the archipelago. The hoped-for result, however, was to be meaningful reforms, assimilation rather than a separation from Mother Spain, wherein Filipinos had standing equal to any other Spaniard. The Propagandists were especially keen on abrogating the role of the friar orders in civil government, removing them from their curacies, and replacing them with Filipino secular priests. In Spain, they allied themselves with anti-clerical factions.

Testimony by Fr. Juan Villegas, a Franciscan, before the Philippine Commission in 1900, at the start of the United States colonial era, catalogued the powers that his *confrères* wielded during Spanish colonial times: "He was inspector of primary schools; president of the health board and board of charities; president of the board of urban taxation. . . . He certified to the correctness of cedulas [tax certificates] . . . was president of the board of statistics. . . . The priest also certified as to the civil status of persons." Before the same commission, a certain Florentino Torres stated: "The local authorities took no step, obeyed no superior orders and did not perform the duties of their office without previous advice, permission, or knowledge of the friar curate, since the protection of the latter sufficed at times to defy the anger of the governor of the province and paralyze or evade the action of justice." Such evidentiary testimony bore out the fictional world eloquently detailed two decades earlier in Rizal's novels.

In summary, as the historian Reynaldo Ileto put it, in his *Filipinos and Their Revolution*, "The Spanish priest was the equivalent of the god-king elsewhere in Southeast Asia." Thus, notwithstanding their excesses, the friars constituted the de facto bulwark of Spanish colonial rule and were therefore indispensable. To further solidify their indispensability, the friars resisted any systematic attempt for the Indios to learn Spanish. The main reason the friars so assiduously learned the various native languages was so that only they could mediate between the indigenous population and the civil state. The very act of mediating, the ability to move in both spheres at the same time, conferred upon them a great deal of power. For in the eyes of the civil authorities, the alternative—allowing native priests to control most curacies—would mean opening the floodgates of nationalism. Originally the slur against the native priest was his alleged incompetence. Now, he was grudgingly perceived as being intelligent but his loyalty to Mother Spain was doubtful. He was likely to be seditious, and, as a high official put it, either "a disgrace for the clergy or . . . a peril for the colony."

And yet, the ilustrados saw themselves as faithful sons of Spain, in a sense, more Spanish than the Spanish. To them, the friars and other avatars of colonial rule were the unfaithful subjects, the subversives. Echoing the plaints of Fr. Burgos, the ilustrados believed that if only the mother country saw them in a positive light and extended to them and to the rest of the Indios the same rights as their brothers in the Iberian Peninsula, then all would be set right.

Three groups formed the nucleus of the Propaganda Movement. There were those who, having been implicated in the 1872 Mutiny and exiled to the Marianas Islands, had made their way to Europe; a decade later came young men seeking higher education; and third were those fleeing persecution in the colony. The nucleus of the Filipino expatriate community in Madrid counted among its earliest members Gregorio Sancianco and the Paterno brothers. Coming from a well-to-do family in the colony, the Paternos held a regular salon at their residence for writers and political figures. One of the brothers, Pedro, was a poet, the themes of whose collection of verse, titled *Sampaguita y Poesias*, published in 1880, were specifically Filipino. Except for the fact that this was the first such book by a Filipino, the verses were apparently forgettable. Pedro also penned a novel, *Ninay*, that, like *Sampaguita*, failed to garner any critical praise. Published in 1907, *Ninay* did have the distinction of being the first novel written in Tagalog.

A Chinese mestizo, Sancianco, on the other hand, wrote *El Progreso de Filipinas* in 1881, a study that examined Philippine colonial society from the standpoint of material progress. Not surprisingly, its author concluded that due to corruption and backward economic and social policies, the country had shown very little development. Government services and the country's infrastructure demanded radical improvements. The tax structure was highly inequitable, and the tribute levied on the Indios was both racist and unfair. He pointed out that those with the least had to pay the most, while the tribute was demanded of everyone in the Philippines, except the Spanish, whether peninsular or insular. The tribute had to be abolished and the present tax system replaced by one directly related to the ability to pay. Since the colony should be considered a province of Spain, it followed that its inhabitants were to be viewed as Spanish citizens and treated accordingly.

Sancianco also assailed the monopoly the religious had over education in the colony. He said students wished for a more rational and secular curriculum, and suggested that the civil government rather than the church take over the tasks of schooling. Though largely ignored, Sancianco's critique of the Philippines under Spanish rule was accurate, its themes propounded later on by ilustrado writers such as Rizal, who occasionally referred to him in his letters.

The Propaganda Movement had reformist rather than revolutionary goals. Among these were: recognition of the colony as a province of Spain; equal treatment of Filipinos; freedom of the press; curtailment of Guardia Civil abuses; representation in the Cortes; and secularization of the parishes. Its main mouthpiece was *La Solidaridad*, a fortnightly first published in Barcelona in February of 1889 and for six years, until late 1895, functioned as the mouthpiece of the Propaganda Movement.

Financed by contributions from the Comité de Propaganda, a Manila-based group, *La Solidaridad* put forth the demands of the Propaganda Movement, singling out the friars as major obstacles to meaningful reform. As the maiden issue put it, the movement's aim was to "combat reaction . . . be receptive to liberal principles . . . and propagate democratic ideals." The paper also printed news about events in the colony, and political views of leading Spanish politicians on the Philippines.

The Propagandists had aims similar to that of a Madrid group, the Asociación Hispano-Filipino, founded on January 12, 1889, principally by a Spanish academic Miguel Morayta. However, the Propagandists, being younger, felt the Madrid group (made up of Españoles Filipinos, mostly retired Spaniards who had once lived in the Philippines) was too accommodating of the authorities. The Asociación did lobby successfully for the passage of some laws such as mandating the teaching of Spanish. Nevertheless, the Asociación and the Propagandists lobbied jointly for their common objectives, e.g., representation in the Cortes, the lifting of censorship of the press, and an end to the arbitrary deportation of colony residents without due process.

Three Filipino expatriates formed the heart of both the publication and the movement: Graciano López Jaena, Marcelo H. del Pilar, and José Rizal. All three wrote for *La Solidaridad*; Rizal, writing in the journal, addressed the Spanish government: "If you persist in your system of banishments, incarcerations, and assaults without cause, if you punish them for your own faults, you make them despair, you remove their abhorrence for revolutions and turmoils, you harden them and you arouse them to struggle."

López Jaena was the editor for its first eight months, before handing over the editorial reins to del Pilar. Back in the islands, López Jaena had penned a satire whose principal character was a Fray (or Friar) Botod. *Botod* in López Jaena's native Hiligaynon—a major Visayan language—means full-bellied and was a none-too-subtle reference to the corpulent lifestyle and avarice of the friars. The work pilloried all the shortcomings of the Spanish clergy. Even though the tale circulated only in *zamizdat* form, its notoriety drew unfavorable clerical attention, prompting in López Jaena a sudden and intense curiosity about life in Spain. He had a reputation as a skillful orator and for having contacts among Spanish liberals and Masons, most if not all of whom were anticlerical. Unfortunately, López Jaena had a fondness for the bottle, hardly helpful to regularly putting out a publication. After a brief but disastrous visit to the islands, López Jaena returned to Spain. He had become a hack, at one point writing for a Spanish broadsheet that was critical of the Propagandists. He died, penniless and a consumptive, in Barcelona, at the age of forty.

Del Pilar, a lawyer from the Tagalog province of Bulacan, whose brother, a secular priest, had been deported to the Marianas in the wake of the 1872 mutiny, and who wrote under the pseudonym of Plaridel, was the real force behind La Solidaridad, soliciting articles from various correspondents, raising funds, writing for the journal itself, and finally taking over the editorial reins from López Jaena. He had also published in 1882 the broadsheet Diariong Tagalog (Tagalog Daily)—the first such publication in the islands. It lasted for only three months. He was an early defender of Rizal's first novel, Noli Me Tangere. Due to his satirical pamphlets, written in Tagalog—unlike the works of Rizal, who wrote his novels in Spanish, a fact which meant a majority of Filipinos couldn't read him (only five percent of the population was fluent in Spanish)—del Pilar was forced to flee the colony in early 1889.

Del Pilàr parodied, for instance, the Ten Commandments and the tyranny of the friars. His First Commandment was "Worship the Friar Above All Else." The Fifth Commandment, "Do Not Kill," became "Thou Shalt Not Die Without Having Sufficient Funds for a Funeral"— an unambiguous reference to the unsavory friar-practice of charging parishioners fees for administering such sacraments as Extreme Unction. His parody of the Lord's Prayer is especially acerbic and begins with "Our Substitute Father, who art in the convent, cursed be your name, your greed be taken away from us, your throat cut open on earth as it is in heaven." Hardly words to warm a friar's heart—or belly.

Other figures who moved around in reformist circles in Spain were Mariano Ponce, who assisted López Jaena and del Pilar with La Solidaridad, and contributed articles to the publication; the painters Juan Luna and Félix Resurrecíon Hidalgo; and Antonio Luna, Juan's brother and future general in the Philippine-American War of 1899. Both painters were critical successes on the continent, Luna's Spoliarium winning a gold medal at a prestigious art exposition in Madrid in 1884, and Hidalgo's Virgenes Cristianas winning the silver. After being acquitted in Paris of shooting his wife and mother-in-law fatally in a jealous rage—a case that provoked widespread scandal—Juan Luna returned to the colony in 1894. Shortly after the revolution against Spain broke out in August of 1896, Luna was implicated and imprisoned, only to be released in 1897. In 1899, he was named a member of a delegation to the United States by the Philippine revolutionary government, headed by Emilio Aguinaldo, to make a case for independence, but the painter died of a heart attack in Hong Kong.

JOSÉ RIZAL

Born in 1861, José Rizal could converse in ten languages and corresponded in six. The most charismatic and well-known member of the Propaganda Movement, Rizal was also a medical doctor, scientist, fencer, and writer who brilliantly articulated the dreams and buried hurts fueling the newfound nationalism. His older brother, Paciano, had been a protégé of Fr. Burgos and had been living with the latter when he was implicated in the Cavite Mutiny. Paciano had described the grisly executions to the young José, eleven years old at the time, which undoubtedly helped shape his later views. Rizal would write the staff of *La Solidaridad*: "Without 1872 there would now be neither Plaridel nor Jaena nor Sancianco, nor the valiant and generous Filipino expatriates in Europe. Without 1872, Rizal would have been a Jesuit and instead of writing the *Noli Me Tangere*, would instead have written something entirely different."

Coming from an upper middle-class family in Calamba Town in Laguna Province, not far from Manila, and whose patriarch, Francisco Mercado, was an inquilino who farmed large tracts of friar land, José Protacio Rizal Mercado y Alonso was a precocious child, the favorite of his mother Teodora Alonso, a sophisticated and devout woman who believed in the virtues of a good education and taught the young boy to read and write even before he started his formal schooling. A prodigious and disciplined learner, Rizal easily shone in the lower grades and, with nothing more to learn in the local schools, was sent to Manila at the age of eleven, to continue his studies, first, at the Jesuit-run Ateneo de Manila and, later, at the Dominican University of Santo Tomás. He moved to the city as José Rizal, "Rizal" being a second surname, and a variant of the Spanish *ricial*, meaning pasture land. His family feared that if he bore the patronym of Mercado, he would be linked to his older brother Paciano and thus indirectly to Fr. Burgos.

Higher education, in which he excelled, graduating summa cum laude from the Ateneo, and during which he was awarded literary prizes for his writing in Spanish, only fed his hunger for broader horizons, which he, along with his generation, knew were not available in the stultifying atmosphere of a conservative dispensation that looked down on Indios. At the age of twenty-one, in 1882, he sought those horizons in Europe. He quickly became part of the Filipino community of students, intellectuals, and political exiles in Spain, and was soon one of the leaders of the Propaganda Movement.

Rizal published his first novel, the Spanish-language *Noli Me Tangere*, in 1887. The novel is a powerful and searing indictment of corruption and abuse in the colony, particularly among the friar orders who epitomized to the novelist as they did to most Filipinos the venality, moral blindness, and arrogance of colonial rule. The novel was banned in the colony—having a copy was grounds for being charged with subversion—but circulated clandestinely. The author returned to Manila for a visit in 1888, one cut short when his family, fearful for his safety, persuaded him to leave. By then, Rizal had acquired something of a rock star's popularity, often followed by crowds when he was seen in public, deepening the distrust the authorities had of this ilustrado.

Returning to Europe, after watching Buffalo Bill's Wild West show in Paris in 1889, Rizal and his companions were impressed by the dignity and agility of the American Indian performers. They decided, part in jest, part in all seriousness, to call themselves "Los Indios Bravos," claiming a term the colonizer meant disparagingly as a badge of honor, a way of empowering themselves. In London, Rizal annotated *Sucesos de Las Islas Filipinas*, by Dr. Antonio de Morga, a 1609 Spanish account of pre-Hispanic culture, to show that a thriving sophisticated culture existed before the advent of the Spanish.

He went on to write *El Filibusterismo* (*The Subversive*), a sequel to the *Noli* and published in 1891. Rizal felt the second novel was darker and more profound than the *Noli*. Dedicated to Gómez, Burgos, and Zamora, the *Fili* (as it is popularly known) concerns its wealthy protagonist, Simoun, disillusioned by the failed reforms he has championed, plotting a violent uprising, and recruiting young men to his cause. The plot fails, however, and the would-be revolutionary kills himself. Just as with the *Noli*, the second novel added fuel to the fire of friar hatred directed at Rizal, and was proscribed as well.

La Liga Filipina and the Katipunan

After his stay in London, during which he was made honorary president of *La Solidaridad*, Rizal decided to carry on the struggle for reforms back in the colony. He likened it to a doctor visiting the sick patient. He left Europe for good, and sailed for Hong Kong in October of 1891, where he waited to see how the political winds blew in Manila. In the British colony, he seriously explored the Utopian possibility of establishing a Filipino community in Sandakan, Borneo. He wanted to create a sanctuary for himself and his family, as well as the people of Calamba, his hometown, who had been dispossessed of their lands by the Dominican friars. Even though the British North Borneo Charter Company was amenable to having these prospective immigrants settle on 5,000 acres of land, rent-free for three years, the financial costs involved and the almost certain refusal of the Spanish colonial government to allow such a move in the end doomed Rizal's endeavor to have the country come to him rather than he to the country.

He decided to proceed to Manila by late June of 1892. Barely a week after his arrival he founded La Liga Filipina, its aim to disseminate the Propaganda Movement's call for reformist, nonviolent ideals. Among other goals, La Liga Filipina advocated the unification of the archipelago into a political and cultural whole; development of agriculture, education and industry; and the eradication of injustice. Though these were hardly radical aims, the existence of the league provided the excuse his powerful enemies had been waiting for, and they complained to Governor General Despujol. On his orders, Rizal was arrested just four days after La Liga's initial meeting. The government exiled him to Dapitan, a coastal town and Jesuit mission in northwest Mindanao and far from Manila. His enforced departure from Manila on July 15, 1892, effectively ended the reformist movement.

Rizal's four years in exile turned out to be some of the most peaceful in his life. In Dapitan, he set up a water system, a school for boys, and an eye clinic as well, where he treated the residents of the town for free. In the square fronting the town church, he constructed an earthen relief map of Mindanao. It was in Dapitan where he met the young Josephine Bracken, an Irish-Chinese mestiza who had accompanied her stepfather from Hong Kong to Dapitan so the latter could be operated on by Rizal, whose fame as an ophtalmologist had spread beyond national boundaries. Bracken would be his lover and companion in this last period of his life.

ON THE EVE OF THE REVOLUTION

This last decade of the nineteenth century is unprecedented. Chaos, social upheaval, disease, hunger, and senseless deaths, but also hopes, dreams, a sudden sense of new direction—birth pangs of a nascent nation, death throes of an all but extinct formal colonial order. On the global stage, an aging empire is dying, and a new one is about to rise from its ashes. In that age of turbulence, life goes on for the Filipino, but now he begins to imagine himself in terms of a national identity, and regardless has a storehouse of customs—but customs that reflect an improvisatory sense, the different facets, the different streams, of life in the Philippines at the time, blending then as now the indigenous and the foreign, the alien and the familiar, in a word, "Filipinizing" them.

In 1894 the population of the colony was estimated, based on parish registration, to be between 6 million and 7 million. To these need to be added about a million non-Christians, such as the indigenous tribes of the interior, the Chinese, the Mindanao Muslims, and foreigners residing in the colony. The 1894 tally also counted 2,751 religious and lay clergy, and 21,513 military personnel. Of the latter, fewer than three thousand were Spanish; the rest were native conscripts. By the close of the century the peninsulares were believed to number approximately twenty thousand.

If the native had changed, if his or her way of life had been altered, not so the apparatus of colonial administration. The governor general was of course the top of the heap, with two advisory bodies: the *Junta de Autoridades*, or Board of Authorities, and the *Consejo de Administracíon*, or Council of Administration. Additionally, there were four types of regional governments: civil; politico-military provinces; politico-military commands; and district commands.

There were also the *ayuntamientos*. In modern parlance these would be metropolitan districts, of which there were eight, Manila being the oldest and largest. Governing an ayuntamiento were two *alcaldes en ordinario*, elected by Spanish residents; a city council; an *alguacil*, in charge of peace and order; and a scrivener, responsible for record keeping and answerable to the governor general and *alcalde mayor*, or governor of the province. Then came the municipalities, or townships, made up of *cabecerias de barangay*, an agglomeration of barangays, each consisting of forty to fifty families and headed by a *cabeza de barangay*, or barangay chief. The latter had traditionally been drawn from the ranks of pre-Hispanic datu families but over time were appointed on the recommendation of the municipal government. The *gobernadorcillo*, or mayor, along with the cabezas de barangay and landowners, made up the principalia.

As it is, the feudal system, with all its exploitative features, championed avidly both by the Spanish colonial authorities (except for the occasional liberal governor general) and the religious, remained intact, essentially unchanged since the conquest that began in the late sixteenth century. Despite reform laws passed in the home country, the colonial administrators could basically pick and choose which features to implement in the islands. An instructive example was the liberalizing measure provided by the Becerra Law of 1889, which provided for the establishment of more ayuntamientos wherever there was civil government. At that time, there were eighteen provinces with a purely civil government, but the then-governor general Valeriano Weyler (1888-91) believed that only in seven of these provinces were there sufficient personnel qualified to carry out the tasks of civil government. Moreover, rather than allowing elections so representatives could be chosen—as provided by the law—Weyler appointed individuals he deemed capable (and loyal both to him and to colonial strictures) to these positions. Thus, the very intent of the law, of providing an opportunity for the locals to acquire exposure and training in self-government no matter how limited, was thwarted.

In contrast, Puerto Rico already had some form of elections while Cuba had the status of an assimilated province. Before the outbreak of the Spanish-American War of 1898, there were already two major political parties in Puerto Rico, the Incondicionales, or Spanish party, and the nativist Autonomist Party. Months before the 1898 war began, the Autonomists won island elections. Thus, the Puerto Ricans enjoyed a certain degree of self-government, but still within the protective embrace of Madrid. In contrast, in the Philippines, any putative attempts at reform and eventual self-government were stifled, mostly at the behest of the almighty friar orders that had in essence become the state. Only when the Philippine Revolution of 1896 began were there half-hearted efforts toward democratic reform, and by then, of course, these were meaningless.

Nor had colonial rule meant a significant transformation of the colony from being mainly a source of raw material to one where industrialization took firm root. What the Spanish focused on throughout colonial occupation was extraction of whatever was of value in the islands, whether these were precious metals or spices or tobacco, to be sold or traded. As well, the Spanish viewed the islands as a trading conduit in Asia, particularly with regard to China. Even with the introduction of agricultural machinery and cash crops, the emphasis continued to be trade for short-term purposes rather any far-reaching industrialization. Essentially, the Spaniards made most of their fortunes in the Philippines from an extractive economy, to the clear detriment of the local population. It was after all what they had done in their New World colonies, whose immense wealth of raw material—gold and silver— lulled the Spanish into avoiding the path of industrialization, and thus were outstripped in this by the Netherlands and Great Britain.

In terms of the religious sphere, towards the end of Spanish occupation, the archipelago was divided into five dioceses: one metropolitan area, Manila, and four suffragan, or subordinate, bishoprics: Nueva Segovia (Vigan), Nueva Caceres (Bicol), Cebu, and Jaro. Each diocese was supposed to oversee the activities of both regular and secular clergies active within its jurisdiction, but time and again the friar orders, as has been previously described, were well aware of their indispensable role in colonial government and resisted the right of diocesan visitation—perhaps the most obvious symbol of civil oversight. The regular orders in the islands were made up of the friaries (the Augustinians, Recollects, Franciscans, and the Dominicans) as well as the Jesuits.

The immense wealth the religious orders accumulated was strikingly evident in their landholdings at the end of the Spanish colonial era. The friars owned almost 400,000 acres, or about one-fifteenth of cultivated land. In Manila and outlying districts, lands owned by the religious totaled more than 110,000 acres. The largest friar hacienda, run by the Dominicans, was in Calamba (where José Rizal's parents were inquilinos) with 35,000 acres.

While the European Propagandists soldiered on in Spain, the government turned a deaf ear to their efforts, though individual public officials were sympathetic. The fact that the once mighty Spanish empire was now reduced to small island colonies only strengthened the resolve of the Spanish ultranationalists to hold on to the remnants. Consequently, the authority of the Spanish friars in the Philippines was rendered well-nigh impregnable, as they were seen as the main bulwark against nationalist feelings. With the friars as parish priests, the Archbishop of Manila had little to no canonical authority over them. He was forced to consult the provincials of the four friar orders on all matters pertaining to the church, thus guaranteeing the depth and continuation of friar influence on Philippine society.

One of the Liga's members was a young working-class firebrand and Tondo warehouse worker by the name of Andrés Bonifacio, who revered Rizal. At first Bonifacio worked actively on behalf of the Liga, recruiting members. But the leadership of La Liga, fearful that the new members Bonifacio had brought in were more inclined to revolution than assimilation, dissolved the organization. Its more conservative members (mostly from the upper middle class) continued to support the Propagandists in Spain, mainly to ensure publication of *La Solidaridad*.

Bonifacio, on the other hand, as with the newer and more uncompromising members, drawn from the lower middle and working classes, saw reforms, even if they were to be granted by the despotic Spanish regime, as symbolic rather than substantial. Orphaned at an early age, Bonifacio read avidly, keeping abreast of the Propagandists' activities through *La Solidaridad*. He had Rizal's novels; *Les Miserables* by Victor Hugo; Eugène Sue's *The Wandering Jew*; and texts on the French Revolution, international law, and religion. The ideals of the French Revolution, in particular, seemed to have inspired him to think along mass mobilization and the resort to arms. He had read del Pilar's satires, and it was the satirist who seemed to have influenced Bonifacio ideologically, for the hard-hitting writer was not averse to armed revolution.

Bonifacio, along with the new recruits, consequently shifted the orientation of the mass movement towards complete independence from Spain. He founded in 1892 the secret revolutionary society dedicated to overthrowing the colonial yoke: *Ang Kataastaasang Kagalagalangan Katipunan ng mga Anak ng Bayan*—the Highest, Most Honorable Society of the Country's Sons and Daughters, the KKK, or simply the Katipunan. It would be the explosive catalyst that would end Iberian despotism, friar abuse, and establish a free state.

Economic conditions exacerbated the social and political oppression suffered by the vast majority of the populace. There was a sizeable lumpenproletariat in Manila, made up of thousands of workers, drawn there (as today) by the possibility of jobs, whether in the tobacco industry, in the port area, or in other factories that had sprung up due to increased trade and demands for Philippine raw materials. In the country-side, the growing landlessness increased the ranks of tenant farmers now working plots of land they had once owned but had had taken away from them by the manipulations of friar estates, unscrupulous landowners, and the rapidly rising class of Chinese mestizos. Landlessness of course prompted many to simply pack up and seek their fortune in the cities.

The Katipunan didn't lack for recruits. With many of its leaders members of Masonic lodges (Rizal himself was a Mason, with his Masonic name being *Dimasalang*, a Tagalog approximation of *Noli Me Tangere*), would-be revolutionaries underwent initiation rites that had a Masonic tinge. They were blindfolded and led to a dimly lit room that had a skull, a revolver, and a cutlass. If the applicant responded satisfactorily to questions put to him, he was then initiated into the secret society by means of a blood compact. From an incision in his arm, the initiate drew blood to write his name. The initiate also took on a new name—his nom de guerre. The newly inducted member would initially belong to the first of three Katipunan ranks, the *Katipun*. He could aspire to the next higher level, the *Kawal* (or Warrior), and thence the highest, the *Bayani* (Hero).

The Katipunan stressed brotherhood and ethical behavior. Many of its tenets clearly reflected the legacies of the Enlightenment and both the American and French revolutions: All men were equal and no one was superior to anyone else in terms of human dignity; the oppressed needed to be defended against the oppressor; and a man was great because he neither oppressed nor aided the oppressor and knew how to love and defend his country. Anticipating both the modernist feminist revolution and Mao Tse-Tung's maxim that "women hold up half of heaven," while also reflecting pre-Hispanic values, one tenet declared women to be partners, companions who shouldered equally the burdens of life. In the Katipunan's *Cartilla*, or *Primer*, written by Emilio Jacinto—Bonifacio's university-educated adviser who refused to give up the struggle even after Bonifacio's execution by his soon-to-be-rival General Emilio Aguinaldo—the revolutionary society enjoined its members to "consider your wife not as a mere plaything, but as a partner, a companion in the hardships of life; be considerate towards her weakness and think of the mother that cared for you in your childhood. What you would not want others do to your wife, daughter, and sister, do not do to the wife, daughter, and sister of another."

That the Katipunan explicitly referred to how women should be treated reflected the fact that the vital social role of women had enjoyed prior to colonial rule had continually been under assault by the aggressive patriarchal attitudes and values espoused by the Spanish, most intensely and consistently by the religious orders. These men of the cloth, reflecting the ultra-masculine ethos of Roman Catholicism by way of Inquisitorial Spain, saw the essentially egalitarian relationships between the sexes as aberrations, if not abominations. For women such as the babaylan to be the mediators between the visible world and that of the spirit; to be perceived as healers; to be called upon as a villager lay dying; for them to have as much right to sexual pleasure as men— all these female prerogatives were anathema to the friars, and a threat to their primacy. Male authority had to reign supreme, whether in matrimony, government, or religion. By the time of the 1896 Revolution, the "good" Filipina was a paragon of modesty, keeper of repressed longings, and unswervingly faithful to the men in her life, whether to the husband, son, or Christ on the cross. With the Katipunan, there was a deliberate effort to do away with the restrictions on women's roles. They may not have borne arms—at least not many did—but they participated otherwise as actively in the revolution as the men. Hilaria Aguinaldo, Emilio Aguinaldo's wife, for instance, organized the first chapter of the Red Cross in the country.

THE CRY OF BALINTAWAK

Under Bonifacio's stewardship—he was referred to as the *Supremo*— the Katipunan combined liberal ideas with plans for armed struggle. The society began to store weapons in various safe places in preparation for the revolution. The Katipunan grew rapidly, and though Manila was rife with rumors about the existence of a revolutionary society, no hard evidence could be produced. Governor General Ramón Blanco consequently dismissed the reports as the paranoid musings of the friars. That hard evidence was supplied when a low-ranking disgruntled Katipunero Teodoro Patiño unburdened himself to his devoutly Catholic sister about plans for an armed uprising. The information quickly reached the curate of the Tondo parish, Fr. Mariano Gil. The friar convinced Patiño (most likely under threat of excommunication), a typesetter at the newspaper, *Diario de Manila,* to lead him to the offices and show him where papers and other paraphernalia pertaining to the Katipunan had been hidden.

The untimely discovery forced the Katipunan to proclaim the need for revolution on August 23, 1896 at a place called Pugad Lawin (Hawk's Nest), at the home of Melchora Aquino, a self-taught eighty-four-year-old widow who fed, housed, and otherwise took care of the Katipuneros when fighting broke out. The grand dame of the revolution, she was known affectionately as Tandang Sora (Old Sora). Subsequently imprisoned by the Spanish and interrogated as to Katipunan activities, the octogenarian wouldn't talk. She was exiled to the Marianas and allowed to return once the United States of America had taken over the country. Still, she refused to pledge allegiance to the United States, and died in 1919 at the age of 107, with American colonial rule firmly in place.

In the yard of her home, Bonifacio and his fellow Katipuneros tore up their *cedulas*, or tax ID certificates, indicating a decisive split with Spain. (In 1884, a graduated poll tax, known as the *cedula personal*, was created to replace the age-old tribute. The cedula was proof of payment.) The revolution, initially confined to the Tagalog provinces, quickly spread to other regions. Attacks against government buildings and garrisons occurred in places such as the Camarines provinces, Zambales, and, to the southwest, Palawan Island.

Not surprisingly, Governor General Ramón Blanco proclaimed a state of war. Those suspected of being members of the Katipunan were imprisoned and tortured, with many being put to death. Among the most notorious instances of mass execution were two that took place on January 4 and 11, 1897—by then Blanco, perceived by the friars as insufficiently hawk-like, had been replaced by Camilo Polavieja, a battle-tested veteran who rarely brooked compromise. The first group, consisting of fifteen men, was known as the Bicol Martyrs, after the southern Luzon region whence they hailed originally. Included were three secular Filipino clerics. The second group came to be called the Thirteen Martyrs of Bagumbayan, after the site of their execution, now part of Rizal Park. These were men arrested after the Cry at Balintawak on charges of treason, and included civic leaders, professionals, and members of the Katipunan.

The most prominent victim of the regime was Dr. José Rizal. The previous year, Rizal had requested permission to act as a volunteer medic with Spanish forces in Cuba, where revolutionary forces under

José Martí sought independence, a revolution that would provide the U.S. the needed pretext of declaring war on Spain. Acting on the suggestion of his Austrian friend and faithful correspondent Ferdinand Blumentritt, Rizal believed his petition would dispel the notion that he was disloyal to Mother Spain.

Permission to sail to Cuba was granted in 1896, before the Revolution broke out. Rizal sailed to Manila and there, on September 3, shortly after the Revolution began, boarded a ship for Europe, with letters of recommendation from Governor Blanco. In one, addressed to the Spanish Minister of War, Blanco wrote that Rizal was "in my judgment, more deserving of pardon and benevolence since it appears that he is in no way involved in the uprising." Nevertheless, en route—by then the Revolution was in full throttle—on the orders of the same Blanco, who was under pressure from Spanish military officers to bring the physician/novelist back, Rizal was arrested for his alleged role in the uprising. Once in Barcelona, after a short stay in Montjuich Prison, he was sent back to Manila under guard. After imprisonment at Fort Santiago, and a trial closed to the public, Rizal was found guilty of fomenting rebellion. The fact that one of the passwords used by Katipuneros was "Rizal" provided damning circumstantial evidence of his alleged complicity.

The irony was that Rizal, while in exile at Dapitan, had been approached in early 1896 by Dr. Pio Valenzuela, an emissary of the Katipunan, seeking his advice and, more importantly, his imprimatur for the planned uprising. Though the protagonist Simoun in his second novel *El Filibusterismo* had argued that only violence could overthrow the Spanish regime, Rizal believed the country was not yet prepared for such a radical step, that it would only result in the tragic loss of innocent lives. He informed Valenzuela that he would not be a party to the impending revolution. Like other members of the Propaganda Movement, he saw evolutionary reform as the gradual but sure way to independence. In his stress on nonviolence, Rizal anticipated Gandhi's policy of passive resistance that proved effective in securing independence for the Indian subcontinent.

As seen in an iconic photograph of the execution (taken by the Spanish Creole photographer Manuel Arias Rodriguez, whose photo documentation of the conflict between Filipinos and the Spanish is invaluable), at dawn of December 30, 1896, clad in a morning coat and a black bowler hat, Rizal was executed by firing squad at the Luneta. Behind the firing squad made up of Filipinos were Spanish riflemen, ready to gun down the Indios should they refuse to fire. Rizal had asked the officer in charge of the firing squad if he could face the riflemen but was denied permission. Upon being hit, eyewitnesses said he managed to twist his body around and fall as he had wanted to: face up. In a possibly apocryphal version of his death—and a testament to how potent a symbol his martyrdom had immediately become—the more moved of the onlookers rushed forward to dip their handkerchiefs in his blood, now considered sacred.

Unbeknownst to his jailers, the day before his execution, Rizal had managed to conceal a document in an alcohol stove he gave to his sister, whispering to her in English that he had something hidden in it. The document turned out to be a poem, *Mi Ultimo Adios* (*My Last Farewell*), a moving and eloquent record of his thoughts about his country—as well as his love for Josephine Bracken. (Bracken joined the revolutionary army briefly but left the country for Hong Kong in May of 1897.) The poem quickly became famous, its opening line known to every school child in the country: *"Adios patria adorada, region del sol querida"* ("Farewell, beloved country, land cherished by the sun").[*]

Aware of how scarce his manpower resources were and how the Cuban Revolution was drawing in more Spanish troops, and with the possibility of native soldiers joining their brother Filipinos in open revolt, Blanco requested a thousand soldiers from Spain and permission to form militias of volunteers drawn from the Spanish community in the colony. Surprisingly more aware of the need for a surge in troops, Madrid sent approximately double the number of soldiers requested. Towards the close of 1896, a little more than two thousand troops disembarked at Manila, almost at the same time as the arrival of Blanco's successor, Camilo Polavieja.

The reinforcements were welcomed as saviors by the Spanish community and by civil and religious authorities in festive, even giddy, rites. In a welcoming speech, the president of the Casino Español, the preeminent Spanish club in Manila, spewed vitriol on the Indio revolutionaries: "You arrive in time; the cannibals of the forest are still there; the wild

---

[*] *Mi Ultimo Adios* has at least 35 translations in English, 46 in Philippine languages, and 38 in other languages, from Indonesian and Hindi, to Romanian and Wolof.

beast hides in his lair; the hour has come to finish with the savages. . . . Destroy! Kill! Do not pardon." Despite the increase in troop strength, it was too little too late. The repressive measures only stoked the fire of rebellion. To the long-suffering populace, such measures were harsher only by degrees and not substantially different from what they faced in pre-revolutionary times. They were up to the task of enduring whatever the Spanish could throw at them. Too, where ethnic and regional rivalries divided them in the past, now they began to have a sense, even if tenuous, of a collective whole. By the end of the year, the fire of revolution engulfed the country. And while the revolution had still to coalesce effectively, nonetheless it would only be a matter of time before it did.

Bonifacio versus Aguinaldo

On the ground, Bonifacio, though an inspirational figure, proved to be ineffective as a military strategist, his forces' attacks on towns and garrisons ill-planned and ill-fated. As the revolution blundered on, Bonifacio's reputation diminished almost in reverse proportion as that of another member of the Katipunan, Emilio Aguinaldo, was on the rise. Inducted by Bonifacio into the Katipunan, Aguinaldo was the gobenadorcillo of Kawit Town, in nearby Cavite Province (the same province where the 1872 Mutiny had taken place). Under Aguinaldo's leadership, the Cavite rebels scored victories against the Spanish.

After the initial successes of the Katipunan in Cavite, Governor General Polavieja, having taken over from Blanco, mounted a counteroffensive that regained ground. The two main factions of the Katipunan in the province—Magdalo, under Aguinaldo, and Magdiwang, pro-Bonifacio—agreed to meet. Bonifacio and some of his staff traveled to the town of Tejeros, where elections were held to determine who should lead the revolution. Along the way, many onlookers hailed Bonifacio as the "King of the Tagalogs," a testament to his popularity. By this time, however, it was clear to everyone that Aguinaldo was far superior as a military strategist than the Supremo. The added fact that the elections were being held in Cavite, Aguinaldo's home turf, meant the gathering was dominated by pro-Aguinaldo members. Unsurprisingly, Aguinaldo won the election, while Bonifacio was elected as Minister of Interior, more of a ceremonial office. Outmaneuvered and provoked by questions of his competence, and nearly coming to blows with his interlocutors, Bonifacio, asserting his authority as founder and head of the

Katipunan, refused to recognize the legitimacy of the Tejeros Convention and stormed out of the hall.

Aguinaldo was sworn in as president of the revolutionary government shortly after; his Cabinet took shape, all its members from Cavite, a fact that spoke to how regionalism played a role in Aguinaldo's consolidation of power. (This would have been obvious to Bonifacio but which he ignored, probably banking on his stature as founder of the Katipunan to outweigh everything else.) The lone exception was General Artemio Ricarte, who hailed from the Ilocos region up north but was now a permanent resident of the province. Bonifacio and his followers continued to oppose the Aguinaldo government even though they were at a disadvantage, not being from the province and therefore having little support there. Even the supposedly pro-Bonifacio Magdiwang wing threw its support behind Aguinaldo. Aguinaldo had him arrested, and the founder of the Katipunan and his brother Procopio were brought to trial before a military court supervised by their now-sworn enemies. The two were quickly found guilty of sedition and treason. On May 10, 1897, the Bonifacio brothers were executed in the woods of Mt. Buntis. The Supremo's widow, Gregoria de Jesus, evaded capture and returned to Manila, where she married Julio Nakpil, a Katipunan officer loyal to Bonifacio and active in the revolution against Spain. She resumed revolutionary activities, principally deciphering messages sent in code by members of the Katipunan in the field. She also knew how to ride and use firearms, and took part in a number of encounters.

The leadership was now firmly in the hands of propertied men, members of the principalia, rather than the working-class forces that Bonifacio had represented. Would this change the direction of the armed struggle against Spain? Not in the short term, but as the drive for independence from a Spain determined to hold on to the vestiges of its once grand empire proved to be complicated, it finally did veer towards compromise. As Renato Constantino puts it in his *A Past Revisited*, "There was only one logical outcome of the triumph of the elite. Leading the Revolution meant leading it to suit the desires of those who had interests to defend. Such a leadership could offer only a vacillating attitude towards the enemy."

One Revolution, Two Wars

Undisputed as the leader of the revolution, Aguinaldo and his forces retreated south to Batangas Province, as the Spanish counter-attacks reclaimed territory. They then moved to Biak-na-Bato in Bulacan Province, north of Manila, where a constitution, based on the Cuban Constitution of Jimaguayu, was drawn up on November 2, 1897, for the republic that had been founded earlier that April, in Cavite province. A little more than a month after, however, through the mediation of Pedro Paterno (author of *Sampaguita* and *Ninay*), both sides in the conflict negotiated to try to end the conflict. By December 15, 1897, the Treaty of Biak-na-Bato was signed between the Spanish colonial government and Aguinaldo.

Under the Treaty, Aguinaldo and his cabinet agreed to go into exile upon being indemnified $400,000: $200,000 to the revolutionary army, and $200,000 more when the surrendered arms reached an agreed-upon total. An additional $900,000 would be used to compensate non-combatant Filipino families who had suffered losses during the fighting. Aguinaldo and several of his closest associates sailed for Hong Kong on December 27, 1897, where the indemnity was deposited in banks. According to some sources, the general's intent was to use the funds to purchase war materiel and continue the fight against Spain. But his detractors held that time and the odds favored the revolutionary forces, creating considerable suspicion that the treaty was essentially a sell-out.

Be that as it may, it was an illusory peace, as the Spanish barely complied with the treaty's terms, nor did the revolutionary forces lay down their arms. Besides, the revolution could no longer be bound by the policies of Aguinaldo and his Cabinet. The genie had been let out of the bottle. Now there was a near-universal desire to be rid of Spanish rule. The fighting continued in Central and Northern Luzon, and in parts of the Visayas. But events moved fast. On February 15, 1898, the *USS Maine* exploded in the harbor of Havana. In a feverish exercise of yellow journalism, the U.S. press stoked public outrage, and the United States used the *Maine* as a pretext to declare war on Spain in April. And so the stage was set for the rise of the United States as a global power and the beginning of what is often referred to as the American Century.

4. AMERICANIZATION AND ITS DISCONTENTS, 1899-1946

"The Person Sitting in Darkness is almost sure to say: 'There is something curious about this—curious and unaccountable. There must be two Americas: one that sets the captive free, and one that takes a once-captive's new freedom away from him, and picks a quarrel with him with nothing to found it on; then kills him to get his land.'"

—Mark Twain, "To the Person Sitting in Darkness"

THE WANING OF AN AGE:
THE SPANISH-AMERICAN WAR

I N EARLY 1898, IN RESPONSE TO THE ONGOING CUBAN WAR OF INDE-
pendence against Spain, the United States government ordered the
battleship *USS Maine* to Havana—a move meant to signal Spain
that the U.S. sympathized with the Cuban rebels and that it intended to
protect U.S. interests in the Caribbean island. The ship was blown up
on February 15, 1898, while at anchor off Havana, killing 266 men. At
the time the cause was unknown—though an investigation in 1976 by
Admiral Hyman Rickover of the U.S. Navy determined that the explosion was an accident, caused by a faulty coal bunker—but U.S. newspapers immediately blamed the Spanish. The rallying cry for the moment
was "Remember the Maine! To hell with Spain!" William Randolph
Hearst, owner and publisher of the *New York Journal*, famously said to
Frederic Remington, the paper's well-known illustrator, "You furnish
the pictures and I'll furnish the war!"

And that Hearst and the media did. The explosion was the perfect
excuse for a war, and even though Spain had offered an immediate
armistice and considerable autonomy for the Cubans, the McKinley
government was undeterred from its mission, declaring war on April 25.
The conflict was just the right opportunity for a young giant, eager to
participate in the "Great Game" of empire building. It heralded the
beginning of what has since come to be known as the American
Century. Even before the formal declaration of hostilities, Theodore
Roosevelt, Undersecretary of the Navy—filling in for Secretary John D.
Long, who was on leave—ordered U.S. warships under the command of
Commodore George Dewey to Hong Kong in late February and there
await battle orders. Once at berth in Hong Kong, in anticipation of the
war, Dewey requested troop reinforcements from Washington. With the

declaration of war, he and his fleet steamed to Manila and on May 1, annihilated an aging Spanish fleet, with only one loss of life: an American sailor felled by heat stroke.

The lopsided victory essentially sealed the fate of Spanish rule. It was an outcome easily predicted: the Spanish empire was on its last legs, plagued by a significant trade deficit and political instability at home. American consular authorities had already contacted Aguinaldo in Singapore and led him to believe that the North American nation was coming to the revolution's assistance and would engage the Spanish on behalf of what was hoped would soon be an independent country. Nothing was ever put in writing, however, leading to denials later on the part of the consular officials involved.

Aguinaldo followed shortly on May 19, brought back from Hong Kong to the islands by an American gunboat. Less than a week later, on May 24, 1898, he declared the establishment of a dictatorial government. It was to last until a Constitutional Assembly could be formed, a preliminary step in forming a republic, with a president and a cabinet. At first, cordiality characterized relations between Aguinaldo and his Philippine revolutionary forces and Dewey and his troops. A month after he arrived, on June 12, 1898, Aguinaldo proclaimed from his home province of Cavite an independent Philippine republic. By then, Filipinos had defeated the Spanish in most of the archipelago and had ringed the Walled City—the king piece still in the hands of the Spanish but perilously close to being checkmated by Aguinaldo.

Thus the stage was set for the subsequent and inevitable war between a fledgling nation—the first in Asia to raise the banner of revolution against a Western power—and a North American republic, itself founded on revolution and with a constitution that had served as a model and inspiration to others around the globe as well as to the Filipinos, its troops now set to deprive those same Filipinos of their right to freedom.

In setting its sights on Spanish colonies in the last decade of the nineteenth century, the United States made it clear to the European powers that it would not be excluded in claiming its share of colonies so as to acquire markets and sources of raw materials. Overseas expansion was viewed by both U.S. politicians and entrepreneurs as a way out of the economic crisis that befell the U.S. in 1893. But taking over the former Spanish colony in Southeast Asia was not a foregone conclusion. France, Germany, England, and Japan showed proprietary as well as predatory interest in the islands, having sent warships to Manila Bay, to the great annoyance of Commodore Dewey. However, the war that erupted in early 1899 between the United States and the fledgling Republic of the Philippines, and the increase in U.S. troops, effectively curtailed foreign interest, at least until the outbreak of World War II.

The entry of the United States obviously complicated the picture, however. On one level, Spanish colonialism was being confronted by American imperialism, eager to administer the coup de grace to the old order. On another level, the Philippine Revolution was once more under the leadership of Aguinaldo and his fellow principalia—a revolution that had only grown stronger and had the Spanish on the ropes. In an attempt to delay the inevitable, the Spanish proposed the formation of a consultative assembly to be made up of the elite, and to bestow on Aguinaldo the rank of brigadier general if he would join the Spanish army. Both offers were refused.

On the ground, Aguinaldo and his army consolidated their gains, capturing Spanish garrisons in quick succession and, by the beginning of July 1898, controlled virtually the entire colony, except for the capital, Manila, to which it laid siege, alongside, albeit uneasily, U.S. troops. In these early stages, the Filipinos were not averse to American protection, regardless of whether the rank and file viewed the North Americans as genuinely sympathetic with their goals as set out by the Katipunan. In the meantime, the United States forces played for time until more troops arrived. By late July, twelve thousand troops were on hand, and thereafter more troops began to arrive regularly.

Aguinaldo declared the independence of the Philippines on June 12—Commodore Dewey was invited to the momentous occasion but he begged off, saying it was mail day—and for the first time, the Philippine flag was displayed and the national anthem sung. In a nod to the United States, still seen as an omnipotent ally, the declaration stated: "Under the protection of the mighty and humane North American Nation, we proclaim and solemnly declare, in the name and by authority of the inhabitants of all these Philippine Islands, that they are and have the right to be free and independent; that they are released from all obedience to the crown of Spain; that every political tie between the two is and must be completely severed and annulled; and that, like all free and independent states, they have complete authority to make war, conclude peace, establish treaties of commerce, enter into alliance, regulate commerce, and execute all other acts and things that independent states have the right to do." Aguinaldo then began appointing his first cabinet ministers, in preparation for the business of governing a full-blown republic.

In these formative months, Apolinario Mabini, a brilliant thirty-four-year-old lawyer of peasant origins from the southern Tagalog province of Batangas, became Aguinaldo's political adviser. Dubbed the Sublime Paralytic due to paralysis of the lower limbs, Mabini was carted by relays of men to Cavite. It wasn't long before he was seen as the brains of the revolution, for his ability to navigate the complex fields of diplomacy and help create a government to suit the temper of the times. He drafted decrees for Aguinaldo and persuaded the latter to move from a dictatorship to a revolutionary government. By June 23, 1898, such an administration was formed, with Aguinaldo as president. Local governments were established, keeping in place the administrative structures set up by the Spanish.

Mabini was a Freemason and a member of Rizal's La Liga Filipina. Initially opposed to armed struggle, he believed in the advocacy of reforms and had been a correspondent for Marcelo H. del Pilar's *La Solidaridad* in Barcelona, enabling its expatriate readers and the Spanish to know what was going on in Manila. He quickly realized that Spain, having resisted instituting reforms agreed to under the Biak-na-Bato Treaty, would never acquiesce to handing over power; revolution was the only recourse. Envious of his closeness to Aguinaldo, and probably out of snobbery, other members of Aguinaldo's cabinet spread the canard that Mabini's paralysis was due to his having contracted syphilis, in an attempt to besmirch his character.

The Aguinaldo government disseminated information about the emergent state through two publications: *El Heraldo de la Revolucion*—later to be called *Gaceta de Filipinas*—and *La Independencia*, whose founder and editor was General Antonio Luna. These served as outlets for exhortatory articles and official communiqués, as well as news articles; more importantly, the two papers presented a portrait of a legitimate, functioning government.

Even though American forces had been beefed up, Filipino troops controlled the major approaches to Intramuros and could have easily forced its defenders to surrender by cutting off food and water supplies, but they held back. The Spanish, to whom surrendering to a people they had viewed for 333 years as inferior and incapable of self-rule would have been an unbearable humiliation, cut a deal with the Americans. By early August General Fermin Jaudenes, in command of Intramuros's defense, was in backroom negotiations with Dewey to arrange a mock battle for the Walled City in which the newcomers would win but in a way that saved face for the Spanish. After a sham battle on August 13, 1898, to preserve their honor, the Spanish garrison defending Intramuros yielded to the Westerners. The scripted battle went off as planned, though not without six American and forty-nine Spanish casualties. The Yankees claimed Manila that same day and refused entry to Philippine troops, on the grounds that the Spanish were fearful of being killed en masse by vengeful Filipino soldiers.

The actions of the U.S. military confirmed the worst fears of the Aguinaldo government: that the United States was out to claim the colony for itself. Now with Manila in the hands of the U.S., and Spain surrendering to the North Americans, erstwhile allies faced each other in an uneasy standoff. Seeking to nullify U.S. gains, Aguinaldo sought diplomatic recognition from foreign governments; it dispatched Felipé Agoncillo as its representative, first, to Washington, D.C., and then to Paris, where Spain and the United States met in October 1898 for a conference to formally end the Spanish-American War, and to determine the conditions under which the victor would receive the spoils. Protesting that there was already in place a legitimate government, Agoncillo was ignored, and refused a place at the bargaining table. On December 10, 1898, the Treaty of Paris was formally signed, setting out these terms: Spain would relinquish Cuba, Puerto Rico, the Philippines, and the Marianas (Guam). In return, the United States would indemnify Spain $20 million—or a little less than $3 per Filipino, the population of the archipelago then estimated at 7 million. The treaty also allowed the Spanish ten-year access to Philippine ports and goods for the purposes of trade. For the treaty to take effect, the United States Congress needed to ratify it, and its approval was by no means sure. A vote was scheduled for February 6, 1899.

Spain agreed to hand over control of Las Islas Filipinas, as well as Guam and Puerto Rico, to the United States. The U.S. allowed Cuba its independence, but burdened it with the Platt Amendment, which provided that Cuba cede territory to the United States for use as military bases—Guantánamo, principally—and the right to intervene in Cuba to preserve life, property, and liberty, essentially whenever Washington deemed such intervention necessary. The amendment also barred Cuba from making a treaty with another nation, giving the U.S. effective control over its foreign affairs. Signed into law by President McKinley in 1901, these provisions were incorporated into the Cuban Constitution, rendering the island nation a U.S. protectorate and guaranteeing U.S. imperial hegemony by indirect, rather than direct, means. (These provisions would later be repealed by the Cubans in 1934.)

A Lull on the Battlefield

Determined to assert control, in September of 1898 Aguinaldo had moved the provisional government to Malolos, Bulacan, a province bordering Manila to the north. There he convened a congress—the consultative body Mabini had proposed—at the hoary Barasoain Church. There trooped eight-five representatives (mostly men of property) from provinces controlled by the Aguinaldo government. They set about drafting a Constitution, though this was essentially entrusted to one delegate, Felipé Calderón. Drawing from the constitutions of several South American countries as well as that of the United States, Calderón wrote a draft that proposed a unicameral legislature, and made the National Assembly, essentially the legislature, the dominant branch of government. The rationale, with which most of the Congress agreed, was that the Spanish colonial regime had been marked by an overbearing and tyrannical chief executive, the Governor General. It was hoped that the elevation of the National Assembly as preeminent branch, to be made up of elected representatives, would avoid this pitfall.

Mabini opposed the adoption of a constitution. To him, the Malolos Congress was an interim body, its raison d'etre to act as a consultant and propose policies to Aguinaldo's revolutionary government, especially with regard to possible war with the United States, whom Mabini had from the outset mistrusted. Once a permanent government had come into being, a true constitution could be drawn up. How the Congress would act was determined in part by class. Mabini came from a peasant background, while Calderón and most others of the Congress were of the elite ilustrado class. Pressed on which course to take, Aguinaldo, himself a property owner and member of the principalia, decided to abide by the wishes of the Congress, which overwhelmingly approved the Calderón-drafted Constitution. Most of its original provisions were endorsed, except for one: an article that made Catholicism the official religion of the state.

In effect, this proposed article would retain what the Spanish had wrought—a devoutly Catholic state. This didn't sit well with those in the Congress who harbored strong anti-clerical sentiments and many of whom certainly would have been Masons. After debates on the pros and cons of the provision, the Congress affirmed by only one vote the principle of separation of church and state. Written in Spanish, the document was adopted and the Philippine Republic inaugurated on January 23, 1899. The Constitution acknowledged that sovereignty resided exclusively with the Filipino people. To Aguinaldo, the Malolos Constitution was "the most glorious expression of the noble aspirations of the Filipino people, a mirror of their culture, and a clear proof before the world of their capacity to govern themselves." Aside from the separation of church and state, its other notable provisions were setting up a system of free and compulsory education; a new fiscal and tax system; the foundation of a navy; a reorganized army; and the establishment of a diplomatic corps. Elected or not, the Malolos delegates were eager to show that they were capable of running the country without outside help.

By then, most of the Spanish forces had sailed for Spain, except for a fifty-man garrison in the small town of Baler, in the province of Tayabas on the largely inaccessible Pacific coast of northeastern Luzon. There for eleven months, from July 1, 1898 to June 2, 1899, the garrison held out in the town church—the only stone building in Baler—refusing to believe the revolution had succeeded, even when Spanish officials visited them. Finally, an article in a Madrid newspaper artfully left behind convinced the commanding officer of the truth, and the longest encounter between the Filipino forces and the Spanish was over. The thirty survivors surrendered and were treated with respect by the Filipino troops. Back in Barcelona, the soldiers were given a hero's welcome. (This event was the basis of a 1945 Spanish film, *Los Ultimos de Filipinas*, or *The Last of the Philippines*, a nostalgic valorization of patriotic duty and the defense of empire, very much in tune with the values of the Franco regime, already in place since 1939.)

Being that Spanish colonial rule had spanned more than three centuries, there remained sizable communities of Spanish families who had lived not just in Manila and its environs but in port cities such as Cebu and Iloilo for generations, had intermarried with the natives, and considered Las Islas Filipinas their home, albeit now to be ruled by English speakers. Such businesses as they had set up—San Miguel Brewery and Tabacalera being two of the more enduring examples—continued to operate. And of course those centuries guaranteed an imprint of Hispanicization and a mestizo culture that had evolved and proved to be ineradicable, especially when it came to matters of faith.

The United States and Spain agreed that Filipinos would be given religious freedom as well as civil rights but conditioned on approval of the U.S. Congress. President McKinley appointed a commission, to be headed by Cornell University president Jacob G. Schurman, to proceed to the newly acquired colony and investigate conditions there. By the time the Schurman Commission arrived in Manila in March of 1899, however, the anticipated war between the United States and a newly minted Republic of the Philippines had been going on for a month.

A Splendid Little War Turns Ugly: The 1899 Philippine-American War

The deliberations and decisions of the Malolos Congress were ignored by the U.S. Less than two weeks after the inauguration of the Philippine Republic, and two days before the U.S. Congress was to vote on ratifying the Treaty of Paris and the takeover of the Philippines, hostilities between the fledgling government and the United States erupted. On February 4, 1899, two American soldiers, Willy Grayson and Orville Miller of the Nebraska Volunteers, shot and killed two Filipino soldiers. Grayson later said the Filipinos disregarded his warnings to halt and identify themselves when they apparently wandered too close to American lines. After the two infantrymen had killed them, Grayson shouted to his comrades-in-arms, "Line up, fellas. The niggers are in here all through these yards!"

With the war conveniently being blamed on the Filipino forces, and public war fever being stoked once more, the Treaty of Paris was ratified by the Senate, but by only one vote. The 1899 Philippine-American War (described by the United States government as a mere "insurrection") was fierce, bloody, and long-drawn out, officially ending in 1902 but in fact continuing for a decade more. It far surpassed in ferocity, cost, and duration the Spanish-American War, which lasted all of four months, though it is this war that is remembered while its more costly 1899 sequel is not.

With the U.S. military moving beyond Manila to conquer and colonize the rest of the country, the Philippine revolutionary army resisted fiercely but, lacking the weaponry, was outgunned. Only half of the estimated 80,000 Filipino soldiers had rifles, with the other half relying on *bolos* (machetes), spears, and homemade guns. Unopposed, Dewey cruised the Pasig River, lobbing 500-pound shells into Filipino fortifications, with predictable and deadly results. In conventional combat, not surprisingly, the Filipinos suffered disproportionate losses. The next day, February 5, Aguinaldo issued a proclamation in which he stated: "I know that war has always produced great losses; I know that the Philippine people have not yet recovered from past losses and are not in the condition to endure others. But I also know by experience how bitter is slavery, and by experience I know that we should sacrifice all on the altar of our honor and of the national integrity so unjustly attacked."

More disheartening to those committed to the revolution were the ilustrado defections to the enemy in May, attracted by offers from the Schurman Commission for positions in the government being cobbled together. Cayetano Arellano, for instance, was appointed to the Supreme Court in Manila. Another noteworthy defection was that of Trinidad H. Pardo de Tavera, a member of the ilustrado expatriate community in Europe, who founded *La Democracia*, a decidedly pro-American paper.

Later on, de Tavera, along with other wealthy ilustrados who had supported the revolution against Spain, helped establish the Federalista Party, which initially sought only statehood but changed that to gradual independence when the original stance failed to attract any significant public following. Such defections were not altogether surprising, as the ilustrados as a whole had always been reformists rather than revolutionaries; the United States, it seemed to them, would grant the reforms they had long and vainly sought from Spain.

In April of 1900, the second Philippine Commission arrived, headed by William H. Taft, to put into place the Schurman Commission recommendations. Taking on legislative powers, the Taft Commission formally set up colonial rule. Taft—a massive six-footer who weighed 340 pounds—persuaded de Tavera, and two other ilustrados, José Luzuriaga and Benito Legarda, Sr., to sit on the Commission, a seductive signal to the landed elite that they could have a hand in ruling the colony. The next year, Taft was named by President McKinley as the first governor general of the islands, along with several Americans to serve in his cabinet. All this went on even as the war raged outside the few pacified areas.

Racism accentuated the cruel and brutal character of the U.S. war of conquest, marked by the use of torture, the killing of prisoners, and genocidal tendencies. The Spanish colonizers had been booted out, but not in opposition to their beliefs or practices. The U.S. forces were contemptuous of Filipinos and described them as "barbarians" and "savages," reflecting the prejudices and xenophobia of the larger American society, one that routinely portrayed Chinese and Japanese immigrants as a "Yellow Peril." The U.S. soldiers fashioned an epithet just for the Filipino: "Gugu"—from *gago*, the Tagalog word for "stupid"—which more than half a century later would morph into "gook" to accommodate the Koreans and the Vietnamese.

Soldiers on the march often sang these lyrics:

Damn, damn the Filipino
Pockmarked Khakiac ladrone [thief]!
Underneath the starry flag
Civilize him with a Krag
And return us to our beloved home!

Many of the U.S. officers were veterans of the genocidal campaigns against Native American nations, and in the Filipino enemy they discerned unmistakable likenesses. And so did Roosevelt: on the campaign trail for the vice-presidency of the United States, he likened the rebels to the Apaches and the Comanches.

African-Americans serving in the U.S. expeditionary forces were caught in a bind. On one hand, these Buffalo Soldiers—so-called for their bravery during U.S. wars against Native Americans—felt that they needed to show they were just as patriotic and courageous as the white soldiers. On the other hand, racial and social affinities between them and Filipinos were too obvious to be ignored, a fact brought home when white soldiers often called Filipinos "niggers." Similar debates took place in African-American communities back in the United States. In Boston, black anti-imperialists adopted resolutions opposing the war. One such resolution declared: "Resolved, that while the rights of colored citizens in the South, sacredly guaranteed them by the amendment of the Constitution, are shamefully disregarded; and while the frequent lynching of Negroes who are denied a civilized trial are a reproach to the Republican government, the duty of the president and the country is to reform these crying domestic wrongs and not to attempt the civilization of alien peoples by powder and shot."

Many black soldiers defected, the most celebrated (or infamous, depending on one's perspective) being David Fagan. The twenty-four-year-old Fagan became an officer under the command of General José Alejandrino in Central Luzon. For two years, he proved to be a thorn in the side of his fellow Americans, so much so that his exploits became legendary, with an article in the *New York Times* characterizing him as a "cunning and highly skilled guerrilla officer who harassed and evaded large conventional American units." The U.S. military offered $600 for his capture, dead or alive. On December 5, 1901, a Tagalog hunter offered U.S. officers the severed head of someone he claimed was Fagan. The identity was never confirmed, nor was there a record of reward money being paid. Fagan's fate to this day remains shrouded in mystery.

At a military disadvantage when confronting the U.S. military in open battle, the Philippine revolutionaries ceded ground, and Aguinaldo and his staff resorted to guerrilla warfare. The switch prompted the U.S. military to label this "uncivilized"—a charge refuted by Mabini, who pointed out that the Filipinos had no choice since they were poorly armed, that they had to continue to resist since their freedom was being threatened, and that "humiliating peace is tolerated only in uncivilized countries." The war might have progressed differently if General Antonio Luna, Aguinaldo's most capable field commander, had not been assassinated by Filipino soldiers in June of 1899. Luna was a wealthy ilustrado, and brother to the famous painter Juan Luna. Though Antonio had stayed on the sidelines in the 1898 revolution, shortly before the war broke out between the Philippines and the United States, he offered his services to Aguinaldo and proved his mettle as a brave and savvy officer. He was soon heading Central Luzon military operations—the main theater at this point in the war. However, Luna, notorious for his volatile temper and tart tongue, incurred the wrath of several influential military officers. Even the normally unflappable Mabini complained of Luna's mercurial disposition but knew that in this general he had an important ilustrado ally against accepting any compromise with the Americans, one who moreover declared impassionedly, whenever the occasion presented itself, his devotion to the goal of independence. Luna said that everywhere he went he asked the people if they wanted autonomy. According to him, their steadfast answer was: "Long live independence. May autonomy die!"

On June 5, Luna—already falsely rumored to be contemplating a coup against the Supremo—rode to Cabanatuan, in the Central Luzon province of Nueva Ecija, in response to a note alleged to have been written by Aguinaldo inviting him to meet and discuss strategy. When Luna arrived, Aguinaldo was nowhere to be seen; Luna was stabbed and shot by soldiers from Aguinaldo's hometown of Kawit—the same soldiers Luna had once vehemently upbraided for some breach of protocol and which censure still rankled. He was buried with full military honors, but his killers were never brought to justice.

The War of Words

In the meantime, the propaganda war was in full swing. The Schurman Commission stressed that the U.S. was on a mission civilatrice, to render the Filipinos "among the most civilized peoples of the world." But setting aside its stated altruistic aims, U.S. intentions towards the Philippines were remarkably similar to Spain's: to exploit the Philippines as a market and source of raw materials, and to utilize the islands as a steppingstone from which to gain access to the markets of China. The new imperialists were, however, not so unvarnished in their stated reasons for holding on to the Southeast Asian archipelago. They pictured themselves as reluctant colonizers impelled more by a Christian sense of duty than the desire for material gain. Conquest may have been painful, but was essential were the country to move forward. President McKinley's famous peroration to a group of Protestant clergymen puts it rather melodramatically:

> When I next realized that the Philippines had dropped into our laps I confess I did not know what to do with them. . . . I walked the floor of the White House night after night until midnight; and I'm not ashamed to tell you, gentlemen, that I went down on my knees and prayed the Almighty God for light and guidance more than one night. And one night late it came to me this way—I don't know how it was, but it came: . . . that there was nothing left for us to do but to take them all, and to educate the Filipinos, and uplift and civilize and Christianize them, and by God's grace do the very best we could by them, as our fellow-men for whom Christ also died. And then I went to bed, and went to sleep, and slept soundly, and the next morning I sent for the chief engineer of the War Department (our map maker), and I told him to put the Philippines on the map of the United States, and there they are, and there they will stay while I am president!

McKinley conveniently overlooked the fact that the islands had been Catholic for more than three hundred years.

The need to "uplift and civilize" the Filipinos would be the theme incessantly harped on every time U.S. imperialism was questioned. While self-serving, such justification was closely linked to the unshakeable belief in racial superiority that permeated the U.S. war effort—one that Rudyard Kipling endorsed. Kipling wrote his poem "White Man's Burden" precisely to encourage the United States in its colonial endeavor (the poem's subtitle is "The United States and the Philippines"):

> Take up the White Man's Burden
> Send forth the best ye breed
> Go bind your sons to exile
> To serve your captives' needs
> To wait in heavy harness

On fluttered folk and wild
Your new-caught sullen peoples
Half-devil and half-child . . .

As the Americans envisioned it, colonial rule would be tutelary in intent and benign in execution. Washington, after all, sought only "to spread peace and happiness . . . freedom . . . and self-government." At a speech in Boston, Senator Alfred Beveridge had declared that the United States was "a conquering race. . . . we must obey our blood and occupy new markets and, if necessary, new lands." Once the Spanish were vanquished, and the prospect of war with the Aguinaldo regime seemed imminent, the same senator thundered in Indianapolis, in response to the rhetorical question of ruling a people without their consent: "Would not the people of the Philippines prefer the just, humane, civilizing government of this Republic to the savage, bloody rule of pillage and extortion from which we have rescued them?"

In May, two months after it began its investigations, with most of its information derived from a small number of the conservative elite, including former members of the Malolos Congress eager for rapprochement with the United States, the commission recommended the appointment of a governor general who, like his Spanish predecessors, would be the paramount ruler. There would be an advisory group and an independent judiciary. Most importantly, the commission not surprisingly ratified the view that Filipinos were unfit for self-government, that the country was simply a "collection of tribes," and that therefore it was imperative for Americans to stay on and impart the lessons of democracy.

Enough members of the Malolos Congress favored accepting the Schurman offer, which would have rendered the islands an American protectorate. They requested Aguinaldo to dissolve the Mabini Cabinet and form a new one that could secure a peaceful arrangement with the American forces and the government they had been setting up. Instead, Mabini proposed an armistice that General Otis rejected, believing that the "insurrection" would collapse easily. Mabini then issued a statement urging the people to continue the struggle. Mabini was eventually captured by the Americans in late December of 1899. Refusing to pledge allegiance to the United States, he was exiled to the Marianas. His fragile health worsening in the unfamiliar setting, he finally agreed to take the oath of allegiance to the United States in early 1903, and thus was allowed to return to the Philippines, where he died in May.

Negotiations on autonomy broke down, and the war continued. In the meantime, the Aguinaldo government kept an eye out for political developments in the U.S. that might mean favorable concessions for the Philippines. The November presidential elections of 1900 between McKinley and William Jennings Bryan were seen as an opportunity for the anti-imperialist forces in the U.S. to win, but Bryan was defeated.

The war was still going badly for the Filipinos, forcing Aguinaldo and his staff to keep moving north, to the mountainous terrain of the Cordilleras. By November 1899, he and his army focused on defensive tactics. The Supremo was nearly caught at the mountain pass of Tirad, in Ilocos Sur, but General Gregorio del Pilar, commander of Aguinaldo's rear guard of sixty riflemen, delayed the 900 American troops at the cost of his own life, enabling Aguinaldo to escape. Dead at the age of twenty-four, his body left to lie on the rocky soil, stripped of most of his clothing and decorations by the victorious soldiers, del Pilar was the nephew of the Propagandist Marcelo H. del Pilar and the youngest general in Aguinaldo's army, earning him the sobriquet of the Boy General. Aguinaldo and his men finally found refuge in the mountain stronghold of Palanan, Isabela Province, on the remote rocky northeastern coast of Luzon.

At the outset, General Elwood Otis assured Washington that the war would be over in a few weeks, especially after his forces had taken Malolos, yet he kept requesting more troops as the weeks turned into months. Gaining ground was easy enough, but it didn't take long for the U.S. command to realize they were in danger of stretching their forces too thinly as they struck deeper into the countryside, where it proved harder to defend themselves against guerrilla attacks. Instead of set engagements, the Filipino guerrillas could choose the time and place for ambushes and didn't require the logistical support the Yankee soldiers did, for the simple reason that the Filipinos could and did rely on the local population for their supplies as well as hide among them in plain sight. Too, the locals resisted providing information that would have aided the invaders. The Aguinaldo government had the support of the masses, overwhelmingly based outside the few urban areas and who, having borne the brunt of Spanish abuse, were not about to yield meekly to strangers who looked and behaved like their Spanish predecessors.

THE CONDUCT OF THE WAR

Early on, a General Shafter proved to be prescient regarding the way war had to be waged: "It may be necessary to kill half of the Filipinos in order that the remaining half of the population may be advanced to a higher plane of life than their present semi-barbarous state affords." The U.S. forces grew increasingly frustrated as they proved unable to infiltrate guerrilla networks and disrupt the workings of shadow governments. In towns and villages, the Filipinos practiced what came to be derisively referred to by U.S. soldiers as "amigo warfare"—friend by day, foe by night. In areas that were considered "pacified"—under U.S. military control, and with a local government sympathetic or at least seemingly cooperative with the U.S.—the residents never outwardly resisted and often seemed to abet occupation but in reality constantly sought to undermine that same occupation, either by being actively involved as guerrillas, or providing the guerrillas shelter and support, a majority of whom after all were friends and relatives. Such frustration on the part of the invader, combined with a racist outlook on Filipinos—"half-devil, half-child"—provided the rationale for indiscriminate warfare and torture.

In spite of press censorship, reports filtered back to the United States that detailed wartime atrocities, such as the burning of villages; the indiscriminate killing of civilians; the execution of prisoners where a take-no-prisoner policy was in place; and the use of torture. In an article for *Harper's Weekly*, a correspondent by the name of John Bass described the incompetence of Otis, the military tactics used as unsuitable to the tropical climate, and the obvious sympathy the locals had for the insurgents. He candidly observed that the "the sooner the people of the United States find out that the peoples of the Philippines do not wish to be governed by us, the better."

One major source of unfiltered information were the letters soldiers wrote home to their families, recounting their horrific experiences. These graphic details would often land in the pages of hometown newspapers. From Anthony Michea, of the Third Artillery: "We bombarded a place called Malabon [a suburb of Manila], and then we went in and killed every native we met, men, women, and children." And Charles R. Wyland, of Company C, Washington Volunteers, observed: "I have seen a shell from our artillery strike a bunch of Filipinos, and then they would go scattering through the air, legs, arms, heads, all disconnected. And such sights actually make our boys laugh and yell, 'That shot was a peach.'"

Two methods of dealing with amigo warfare were particularly harsh. The more sweeping one was the policy of hamletting, practiced by the Spanish in Cuba and known as *reconcentrado*, a technique that would be repeated during the Vietnam War more than half a century later. In early 1901, for example, the U.S. military herded the entire population of one island, Marinduque, into five concentration camps. But the most brutal example was perhaps the pacification of the provinces of Batangas, Laguna, Cavite, and Tayabas (now Quezon) as directed by Major General Franklin Bell, who had earlier introduced the residents of the Ilocos region to the benefits of reconcentration.

Bell was determined to hunt down the hold-out General Malvar, who commanded five thousand guerrillas and effectively controlled local governments. In early December 1901, Bell had the population forcibly evacuated into designated centers or towns that were transformed into virtual prison camps. The Filipinos were ordered to move into specified zones and to bring whatever they could of their property. Anything left behind would be subject to confiscation or destruction. This meant that the outlying villages and their adjacent farm fields were abandoned, the idea being to deprive the guerrillas civilian cover while at the same time keeping a close watch on the quarantined villagers who themselves could be rebels. Locals had to demonstrate that they were "active" friends, e.g., providing information to Bell's forces as to the whereabouts of the guerrillas. Curfews were put in place and boundaries set up outside each camp, with a no-man's land beyond that—one that was termed morbidly a "zone of death," for anyone caught in it after curfew was likely to get shot, no questions asked.

In this manner, the region was turned upside down and laid waste to, as abandoned villages were often put to the torch—particularly if these were suspected of having harbored guerrillas—wells poisoned, and livestock either starved or killed. Ninety percent of the region's *carabaos*, or water buffalos, perished, and rice production plummeted to just a fourth of its pre-reconcentrado levels. Unable to attend to their fields, the huddled population suffered an inordinate rate of death due to malnutrition and disease, such as dengue fever and malaria. In Batangas alone, 54,000 civilians died by the end of 1901. Overall, it is estimated that at least 100,000 people perished due to Bell's iron-fisted rule.

In April 1902, General Malvar surrendered to the U.S. forces, his capitulation taken as a conclusive sign that the fighting was over, and that the remaining resisters were simply bandits and thieves, taking advantage of the war to practice their ancient trade under the guise of nationalism. On July 4, 1902, President Theodore Roosevelt declared the war, or "insurrection," over. It wasn't, of course. Enough revolutionary leaders continued the war of resistance, such as Generals Sakay, Ola, and Bulan.

Similar tactics were exercised in the Visayan island of Samar. One town in particular provoked a scorched-earth policy from the commanding officer for the region, General Jacob Smith. Balangiga was a coastal town in the southern part of the island, where seventy-four U.S. troops were garrisoned. The troops routinely abused the townspeople, often forcing them into open-air holding pens even in rainy weather. This prompted clandestine plans for retaliation. On the morning of September 28, 1901, as the men were sitting down to breakfast, Filipino guerrillas, some of them disguised as women, burst into the mess hall and, armed mainly with bolos, attacked. Both commanding officers were boloed to death, forty-six more were killed, and twenty-two seriously wounded. Only four escaped. Retaliation was swift and brutal. General Smith declared his intention to turn the province into a "howling wilderness," telling his men, "I want no prisoners. I wish you to kill and burn; the more you kill and burn, the more you will please me." According to his instructions, anyone over ten was fair game. A food and trade blockade was instituted, villages were burned, noncombatants were shot, and, as with General Bell's policy, Filipinos had to actively show that they were friends; one surefire way of doing so was by turning informer. In 1902, General Smith was court-martialed and found guilty. His punishment? An admonition and forced retirement.*

---

* Three church bells were confiscated by the U.S. troops. One is with the 9th Infantry Regiment at its base in South Korea, while the other two are on a military base in Cheyenne, Wyoming. The Philippine government has tried unsuccessfully to have the bells returned to the town of Balangiga.

Just as brutal a retaliation visited on the indigenous population elsewhere was the 1906 massacre of 600 Moros—men, women, and children—at Bud Dajo, a dormant volcano on the island of Jolo off the southern coast of Mindanao. The indiscriminate slaughter, presided over by General Leonard Wood, was a response to the killing of several U.S. soldiers a few days earlier. In Mindanao, in a six-month period, Moros had launched various assaults on American emplacements. Two hundred smaller engagements alone had also taken place in 1901. The war against the Moros was different since it had echoes of the religious Crusades against the Muslims in the Holy Land, whereas elsewhere in the archipelago the war was a secular affair, being against Filipinos who were themselves fellow Christians, though the conduct of the war was decidedly un-Christian .

One favored method of torture, practiced on prisoners who were considered to be potential high-value informants, was the so-called "water-cure." In this harsh method of interrogation, the detainee was forced to imbibe huge amounts of water, with soldiers pinioning his limbs, forcing open his mouth, and pouring water through a funnel. Sometimes water was forced down a prisoner's nostrils. Once the detainee was primed, he would be pummeled or kicked, the liquid being forcibly and painfully ejected. Though reluctant to give antiwar critics any ammunition, Governor Taft candidly stated before the U.S. Senate in 1902 that "there had been . . . individual instances of water cure, that torture that I believe involves pouring water down the throat so that the man swells and gets the impression that he is going to be suffocated and then he tells what he knows."

Former Sergeant Leroy Hallock, who had witnessed the "cure" administered to at least a dozen insurgents, was more graphic: "They would swell up—their stomachs would swell up pretty large—and I have seen blood come from their mouth [sic] after they had been given a good deal of it." This same Hallock testified to seeing one village of three to four thousand inhabitants being torched, and of knowing of at least half a dozen other such burnings.

When the U.S. military was accused of perpetrating atrocities, a blanket denial was issued, or they were explained away by saying the harsh methods were justified on the grounds that these were necessary against a people who were less than human, and to whom therefore the common standards of humanity, or civilization, could not be applied. (It would be an argument repeated during the Korean and Vietnam wars.) In the case of General Smith, he was court-martialed and found guilty of inciting his troops to cruelties. He was punished with an admonition.

An American congressman, who visited the Philippines and who preferred to remain anonymous, spoke frankly about the results of the pacification campaign. "You never hear of any disturbances in Northern Luzon, because there isn't anybody there to rebel. . . . Our soldiers took no prisoners, they kept no records; they simply swept the country and wherever and whenever they could get hold of a Filipino they killed."

General Elwood Otis proved to be inept and was replaced by General Arthur McArthur, who took over in May of 1900 and served until July 1, 1901. MacArthur was a veteran of the wars against Native Americans. Though he endorsed imperialist goals, he was a realist who knew that the Filipinos had no love for the Americans. He once said that it would take "ten years of bayonet treatment" to pacify the country. He realized that successful guerrilla warfare "depends upon almost complete unity of action of the entire native population. That such unity is a fact is too obvious to admit of discussion; how it is brought about and maintained is not so plain. Intimidation has undoubtedly accomplished much to this end; but fear as the only motive is hardly sufficient to account for the united and apparently spontaneous action of several millions of people."

The war could have dragged on longer but luck helped shorten it when a certain Cecilio Segismundo, a courier from Aguinaldo, was captured by U.S. forces. Segismundo was carrying dispatches to commanders in the field, one of which asked for more men for Aguinaldo's mountain hideout. Under interrogation Segismundo revealed the whereabouts of the revolutionary leader. A plan was formulated to gain entry to his Palanan redoubt without arousing suspicion. Five U.S. soldiers, headed by General Frederick Funston, would pretend to be prisoners of the Macabebes, mercenaries from Pampanga Province, disguised as Filipino troop reinforcements. Accompanying them were some Tagalog turncoats and a Spanish secret service agent, Lazaro Segovia. Forged documents purporting to be from one of Aguinaldo's generals completed their disguise. Departing Manila by boat on February 6, they were brought to the desolate Pacific coast of northeastern Luzon and thence trekked through rainforests and mountain passes until on March 23, 1901, they gained entry into the camp. Brought before the unsuspecting

Aguinaldo, Funston and his men were able to capture the Supremo and his staff.

Barely a week after, on April 1, 1901, Aguinaldo pledged allegiance at Malacañang, where he had been detained, to the United States. MacArthur resigned that same day, with Major General Adna Romanza Chaffee, also a veteran of the wars against Native Americans, taking over. On April 19, Aguinaldo issued a proclamation for peace, which said in part: "The Philippines decidedly wishes peace: be it so. Let the stream of blood cease to flow; let there be an end to tears and desolation. . . . I proclaim before all the world that I cannot remain deaf to the voice of a people yearning for peace nor to the lamentations of thousands of families who long for freedom of their loved ones, which is promised them through the magnanimity of the great American nation." Although the head of the Philippine Republic did desire a free and independent country, he had initially been too trustful of the United States, and ignored signs until it was too late that the North Americans intended to stay. In the end, like most of the ilustrados, Aguinaldo sought compromise even as he and his men bore arms.

Despite Aguinaldo's pronouncement, the war of resistance continued. As a counterinsurgency tactic, the reconcentrado method was used mercilessly. In southern Luzon, Bell's reconcentrado bore fruit: a weakened General Malvar, along with his men, surrendered in April of 1902. With Aguinaldo quiescent and Malvar captured, President Theodore Roosevelt declared the war over on July 4, 1902. Henceforth, revolutionary fighters would be classified as bandits and thieves.

On June 1, 1902, the Philippine Commission passed the Reconcentration Camp Act, rendering official what the military had been utilizing in the field. The Act authorized any provincial governor to reconcentrate in the towns all residents of outlying barrios if "ladrones" or "outlaws" operated in these areas, thereby hoping to dry the rivers in which the guerrilla fish swam. Another prize catch for the U.S. forces was General Macario Sakay. Sakay grew up in Tondo, where he had gotten to know Bonifacio. Joining the Katipunan in 1894, Sakay acted in popular Tagalog verse dramas, which were staged in different neighborhoods in Manila, thus providing the perfect cover for the young Katipunero to move about.

Countering U.S. efforts to brand Filipino fighters as brigands, General Sakay, based in the mountains of the southern Tagalog region, declared himself president of the Philippines in 1903 and decreed that "anybody who contributes or gives aid and comfort to the government of the United States of America will be considered a traitor to this native land." Continuing operations by U.S. troops forced him to move and eventually he agreed to yield. Through an intermediary, Sakay's conditions for his surrender—among them, general amnesty and permission to carry firearms—were accepted by the authorities. He and his followers came down from the mountains to Cavite on July 20, 1906—four years after the war was officially declared over—where they were invited to a banquet at the governor's residence. There, he and his followers were seized and disarmed, accused of crimes under the Brigandage Act and quickly brought to trial. Not surprisingly, he was found guilty, and he and an aide, Colonel Lucio de Vega, were incarcerated at Bilibid Prison in Manila, and hanged on Sept. 13, 1907. Before his death, the revolutionary general declared to the small crowd of witnesses (mostly prison guards and employees), "I want to tell you that we are not bandits and robbers, as the Americans have accused us, but members of the revolutionary force that defended our mother country the Philippines! Farewell! Long live the Republic and may our independence be born in the future! Farewell! Long live the Philippines!"

In the Visayas, a notable case was that of the self-proclaimed Pope of Negros Island, who was a thorn in the side of the U.S. military. Papa Isio, as he was called, was a charismatic peasant who led a band of remontados, the Pulajanes (the Scarlet Ones), and had joined forces with the local elite in opposing the Spanish in the 1898 Revolution. Once war erupted between the Aguinaldo government and the United States, however, the local principalia signaled the U.S. that the island would gladly be a protectorate—a deal that Papa Isio and his followers rejected. The Pulajanes resisted both U.S. occupation and landlord collaboration, burning the haciendas of pro-American hacenderos. Motivated by economic desperation, the ragtag army fought U.S. troops bravely but in 1907, Isio, realizing the futility of armed struggle, gave himself up and was duly sentenced to death.

The religious trappings of Papa Isio and his Pulajanes reflected a desire lodged deep in the psyche of the people, for a more active role in determining both the spiritual and material forces that would guide their lives. Hence, his refusal to go along with the principalia leadership. This discordance between a populist stance and an elitist accommodation in fact marked both the revolution against Spain and the war with the Americans, albeit episodically, e.g., Bonifacio versus Aguinaldo, Mabini versus the Malolos Congress. Even if indirectly, both strains sprung from the 1872 martyrdom of Gomez, Burgos and Zamora and the drive to Filipinize Catholic parishes—an aim that had acted as a spur to revolution. Not surprisingly, native priests sympathized with the revolution, even though the mostly Spanish Church had condemned it.

The Emergence of an Independent Church

Filipino priests had no quarrel with Catholicism itself. How could they, when they were believers in a country that, after more than three centuries, was solidly Catholic. Their quarrel was with the racialization of their ranks; a schism was inevitable. A secular priest from the Ilocos region, Fr. Gregorio Aglipay, thirty-eight years old and the only man of the cloth at the Malolos Congress, served as Military Vicar for Aguinaldo's forces. He supported the goals of the revolution and asked Filipino priests to do the same. He reasoned that with colonial ties to Spain severed, the patronato real was no longer in effect. It was time for Filipino priests to take control of the church in the country.

Aglipay's archbishop, Bernardino Nozaleda—clearly acting more as a loyal Spaniard than a Catholic priest—excommunicated him in January of 1899 even though Aglipay had made clear his intent to remain loyal to the Vatican. On October 23, 1899, Aglipay, with the implicit endorsement of Mabini, who wished to see the establishment of a Filipinized church, still heeding the Vatican but working closely with, rather than against, the Philippine government, organized an ecclesiastical assembly in the province of Tarlac, in Central Luzon. The result was a provisional constitution for a nationalist Catholic church wherein foreign bishops could work in the island only with the approval of Filipino priests—clearly aimed at the Spanish ecclesiastical authorities used to calling the shots in the colony. Subsequent events, especially the war with the United States (in which Aglipay fought as a general) led to the founding of the Iglesia Filipina Independiente (the Philippine Independent Church) in 1902, with Aglipay as its supreme head. Almost two decades later, the church counted a million and a half members, known as Aglipayans.

Instrumental in the formation of the new church was Isabelo de los Reyes, who was from Vigan in the Ilocos region. A distant relative of Rizal, de los Reyes was an activist who had been jailed by both the Spanish and the United States colonial administrations. At the age of twenty-four, by then a practicing journalist, in 1889 he published *El Ilocano*, the first such publication devoted entirely to a Philippine language other than Tagalog. He went on to become a distinguished folklorist who envisioned a nation that encompassed both the un-Hispanicized indigenous and Christianized groups—a nation that transcended ethnicity. Married thrice, the man was as indefatigable in his campaign for independence as he was in siring offspring: he had twenty-eight children. The same year that the PIC was formed he organized the *Union Obrera Democratica* (UOD), the first labor union in the Philippines.

The newly established church embodied one of the revolution's goals: the displacement of the friar orders by Filipino clergy. However, the PIC came into conflict with the U.S. regime over abandoned Roman Catholic churches it had taken over. The authorities sided with the Catholic Church by confirming its ownership of the churches. The separate question of what to do with the friars' huge landed estates— approximately 400,000 acres—was resolved when the Philippine Commission in 1903 was authorized to purchase these. However, instead of selling the lands to those who most needed them and thus helping to solve the land-reform problem, the commission, headed by Taft, allowed wealthy elite families and a few corporations to purchase these choice estates. Thus, for instance, the Spanish-owned Tabacalera company managed to expand its holdings to more than 30,000 acres by 1913.

THE WAR ENDS, THE WAR CONTINUES

For the fledgling nation, the war was tragic, putting on hold national independence. On the Philippine side, the savage conflict left at least 20,000 combatants and at least 250,000—but possibly as many as a million—noncombatants dead from war or war-related causes. By the war's end, more than 4,000 U.S. soldiers had been killed, and 3,000

José Rizal, doctor, scientist, and writer, whose incendiary novels and agitation for reform led to his execution by the Spanish colonial government in 1896.
(LÓPEZ MEMORIAL MUSEUM)

Andrés Bonifacio, a warehouseman in Tondo, who founded the revolutionary society, the Katipunan, in 1892 and launched the war of independence against Spain in 1896.
(LÓPEZ MEMORIAL MUSEUM)

The Philippine revolutionary government in exile in Hong Kong, following the terms of the 1897 Biak-na-Bato Treaty with the Spanish. Its head, Emilio Aguinaldo, is in front, marked no. 1.

Emilio Aguinaldo, general in the 1896 Revolution and the subsequent 1899 Philipine-American War, and first president of the republic.
(AMERICAN HISTORICAL COLLECTION, RIZAL LIBRARY, ATENEO DE MANILA UNIVERSITY)

Members of the Philippine Commission, headed by William Howard Taft (marked no. 4), and members of the first Philippine Assembly, 1907.

Filipino trench casualties of American artillery fire in the 1899 Philippine-American War.
(AMERICAN HISTORICAL COLLECTION, RIZAL LIBRARY, ATENEO DE MANILA UNIVERSITY)

Prisoners of war about to be deported to Guam, during the 1899 Philippine-American War.
(AMERICAN HISTORICAL COLLECTION, RIZAL LIBRARY, ATENEO DE MANILA UNIVERSITY)

General Arthur MacArthur and staff, ca. 1901.
(AMERICAN HISTORICAL COLLECTION, RIZAL LIBRARY, ATENEO DE MANILA UNIVERSITY)

U.S. Army officer David P. Barrows and the Sultan of Sulu, seated, ca. 1903.
(American Historical Collection, Rizal Library, Ateneo de Manila University)

Cordilleran school children with U.S. teachers known as Thomasites, General Leonard Wood (center rear), and William Howard Taft (left rear), ca. 1903.
(American Historical Collection, Rizal Library, Ateneo de Manila University)

President Franklin Delano Roosevelt at the signing of the Constitution of the Philippine Commonwealth in Washington, D.C., March 23, 1935. Sitting left to right: Hon. George H. Dern, Franklin D. Roosevelt, Manuel L. Quezon. Standing left to right: Frank Murphy, Cordell Hull, Key Pittman, Miguel Cuaderno, Pedro Guevarra, Manuel L. Roxas, Francisco A. Delgado, and Claro M. Recto.

Manila street scene during the World War II Japanese occupation, 1942-1945.
(AMERICAN HISTORICAL COLLECTION, RIZAL LIBRARY, ATENEO DE MANILA UNIVERSITY

General Douglas MacArthur wading ashore in Leyte in October of 1944, with Sergio Osmeña to his left, acting president of the Commonwealth, and Carlos P. Romulo to the rear, wearing a helmet.

(AMERICAN HISTORICAL COLLECTION, RIZAL LIBRARY, ATENEO DE MANILA UNIVERSITY)

The Manila post office and nearby bridge in ruins in a city devastated during the Battle of Manila, February-March 1945.

(AMERICAN HISTORICAL COLLECTION, RIZAL LIBRARY, ATENEO DE MANILA UNIVERSITY)

The Philippine flag being raised at the Luneta as the Stars and Stripes is lowered on July 4, 1946, when the Philippines gained its independence from the United States.

Protest against the presence of U.S. bases on Philippine soil, ca. 1960s.
(AMERICAN HISTORICAL COLLECTION, RIZAL LIBRARY, ATENEO DE MANILA UNIVERSITY)

Nancy Reagan and Imelda Marcos chat while their husbands share a laugh and a settee during Governor Ronald Reagan's visit to Manila in 1969.

President Richard M. Nixon at a state dinner held in his honor by President Ferdinand Marcos, 1969. Left to right: Vice president Fernando López, Imelda Marcos, Richard M. Nixon with Ferdinand Jr., Ferdinand Marcos, and Patricia Nixon.
(AMERICAN HISTORICAL COLLECTION, RIZAL LIBRARY, ATENEO DE MANILA UNIVERSITY)

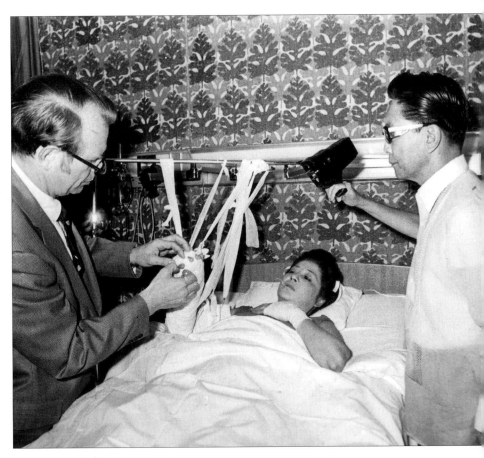

A hospitalized Imelda Marcos being visited by Ferdinand Marcos, following the attempt on her life by a knife-wielding assailant during a live television broadcast on December 7, 1972
(AMERICAN HISTORICAL COLLECTION, RIZAL LIBRARY, ATENEO DE MANILA UNIVERSITY

wounded. A total of approximately 130,000 U.S. troops had served in this, the first war fought by the U.S. on Asian soil. Ostensibly for the liberation of Spanish colonies, the war mutated into one of empire building. First against Spain, and then against the Philippines, the United States aggressively strode to be an imperialist power. The two facets of what in fact was a single war set the stage for subsequent U.S. involvement in the Philippines that continues to this day.

The Debate on the Home Front

The unabashed imperialist Senator Beveridge aligned U.S. expansionism with Divine Will. To subjugate a brown people was to do God's work. Having just returned from a visit to the archipelago, he declared that "we will move forward to our work, not howling out regrets like slaves whipped to their burdens, but with gratitude for a task worthy of our strength and thanksgiving to almighty God that He has marked us as his chosen people, henceforth to lead in the regeneration of the world." More important perhaps was his common observation that the islands lay close to China, the great prize sought by various Western powers, as well as the profits that could be realized from the islands themselves. The colony would serve as a huge economic stimulus package: its subjects would be a captive market for consumer goods turned out by an industrialized United States, with a capacity for production that demanded new markets.

A countervailing force was the Anti-Imperialist League, founded in Boston on June 15, 1898. Its guiding principle was that no government was legitimate which did not have the free consent of the governed. The League spearheaded the anti-war movement, its public visibility owing mainly to its high-profile members, including Mark Twain, the industrialist Andrew Carnegie, the president of Harvard University Charles Eliot, and Samuel Gompers, labor union leader and founder of the American Federation of Labor.

In its platform the League stated:

We earnestly condemn the policy of the present national administration in the Philippines. It seeks to extinguish the spirit of 1776 in those islands. We deplore the sacrifice of our soldiers and sailors, whose bravery deserves admiration even in an unjust war. We denounce the slaughter of the Filipinos as a needless horror. . . . We demand the immediate cessation of the war against liberty, begun by Spain and continued by us. We urge that Congress be promptly convened to announce to the Filipinos our purpose to concede to them the independence for which they have so long fought and which of right is theirs. . . . as greatly as we regret that the blood of Filipinos is on American hands, we more deeply resent the betrayal of American institutions at home.

Between 1899 and 1902, the League distributed documents written by Filipinos. Among these were Emilio Aguinaldo's "The True Version of the Philippine Revolution"; statements to U.S. Congress by Felipé Agoncillo, who had been unceremoniously shunned at the 1898 Treaty of Paris; and even a comparison of policies enumerated by Theodore Roosevelt and Apolinario Mabini. Later, after the war was declared officially over, the League would publish articles from Manila that were pro-independence. In addition, some League members wrote for new Filipino publications in the U.S., including the first, the *Filipino Students Magazine*, founded in 1905.

But opposition was not solely based on altruism. Many League members were in fact imperialists but believed the U.S. could expand without the usual strong-arm tactics of the older empires. Andrew Carnegie, for instance, felt the weight of U.S. capitalism would preempt such antiquated methods just by economic domination. There were those who opposed annexation for fear that Anglo-Saxon blood would be contaminated. Certain sectors of labor perceived immigrants as forming a pool of cheap labor that would drive down wages, while agricultural enterprises feared the importation of duty-free agricultural products and the unfair competition this would generate. A middle way was espoused by the Philippine Progress League, also known as the Philippine Independence League. Less militant and hardly as popular as the AIL, the PPL proposed making the Philippines another Cuba—allowing it self-government but as a U.S. dependency.

Though the pros and cons of U.S. conduct abroad was vigorously debated, it did nothing to stop the war. Might did make right, and the islands came under the dominion of the Stars and Stripes. As anticipated by the pro-annexation forces, the Philippines became an important market for U.S. goods and in 1900 provided the base enabling the McKinley administration to send U.S. troops to China to help put down the Boxer rebellion, an uprising of Chinese nationalists desirous of closing China to foreign capital and manufacture.

Educating Big Brother

Stoking the U.S. public's patriotic fervor for this "civilizing" war were purported film documentaries that were in fact reenactments—obvious to today's film audiences but likely not to filmgoers then, since cinema was still in its early stages. Thomas Alva Edison's studio made six newsreels about scenes from the war, in its West Orange lot in New Jersey. African-Americans stood in for Filipino soldiers, since Filipinos were routinely thought of as blacks. Inevitably, the reenactments ended with the white U.S. soldiers triumphant. These reels, amongst the earliest instances of film as propaganda, thus helped reinforce pro-war sentiments, with its jingoistic emphasis on racial superiority, among the public.

An effective tool in cultivating public sentiment favoring colonial-era philosophies that mixed so-called enlightened rule with the benefits of new markets and technology was the St. Louis World's Fair. Opened in April and lasting to December of 1904, the fair was meant to commemorate the centennial of the Louisiana Purchase. Sprawled across 1,200 acres and with more than 1,500 buildings, it was the largest of its kind in the world. Intended as a showcase of progress under U.S. rule, as well as to promote its global expansion both of trade and territory, the fair was a huge hit. And no other display was as popular as the Philippine Exhibit, which occupied 47 acres and constituted the fair's largest. Approximately 1,100 Filipinos, of different ethnic groups, from Igorots to Visayans, from Mangyans to Moros, were brought over, presumably to educate the public but in reality served as freakish entertainment. The mood was expansive: the barbarians were no longer at the gates since they had been invited in. More than 400 Philippine Scouts and officers were on hand, to watch over their fellow Filipinos as well as to embody the new social order—the triumph of light over darkness—that American colonial rule supposedly had brought to the islands.

A disturbing aspect of the Philippine section was the consumption by Igorots of dogs. Traditionally this was done only on ritual occasions, but in St. Louis the Igorots were required to consume them daily, rendering meaningless a ritual act and adding another stereotype to the impressive roster already lodged in the Yankee mind. Other ethnicities were on display, too, from Native Americans—the latter were positioned just across the Philippine Exhibit—to Indians and Africans. The ethnocentric, racist display in St. Louis came seventeen years after a similar but smaller exhibition in Madrid, the Philippine Exposition of 1887. The centerpiece of that was an assemblage of island dwellings and about thirty Indios, a mix of Muslims and non-Christian tribespeople. The exhibition had been organized in part by the Manila-based Dominican Brother Pedro Payo, who intended the display of Filipinos as proof positive that the colony was still largely "uncivilized" and demanded tutoring, particularly the religious kind. The reaction of the Madrid ilustrados anticipated that of the thoughtful observer in 1904: that the colonizer (in this case the Spanish) wished to strengthen rather than diminish the perception that the Filipinos were a backward and savage lot, thus justifying continuing dominion over them.

Educating the Little Brown Brother

Mass social and political movements in the islands during the American colonial period were subject to strict surveillance and militarization, impeding their growth and effectiveness. Both local politicians and U.S. colonial administrators, in their debates about self-rule, consciously and unconsciously kept the notion of independence from the U.S. alive in the public mind. The overt Filipinization of the colonial administration, though American control was very much in place, proved to be a powerful incentive to those who had always been ambivalent about armed resistance. President William McKinley's policy of Benevolent Assimilation was built on the premise that Filipinos would gradually be incorporated into the Pax and Via Americana through peaceful indoctrination in the principles of self-government and a cultural frame of mind distinctly Westernized and attuned to the same cultural models as the United States. The idea was to encourage the "little brown brothers," as Filipinos were blithely and patronizingly referred to, to emulate and identify with their bigger white brothers, thus transforming hostility into acceptance and, it was hoped, admiration.

Mass education in English was undertaken early on, even when military rule was still in place, for both General Otis and General

MacArthur viewed educating their colonial charges as an effective means of pacification. In 1901, the Second Philippine Commission, chaired by William H. Taft, performing legislative functions and supervising the establishment of local government, directed that free primary education in English be provided to the public and that Filipino teachers be trained to take over the duties borne by military men and U.S. civilian teachers, known as the Thomasites, after the USS *Thomas*, the former warship that had brought them over on August 21, 1901. That initial group consisted of 509 young men and women, an evangelizing army eager to indoctrinate the school-boys and -girls of the islands in American ways and thus help heal the wounds of war by refashioning brown folk into the image of the colonizer. For that reason English would be the medium of instruction. A common language rendered identification much easier; it wouldn't be too long before Filipino kids started to dream of snow, yearn for apples, and idolize fair-skinned Hollywood stars. On the practical side, English instruction would also ensure a steady supply of English-proficient civil and military personnel. The eagerness of the Thomasites to teach English to Filipinos stood in stark contrast to the Spanish who for the most part disdained to impart their language to the Indios.

Education was the perfect tool for colonial administrators, as it embodied the tutelary basis of colonialism. Fred Atkinson, the first General Superintendent of Education in the Philippines, echoed that rationale when he talked about the U.S. mission in the islands: "The Filipino people . . . are children, and childlike, do not know what is best for them. . . . In the ideal spirit of preparing them for the work of governing themselves finally, their American guardianship has begun."

In 1903, the colonial government set up a program for qualified Filipinos to be sent to the United States and there earn their university degrees. The idea was to produce trained people who would return and take over the tasks of civil administration. Called *pensionados* (literally, pensioners but here meaning those sent to boarding school), by 1912, over 200 men and women had received their higher-education degrees. The pensionados were usually drawn from middle- to upper-middle-class families, thus reinforcing class ties between the local elites and their U.S. patrons. With landlords, wealthy entrepreneurs, and the bourgeoisie favoring accommodation to U.S. rule, the only sectors of society that consistently opposed such rule were the working class and the peasantry. Gaining the least they despaired the most.

On a parallel track, Taft inaugurated a policy of "the Philippines for the Filipinos." Fostering a kinship between the new colonizer and the Filipinos would, Taft believed, not only make Filipinos consumers of American products but also tamp down the fires of insurgent nationalism. Autonomy or even independence could then be sought, within rules set down by the United States. As long as the United States was in control, it could afford to put a kindlier face on military and civil repression. Such assimilationist tactics combined with free-trade policies would all but guarantee the Philippines would eventually become economically dependent on the United States while acting as a source of raw materials and expatriated profits—a tutelary endeavor that benefited the tutor more than the tutee.

The year after Taft took office, in 1902, the Organic Act of the Philippine Islands was passed by U.S. Congress. The act set up a legal framework with a marked emphasis on a colonial economy that would facilitate the operation of U.S. businesses and investment enterprises. It also mandated the creation of the Philippine Assembly, subordinate to the Philippine Commission, and set up posts for two resident commissioners to the United States. There would be a clear separation of church and state—as had been called for in the Malolos Constitution. The advantage to the Roman Catholic Church was that this precluded government intervention in appointments and the creation of parishes. The downside was that public aid ceased, and priests no longer had rights and privileges when it came to public affairs.

THE CAMPAIGN FOR INDEPENDENCE

Despite the virtues of democracy and freedom being trumpeted, the Sedition Law of 1901 prohibited the public manifestation of nationalistic feelings. Whether "orally or by writing or printing," the advocacy of independence was banned. Part of the reason was that the Philippine-American War was still raging outside of so-called "pacified" areas. In a famous case, the authorities arrested the playwright Aurelio Tolentino (a pioneer member of the Katipunan), accusing him of sedition and libel. His nationalist drama, *Kahapon, Ngayon, at Bukas* (*Yesterday,*

Today, and Tomorrow), had been staged in 1903 at a Manila theater. In one scene, a character took down the American flag and trampled it, much to the anger of Americans in the audience. The theater was subsequently shut down. Found guilty, Tolentino was imprisoned briefly. The playwright was unrepentant: until his death in 1915, he continued to write plays and poems that portrayed Uncle Sam as a villainous character.

By late 1907—five years after the official "Mission Accomplished" of 1902—Governor General James Smith had informed President Theodore Roosevelt that a complete peace now existed, even though there were still clashes between Muslims and American forces in Mindanao. (That island was to remain under military rule until 1914, when Manila created the Department of Mindanao and Sulu as the local administrative body.) Elections had been held earlier on July 30, 1907, for the Philippine Assembly. Competing political parties could now openly and legally advocate for independence. Two young politicians came to dominate the Assembly and the local political scene until the outbreak of World War II: Sergio Osmeña from Cebu and Manuel L. Quezon, from Tayabas (now Quezon) Province. A Spanish mestizo, Quezon was a lieutenant in Aguinaldo's army and had given up once the Supremo had issued his call to lay down arms. A Chinese mestizo, Osmeña was a journalist who supported the nationalist struggle. Both were appointed governors of their respective provinces, and their administrative capabilities and in particular their successful handling of local rebellions drew the attention of the colonial establishment.

Two parties campaigned for ascendance: the Nacionalistas, whose platform centered on immediate independence; and the Federalistas — one of whose founders was Pardo de Tavera—whose initial goal was limited to statehood but later shifted to gradual independence. The voter base excluded the majority of Filipinos, being limited to those literate either in Spanish or English and with property valued at P500, a substantial sum in those days. Out of a population of more than 7 million, only 104,966 were registered to vote, and only 98,251—less than 2 percent of the population—went to the polls. In effect, it was the elite voting the elite in. Standard bearers for the Nacionalistas were Quezon and Osmeña, both of whom won easily, with the latter getting the nod for Speaker of the Assembly. The Assembly was formally inaugurated on October 16, 1907, and came to be dominated by Nacionalistas. Constituting the lower branch of the legislative body of the colonial government—above it were the Commission and the governor general—the Philippine Assembly spearheaded the drive for independence. That too was the main task set by Quezon, as one of two Resident Commissioners to the United States Congress from 1909 to 1916.

With the encouragement of Quezon, in 1913 President Woodrow Wilson appointed Francis Burton Harrison governor general of the islands. Harrison continued Taft's "Philippines for Filipinos" under a policy known as "Filipinization." Filipinos became the majority in the Philippine Commission, thereby ensuring full control of the legislative branch of the government. Harrison also appointed Filipinos to the judiciary and to important posts in the bureaucracy. Certain departments remained, however, under direct U.S. control, including education, the military, prisons, forestry, health, and the Metropolitan Water District. Harrison also ordered that the administration of Muslim Mindanao and the northern Luzon highlands of the Cordilleras be transferred from the U.S. Army to Filipino colonial officials, incorporating (in theory, at any rate), these regions into the mainstream. Especially for the Muslims, this forestalled any move towards separation from the Philippine state, but would be revived during the martial-law regime of Ferdinand Marcos in the 1970s.

Quezon also lobbied for the Philippine Autonomy Act of 1916, otherwise known as the Jones Bill. This abolished the Philippine Commission and established a bicameral legislature. The Senate or Upper House would have twenty-two nationally elected members and two appointees to represent the non-Christian minorities. The lower house, formerly the Philippine Assembly, would have eighty elected members and nine appointees. Quezon resigned from the Assembly to run for the Senate, won easily, and was elected Senate President. Osmeña retained his speakership of the lower house.

The Jones Bill also affirmed the U.S. goal of independence for the colony but set no date. Quezon's support for this bill, and his belief that independence be withheld until a majority of the population was literate, undermined the Anti-Imperialist League's faith in him as a staunch anti-imperialist. That seemed to be the final straw for the League, which in any case had seen its membership dwindle. In 1921, the League folded its tents quietly.

Governor Harrison reorganized the executive branch, now with six executive departments making up the cabinet. At the same time, the government acquired a controlling interest in a number of businesses, such as the Manila Railroad, and set up the Philippine National Bank. In 1919, the first Independence Mission to the United States was formed, headed by Senator Quezon. In Washington, Quezon and company found President Warren G. Harding, a Republican who had succeeded Woodrow Wilson, not so welcoming, or receptive to the idea of independence anytime soon. Harding dispatched a fact-finding mission, made up of General Leonard Wood (the same general in charge of U.S. troops responsible for the 1906 massacre at Bud Dajo) and former Governor General Cameron Forbes (a grandson of Ralph Waldo Emerson), to determine the readiness of the colony for self-government. The two concluded that in spite of advances, the colony was not quite ready for independence. Subsequently, President Harding appointed Wood as Burton Harrison's replacement.

In contrast to the affability of Harrison and his policy of Filipinization, Wood (1921-27) proved to be autocratic, probably due to his military training and temperament—diametrically opposed to the democratic spirit. He had the rather odd practice of having on hand an American witness whenever discussing weighty issues with Filipino leaders. As can be imagined, such an obvious sign of mistrust didn't sit very well with them. Filipino politicians filed complaints against him with Harding's successor, President Calvin Coolidge, but to no avail.

Wood, a Republican, believed firmly in the role of private capital in the development of the national economy. To stimulate the growth of agribusiness, he favored the relaxation of restrictions on foreign ownership of land. Furthermore, he proposed the privatization of government-owned enterprises. The liberalization of controls was opposed by the Filipino legislators, headed by Quezon and Osmeña, who saw in these proposals a Trojan horse, by which the entry of capital-rich foreign investors and their subsequent control of the economy would be facilitated. Quezon, irritated by what he perceived to be Wood's intransigence, uttered the most memorable comment of his political career: "I would prefer a government run like hell by Filipinos than one run like heaven by Americans."

At an impasse with Filipino leaders, Wood returned to the U.S. for a brain operation in 1927, but the operation was a failure and Wood died. Henry Stimson replaced him and managed to restore more cordial relations with influential Filipino leaders.

The Depression

Due to the financial meltdown that led to the Great Depression of 1929, economic interests propelled U.S. private industry (agriculture, primarily) to push for Philippine independence. The change in status for the colony, it was hoped, would lead to the termination of duty-free exports from the Philippines. Independence would also result in stricter immigration controls vis à vis Filipino workers, now able to enter the U.S. freely and who were seen as unfairly competing on the labor market for jobs, depriving U.S. citizens of economic opportunities.

Cheap Filipino labor had in fact been coming in since 1906, when fifteen young Filipinos boarded a ship for Hawaii, initiating an exodus of Filipinos who would in the beginning provide a steady supply of labor for the farms and agricultural enterprises in Hawaii, and later for the West Coast. Filipino immigrant communities formed mostly bachelor societies—women were discouraged from emigrating, primarily to forestall the formation of families and the putting down of roots—and would essentially remain so until the end of World War II. These pioneers and the men who followed in their footsteps came to be called the *manong*, or "elder brother." By 1926, approximately 150,000 Filipinos had emigrated to work in the United States, with a spike in the exodus fueled by the Immigration Act of 1924, which banned further immigration of Japanese to Hawaii. By 1930, during the Great Depression, 75,000 manong were eking out a living in Hawaii while 60,000 worked the farms, orchards, and canneries on the West Coast, including Alaska. For most of those going to the mainland, California was the favored destination.

Though Filipinos swore allegiance to the United States, they were not citizens but rather "nationals." In this in-between state, they were defined as Philippine citizens, under the protection of the U.S., free to enter the country and look for work. On the other hand, they couldn't vote, own land, or marry white women. Anti-miscegenation laws in the West Coast banned marriages between white women and Negroes, Mongolians, or mulattoes—with Filipinos being classified as Mongolians. When the courts in 1931 ruled that Filipinos were not Mongolians, California legislators craftily added the phrase "or member of the

Malay race" to maintain the racial ban. Being seen in public in the company of a white woman a Filipino male (or for that matter, any Asian male) was liable to be harassed and even physically assaulted by those who took offense at such racial mixing. Anti-Filipino prejudice reflected the larger anti-Asian sentiment as expressed, for instance, in the Chinese Exclusion Act of 1882. Labor camps were often attacked by white vigilantes, with serious injuries and some deaths resulting.

The most eloquent chronicler of the travails of Filipino immigrant life before World War II was the fiction writer and poet Carlos Bulosan who, like the vast majority of nationals leaving for the United States, came from peasant stock. Largely self-educated, Bulosan, an Ilocano, penned the now classic, largely autobiographical novel *America Is in the Heart*, an intense and often feverish account of a young Filipino labor organizer's political and social awakening to the harsh realities of living in a society where racism was a constant, corrosive factor, exacerbated by the Great Depression. Bulosan himself was a labor organizer and activist and had been involved in efforts to unionize farm workers that helped pave the way for the birth of the United Farm Workers, headed by César Chávez, a Mexican, with the vice president being Philip Vera Cruz, a Filipino. Bulosan's activism landed him on the FBI's blacklist. Plagued by ill health and broke, he died of consumption in Seattle in 1956, at the age of 43.

More than half a century after Bulosan's demise, at the end of 2009, an estimated 4 million Filipinos lived in the United States, the second-largest Asian-American group after the Chinese. These U.S.-based Filipinos have a median household annual income of close to $66,000 and are ranked second to U.S.-based Indians, who have the highest income of all U.S. households at more than $68,000. The Philippine diaspora totals approximately 11 million, spread throughout the globe, from North America to the Middle East to the Scandinavian countries, with occupations ranging from doctors, nurses, and computer engineers to domestic workers and merchant marines.

The Tydings-McDuffie Act

In 1932, a new independence team proceeded to Washington, made up of Osmeña, now a senator, and Manuel Roxas, an up-and-coming congressman. Nicknamed the OsRox Mission, it lobbied for the passage of the Hare-Hawes-Cutting Bill, which set out the specifics of independence—absent from the Jones Bill. In Manila, however, the Philippine Legislature opposed it, with the opposition headed chiefly by Manuel Quezon. He cited a provision that would allow the United States to retain military bases in the country as inimical to true independence. In reality, he viewed approval of the bill as politically disadvantageous to his ascension, Quezon himself not having been its chief architect. With support from sugar planters, who didn't want independence at all, and revolutionary figures such as Aguinaldo and Ricarte, who wanted immediate independence, Quezon convinced the legislature to defeat the bill. (Ricarte was still a revered figure, who, rather than pledge allegiance to the United States, chose exile in Yokohama, Japan, where he made a living running a coffeehouse and teaching Spanish on the side.) Quezon then proceeded to Washington and helped push for the 1934 Tydings-McDuffie Act, which was virtually identical to the Hare-Hawes-Cutting Bill. The difference, of course, was that this time it was his name associated with the bill.

The act provided for a ten-year transition period before independence would be granted—and during that transition period the colony would be accorded commonwealth status. As provided by the act, a constitutional convention was formed, headed by Claro M. Recto, a Quezon protégé. The body drafted a constitution that was then submitted to the U.S. for approval. Franklin Delano Roosevelt gave his imprimatur in March of 1935 and by May 14, it was ratified by the Philippine electorate. The form of government was based on that of the United States, with a bicameral congress and three separate branches of goverment: the executive, legislative, and judicial. The act also classified Filipinos as foreigners for the purpose of immigration, setting a quota of fifty for entry to the U.S.

Not surprisingly, the arrangement benefited the United States more than it did the Philippines. Free trade was to continue from 1935 to 1940, with certain restrictions on Philippine exports to the U.S., but with no such restrictions on U.S. exports to the Philippines. It was easy to see why: in 1934, the colony was the ninth largest market for U.S. goods, and the first for such exports as cigarettes, galvanized iron and steel sheets, paints, canned milk, and soap. In 1935, American investments in the archipelago were worth $200 million.

The United States was ensuring that its economic advantages would not be lost even when the Philippines gained its independence. Thus, the

1935 Constitution protected the interests of U.S. citizens and corporations, according these the same property rights as Filipinos. Moreover, independence was to be hedged with so many restrictions that essentially rendered the country a U.S. protectorate—as had been the case with Cuba. The trade preferences would have been disastrous for the country, and vested interests on both sides of the Pacific did little to change these. While remedial legislation was being considered, true economic development remained a mirage.

Domestically, labor and agrarian unrest continued to be a major source of concern to local governments and colonial rule. The lack of serious industrialization meant limited work opportunities, compounded by the fact that most arable land was concentrated in the hands of a few. Employment was available but mostly in low-paying jobs in agriculture. By 1938, out of a workforce of 4 million, more than three-fourths, made up of day laborers and sharecroppers, worked on farms and plantations. Clearly, any unrest among the ranks of agricultural toilers would seriously affect the economic and political stability of society. The landed estates of the friars, which could have diminished the seriousness of land issues through sales to low-income farmers, were instead sold, as noted earlier, mainly to landlords and agribusiness.

As in Spanish times, quasi-mystical peasant sects arose in response, often headed by individuals with messianic goals, but these rarely constituted a threat to public order. Unlike under Spanish colonial rule, however, owing to a heightened sense of nationalist unity, this time there arose labor unions such as the Union Obrera Democrata. With its roots in labor activism of the past two decades, and in Partido Obrero de Filipinas, a pro-labor party founded in 1924, the Partido Komunista ng Pilipinas (PKP) or Philippine Communist Party, was formally organized on November 17, 1930, by Crisanto Evangelista, a labor militant. Active in peasant and labor organizations, and a firm believer in aggressive politics, the PKP quickly found itself hounded by the government. The Philippine Supreme Court declared the party illegal on October 26, 1932, forcing its key members to lead a clandestine life. Nevertheless it helped unify diverse peasant movements, especially in Central Luzon, a unity helped along when the PKP and the Socialist Party of the Philippines, founded in 1932 by Pedro Abad Santos, merged in 1938. With the outbreak of World War, II it went underground, along with other legal parties and individual Filipinos.

But perhaps the movement with the most impact in the turbulent, Depression-plagued decade prior to World War II was the Sakdal (Indictment) movement, founded and led by Benigno Ramos. Ramos had been a protégé of Quezon when the latter was Senate President, but they had a falling out in 1930 when Quezon would not support a student protest against well-publicized anti-Filipino remarks by an American schoolteacher. Ramos subsequently established the Tagalog-language *Sakdal*, a weekly that regularly printed broadsides against Quezon, Osmeña, and their fellow politicians; American colonial administrators; and other pillars of the establishment. The publication grew to be enormously popular, its readership providing the base for the Sakdalista Party, established in 1933 and not surprisingly headed by Ramos.

In the 1934 elections, Ramos and the Sakdalista candidates offered themselves as an alternative to the mainstream parties. The party platform called for immediate independence by December 1935, the curtailment of American control of the economy, overhaul of an educational system that was seen as too colonial, rejection of U.S. military bases in the country, and a redistribution of land. Harassed regularly by the government, the party nevertheless won three seats for the House of Representatives, a governorship, and several municipal offices. The Sakdal leaders lost no time embarking on a campaign for the people to boycott the forthcoming plebiscite on the proposed Commonwealth Constitution.

The government deemed such a campaign seditious, arrested a number of Sakdalistas, and cancelled permits for public rallies. These provocations resulted in violent uprisings in two days in May 1935, by close to sixty thousand peasants in about twenty towns in the Tagalog provinces. The Philippine Constabulary units put down the rebellion violently, with fifty-seven peasant casualties, as the protesters were poorly armed and disorganized. Through such aggressive establishment tactics and with Benigno Ramos in Japan meeting with militaristic elements in Tokyo, the influence of the Sakdalistas quickly evaporated. Ramos remained in Japan until 1938; by then, the party he had founded was history—but not its profound resentments.

The Commonwealth

The Philippine Commonwealth was inaugurated on November 15, 1935, following the timetable set down by the Tydings-McDuffie Act, with Quezon and Osmeña elected as its president and vice president, respectively. The post of governor general metamorphosed into that of U.S. high commissioner, with Frank Murphy thus being the last colonial governor general and the first commissioner of the commonwealth. President Quezon took on General Douglas MacArthur (Arthur MacArthur's son) as military adviser to his government, with the title of field marshal came with five stars, the first American general to be so ranked. MacArthur would assume his new duties once he had stepped down as chief of staff of the U.S. military. He was to be aided in planning for the archipelago's defense by Major Dwight Eisenhower.

Quezon and his wife had taken a liking to MacArthur when the latter had been posted to the islands from 1922 to 1924, as commander of the Military District of Manila, accompanied by his first wife Louise Brooks, a wealthy divorcée. MacArthur was reassigned to the colony—without Louise as they had already separated and then divorced in 1929—as department commander from 1928 to 1930. He was recalled to Washington in August 1930, having been appointed chief of staff by President Herbert Hoover. On his return, he arranged for his Filipina mestiza mistress, Isabel Rosario Cooper, otherwise know as Dimples, to be lodged discreetly at an apartment in Georgetown.

It was not uncommon for U.S. military men posted to the colony to have romantic liaisons with the local women; while winked at, such relationships were officially frowned upon. But there was one person whose disapproval MacArthur feared more than anything else: his mother, who was living with him at his official quarters. He broke off with Dimples after four years, once two reporters, whom he was suing for libel, got wind of Dimples's existence and threatened to reveal the relationship if MacArthur didn't drop the court case.* And so he did.

Under the National Defense Act, MacArthur was charged with building up an army of 300,000 troops, though in his typical grandiose manner, he declared he would have 400,00 by 1946. At the moment, he had only 10,000 in the islands.

---

* The two journalists were Drew Pearson and Robert S. Allen. They had criticized the government's violent dispersal of several thousand Bonus Marchers—World War I veterans who had encamped in the summer of 1932 with their families near the Capitol—demanding immediate cash redemption of certificates they has been given for their service. MacArthur had been in charge of the dispersal.

The next year, 1936, as a gesture to nationalists, the Quezon government set up the Institute of National Language, whose primary goal was to adopt and develop a national tongue based on one of the principal native languages. By 1937, Tagalog, the language of the capital region (and of Quezon), was chosen as the basis of the national language, to be called "Pilipino"—much to the dismay of Cebuanos, who claimed to have more speakers than the Tagalogs and who were acutely aware that in spite of Cebu being the first Spanish settlement in the country, here they were, still overlooked almost four hundred years on. That same year, women were granted the right to vote.

In the 1938 elections for the legislature, Quezon and Osmeña's Nacionalistas dominated, with the opposition winning only five out of 98 seats. In 1940, the terms for the presidency and vice-presidency were changed from one six-year term with no reelection to one term of four years, with one reelection allowed—an amendment clearly meant to benefit the incumbents. Later that year, to no one's surprise, Quezon and Osmeña were reelected.

Free Rather than Fair Trade

Free trade enabled big business interests in the colony to prosper; understandably, the American business community in Manila had misgivings about the colony getting independence from the United States. In little more than three decades since the start of colonial rule, the growth of imports from the United States was tremendous, increasing ninety one times while in comparison exports to the U.S. grew thirty-two times. Eighty percent of Philippine export products were meant for the U.S. market. And 65 percent of goods brought in were from the United States. An over-reliance on the U.S. market thus made Filipino exporters uneasy about the prospects of independence. More importantly, it sidelined the need for industrialization.

In public, Filipino politicians declared that free trade would hurt the economic interests of the Filipinos, that such a policy favored vested economic interests, opening the country's commerce, industry, and agriculture to domination by American enterprises. In private, the opposition was much more muted, and after intense lobbying, most politicians acquiesced to free-trade policies, in order to protect their careers. At the same time, the easy access to American products worked against the emergence and development of local industry while cultivating in the

Filipino consumer a marked preference for such products. Indeed, "Stateside" came to be a term that connoted a preference for U.S.-made products.

Hence the establishment of a commonwealth that would ostensibly lead to independence was hedged with enough restrictions so as to ease the worries of powerful U.S. economic interests. Independence would be granted but Philippine products would be at a disadvantage. At the same time, the Commonwealth Constitution protected U.S. business interests so that the colony would still be a rich source of profits—as well as a base, still, for extending U.S. reach in Asia and the Middle East. In essence, the country was slowly but surely being transformed into a neo-colony, independent formally but still largely tied to the apron strings of America.

Land continued to be a burning issue in the countryside, with land policy mostly conservative. Although the colonial government declared its desire to broaden the base of independent ownership, American interests clearly lay in not disturbing—and indeed strengthening—the system of landownership that had developed under Spain. And the ruling elite saw no reason to disrupt what had been a hugely profitable arrangement for so long. The same obstacles that had prevented a fair and equitable redistribution of land in the Spanish colonial era were still operative: poverty and ignorance, the resulting failure of many individual tillers to acquire the necessary land titles, and aggressive landlord resistance.

WORLD WAR II AND THE GREATER EAST ASIA CO-PROSPERITY SPHERE

The 1930s were a time of political turmoil in Japan (as they were in Germany and Spain). With very few natural resources, an expanding population, and an increasing industrial output, the Japanese desperately needed foreign markets and access to raw materials. Its sizable commercial interests in Manchuria were under threat from Chinese nationalists. Domestically pro-fascist elements came to dominate the military and political spheres. Plans were then made for a southward expansion, a policy referred to originally as *Nan'yo* that later became the more sinister-sounding "Greater East Asia Co-Prosperity Sphere."

Due to construction of a highway leading up to Baguio City, the hill station the Americans had decided to build in the Cordilleras in northern Luzon, Japanese laborers were brought in, so that by 1903, the Japanese community in the islands numbered more than 1,000. By the 1920s, the Japanese began to arrive in greater numbers; by the 1930s they were a commercial presence in the archipelago. (Such presence included a number of Japanese brothels in Manila and Davao, with Japanese prostitutes catering mainly to non-Filipino customers.) Trade between the colony and Japan was worth $17 million in 1931. Japanese entrepreneurs were especially active in the hemp, lumber, and fishing industries.

In Davao, on the island of Mindanao, a sizable Japanese community had sprung up. At 18,000 strong, the Davao Japanese, a majority of whom came from Okinawa, controlled approximately 60,000 hectares—two-thirds of commercial agricultural land in the province. Employing 12,000 laborers, the Japanese had become the mainstay of economic development in Mindanao—aided by high-level, Japanese-paid lobbyists in the Quezon administration—and had helped make Davao the largest exporter of hemp in the world. Japanese entrepreneurs were active as well in the mining industry, establishing at least four mines. By 1934, Japanese merchants controlled 27 percent of the retail trade, 50 percent of the textile industry; 80 percent of the iron ore Philippine mines were producing was shipped to Japan. All these fueled suspicions that Japan was girding for war..

While there was a growing awareness in the commonwealth of the threat posed by Japanese fascism, much of the Spanish community in the islands sympathized, if not openly supported, Generalissimo Francisco Franco and the fascist Falangists, who had emerged victorious at the conclusion of the Spanish Civil War in 1938. One exception was the order of Capuchin monks, who were mostly from the Basque region, known for its fierce anti-Franco sentiments. The Casino Español, a bastion of Spanish conservatism in Manila, took down the Republican flag and raised that of Franco's. The Catholic Church hierarchy as well as the leading Spanish businessmen and landowners, who were also close to and identified with the U.S. colonial rulers, approved heartily of Franco's anti-Communist, anti-Republican campaign. They would be buoyed up later on by Washington's recognition of the Franco regime.

With a militaristic and expansionist government in place, Japan invaded China's Manchuria Province in 1937. With the onset of war in Europe and Hitler's takeover of France, the Japanese Imperial Army pushed into French Indochina and used that as a base from which to launch further incursions into China. In retaliation, the United States in October of 1940 halted the export of steel to Japan—an act the Japanese government deemed unfriendly. On July 26, 1941, Washington froze Japanese assets in the United States, and in August President Franklin Delano Roosevelt declared his government's opposition to involuntary regime change and demanded that Japan withdraw its forces from Indochina and China.

Later that year, trade negotiations were resumed between the two countries in a last-ditch effort to prevent further deterioration in relations that could lead to war. But by the end of November, the talks had proved useless. Preparations in the Philippines for an impending war were woefully inadequate. Quezon admitted to insufficient food stocks, fuel, and air raid shelters. MacArthur seemed to have buried his head in the sand, confident as late as November 1941 that if the Japanese attacked, it would be at the earliest in the spring of 1942.

MacArthur was off by a season. World War II commenced for the United States and the rest of Asia when the Japanese bombed Pearl Harbor in Hawaii on December 7, 1941 (December 8 in Manila). Bombing of Manila followed nine hours later. By 3 a.m., MacArthur knew of the surprise attack on Pearl Harbor but inexplicably took no action. As a result, slightly past noon, Japanese warplanes found most of the U.S. planes on the ground. At least half of MacArthur's air fleet was destroyed, the tragic result of nine hours of indecision. Both raids provided the dramatic opening salvo in Japan's campaign to build the Greater East Asia Co-Prosperity Sphere and thus unite Asian countries under the Rising Sun.

It was painfully evident that MacArthur had failed to build up a prepared army. The Japanese blitzkrieg was mostly uncontested, with Japanese troops landing in northern and southern Luzon, as well as in Davao. To spare Manila harm, MacArthur declared it an open city on December 26. By this time, he and other commonwealth officials were on Corregidor Island, including Quezon, Osmeña, and their families, while in Bataan, on Luzon, U.S. and Filipino troops regrouped. By early 1942, McArthur, Quezon, Osmena et al. had slipped away to Australia, thence to Washington, where a government-in-exile was quickly formed by the summer of 1942. Before MacArthur and Quezon went on their separate journeys out of the islands, the Philippine government, under the direction of Quezon, paid MacArthur $500,000 for his services to the commonwealth.

MacArthur was free to accept any sum of money from the Philippine government as his employer. However, once he had been reactivated in July of 1941 as an officer in the U.S. military, he was bound by army regulations that prohibited its members from accepting such cash gifts. This violation of army ethical rules was never made public, nor did President Roosevelt raise any objections

Less than a month after Japanese planes began their invasion, their ground forces rolled into Manila on January 2, 1942, and proceeded to set up a mechanism for administrative rule that would on one hand seem to give Filipinos their independence and on the other ensure that the country would be part of the Greater East Asia Co-Prosperity Sphere. As with the Spanish and the Americans, the Japanese declared that everything they were doing was for the benefit of the natives—which worried the natives no end.

In the United States, President Franklin Delano Roosevelt signed an executive order that awarded Filipinos full veterans benefits if they enlisted in the U.S. Armed Forces. In California alone, 16,000 signed up; about 9,000 formed the First and Second Filipino Infantry Regiments. Overall, approximately 250,000 Filipinos fought alongside U.S. troops in the Pacific War. However, FDR and his military advisers, including General Dwight Eisenhower, decided to focus on the European/Atlantic theater before attending to the war in the Pacific. Eisenhower in particular argued that sufficient forces to recapture the Philippines could not be assembled without hurting the war effort in Europe and the Atlantic. Consequently, in spite of a gallant, against-all-odds defense, on April 9, 1942, the beleaguered Filipino and U.S. soldiers in Bataan surrendered to the Japanese. Many men under arms, however, were able to escape to nearby Corregidor. Those who surrendered were forced to march from Mariveles, Bataan, to San Fernando, Pampanga, and thence to prison camps in Capas, Tarlac, in Central Luzon.

The march was one of the grimmer episodes of the Pacific War and has been described aptly as the "Death March," for the prisoners trudged in the torrid summer heat—April and May are the cruelest months of the Philippine summer—with no food or drink. Stragglers were more often than not bayoneted or shot on the spot. Of the estimated 85,000-90,000 surrendered soldiers, approximately 25,000 perished before reaching San Fernando. From San Fernando, the prisoners were herded into trains that took them to Capas. In barracks meant for 20,000 occupants, 60,000 were crammed. Of those 60,000, by war's end, about 45,000 had died due to illness, starvation, and exhaustion. Meanwhile the 11,000 troops on Corregidor, under the leadership of Lt. General Jonathan Wainwright, battled valiantly, but on May 6, 1942, he and his men surrendered to the Japanese, and with that, the Japanese takeover of the archipelago was complete.

A puppet government was installed, with the formation first of the Philippine Executive Commission, made up of politically well-placed Filipinos, among them Chief Justice of the Supreme Court José P. Laurel, later to become the nominal president of the country. Jorge Vargas, Quezon's executive secretary and appointed mayor of Manila just before Quezon's departure, was named head of the commission. Pragmatic above all else, a significant portion of the elite—fourteen out of twenty-four senators and thirty-five out of ninety-eight representatives—collaborated with the Japanese command, to ensure retention of their political and economic power. Collaboration, of course, was not limited to politicians. Quite a number of fortunes were made on the black market by unscrupulous businessmen supplying the Japanese with whatever materials were needed.

Focusing on the Japanese promise of independence, as declared by Premier Hideki Tojo, enabled elite collaborators to cite this as justification for cooperating with this new invader. Vargas, for instance, expressed his "confidence and trust in the true and benevolent intentions of the Japanese Imperial Forces," while Congressman Benigno Aquino Sr. declared that Filipinos were Asians, "not Europeans or Anglo-Saxons." And in a letter to the Japanese high command, a virtual political Who's Who stated their intent "to obey to the best of our ability and within the means at our disposal the orders issued by the Imperial Japanese Forces for the . . . well-being of our people."

In reality, the promise of self-rule and a cultural renaissance was broken right from the start. All institutions that governed or influenced public life and perceptions were controlled by the military. This meant a media—newspapers, radio, even printing presses—that served the propaganda needs of the Japanese. The same process was repeated for education, government offices, and churches.

Just as the United States had done with English, the puppet government ordered the teaching of Japanese, or Nippongo. The Americans were portrayed as purveyors of decadence who had placed an undue emphasis on individual rights. According to General Hayashi Yoshide, director of the Japanese Military Administration (JMA), the United States had led the country down the path of "deceit and misguidance." The lesson was clear: Filipinos needed to rehabilitate themselves.

A major role for the Philippines, as with other Asian countries taken over by the Japanese military, was to provide much needed resources for Japan's war effort, whether in the building of weapons or in feeding its troops, which at its height, numbered more than 250,000 in the islands. The diverting of crops, especially rice, to the soldiers meant great hardships for the masses. The miseries they suffered, and the many acts of brutality inflicted on them by soldiers in His Majesty's Imperial Army, undercut the stated aims of Filipinizing the Philippines, strengthening rather than weakening pro-American sentiments. Since real power lay in the hands of the Japanese military, martial law was in effect.

To stress that the Japanese were serious about liberating the Philippines from colonial rule and to wean Filipinos from pro-U.S. leanings, independence was to be granted earlier than 1946, the date promised by the United States. A hastily assembled Preparatory Commission for Philippine Independence drafted a new constitution that was speedily ratified in September of 1943, the ink barely dry on the document. Delegates to a National Assembly were elected, as decreed by the new constitution, and in turn the delegates elected Laurel as the president.

With the Allied offensive in full swing, and U.S. forces retaking strategic islands such as Saipan, bringing them within striking range of the Philippines and Japan, the tide started to turn against the Japanese. Nevertheless, on October 14, 1943, in front of crowds assembled by the Kapisanan sa Paglilinkod sa Bagong Pilipinas (KALIBAPI) or Association for Serving the New Philippines—in reality, a nationwide surveillance network—the new Republic of the Philippines was inaugurated. To appeal to nationalists, the Japanese had brought Artemio Ricarte back to Manila from exile in Yokohama, where he and his wife made a living running a coffeehouse. Ricarte, already in his late seventies and a former general in Aguinaldo's army known as "El Vibora," or "The Viper," had steadfastly refused to pledge allegiance to the United States. Supportive of the Japanese, he was a living symbol of the Filipino struggle for independence. He was on hand to assist in the raising of the Japanese flag on that fateful day, alongside the Philippine flag as an allegedly independent Philippine state was declared. Ricarte's time had passed, however, and he no longer had the following he had had three decades earlier. Fleeing the American army towards the end of the war, he died of dysentery in the Cordilleras.

Mimicking a regular government, administrative machinery was set in place, along with a judiciary. Filipino diplomats were posted abroad wherever the Japanese reigned supreme. On the local level, the Japanese instituted a system of neighborhood associations that served as distribution points for commodities and a source of labor and spectators at official public events. More important, these associations constituted a widespread surveillance network, organized by the Kalibapi, which had displaced political parties, depicted as mere mouthpieces for American propaganda. The organization also included a sub-branch for younger members. Launched on December 30, 1942, the death anniversary of José Rizal and a nod to nationalism, Kalibapi was headed by Benigno S. Aquino, father of Senator Benigno Aquino, Jr., later to become the most famous political opponent of Ferdinand Marcos in the 1970s.

Along with abusive and often violent Japanese soldiers, the Kalibapi rendered Japanese rule despicable to ordinary Filipinos. Where before they might have viewed the United States in a similar light given the horrors of the 1899 Philippine-American War, now they came increasingly to long for the return of the Americans. Complementing the Kalibapi's efforts was a more insidious organization, the Makabayang Katipunan ng Mga Pilipino (MaKaPili) or Patriotic Society of Filipinos, which was formed by Benigno Ramos, founder of the Sakdal movement, and a long-time sympathizer of the Japanese. The Makapili were armed and collaborated with the occupiers by pointing out those who were working with the underground or who otherwise displayed anti-Japanese sentiments. Often, Makapili members—hooded in public, to protect their identities—used their position to simply settle old scores.

Resistance to the Japanese was widespread. Guerrilla bands and underground intelligence units, most headed by USAFFE officers, were everywhere, an ubiquitous threat to the fragile stability of Japanese rule. For the most part, the resistance hewed to U.S. plans for retaking the islands. One group, though, was steadfast in its opposition both to Japanese and to U.S. rule: the *Hukbo ng Bayan Laban sa Hapon*

(Hukbalahap, or Huks), or the Anti-Japanese People's Army. Organized in March of 1942, the Huks constituted the military arm of the Partidong Komunista ng Pilipinas and at its peak counted 10,000 members. The Communist Huk leadership couched their appeal to the peasants and farmers in terms of long-needed socio-economic reforms rather than hard-core ideological lines. These left-wing resistance fighters were most active in Central Luzon, where they set up the Barrio United Defense Corps, or BUDC, to act as local government units.

The BUDC was critical to the economic survival of a community, making sure, for instance, that the harvesting of rice was done quickly and the grain distributed before the landowner and the Japanese got their hands on it. While the Huks were nationalists, for tactical reasons, they didn't oppose the USAFFE-led units since they had a common enemy. However, not a few of the pro-American groups were hostile towards the Huks and, as the war drew to a close, would attack them when the occasion presented itself.

RECONQUEST: MACARTHUR'S RETURN

General Douglas MacArthur had famously said, upon arriving in Australia in 1942, "I have come through and I shall return." It would be two-and-a-half years before he could make good on his promise, as, despite the government-in-exile's and his arguments, Roosevelt had decided first to focus on the European phase of the war. On October 20, 1944, Leyte Island was retaken by U.S. forces and thence the reconquest of the rest of the islands was undertaken. Accompanied by Sergio Osmeña (now the acting president, Quezon having died in August of that year in upstate New York) and Carlos P. Romulo, the signatory for the Philippines to the United Nations charter on its founding in 1946, the good general declared from Tacloban City, Leyte's capital, "People of the Philippines, I have returned."

MacArthur's dramatic announcement was made even more so by the largest naval battle of World War II and one of the largest in history: the Battle of Leyte Gulf, actually four separate engagements between U.S. and Japanese warships, from October 23, 1944 to October 26. Two hundred seventy-six warships fought it out, with the U.S. enjoying numerical superiority: 209 on the U.S. side and 67 on the Japanese. Japan lost four aircraft carriers, three battleships, ten cruisers, and eleven destroyers.

Such losses crippled the Japanese navy, no longer an effective deterrent to U.S. attack on the homeland. The battle also witnessed the first use of the kamikaze (Japanese for "divine wind"), with planes converted into suicide weapons. Before the United States had secured total control of the air, kamikazes had sunk sixteen U.S. ships and damaged another eighty.

Prior to the beach landing on Leyte, U.S. bombers had already struck in a south-to-north pattern, hitting Davao, the Visayas, and Manila. In early January of 1945, U.S. forces stormed ashore on the west coast of northern Luzon, and subsequently, in southern Luzon. By the first week of February U.S. armored columns were entering Manila from the north. The battle to oust the Japanese from the historic city was fierce and apocalyptic—the fiercest urban battleground in the Pacific theater, akin to the battle for Stalingrad. Innumerable accounts tell of Japanese soldiers committing atrocities during their retreat, while for their part U.S. artillery indiscriminately pounded Intramuros, the historic matrix of Manila, to rubble. The city south of the Pasig River was essentially obliterated. The month-long fighting in Manila, from February 3 to March 3, 1945, was hand-to-hand and street-to-street, with 1,010 U.S. soldiers killed, and more than 5,000 wounded. Japanese casualties were 12,000. Of the civilian population, approximately 100,000 perished. Not taking into account the U.S. atomic bombing of Hiroshima and Nagasaki cities later that August, the devastation of Manila ranked second only to Warsaw. On July 5, 1945, the archipelago was finally wrested from Japanese occupation.

The commanding general of the Japanese Imperial Army in the islands, General Tomoyuki Yamashita—known as the "Tiger of Malaya," for his capture of Malaya and Singapore from more than 100,000 troops under British command—was charged with war crimes, particularly with the atrocities inflicted by the Japanese army on civilians in the bloodbath that was the Battle of Manila. The general's defense was that he was no longer in Manila when the U.S. began its efforts to reclaim the historic city. He had, with most of his troops, in fact retreated to the mountainous north, where he planned to offer fierce resistance and thus delay significantly the inevitable advance on Japan, once the Philippines had been secured by the United States. Left in charge of Manila's defense was Rear Admiral Sanji Iwabuchi who, contrary to Yamashita's orders, decided to defend the city to the death. And it was, with disastrous results.

MacArthur ordered a trial, had a court set up, and determined the rules under which it was to operate. After a three-week trial, Yamashita was found guilty and sentenced to die by hanging. The conviction was appealed by his defense team first, to the Philippine Supreme Court, and then to the U.S. Supreme Court, the main argument being that Yamashita couldn't possibly have had a fair trial under the conditions set up by MacArthur, the commander of enemy forces. In a 7-2 decision, the Court affirmed the verdict, with the two dissenters calling the execution "legalized lynching." The sentence was carried out near Manila on February 23, 1946, five months after the Japanese had officially surrendered to the Allied forces on September 2, 1945, on the battleship USS *Missouri*, anchored at Tokyo Bay.

5. THE REPUBLIC: PERILS OF INDEPENDENCE, 1946-1972

"The security interests of the United States require that the Philippines become and remain stable, anti-communist, pro-American, and an example for the rest of the world of the intention of the United States to encourage the establishment of progressive and responsible governments. This entails the reassertion of U.S. influence to the extent required to eliminate prevalent corruption, provide efficient administrative services, and restore public faith in the concept of government in the best interests of the people. . . . [The United States should] continue to assume responsibility for the external defense of the Islands and be prepared to commit United States forces, if necessary, to prevent Communist control of the Philippines."

—U.S. National Security Report, November 10, 1950

THE IMMEDIATE AFTERMATH OF THE WAR

THE BLOODY CAMPAIGN TO WREST THE PHILIPPINES AWAY FROM the Japanese left the country in ruins, with the archipelago facing the seemingly insurmountable task of rebuilding. Manila was a shell of its pre-war grandeur, its heart, Intramuros, gutted. In an initial estimate of the damages caused by war, the Philippine Bureau of Census and Statistics put these at close to $3 billion. Later the Philippines would file claims on the Japanese government for $4 billion.

Claims from all the countries damaged by the Pacific War totaled $54 billion, an enormous amount that Japan would find all but impossible to pay. The Allied reparations committee, however, could not agree on the amount Japan could pay. In the interim, the U.S. government authorized MacArthur, virtual emperor of Japan during the U.S. occupation, to compel the Japanese to make payments. Most of these interim payments were in the form of industrial equipment. Additionally, Japanese assets in the different countries could be seized by their respective governments.

However, in 1949, the U.S. unilaterally dropped its demands for payments, but the Philippines and other war-damaged countries objected. In light of ideological battle lines being drawn between the Soviet Union and the U.S., Japan was now seen as a vital cornerstone in Asia against the Soviet Union. Its economic recovery, unhampered by reparations, was crucial. In 1952, Japan signed a peace treaty with forty-nine nations, including the United States. The treaty provided that Japan would negotiate separately with not just the Philippines but other war-damaged countries such as Burma, Indonesia, and Thailand. Four years later, Japan and the Philippines agreed to a reparations program wherein Japan would provide $500 million in free goods over a ten-year period; $30 million in technical services; $20 million in payments to war widows and orphans; and $250 million in long-term loans over a period of twenty years, to end in 1977. From the Japanese perspective, the reparations process would help reopen markets heretofore closed to them, and thus gain access to much-needed raw materials.

While Osmeña was nominally the president of the commonwealth, Douglas MacArthur, as commander of the U.S. forces, called the shots. He had at his disposal men, money, and materials, and he used them strategically to once again insure firm U.S. control before Philippine independence would be declared on July 4, 1946. To do that, and to get a government up and running as soon as possible, he and his staff overlooked potential charges of collaboration against those of the political elite who had worked with the Japanese. MacArthur was especially keen on Manuel Roxas, his aide before the war and whom he much preferred to the fastidious and more independent-minded Osmeña, who had succeeded Quezon as president of the commonwealth when the latter died of chronic tuberculosis at Lake Saranac, New York, in August of 1944.

Roxas's star had risen fast in the pre-war political firmament: a politician from Capiz Province in the Visayas, he occupied the speakership of the Philippine Assembly in 1922 at the age of thirty. He worked with Osmeña on the Hare-Hawes-Cutting Bill, and later became secretary of finance under Quezon, becoming his trusted personal adviser. He was elected senator in 1941 and the outbreak of World War II saw him as a lieutenant colonel in the United States Armed Forces in the Far East (USAFFE). He was captured by the Japanese in Mindanao in 1942, and he subsequently served in the puppet government set up by the Japanese, as the chair of the Economic Planning Board. Towards the end of the war, he escaped or was released by the Japanese High Command headed by General Tomoyuki Yamashita, who had, along with the cabinet, fled to the mountain resort city of Baguio in the north.

MacArthur pushed for early presidential elections. But Roxas couldn't very well run as the standard bearer of the Nacionalistas, since Osmeña, the party leader, was running for the presidency as well. Roxas thus broke away and founded the Liberal Party in January of 1946, making it the second-oldest political party in the country. The Nacionalistas Party had been around since 1907 when it was founded, and it dominated the political scene until the outbreak of World War II.

Arguments were made that a two-party system was imperative for a democracy to flourish. Nonetheless it was the pursuit of personal ambition that motivated Roxas, thus setting a precedent regularly followed by those whose own ambitions were stymied by their party. Each party's platforms were strikingly similar, and voters were asked to heed the call of one rather than the other not because of ideological differences, but because, pledged to the same ends, one party could achieve these more effectively than the other. In short, no major differences characterized the Nacionalistas from the Liberals and postwar party politics became almost exclusively personal politics. With the implicit view that governance was primarily for the benefit of those in power, the system encouraged personal and individual rather than party loyalty, with turncoats rewarded rather than punished. Short-term interests invariably prevailed over long-term ones.

The left threw its support behind Osmeña, viewing Roxas with deep suspicion due to his wartime collaboration with the Japanese as a high official in the Japanese-sponsored Philippine Republic. The fact that General MacArthur cleared him of treason—in unseemly haste, it seemed to MacArthur's critics—only added fuel to the fire. Collaboration between Filipinos and the Japanese proved to be a more complicated issue than originally thought. Osmeña emphasized that the whole matter had to be examined judiciously, without a rush to judgment that would view all those who worked with and for the Japanese at different levels and capacities in the same treasonous light. Civil servants for example had to keep on working, to insure the everyday workings of government, which was not necessarily true of politicians.

Rebuilding meant not only physical rehabilitation and the resuscitation of a moribund economy, but settling the issue of collaboration. Given that a significant number of the ruling elite had worked with the Japanese, many of whom were known, if not close, to General MacArthur, this issue was political dynamite. With the government in Washington initially desirous that those accused be tried for collaboration, a People's Court was instituted precisely for this, but it was doomed from the start. For one thing, only fifteen judges were on hand to try 5,603 cases. It was a virtually impossible task. Moreover, twenty-five government prosecutors were permitted only six months to argue all the cases. For another, MacArthur had pre-emptively exonerated Manuel Roxas, a pre-war friend.

While the matter of collaboration was still being discussed, the commonwealth government held elections in April of 1946, with Roxas and Quirino vying against Osmeña and Eulogio Rodriguez, and winning. Sixteen senators were also elected, along with ninety-eight congressmen, the full slate of the House of Representatives. While Roxas's Liberal Party dominated, seven senators were from the opposition as were thirty-eight of the ninety-eight congressmen.

Three months later, on July 4, 1946, independence-day rituals were held at the Luneta, not far from the historic Manila Hotel and the U.S. Army and Navy Club, and fronting Manila Bay where in 1898 Spanish gunboats were easily defeated. The United States relinquished its titular and tutelary hold on the country choosing the same date of its own independence to do so. The Stars and Stripes was lowered, and the Philippine flag, with its golden-rayed sun, raised in its place. The population of a still bleeding nation stood at 18 million. With Roxas and Quirino as its president and vice president respectively, the Republic of the Philippines was finally independent of the United States, its colonial master the past half-century.

But was it truly independent?

Having its own flag fly over the nation did not automatically mean the United States had relinquished control over these Southeast Asian islands, only that the means of control had become less overt. Rather than a clean, selfless hand-off—which was what had been promised— that day marked the transition of a colony to a neo-colony, similar to what befell Cuba at the end of the Spanish-American War.

The status of the Philippines was closer to what the unlamented Federalistas (the country's earliest political party, established in 1900) desired. The Federalistas had quickly acknowledged American sovereignty even as the Philippine-American War was raging and campaigned for an autonomous government along the lines of a protectorate. After a certain amount of time had passed, the party had planned to campaign for statehood rather than independence. Half a century later, the country's status had come full circle.

By winning the presidency and vice-presidency of the Commonwealth in April of 1946, Roxas and his running mate, Elpidio Quirino, under the banner of the Liberal Party, effectively ended Osmeña's political career. The tandem presided over the transference of sovereignty from the United States to the newly formed republic on July 4, 1946.

Roxas and Quirino were thus the last president and vice president of the commonwealth, and the first president and vice president under the postcolonial dispensation. Roxas didn't serve out the full four-year term, however, as he died of a heart attack while giving a speech in 1948 at Clark Air Force Base. It was only fitting that the unabashedly pro-U.S. Roxas passed away on American ground. Earlier that year, as expected, he had granted amnesty to all collaborators. There had been 5,603 cases filed, but only 156 had resulted in convictions, with only one relatively prominent figure convicted.

The aftermath of the war offered unparalleled opportunities to remake Philippine society economically and socially. But Douglas MacArthur was too close to the pre-war Philippine elite to initiate any far-reaching reforms. As mentioned in the previous chapter, the half-million dollar gift from President Quezon just before MacArthur had left the islands in 1942 was emblematic of such ties. The pre-war status quo was what the conservatives wanted, and it was what they got. In contrast, as commander of Occupied Japan, from 1945 to 1951, MacArthur and his staff introduced land reform, helped break up the *zaibatsu* (the monopolistic industrial combines), and drafted labor laws, among other elements of change. MacArthur could afford to be dispassionate in his role as military ruler, an American shogun in Japan, having no personal or professional ties with Japan's ruling elite. However, he did exonerate Emperor Hirohito and the rest of the imperial family for any responsibility for the war. He also accorded immunity to the Japanese bacteriological research units in exchange for data based on gruesome human experiments.

That the United States was less altruistic with the Philippines can be seen in the number of strings it attached to the formal cessation of colonial rule. The new republic, having suffered a horrific three-and-a-half years of war due to its status as a U.S. colony, was in no position to refuse. Among those strings were economic agreements that favored the U.S. and a 99-year bases lease that placed significant chunks of Philippine territory under U.S. suzerainty.

In the interim President Harry Truman had decided to leave the issue of collaboration up to the civil authorities in Manila, ostensibly to display trust in the Philippine government to do the right thing but it was in effect a policy of appeasement. He did so on the recommendation of MacArthur, who knew that, despite popular sentiment calling for retribution against those who had worked with the Japanese occupiers, the political establishment would not condemn its own. Any sustained investigation into their wartime activities would embarrass and alienate the pre-war elite who were back in the saddle. At the start of 1948, Roxas declared an amnesty for all suspected collaborators, sidestepping the thorny dilemma and effectively curtailing the existence of the People's Court. The amnesty appeased many of Roxas's powerful supporters, landlords, and other wealthy and socially prominent individuals who were suspected of wartime collaboration.

THE COLD WAR

Why was the politically explosive issue of collaboration allowed to wither away? Quite simply, the Cold War and the perceived threat of Communism emerged as the two most crucial and related issues the United States believed it had to deal with. With ideological fault lines being drawn up globally between the Soviet Union and its allies on one hand and the United States and its allies on the other—between the Free World and the Iron Curtain, in the jargon of the day—Washington's overriding anti-Communism translated into continued support of the traditional Philippine oligarchy, whose own anti-Communist feelings were beyond reproach if only because this was what was expected of them. Besides, the hardships of World War II and the brutality of Japanese occupation transformed the image of the Americans from colonial oppressors to liberators. Except for the Huks, with their roots in anti-imperialism, most guerrilla groups viewed the Japanese as the only enemy. Harboring doubts that the postwar dispensation would be any kinder towards their socialist goals, the Huks held on to their arms, ready to use them once more if no substantial reforms were undertaken by the government.

Washington was relying on the oligarchy to restore order, fight Communism, and to assure stable leadership in independence, equating stability with democracy. Roxas may have been a collaborator but more importantly this economic expert was anti-Communist and would align the Philippines with the United States. It thus became increasingly difficult to criticize the establishment without being thought of as a commie sympathizer.

In the immediate aftermath of the war, the need for the ruling establishment's unconditional support for U.S. Cold War policies meant

U.S. authorities conveniently overlooked instances of corruption. In one notorious case, war surplus property that had been stockpiled for the planned invasion of Japan and valued at $137 million was to be sold off by a government commission, dominated by Roxas's Liberal Party, over a period of three years, from 1946 to 1949. At the end official sales tallied only $37 million; the question of where the balance of $100 million went was never satisfactorily answered. According to the *American Chamber of Commerce Journal*, this "constituted the biggest windfall in Philippine history."

There had been precedents, of course, during the Japanese Occupation, with the black market enabling many an unscrupulous businessman and/or politician to realize vast profits. And so a pattern of corruption was set that permeated the different levels of government bureaucracy, where appropriations for public services and programs, especially in rural areas, were inevitably depleted due to kickbacks and bribes—a pattern that continues to plague the government to this day.

Now the enemy as defined by the Cold War was Communism. Washington looked in alarm at the postwar emergence of the Soviet Union as a superpower. At the same time, two developments in mainland Asia provoked further anxiety: the defeat of the Chinese Nationalists headed by Chiang Kai-shek and the establishment in 1949 of a Chinese Communist regime under Mao Tse-tung; and the outbreak of the Korean War in 1950.

The Korean War—which is, even in the twenty-first century, unfinished—began in June of 1950, when the army of the Democratic People's Republic of North Korea under Kim Il-sung crossed the 38th parallel into the Republic of Korea. The war was the culmination of escalating conflicts between the two halves of a country that had been divided right after World War II once it had been freed of Japanese colonial rule, which had begun in 1910. Truman announced that U.S. forces would be sent to Korea and used this opportunity to order that aid to France's colonial war in Indochina be stepped up, that the U.S. Seventh Fleet defend Formosa should Communist China attack, and that United States forces in the Philippines be strengthened and military assistance to the Philippine government be accelerated. The Korean War marked the first conflict where Cold War antagonists openly backed one side or the other, thus becoming not just a war to unify the country but a proxy one as well between the two superpowers.

The war was also the first time that the United Nations decided to use force—to intervene on behalf of Syngman Rhee's South Korea, with the United States leading the way. President Quirino authorized the sending of the Philippine Expeditionary Force to Korea (PEFTOK) of more than 7,000 troops. After stunning victories and swift advances into South Korea by North Korea, the UN forces, led by General MacArthur, counterattacked, pushing the North Korean forces back across the border. Rather than stopping at the border, MacArthur's forces undertook incursions into North Korea. China, feeling that its own security was under threat, responded militarily, sending in its own troops to fight alongside the North Koreans. It was a war of bloody stalemates. Because MacArthur had dared publicly rebuke President Truman's war policies, he was fired. The general had wanted to escalate the war by invading China and using atom bombs to create a nuclear fallout zone as a barrier. Such tactics would have widened the scope of the war and brought the Soviet Union into the fray—an outcome Truman wished to avoid. An armistice was finally signed on July 27, 1953—an armistice that has never led to a cessation of hostilities, merely their suspension.

The Korean War and the French troubles with Ho Chi Minh seemed to exemplify the "domino theory," first expounded by President Dwight D. Eisenhower in an April 1954 news conference on Indochina: "Finally you have broader considerations that might follow what you would call the 'falling domino' principle. . . . You knock over the first ones and what will happen to the last one is the certainty that it will go over very quickly. So you could have the beginning of a disintegration that would have the most profound influence."

U.S. Bases Agreement

A crucial element of U.S. Cold War strategy in Asia was the retention of bases in its former colony. While General Dwight David Eisenhower had advocated for the withdrawal of all U.S. forces from the Philippines— he believed that positive relations between the two countries overrode the bases' importance—his was a decidedly minority view. While official rhetoric extolled the "special relationship" between the two countries, with shared goals of promoting the democratic way of life, U.S. policy was decidedly less sentimental, assessing the value of the island nation primarily in relation to Cold War politics. Perhaps no one was more hard-nosed in this regard than the influential veteran diplomat and political scientist George Kennan. He was one of the principal architects of U.S. foreign policy during the early stages of the Cold War, arguing for a policy of containment when it came to the Soviet Union and its allies, whom he regarded as expansionist. Kennan was straightforward enough to dispense with platitudes when defining what the official U.S. attitude towards the Philippines should be. He stated: "We should cease to talk about vague and—for the Far East—unreal objectives such as human rights, the raising of living standards, and democratization. The day is not far off when we are going to have to deal in straight power concepts. The less we are then hampered by idealistic slogans, the better." Kennan suggested a hands-off policy when it came to the country's internal affairs, as long as it continued to serve U.S. security needs in Southeast Asia.

In a post-World War II planet, the United States was eager to build a network of bases overseas, to maintain U.S. hegemony and serve principally as a bulwark against the Soviet Union and to a lesser extent against newly independent former colonies that did not necessarily accept the U.S. interpretation of what a world order should be. These nations, usually referred to as the Third World, came to be regarded as satellites of one superpower or the other, rarely as independent ships of state. Asia, Africa, and Latin America often became sites of proxy wars, that is, wars rooted in local causes but in which the superpowers got involved as a way of advancing their own interests without their own boots on the ground. Another term for these sorts of wars was Low Intensity Conflict (LIC)—low intensity, that is, for the superpower though not for the actual combatants.

Thus, the Philippines' transformation to a neo-colony, with the United States still very much a dominant player in both its internal and external affairs. The fact that there were in 1949 installed a Communist regime in China, an anti-Communist government in Taiwan, and neutral and possibly leftist governments in both India and Indonesia only made the case for continued U.S. military bases in the region more compelling—from Washington's perspective.

Adding to U.S. anxiety about Communism in the region was a guerrilla war between the Commonwealth forces in Malaya and the Malayan National Liberation Army (MNLA), the military arm of the Malayan Communist Party made up mostly of ethnic Chinese. Like the Huks, the MNLA was an outgrowth of the Malayan People's Anti-

Japanese Army. The conflict, begun in 1948, ended in 1960, with the capitulation of the MNLA.

While there was no question that the newly installed Roxas administration was in lockstep with the United States, still, talks on the status of U.S. bases in the country dragged on for eight months. To prod along recalcitrant Philippine officials, President Truman threatened to withdraw all U.S. forces, even as the country was still in ruins and as Malacañang was struggling to cope with a resurging Huk movement. This did the trick. Knowing that U.S. military aid was essential if he were to crush the Huks, who were fast on their way to becoming a major headache, and were U.S. troops to be pulled out, other forms of aid would lessen if not disappear altogether, Roxas reassured the U.S. of his government's commitment to keeping U.S. bases.

On March 14, 1947, the two countries signed the Military Bases Agreement (MBA). The lease on all United States bases in the Philippines was extended to ninety-nine years, subject to extension thereafter. The agreement gave the U.S. control over twenty-three bases, sixteen in active use and seven others held in reserve, to be activated should the need arise. Facilities ranged from Sangley Naval Base in Cavite to Camp John Hay Rest and Recreation Center in Baguio City, from Subic Bay Naval Base (SBNB) in Olongapo, Zambales Province, to Clark Air Force Base (CAFB) in Angeles City, Pampanga Province.

Subic and Clark were the largest U.S. bases outside the United States. Clark covered 14.3 square miles, with access to a reservation of 230 square miles, which included the Crow Valley aerial warfare range. What began as the army base Ft. Stotsenburg in 1903 was now the largest American base overseas, bigger than the entire island of Grenada. Outside of Japan and Korea, Clark Air Base was the sole major operational U.S. Air Force installation in the far West Pacific, able to handle all aircraft, including the largest military transports. Navy planners considered it a superb logistic-support base, essential to maintaining U.S. combat readiness.

Subic Bay, eyed as early as 1572 by Miguel de Legazpi's grandson, Juan de Salcedo, as an excellent deep-water port, had been developed as an arsenal by the Spanish in 1885. The U.S. Navy began to use it in 1901, and in 1903, President Theodore Roosevelt designated it and about 100,000 acres as a military reservation. The largest naval installation outside the U.S., Subic offered the Seventh Fleet a unique combination of ship, aircraft, and support facilities, with three major wharves, that could berth even the largest aircraft carriers. Additionally, Subic had the largest ship-repair facility in the Western Pacific, operating 24 hours a day, 365 days a year. Just as important, labor costs in the Philippines were the lowest available to the U.S. Navy.

At the outset, both bases included cities within their jurisdiction: Angeles for Clark, and Olongapo for Subic, though the two cities later on regained their autonomy. The bases agreement prohibited the Philippines from granting base rights to any other country and placed no restriction on the uses to which the U.S. could put the bases, nor the types of weapons that it could deploy or store there. Additionally, the MBA allowed the United States to recruit Filipinos into the U.S. Armed Forces.

For close to five decades, the United States was sovereign within the bases, able to use them with fewer restrictions than anywhere else it had bases. A principal function for them of course was as springboards for U.S. intervention in Asia. Projecting American might—and later, protecting its interests—in Asia had always been an integral part of U.S. design. Prior to World War II, U.S. military units had been dispatched on three occasions from the colony: in 1900, to China, to help crush the Boxer Rebellion; during the Russian civil war in 1918 to 1920, to Siberia; and in 1927, to Shanghai, to help protect the Western expatriate community known as the International Settlement.

Corollary to the MBA was the Military Assistance Agreement (MAA) of March 21, 1947. The MAA stipulated that a U.S. military advisory group, known as the Joint U.S. Military Advisory Group, or JUSMAG, be attached to the Philippine Armed Forces. The agreement also provided for the training of selected Philippine military personnel in the U.S. As with Cuba's Platt Amendment, the Philippines agreed not to accept military aid or advisers from elsewhere unless Washington consented.

With the U.S. bases and military assistance touted in part as necessary for the defense of the archipelago, the question arose, who exactly were the Philippines' external enemies? Not being part of continental Asia, the country was secure from land-border infiltration. Furthermore, the country had had no historic or traditional enemies, except those who warred with Spain and later the United States, their former colonizers. The only credible threat to the stability of the country and the government would be from within, from its own population, and it was in the domestic arena where U.S. military assistance could be and was often utilized.

Through such measures, the United States insured that it would continue to play a dominant role in Philippine political life well beyond July 4, 1946. While such a strategy was anchored in the realpolitik of the Cold War it had its roots in the imperialism that underscored U.S. occupation at the start of the twentieth century.

THE HUK RESURGENCE

The U.S. obsession of containing, at times confronting, Communism globally, cast the Philippines in a new light. Touted as America's show-case of democracy in Asia, the newly independent nation had to be kept free of Communism. The threat the Hukbalahaps represented was at the least embarrassing, and at the most disastrous to American strategic interests in Southeast Asia. Believing Malacañang ill-prepared for the Huks while engaged in building a nation that would be a staunch U.S. ally, Washington intervened.

For the Huks and the peasants and tenant farmers, the most press-ing issue, as it was even in Spanish colonial times, was land or the lack thereof, and the inequitable ways of farm-income distribution. Though semi-feudal conditions had long been part of the rural social fabric, with cyclical debt plaguing peasant families, still, the fact that landowners lived in their haciendas meant that paternalism (the old model for benevolent assimilation) allowed tenant farmers a basic security that supplemented their own meager resources. It softened the exploitative system, keeping in check but not quite eradicating discontent.

That changed when the incidence of absentee landlordism grew. In conformity with the 1898 Treaty of Paris, the U.S. government had agreed to buy the huge landed estates of the Spanish friars. And it did, in 1903, with funds raised through the sale of Philippine government bonds. In turn, these estates, totaling close to 400,000 acres, were to be sold mainly to the landless. In reality, most of the landless peasants could ill afford to buy the proffered parcels of land. Those who did had no institutional support (government or private) to make the tran-sition from tenancy to landowners. In the end, a majority were forced to sell their small plots to wealthy landowners, to caciques and middle-class elements that had grown during the American occupation. Many if not most of the new landowners chose to continue living in towns and cities, delegating the task of managing their lands to their managers, an arrangement that often led to abuse and more importantly to the breakdown of traditional landlord-tenant relations. Inevitably, the gap between these two social classes grew wider.

Moreover, to the tenant farmers and sharecroppers, the political freedoms and sense of emancipation that American colonial rule promised to bring were nowhere in evidence. Coupled with two new bills that threatened to further weaken an already weakened economy—the Philippine Rehabilitation Act (PRA) and the Philippine Trade Act (PTA), to be discussed shortly—the Huks and the PKP felt they had no other option but to take up arms once again, as they had during the war against the Japanese.

In this regard, MacArthur could have helped defuse the explosive social situation had he pushed for meaningful land reform, as he and Occupation authorities under his command were to do later on in Japan. But the general was too close to the oligarchy to institute any deep-seated changes. He had served in the archipelago at the behest of Quezon and had enjoyed rapport with, and the support of, society's elite. From 1935, when he accepted Quezon's offer to build the Philippine army, until the outbreak of the war in 1941, the general and his wife lived in a magnificent penthouse with seven air-conditioned rooms at the luxurious Manila Hotel, fronting Manila Bay and near both the U.S. Embassy and the Army and Navy Club—a neat, roseate triangulation of a colonial world where most natives rarely intruded and then only to serve. The five-star accommodations were considered part of his compensation as a government employee; not only was he accorded the title Field Marshall by Quezon, he was also designated honorary General Manager of the hotel. Clearly, enjoying demigod status, MacArthur was not about to bite the hand that had fed him so well while in the Philippines.

To insure the passage of laws meant to preserve the U.S.-favored role in the Philippines, Roxas and the Liberal Party needed to undermine if not sideline the opposition in both chambers of Congress. The Nacionalista Party, having been weakened by Roxas's defection, had joined forces with the Democratic Alliance, an anti-collaboration party and among whose leaders were Communists. While the elections went to the

Liberals, six Alliance candidates were elected to the House of Representatives. In the Senate three were known to oppose the proposed bills.

Before the elected Congress in 1946 were the Philippine Rehabilitation Act (PRA) and the Philippine Trade Act (PTA). The PRA set limits on compensation. The estimated cost of restoration was P8 billion, or $4 billion. Of this, the PRA would provide a total of $1.24 billion, broken down into $620 million to compensate for war-related damages; $100 million worth of army surplus and construction equipment; $120 million for infrastructure and public buildings; and $400 million for individuals and businesses that could document losses due to the war.

There would also be $200 million for the Philippine Army but with the proviso that benefits for the 200,000 Filipinos who had fought with the U.S. forces against the Japanese be withdrawn—benefits that had been promised by President Franklin Roosevelt in 1941. The Rescission Act of 1946, signed into law by President Harry Truman, stipulated that Filipino veterans who had served the U.S. military, either in their capacity as regulars in the Philippine commonwealth army or as guerrillas in units recognized by the U.S. military, should not be deemed to have been in active military, naval, or air service for the purposes of any law of the United States conferring rights, privileges, or benefits upon any person by reason of such service. Of all the countries allied with the United States during the war, only Filipino veterans were denied these benefits. (In 2009, this injustice was partly rectified when the American Recovery and Reinvestment Act provided a lump sum of $15,000 for veterans who were U.S. citizens, and $9,000 for non-U.S. citizens. More than sixty years after the war, the number of survivors had dwindled to 15,000.)

The PTA, also known as the Bell Trade Act, guaranteed duty-free exports to the U.S. for eight years, after which tariffs would be imposed on a gradual scale until 1974, when Philippine exports would be subject to full tariffs. The PTA also restricted the Philippines from manufacturing goods that could compete with those made in the United States, thus providing U.S. imports an unfair advantage, and stifling the incentive to industrialize. The bill's most blatantly exploitative provision, however, was, the infamous "Parity" provision, which extended to U.S. investors the same rights that Filipino citizens had to develop the country's resources and to operate public utility companies. Such a provision ran counter to the Constitutional requirement that sixty percent of corporations formed to develop these natural resources had to be owned by Filipinos. This meant that in reserved areas U.S. citizens could have ownership up to 100 percent, whereas other foreign nationals were limited to 40 percent—effectively discouraging foreign investment that was not American. The 1935 Constitution needed to be amended, a process that had to be approved by a majority vote in the legislature. It was made clear to the Roxas administration that this arrangement was a condition for rehabilitation aid. In turn, to make sure that the bills were passed, the Roxas administration through the Liberal Party-dominated Congress refused to seat seven representatives from Central Luzon, and three senators, all of whom had spoken out against parity.

The Roxas government drummed up false charges against these legislators, claiming that they had won their respective electoral contests fraudulently and through violence, sidestepping the Electoral Tribunal created precisely to handle these kinds of cases. Even with the purge, however, the amendment to the Constitution barely passed, by a plurality of one vote.

One of those denied his seat, pending the outcome of investigation into the charges (eventually dismissed), was Senator Ramon Diokno, who had been one of Quezon's chief campaign strategists. He had this to say:

This continuance of American control, however, could not have been achieved without the solicitous assistance of the Filipinos that now rule our country. The Roxas government, which is headed by collaborators, obviously felt that it could not survive unless it accepted the Trade Act in order to open the way for American financial and military aid. It needed money not only for material rehabilitation, but for the maintenance of an expensive governmental system. . . . The Roxas government chose to sacrifice Philippine independence for the sake of the advantage to be gained from American political and military support. This decision was not surprising, inasmuch as these were the same Filipinos that had worked readily with the Japanese, and that would have been removed from political and economic influence if President Roosevelt's directive against collaborators had been carried out. Manuel Roxas himself violated his oath as General in the United States Army by advising puppet-president José Laurel to declare war against the United States and its Allies during the Japanese occupation.

Luis Taruc, the Huk commander-in-chief of the Hukbalahap, was one of the congressmen unseated. From a peasant family in Pampanga, Taruc dropped out of college and, influenced by the increasing radicalism of the peasantry, joined the PKP at the age of twenty-two. He distinguished himself during the war as a guerrilla fighter against the Japanese. The response of the Huks to this latest drawback was rebellion, met by a crackdown by the Roxas regime. The Huks were able to reorganize easily, and win support. The movement was concentrated mainly in Central Luzon, though it had pockets of support in the Southern Tagalog regions and on Panay Island in the Visayas. The Huks, forged in the crucible of the war and buoyed by the successful 1949 Chinese Communist victory, emerged as a serious threat to Manila. They had proven to be a formidable foe of the Japanese, engaging them in 1,200 conflicts and killing approximately 25,000 enemy soldiers and those Filipinos believed to have collaborated with them. By war's end, armed Huks numbered 20,000, with 50,000 in reserve. The thought of a pro-Soviet, pro-China Malacañang induced sleepless nights in Washington, moving it to interfere.

During the war, the Huks had raised the political consciousness of the peasants even as they positioned themselves in Central Luzon. By 1944, the Huks controlled significant areas of Central Luzon, anticipating a possible modus vivendi with the American-controlled Commonwealth government once the war was over. But the U.S. Army's Counter-Intelligence Corps (CIC), in tandem with the Philippine Civil Affairs Unit (PCAU), had other ideas, replacing the Huks with pro-American individuals, often drawn from USAFFE-led guerrilla groups and from the more conservative, upper class echelons of the local society, even if many of the latter had served the Japanese. Thus, where the Huks and their supporters had been instrumental in fighting Japanese rule, they were excluded. They were disarmed as well, and often their leaders arrested and the BUDCs dismantled. In at least one case, members of a Huk unit were simply executed.

The hardening of ideological lines reflected Cold War realities, with pro-U.S. forces displaying an unremitting hostility towards any group professing Communist beliefs. After the war, Taruc and Casto Alejandrino, one of the founders of the Hukbalahap, had been imprisoned briefly by the U.S. military at the Iwahig Penal Colony on Palawan Island. The Solicitor General at the time, however, Lorenzo Tanada (later to become a prominent senator), found no basis for their detention, and the two were released.

The Roxas government instituted an all-out campaign of military suppression against the PKP and the Huk veterans. For a while, Roxas attempted a pacification campaign, sending out mixed signals, but in the end, demanding that the Huks surrender all their arms. In a last-ditch effort, the Huk and PKP organizations responded with a memo to the president urging that all steps be taken to forge a peaceful resolution, asking, among other things, that private armies—landlord-sponsored and financed, and often the flashpoint of physical confrontations—be disbanded, all charges against the Huks for initiatives taken during the war be dismissed, that the Democratic Alliance congressmen be allowed their seats in Congress, and that civil liberties be restored.

The government's response was to increase militarization of Central Luzon. Secret orders were issued for the arrest of Huk top leaders. Warnings went out to them, but failed to reach one influential peasant leader, Juan Feleo, who was abducted by men in Military Police uniforms and subsequently murdered. The Huks responded by reconstituting their armed squadrons and renaming themselves the *Hukbong Magpalaya ng Bayan* (HMB), or People's Liberation Army. They engaged both the Military Police and private armies when barrios were raided. Veterans of the war against the Japanese and with a tested organizational structure, the Huks usually got the better of government forces.

The Huks renewed the peasantry's struggle over social issues such as land reform, health care, and decent wages. Initially hesitant to support the Huks—it believed the revolution would begin in the cities—the PKP saw in this agrarian uprising a golden opportunity to seize state power. Thus the revocation of the parity amendment and the withdrawal of American military bases were added to the Huk agenda. Both the Huks and the PKP leadership saw how fruitless parliamentary struggle had been. With a restive, disillusioned peasant population of close to two million in Central Luzon, the Huks numbered twelve to fifteen thousand armed fighters.

These developments were worrisome not just to Manila but to Washington. Under the 1947 Military Assistance Pact, and through the Joint U.S. Military Advisory Group (JUSMAG), an anti-Huk counterinsurgency campaign was put into place. Roxas died suddenly on April 15, 1948, and Elpidio Quirino took over the presidency.

The Odd Couple

Quirino granted amnesty to the Huks, but faulty implementation led to its failure. The insurgency resumed. Pressured by the U.S. military and the ambassador, Quirino appointed a young congressman, Ramón Magsaysay, to the post of Secretary of National Defense. Against the backdrop of the Cold War, fearful that the Philippines—a country that the U.S. had touted as its showcase of democracy in Asia—might turn Communist, as had China in 1949, the U.S. government through the CIA took an increasingly active role in the counterinsurgency tactics of the AFP. In August Truman had recommended an increase in aid to the Philippines as well as to Southeast Asia, to combat Communist influence and aggression, specifically during the Korean War. Thus, aid in 1951 was four times that of the previous year.

Instrumental in setting up the military programs, including psychological war operations, was Air Force Colonel Edward Lansdale, a former advertising executive and now CIA covert operations specialist—and the model for Alden Pyle, the young American diplomat in Graham Greene's *The Quiet American*, as well as Colonel Hillandale in William Lederer and Eugene Burdick's *The Ugly American*. Shortly after Magsaysay's appointment, Lansdale arrived in Manila and promptly orchestrated the anti-Huk campaign, living out of a suitcase at the defense headquarters, and calling the defense chief "brother"—his younger one, clearly.

Under Lansdale's tutelage, Magsaysay revitalized the Armed Forces of the Philippines, weeding out corrupt and abusive personnel and instilling a sense of professionalism in the ranks. The tasks he and his soldiers faced were formidable. The Huks were popular not simply because they were themselves farmers and peasants but because they had taken steps to remedy social inequities. They provided rudimentary but strict and consistent governance, where none had existed. To the disaffected rural poor, the government in distant Manila seemed to care for them only during elections, when for a brief moment the common *tao* was king and queen. To counter this and no doubt drawing from his advertising expertise, Lansdale put into practice a "hearts-and-minds" strategy, wherein government programs for the welfare of the peasantry were put into place, court cases speeded up, and army units undertook such projects as digging for artesian wells and extending medical care.

Too, Magsaysay often accompanied the troops on their missions, whether in combat or to visit a remote barrio. He and Lansdale made sure these forays were covered by the media, so that every photograph of the Secretary of Defense presiding over the surrender of Huks was a particularly effective bullet in the propaganda war, transforming Magsaysay into the common man's hero. In addition, part of the counterinsurgency success was the government offer of land in Mindanao for the landless Huk fighter. From 1954 to 1963, the government resettled 20,500 families of the Huks—a resettlement program that decades later would contribute to the conflict between the indigenous Muslim and non-Muslim tribes on one hand, and, on the other, descendants of the original Christian settlers over land rights.

One effective psychological warfare and counterinsurgency tactic Lansdale pioneered was to employ traditional beliefs in *aswang*, or vampires, to scare the Huks and their peasant sympathizers. Army patrols would ambush a Huk and, through two puncture marks in his neck, drain the corpse of blood, leaving it on a trail. Fellow Huks or villagers discovering the body would then steer clear of the area, fearing the presence of *aswang*. *New York Times* correspondent Raymond Bonner, in his book on the Marcos regime, *Waltzing with a Dictator*, describes how "Lansdale concocted his 'eye of God' scheme, which he had borrowed from the ancient Egyptian practice of painting watchful eyes on the tombs of pharaohs to scare away would-be plunderers. Lansdale made a sketch of these eyes, and at night members of his team would slip into villages and paint them on a wall facing the house of a suspected Huk." Other psychological-war tactics included flying airplanes above the clouds over Huk-controlled areas, with broadcasts in native languages to make the villagers believe they were hearing directly from the spirit world; and spreading rumors about the presence of *aswang* in the area.

The combination of psychological warfare, hearts-and-minds programs, and old-fashioned military operations proved to be highly effective, setting the prototype for future counterinsurgency wars, most notably in Vietnam, but also in Latin America. U.S. involvement in Vietnam in all likelihood would have been radically different without this earlier intervention in the Philippines. The success in breaking the back of the Huk insurgency, though, was as much Magsaysay's doing as the CIA's. He had become the humane face of the anti-Huk program, a veteran guerrilla fighter who in his interactions with the rural folk lent a sympathetic ear to their too-common tales of high rents and landlord abuse, making free legal services available to them. According to a former Huk fighter, Alfredo B. Saulo, Magsaysay was aided tremendously when "Tarcisio Rizal, alias Arthur, a grandson of the national hero and disenchanted Huk commander, approached Magsaysay and gave him vital information on the whereabouts of the CPP [Communist Party of the Philippines] hierarchy in Manila." The information led to the arrest of many of the top leaders of the insurgency, dealing the Huks a severe blow from which they never recovered. Many of the guerrillas simply resumed their lives, and a significant number accepted the government's offer of land in Mindanao and Palawan.

With the backing of Washington, Magsaysay decided to seek the presidency. Lansdale and his CIA colleagues managed the campaign—from behind the scenes, of course. One of the CIA operatives helping in the campaign and occasionally writing Magsaysay's speeches was David Sternberg, whose cover was as the correspondent for the *Christian Science Monitor*. Magsaysay defected from the Quirino-led Liberal Party to the Nacionalistas in 1952, along with Carlos P. Garcia, a congressman from the island of Bohol as his vice presidential mate. In the campaign against President Quirino, the Magsaysay camp relied on the catchy motto, "Magsaysay Is My Guy." This could have very well referred to Lansdale's control over the former Defense Secretary's candidacy, including the writing of his speeches by CIA operatives. Lansdale made sure that cash flowed in not only from Langley, Virginia, but from American expatriates in the Philippines. Magsaysay, too, had become their guy.

Magsaysay won the presidency handily. He had put to good use his experience as Defense Secretary. Unlike the politicians of the old ilustrado order, of which Quirino was a member, Magsaysay conducted a vigorous grass-roots campaign, visiting more barrios and sitios than other politicians. He dressed simply, ate with his hands when eating with the local folk, and tried to project the persona of a common *tao*. This was in stark contrast with Quirino, who favored white suits—appealing perhaps to the urban and moneyed classes but not to the countryside, where the vast majority of the population lived.

During his term, the third president of the Republic struck a populist tone, declaring that "bare feet will always be welcome at the president's palace." At the same time, he was still very much Washington's guy. He was instrumental in the formation of the Southeast Asia Treaty Organization. Also known as the Manila Pact, since it was first drafted there in September of 1954, SEATO was formally established in Bangkok the next year, where its headquarters were to be located. Meant primarily as an anti-Communist organization and part of the Cold War geopolitical strategy of containment, SEATO had eight members: the Philippines, Thailand, Pakistan, the United States, France, the United Kingdom, Australia, and New Zealand. The organization included Western powers who were not coincidentally former colonial powers, to signal its internationalization. Pakistan,while strictly speaking, not part of Southeast Asia, linked SEATO member states to CENTO, or the Central Treaty Organization, another anti-Communist body. SEATO was largely ineffective, as unanimity was required for it to intervene in any of its member countries and an attack on one was not automatically considered an attack on all. This would prove to be frustrating when the United States got increasingly involved in a ground war in Vietnam. The organization was finally dissolved in 1977, its relevance long gone when the Association of Southeast Asian Nations (ASEAN) was formed in 1967. Formed originally by Indonesia, Malaysia, the Philippines, Singapore, and Thailand, and later on admitting five other Southeast Asian countries, the organization has no Western nation members. Some of its aims are to foster economic growth, promote peace and stability in the region, and encourage cultural development.

Partly as unofficial representative of the United States and partly out of self-interest, the Philippines participated in the 1955 Bandung Conference of Afro-Asian states held in Bandung, Indonesia. The conference brought together nations newly independent from colonial shackles, desirous of seeking a third way or neutrality, and in many instances, hostile to the U.S. but also wary of the Soviet Union. The conference aimed to cultivate economic and cultural ties between the attending states, and to resist any colonial or neocolonial policies the superpowers and their allies might seek to impose on them. The Philippines was one of the few in attendance that viewed the United States in a positive light.

During the Magsaysay administration the Philippine Trade Act of 1946 was revised via the Laurel Langley Agreement of 1955. This new legislation eliminated some of the more odious language that demeaned Philippine sovereignty, though this was more style than substance. In force for the next two decades, the agreement still protected U.S. investments in the former colony but now extended the same degree of reciprocity to those Filipinos wishing to invest in the United States. Considering the huge disparities in capital available respectively to U.S. citizens and to Filipinos, this was akin to what Anatole France once said about pre-Revolutionary France's Legislation: "The law in its majestic equality forbids the rich as well as the poor to sleep under bridges and to steal bread." As a sop to the sugar barons who were an influential bloc in the Philippine Congress, the U.S. agreed to pay higher prices for their sugar than could be had on the international market, thus providing a tremendous windfall for the sugar planters.

Because of Lansdale and the CIA's influence on Magsaysay—the president had appointed his mentor as military adviser—U.S. programs directed at other Southeast Asian countries could be run through a pliant Philippine government, which would provide legitimate cover. In the 1950s the situation in French Indochina—Vietnam, Cambodia, and Laos—in particular, the Communist insurgency led by Ho Chi Minh, worried the United States. In 1954 Lansdale (now stationed in Saigon as an adviser to the South Vietnamese president Ngo Dinh Diem) set up the Freedom Company of the Philippines, through which Filipino personnel were sent to South Vietnam to help the regime. Magsaysay was the company's honorary president. Under cover of a public service organization and having a contract with the host government, Filipinos (and the CIA) assisted Diem's government, at one point training his Presidential Guard Battalion, and ran the huge Operation Brotherhood activity.

The latter began as a humanitarian, largely Philippine, project in 1954, thought of by the Philippine Jaycees to alleviate the miserable conditions of refugees fleeing North Vietnam into South Vietnam. Operation Brotherhood functioned in Vietnam for two years, primarily through medical missions, then moved its operations to Laos at the end of 1956. Operation Brotherhood was yet another plausible cover to operate against the Communists and assist the Diem regime. It was only in Vietnam where Filipinos worked successfully. In the rest of Southeast Asia, they were perceived as being too pro-American, and their very presence in Vietnam seemed to confirm this.

Confident in the friendship of Magsaysay, the U.S. didn't shy away from the use of U.S. bases in the 1950s, for covert operations against perceived anti-U.S., pro-Communist forces not just within the Philippines—the anti-Huk campaign being the most well-known—but in Southeast Asia as well. Civil Air Transport, for instance, was an airline owned by the CIA that flew out of Clark Air Base to ferry support to Indonesian right-wing army officers in their failed attempt in the late 1950s to unseat President Sukarno, a key architect of the nonaligned movement among Third World countries and one of the principal organizers of the Bandung Conference.

Magsaysay's presidency was cut short when, on March 17, 1957, he died in a plane crash, returning from Cebu City to Manila. An estimated two million mourners paid their respects to the dead president as his funeral procession wound its way through Manila. His death caused no small amount of confusion, as Magsaysay's personal support and popularity had made various clandestine and not-so-clandestine activities possible, from the formation of SEATO to covert programs in Vietnam and Indonesia, all justified by the ongoing project to convert the former colony into America's much touted showcase of democracy.

Magsaysay's vice president, Carlos P. García, took over for the remainder of Magsaysay's term and went on to win the presidential elections the next year, 1958. His vice president was Diosdado Macapagal, from the province of Pampanga in Central Luzon.

Another Odd Couple

The presidential contest to succeed Magsaysay was a four-man affair: Carlos P. García, a Nacionalista who as vice president, had taken over the presidency; Manuel Manahan, former customs commissioner and a Magsaysay follower; José Yulo, from the Liberal Party; and Senator Claro M. Recto, the head of the Convention that had drafted the 1935 Constitution. The last was the U.S.'s bete noire. Recto was an outspoken nationalist who had served in the pre-war commonwealth government and had become increasingly disillusioned by what he felt was unwarranted U.S. involvement. He advocated a foreign policy that distanced itself from that of the United States. Thus, he felt it was in the best interests of the country to deal with China even if it had gone Communist—heretical thinking as far as the United States was concerned that viewed Mao Tse-tung, an ally of the Soviet Union, as a major ideological enemy. The Korean War was a reminder that Mao's Red Army was willing to mix it up with the U.S. and hold its own.

But most galling to the United States government was Recto's stand against the continued presence of U.S. military bases on Philippine territory. In 1956, Recto wrote that "by granting America extra-territorial rights in the bases, we surrendered to her the power, the jurisdiction, and the sovereignty of the Republic over portions of the national territory whose integrity is guaranteed by . . . the Constitution. So the Agreement, instead of insuring our territorial integrity accomplished the very opposite." U.S. strategy had always been to emphasize the bases as a contribution to Philippine defense. Recto's stance skewered this position.

In 1957 he emphasized that even American commentators highlighted the use of the bases in the Philippines as a diversion for enemy attacks, especially a nuclear one, that would spare the lives of Americans in the United States. He cited one Hanson Baldwin, an expert on the U.S. military who wrote regularly for *The New York Times*, who believed, according to Recto, that "the role of U.S. overseas bases in the world—bases in the Philippines are among them—is to 'act as magnets for enemy attacks, thus dispersing and weakening his threat to our [United States] cities and fixed installations.'" Recto had only to point to Japan's invasion of the Philippines in 1941 as proof of this fatal attraction.

Recto saw first-hand how Magsaysay's feeling of indebtedness to Washington had influenced Philippine government policy. It was a classic example of *utang na loob*, a social quality, deemed a virtue, whereby a man who had benefited significantly from a patron's intervention was forever in that patron's debt. In Magsaysay's case, he felt beholden to Lansdale and the U.S. for his success in quelling the Huk rebellion and in winning Malacañang. Too, it helped that Magsaysay himself was staunchly anti-Communist.

Recto had broken completely with the popular president and formed the Nationalist Citizens Party. His increasingly nationalist stance worried the CIA. Its operatives blanched at the possibility that a Recto victory would result in Manila dealing openly with Mao's China. The NCP lacked funds, however, and a smooth electoral machinery. The two dominant parties, the LP and the NP, colluded to deny it election inspectors. The conservative Catholic hierarchy had no love for Recto either, as he had in 1955 championed the compulsory reading and teaching in colleges and universities of José Rizal's anticlerical novels. His Rizal bill, as it was known, passed, but exempted students who had religious objections from reading the novels. The proviso in effect enabled Catholic educational institutions (and they were, as in the Spanish colonial era, the dominant force in private education) to simply not include the books on the curriculum, even if there were students who may have wanted to study the life and works of the national hero.

As to be expected, the CIA used its bag of dirty tricks against Recto, and had him labeled as a Communist dupe. According to J. Burckholder Smith, a CIA operative in Manila at the time, the agency spread the word that Recto was "a Chinese communist stooge, an agent infiltrated into the Philippine Senate (shades of Senator Joe McCarthy)." Smith further states that "he had been subjected to various dirty tricks. As I went through the files, I found something that absolutely astounded me. I saw a sealed envelope marked 'Recto Campaign.' I opened it and found it filled with condoms, marked 'courtesy of Claro M. Recto—the People's Friend.' The condoms all had holes in them at the place they could least afford to have them. I tried to find out what purpose the condoms had been supposed to serve. The best I could do was to learn that they were distributed to show how Recto would let you down."

Unlike the condoms, the CIA didn't fail. And so Claro M. Recto, garnering barely 400,000 ballots, lost the presidential election to García. What aided García as well was the fact that, including Recto, three rivals had split the opposition vote.

Relatively unknown, García had been a guerrilla during the war in Bohol, his home province, though he belonged to a unit independent of the USAFFE. Not particularly identified with U.S. interests, unlike Roxas and Magsaysay, García had opposed the Bell Trade Act and the Military

Bases Agreement. As chief executive of the land, this diminutive man proved more independent of U.S. thinking than the late, burly Magsaysay. He proposed re-examining the bases agreement, created a foreign-exchange reserve not wholly reliant on the almighty dollar, and was ready to assume a neutralist stance towards Southeast Asia and the rest of the world.

Most shockingly to those American hands and seasoned politicians who expected residents in Malacañang to be unswervingly loyal to the U.S., he drew up a Filipino First policy. As promulgated by the government National Economic Council, it was a policy "of the government to encourage Filipinos to engage in enterprises and industries vital to economic growth, stability, and security of the country," giving special attention to businesses that might in fact be controlled by non-Filipinos. The policy also laid down stringent rules on the allocation of foreign exchange, favoring Filipinos or corporations that were at least sixty percent controlled by Filipinos.

As to be expected, U.S. and pro-U.S. sectors denounced the Filipino First policy. The U.S. Chamber of Commerce, through its publication, described the program as "nothing less than insane," with "measureless loss and waste, retrogression, and demoralization." A February 27, 1959, issue of the U.S. News and World Report depicted it as "extreme nationalism," going on to say that what the program intended to do was inseparable "from what the Communists say and want."

Even more disturbing to the pro-U.S. sectors was the coalition between García's NP and his former rival for the presidency, Recto and his NCP, gearing up for the 1959 senatorial elections. A mass organization had also sprung up, the National Progress Movement, which aimed to generate support for a nationalist-oriented government, towards which the retention of García was deemed necessary. The NPM ascribed to the sizeable alien communities (Chinese and American) in Philippine society the root causes of "graft corruption in the government and ultimately, in the entire society," for these aliens sought to buy off government authorities and thus extend their influence. The NPM came down particularly hard on Filipinos working to advance foreign interests, describing them as "parasites who feed without contributing to their own national community, its culture and the civilization it may yet attain."

The García and Recto coalition as well as the NPM in effect turned a critical eye on the neocolonial legacies of U.S. rule. Filipinization echoed the earlier policies of the colonial-era William Howard Taft, ironically enough, but this time carried to its logical conclusion: adoption of nationalist programs as envisioned by the Filipino First policy; elimination of the parity amendment to the Constitution; an independent foreign policy; and industrialization. The 1959 elections saw the defeat of former Magsaysay men and pro-U.S. adherents, and the victories of more independent legislators, including the former Solicitor General Lorenzo Tañada.

Emboldened by the 1959 electoral results, President García declared in a major speech in 1960 that the control of the economy by aliens "makes a mockery of our independence and robs it of substance and meaning." It was necessary, therefore, "that Filipinos acquire a major and dominant participation in the national economy of the Philippines." At the same time, he stressed that his government's economic policies were not anti-American, that they were "simply an honest-to-goodness effort of the Filipino people to be masters in their own economic household for exactly the same reason that Americans would be masters of the U.S. national economy . . . In this country there is still room for foreign capital, especially in fields where Filipino capital is deficient or timid."

And what were the results of the Filipino First policy? For one thing, the policy enabled Filipinos to secure 51 percent of foreign exchange allocations by the end of 1959. It liberalized government credit to new Filipino businesses, resulting in fresh infusions of capital into the industrial sector. In December 1959 only 55 percent of new investments were Filipino; by 1961 the figure had jumped to 88 percent.

In the industrial sector, a significant development came with the creation of the Filipino Oil Refining Company in 1959, challenging the dominance of U.S. and other foreign oil companies. There was the Iligan Integrated Steel Mill, Inc., a $1 billion venture, the first stage of a full-fledged Philippine steel industry, which began loan negotiations with the World Bank, the U.S. Export-Import Bank, and other lending institutions. Iligan represented a partnership of government and private Filipino capital and exemplified the García's administration's industrialization policies. In 1960, the Manila Electric Company, or Meralco, a

U.S. owned company founded in 1903, was acquired by a financial group headed by the López family for $66 million. All these developments seemed to augur well for full-scale industrialization.

For the 1961 elections a García-Recto ticket loomed as a real possibility—and a perceived threat to pro-U.S. interests. Claro M. Recto died in Rome, however, of a heart attack on October 2, 1960, leaving the nationalist movement bereft of its leading intellectual and political voice. Not surprisingly, the opposition to García swung behind his vice president Diosdado Macapagal of the Liberal Party. Macapagal, along with the Grand Alliance ticket, whose slate had been defeated in 1959, campaigned on issues such as corruption; the necessity of maintaining an anti-Communist stance (which the nationalist Filipino First was thought to have hurt); development of free and private enterprise; and minimal government interference in the private sector, or the adoption of essentially neo-liberal laissez-faire economic policies. The issue of strict controls over foreign exchange allocations proved damaging to García, for it was one the Macapagal camp exploited, charging the government with using controls as a means of patronage. With Recto no longer on the scene to insist on a strictly nationalist orientation, the García campaign declared that it would gradually ease controls—a concession to free marketers.

Macapagal's campaign team also utilized their candidate's impoverished background as a selling point. He was the "poor boy from Lubao," a small town from Pampanga, the Central Luzon province. He managed to attend law school, and topped the bar exams in 1936. He went on to serve as legal assistant to Quezon. After the war, having served two terms in the House of Representatives, in 1957 he ran as the vice presidential candidate of José Yulo on a ticket that opposed García. Yulo lost to García, but Macapagal won. (In the Philippine electoral system, the vice president is voted in independently of the president.) In contrast García, who had acquired a reputation for poetry as a young man, came from the gentry of Bohol, where his father had served as mayor of their town for four terms.

Macapagal and his running mate Emmanuel Pelaez won the 1961 elections by a substantial margin. President Macapagal immediately signaled his administration's commitment to free enterprise. One of his first acts was to implement decontrol of foreign-exchange allocations and of imports. The government had previously with varying degrees of success attempted to minimize the squandering of dollar reserves by requiring the purchase of a license with which to purchase dollars and thus ship in imports. An inevitable result was a black market in the sale and purchase of such licenses, enabling many, in and out of government, to illicitly amass considerable wealth through the disparity in the official and unofficial exchange rates. With easy money to be made, not much energy was channeled towards setting up new industries. Corruption thus became a potent issue with which Macapagal hammered García during their electoral contest.

On the advice of his cabinet, Macapagal adopted neo-liberal economic policies, and decided to let the peso float, which had until then been pegged at a two-to-one ratio to the dollar. With the new policy, the peso's value dropped to P3.90 to the dollar. Liberalizing trade meant easing or eliminating protectionist measures, resulting in a sharp increase in the shipment of U.S. goods to the country and a corresponding decline in the sales of their counterpart Philippine products. While the devaluation of the peso meant that prices for U.S. products—which were prized, "Stateside" being a mark of approval—increased, it also meant that those domestic industries that had imported equipment and contracted foreign loans now saw their operating costs and more significantly their capital obligations practically double. In addition, the facilitating of credit to local industry, which the García administration allowed, was curbed. As a result, squeezed on both ends, as many as 1,500 Filipino industries that had sprung up because of García's Filipino First policies were driven out of business during Macapagal's tenure, or were absorbed by larger companies, many of these having substantial U.S. investments. The devaluation of the peso inevitably made investment in the Philippines more attractive to foreign capital.

Another unwanted consequence of decontrol, from the point of view of local industry, was the easier repatriation of profits of U.S. companies once restricted under exchange controls. With dollars flowing out, and imports flowing in, the country's foreign reserves declined. To alleviate this, the government began to increase its foreign debt. At the end of García's term, the country's foreign debt stood at a completely manageable $200 million. In 1962, in its first year in office, the Macapagal administration sought and got approved a $300 million loan from the World Bank, the International Monetary Fund, and the U.S. Treasury. Going into Ferdinand Marcos's tenure, by 1972 the country's external debt stood at $2 billion. Macapagal had set a pattern of borrowing that has been followed ever since, essentially adhering to the free-market policies of international lending agencies that encouraged foreign investment by lifting controls, tightening credit, allowing the local currency to float, and reducing spending on social programs.

President Macapagal attempted to address the age-old issue of land reform, getting Congress to enact in 1963 the Agricultural Land Reform Code. It was an ambitious law that sought to abolish sharecropping tenancy, and carve out of large estates smaller family-size farms. The law promised to provide a wide variety of government technical and credit assistance to the beneficiaries of the reform. But a landlord-dominated Congress attached so many conditions and exemptions that beyond reorganizing a number of agencies and redefining their functions so as to streamline their operations, this law achieved little in the way of meaningful change.

In the first half of the 1960s, coincident with the Macapagal administration, nationalism continued to build steam even as government policies reflected the old-order accommodation with the United States. Macapagal was savvy enough to recognize this, and in recognition of the country's revolutionary past, he declared Independence Day June 12—when Aguinaldo in 1898 had proclaimed the independence of the country—rather than the previously designated American-inspired July 4. The latter date was then designated as Philippine-American Friendship Day. There were some grumbles from staunchly pro-American sectors but no serious complaints, as the change, while an important symbolic concession to nationalist sentiment, affected neither the economic nor political arena.

One of the slogans the Macapagal administration touted was for the citizenry to complete the "Unfinished Revolution"—a clear reference to the Bonifacio-led 1896 Katipunan Revolution. As the 1960s wore on, there was a growing awareness as well as critique of how colonial legacies had shaped the cultural landscape, from education and pop culture to the way history had been written and the use of English as the dominant language of national discourse in education, politics, the arts, and the media. The rebelliousness of the decade would be expressed vigorously and dramatically in the latter half, during the tenure of the next president, Ferdinand E. Marcos.

FERDINAND MARCOS: BEFORE MARTIAL LAW

Born on September 11, 1917, in Sarrat Town, Ilocos Norte Province, Ferdinand Edralin Marcos may never have had a political career had he not been able to beat a murder rap against him. The murder victim was Julio Nalundasan, a political rival of his father who had just won the congressional election for the district. He was shot to death one night in 1935, with a .22 caliber bullet. The young Marcos, known to be a member of the University of the Philippines pistol team, came under heavy suspicion. Three years later, in 1938, he was arrested, jailed, and subsequently convicted. By then, Marcos had graduated from the University of the Philippines law school. On appeal—which Marcos wrote in his cell—the Supreme Court overturned the lower court decision in 1940, the same year the future dictator topped the bar. The chief justice was José P. Laurel who would in a little more than two years head the government under Japanese occupation.

After the war, in which he claimed to have led a crack guerrilla unit that scored numerous successes against the Japanese, Marcos had a short stint as a practicing lawyer. He then ran for and won a seat in the House of Representatives in 1949. After two successive terms, he campaigned for the Senate as a Liberal Party candidate in 1959, and managed Macapagal's run for the presidency of the country. By then he had been married to Imelda Romualdez, a statuesque former beauty pageant queen from Tacloban City, capital of the Visayan island of Leyte.

Imelda had gone to Manila in 1953 at the age of twenty-four to stay with her wealthier city cousins and seek some kind of gainful employment. While visiting Congress in 1954—her uncle was then speaker of the house—she met Ferdinand Marcos in the cafeteria. After a whirlwind courtship that lasted all of ten days, the two were married at Manila Cathedral. Initially, Imelda had difficulty in the role of a well-known politician's wife, with its unceasing demands for public appearances with her husband and so little time for herself and her family. At one point, the young and inexperienced Imelda suffered a nervous breakdown and sought treatment in New York City. The treatment was apparently successful, perhaps too successful: she returned to Manila, having made up her mind to fully accept her role as a public figure and the varied and exhausting obligations that came with it. As she grew accustomed to being in the public gaze, and as her husband climbed all the way to the top, she developed sharp political instincts that enabled her to become a powerful player in her own right.

Imelda proved to be a tremendous asset to Ferdinand's campaign for the presidency, for which, in a now time-honored though dubious practice, the ambitious senator switched from the Liberal Party—Macapagal, its head, was running for reelection—to the Nacionalistas. The youthful and glamorous Imelda made most other politicians' wives look positively dowdy. Putting to use her beauty pageant experience, she was soon wowing crowds with her charm and earnest singing, often in duets with her husband. A huge feature of the hustings in Philippine politics is entertaining the crowds that gather to hear different candidates make their pitches. The *palabas*, as these spectacles are known, regularly feature movie and media celebrities, and a candidate who can add some showbiz to his or her oratorical skills is almost sure to win more votes.

The lady from Leyte proved to be a charmer offstage as well. Needing a vice presidential candidate, Marcos had approached Fernando López, the sugar baron and media mogul and one of the richest men in the country. His bailiwick was the Visayas, where Imelda was from. Initially reluctant to be on the Marcos team, he was sweet-talked into it by Imelda. The Marcos-López combination proved to be a winner, and in December of 1965, both men were sworn into office.

Hailed as the Jackie Kennedy of Asia by the Western press, Imelda held considerable cachet with the public, and this was flamboyantly demonstrated in 1966, when the Beatles flew to Manila for a two-concert stopover on July 3, 1966. The next day, July 4, they were scheduled to perform at the open-air Rizal Memorial Stadium. The Fab Four had been invited to Malacañang to have an early lunch before the first concert with Imelda, along with three hundred schoolchildren. There was a mix-up in communications, and the quartet slept through the appointed hour, blissfully unaware that they had disappointed not just the First Lady but a whole bevy of pre-teen Beatles' fans. Word got around about the alleged snub. Departing the next day for New Delhi, the band and their entourage were manhandled as well as booed by outraged crowds. The unfortunate incident would prompt George Harrison to remark that if he were ever to return to Manila, it would be to drop an atomic bomb.

While the country had a highly trained English-speaking professional workforce, there simply weren't enough jobs to keep pace with the influx of graduates that every year flooded the labor market. Coupled with a growing population, chronic bureaucratic inefficiency and endemic government corruption, the Marcos government faced formidable challenges in revitalizing an ailing economy. In his inaugural address, Marcos acknowledged the challenges the country faced, stating, "We have ceased to value order. Government is gripping the iron hand of venality, its treasury is barren, its resources are wasted, its civil service is slothful and indifferent, its armed forces demoralized and its councils sterile." In the manner of John F. Kennedy, to whom he liked to be compared, he exhorted his compatriots to work with him and rise to the occasion: "Not one hero alone do I ask from you, but many— nay, all."

Marcos proved to be a shrewder bargainer than his predecessors when it came to dealing with the United States. Adopting a nationalist tone while maintaining client-state status with the United States, he used in-country U.S. military bases as a bargaining chip to secure more dollars, which his administration deemed rent but which the United States labeled "aid." United States involvement in Vietnam was escalating, and Subic Bay Naval Base and Clark Air Force Base were key staging points for that intervention, as they had been in other, earlier Asian conflicts. In 1966, after intense negotiations, the Lyndon B. Johnson administration and the Philippine government agreed to reduce the bases lease from 99 years to 25 years, to end in 1991 and thereafter be renegotiated.

The war in Vietnam was an economic shot-in-the-arm, at least in the short term, for the economy, particularly for the metropolitan areas in which Clark and Subic were located. Playing up his anti-Communist card, and trumpeting his devotion to democratic principles, Marcos was a master manipulator of U.S.-Philippine relations. Out of self-interest, Washington ignored the increasing levels of corruption, both personal and governmental, within the Marcos administration.

The legitimacy of Marcos's tenure, indeed, of the traditions of centralized political power in an oligarchy and the neocolonial relationship with the United States, was challenged by a dramatic increase in student activism globally along with a resurgence of radical left-wing movements. In particular, 1968 proved to be a watershed year in this respect, an indication of how far the energizing and liberating spirit of a counterculture had spread, one that used drugs regularly and for whom rock'n'roll was a religion. In Chicago, anti-war demonstrators at the Democratic Convention were brutalized by Mayor Richard Daley's cops. In New York City, students occupied Columbia University's administrative offices. Students rioted in Paris and in Prague defied Soviet tanks that rolled in to crush the stirrings of a nascent democratization known as the "Prague Spring." And on the birthday of Mao Tes-tung, December 26, 1968, a young University of the Philippines professor by the name of José Maria Sison founded the breakaway Communist Party of the Philippines in reaction to what he considered the outmoded Soviet-leaning PKP. (He and other student radicals from the University of the Philippines and Lyceum of the Philippines had been recruited in 1964 by a revived PKP.)

Sison, born in Ilocos Sur, was a 1959 graduate of the University of the Philippines and started teaching there as a literature professor. Active in student politics, he founded the radical student group, Kabataan Makabayan (KM), or Nationalist Youth, in 1964. The group organized protests against the Vietnam War as U.S. involvement in that Southeast Asian country was increasing. Its members also regularly demonstrated against Ferdinand Marcos's administration.

The new CPP identified with Mao's China rather than with the Soviet Union, Sison arguing that the Chinese model was closer to home. Not only were the Chinese fellow Asians, but the guerrilla strategy Mao advocated—that of surrounding the cities from the countryside—made tactical sense. Too, the Cultural Revolution, begun in 1966, inspired young left-wing ideologues with its aim of purging classist elements from society and renewing the commitment for the establishment of a proletarian dictatorship. Additionally, many Filipino student activists had visited the People's Republic of China and had forged relationships with the Chinese.

In March of 1969, Bernabe Buscayno, a young Huk guerrilla in Tarlac Province, Central Luzon, and his outfit, unhappy with the Huk leadership, joined forces with Sison to create the New People's Army. The son of dirt-poor tenant farmers whose widowed father had given him and his siblings up for adoption, Buscayno had been radicalized at a young age, and helped organize farm laborers. It wasn't a particularly auspicious beginning, as the twenty-five-year-old Buscayno, with the nom de guerre of Kumander Dante, and his band of about 35 fighters had between them only ten rifles. Nevertheless, the CPP/NPA grew, slowly at first and with painful and at times bloody birth pangs, but surely, through Luzon and the rest of the country—aided immeasurably in its growth by Ferdinand Marcos's declaration of martial law three years later, in 1972.

Nine months after the CPP was founded, in September of 1969, the Cultural Center of the Philippines (CCP) was inaugurated. It was Imelda's personal project—the first of many grandiose projects she would undertake in her long political career and for which she was sardonically said to have an "edifice complex." At the festive opening ceremonies, California Governor Ronald Reagan and his wife Nancy were Imelda's honored guests, beginning a special relationship that would immeasurably benefit the Marcoses during the martial-law era. Critics derided the Center as a waste of money in an impoverished country. The CCP cost $8.5 million—a huge sum in those days—with $3.5 million coming from the U.S. government, which classified the money as war damage claims.

Furthermore, Filipino intellectuals and artists believed the Center was designed to showcase the West rather than fulfill any home-grown aspirations. Indeed, the first months of programming featured internationally known groups like the London Philharmonic Orchestra and the New York Chamber Soloists. There were dance companies from India and operatic troupes from China and Japan. No matter: with the CCP, Imelda made it clear she was at the very least determined to be a national cultural force, a czarina of the arts.

In 1969, Ferdinand Marcos won reelection against Sergio Osmeña Jr., son of the former commonwealth president, thus becoming the first Filipino president to win a second term. However, his 2,000,000-vote margin of victory was glaringly and credibly suspicious. Marcos would probably have won in a by-the-rules contest, since Osmeña was a lackluster politician but in the hardball, no-quarter-given world of Philippine politics, the incumbent was expected to use every resource at his command to guarantee victory, even if it meant overkill. By all accounts, up to that point, the elections were the most corrupt and expensive, rendering government coffers practically bare and resulting in inflation. The results provoked widespread outrage, none more so than among students and workers. By then, Marcos had embarked on a self-mythologizing path, and it was through one such endeavor that student activists were able to get a measure of revenge.

Their instrument happened to be Dovie Beams, a barely known, C-List Hollywood actress who had been hired in 1968 to play the romantic lead on a biopic of Ferdinand Marcos, *Maharlika*. She wound up playing a real-life role as his mistress for two years—a role bigger than any she ever had on the silver screen. Tiring of her, Marcos broke off the relationship at the start of 1970. Imelda by this time had gotten wind of the affair and was furious at this betrayal. Beams, fearing for her life, placed herself under the protection of the U.S. Embassy. Unbeknownst to Marcos, she had tape recorded some of their amorous trysts, as the implications of her romantic entanglement became clear to her. She played some of the tapes at press conferences. Copies were surreptitiously made and leaked to the public. Student activists at the University of the Philippines got hold of a copy, one in which, according to a published account, the president is asking Beams to perform fellatio. The delighted students broadcast it in an endless loop over campus radio, much to the public embarrassment of the presidential family—and the ire of the First Lady. On November 11, 1970, Beams, escorted to the airport by a U.S. consul, boarded a flight back to the U.S.

L'affaire Beams couldn't have come at a worse time, as protests against the Marcos government had reached fever pitch during the First Quarter Storm, or FQS. The FQS was the most violent manifestation of unrest in postwar history up to that point, made up of rallies, protests, and marches held by a coalition of student groups—Sison's Kabataan Makabayan was a major player—labor unions, and farmer organizations between January and March of 1970. The object of their ire was the Marcos government, seen as especially corrupt, and its collaboration with the United States in its war against the Vietnamese. The FQS began on January 26, 1970, on the streets outside of Congress, after Marcos's state-of-the-nation speech. As he and the elegantly attired Imelda exited, they were met by a screaming crowd of 20,000 students, workers, and peasants, mouthing obscenities and displaying papier-mâché crocodiles (symbols of rapacity), hurling rocks and bottles. Never had any of the nation's previous presidents been so embarrassed.

Things came to head on January 30, 1970. Protesters marched to Malacañang and the worst riots in the country's history erupted when the demonstrators attempted to storm Malacañang. Shouting slogans targeting U.S. imperialism and the subservient role of the Philippine state and bemoaning the lack of a true democracy, the demonstrators somehow commandeered a fire truck and rammed it into one of the palace gates. The protesters were dispersed violently by policemen and soldiers, including the Presidential Security Guard. In the ensuing melee, a twenty-three-year-old university student was shot in the head. All day long, protesters and security forces played a cat-and-mouse game in the nearby districts that, with its narrow lanes and sympathetic inhabitants, provided the activists with cover, enough for most of them to ride out the storm. Other marches and demonstrations took place the following weeks, often with the U.S. embassy as the target, but none matched the intensity of that assault on Malacañang.

An even more explosive—literally and figuratively—event took place the next year that made a nervous society even more nervous.

On the humid night of August 21, 1971, the Liberal Party, in opposition to Marcos's Nacionalistas, was holding a campaign rally for its senatorial candidates for elections scheduled for later that year. The outdoor gathering was at Plaza Miranda, Manila's Hyde Park and a historic spot for rallies of all sorts. More than 10,000 supporters were on hand, many, no doubt, there just to enjoy the palabas. Two fragmentation grenades were lobbed onto the stage after 9 p.m., killing a five-year-old child, a photographer, and seven others. Ninety-five were injured, including three of the Liberal candidates and the candidate for the mayoralty of Manila, who lost one of his legs. The blame naturally fell on Marcos and his minions, though years later the CPP head José Maria Sison was thought to have ordered the bombings. Both Marcos and Sison denied the charges. The bombings created tremendous sympathy for the Liberal Party, so that six of the eight Senate seats up for grabs went to the LP, as did the mayoralty of Manila.

By 1972, the Marcos administration repeatedly warned of the fast-spreading Communist threat from within, with Defense Secretary Juan Ponce Enrile leading the chorus. In September, three days after another warning issued by Enrile, two early morning explosions damaged Meralco sub-stations, with little damage. The military blamed Communist plotters. The crowning moment in this *Moro-Moro* (a Spanish colonial-era drama where the ending is utterly predictable) was the fake assassination attempt on Enrile himself. On the fateful day of September 21, 1972, Enrile had decided to ride in his security car, rather than his own, later escaping the fusillade of automatic-weapons fire directed at his car by ambushers. His good fortune was ascribed to God's intervention.

The deity in this case, however, was a two-personned God: Marcos and Enrile himself. The attempted assassination, according to the government, left it no choice but to declare martial law. The next day, September 22, Proclamation 1081 put into place martial law, signed by President Marcos but backdated to September 21, due to the president's superstitious belief in the magical powers of 7 (by which 21 is divisible). Military units fanned out across the city to arrest political opponents, activists, and anyone suspected by the regime of subversion.

The first politician picked up was Senator Benigno Aquino Jr.

6. THE REPUBLIC: THE STRONGMAN AND THE HOUSEWIFE, 1972-1992

"You will probably ask me: will I also apply [land reform] to my family's Hacienda Luisita. My answer is yes; although sugar land is not covered by the land reform law, I shall sit down with my family to explore how the twin goals of maximum productivity and dispersal of ownership and benefits can be exemplified for the rest of the nation in Hacienda Luisita."

—Corazon C. Aquino on land reform while campaigning in Mindanao, January 16, 1986

MARTIAL LAW: THE NEW SOCIETY

SENATOR BENIGNO AQUINO JR., OR NINOY, AS HE LIKED TO BE called by friends and followers, was President Marcos's most charismatic opponent and likely to be the central figure for above-ground opposition to martial law. From the Central Luzon province of Tarlac, he was the son of the late Senator Benigno Aquino, who had served with José Laurel in the Japanese-controlled Philippine government during World War II. The younger Aquino was something of a wunderkind, having worked as a correspondent in the Korean War for the *Manila Chronicle* at the age of seventeen. At twenty-one, he took on a job as an adviser to then Defense Secretary Magsaysay and when the latter was elected president, acted as his emissary to Luis Taruc. After intense negotiations, the Huk chief agreed to an unconditional surrender.

Aquino rose through the political ranks impressively, being elected as mayor of his hometown at the age of twenty-two, the youngest ever in the country's history, as well as being the youngest elected senator later on. He would undoubtedly have been the Liberal Party candidate for president in the 1973 presidential elections, running against Marcos's Nacionalista Party standard bearer, had not the imposition of martial law and one man's megalomaniacal ambitions derailed the nation's normal political processes for a decade and a half. Ninoy was arrested and charged with conspiring against the government, and with illegal possession of firearms. In late 1977, a military tribunal sentenced him to death, a sentence that was immediately suspended as the regime had no desire to canonize its most celebrated prisoner. Aquino would be imprisoned for nearly eight years before being allowed in 1980 to fly with his wife Corazon and children to the U.S. for heart surgery, having suffered a heart attack two months before.

Another well-known opposition senator, Senator José Diokno, was arrested as well. Along with Aquino, Diokno had been one of the more persistent and vocal critics of the Marcos government. Older than Aquino, Diokno had served as justice secretary under President Macapagal and had made a number of powerful enemies in his investigations of corruption, for which he was relieved—a sure sign he was doing his job. Upon his release, Senator Diokno would go on to become a fearless champion of human rights during the repressive years of dictatorial rule. Both senators charged that the spate of bombings (mostly harmless, except for those at Plaza Miranda) and the incessant harping on the internal Communist threat were government tactics meant to create the right circumstances under which martial law could be imposed. A week before the fake ambush on Defense Secretary Enrile, and the subsequent declaration of martial law, Aquino laid bare before the Senate "Oplan Saggitarius," that he said had been leaked to him by his confidential sources. According to Aquino, "Saggitarius" had been prepared by the Armed Forces of the Philippines (AFP) at the behest of the president, by which a series of provocative incidents would be stage-managed so the government could blame violent anti-government factions, and thus justify declaring a state of emergency. Marcos dismissed the accusation as politically motivated and promised that he would seek Senate counsel before such a drastic step were taken.

No such counsel was sought when he did impose martial law. In a press release issued by the president's office on that fateful date, Marcos stated that martial law's immediate aim was to "eliminate the threat of a violent overthrow of our Republic." He added that reform was imperative, and that he was determined to clean up "government of its corrupt and sterile elements," as well as undertake "the liquidation of criminal syndicates and the systematic development of the economy."

Presumably martial law was meant to restore law and order and shore up public trust and confidence in the government's ability to ensure a productive, peaceful, and stable civil state. But in fact, the office of the Philippine president had enough constitutional authority to have the laws enforced strictly, including disbanding the numerous private militias in the provinces that prominent politicians and powerful businessmen employed for security and the intimidation of rivals. Having their own hired guns also made it easier to mock the rule of law and get away with it. The availability of firearms in the immediate aftermath of World War II and the failure of political will in the central government all but encouraged the emergence of clan-based warlords. Martial law wasn't necessary to achieve these goals, but clearly Marcos needed a legitimate reason to stay on in power—the constitution limited a president to two terms. Orchestrating an atmosphere of lawlessness enabled him to proclaim martial law.

He gave the proposed makeover of the country the rather grandiose title of "The New Society," a riff on President Lyndon B. Johnson's "Great Society," and he created the *Kilusan Bagong Lipunan*, or New Society Movement. Marcos envisioned a reinvigorated nation-state that would navigate its way between the violent methods of both left- and right-wing extremists. The path chosen by the New Society would be what Marcos termed "constitutional authoritarianism": by relying on the powers granted to him by the constitution (through the use of its state of emergency provision) the government would undercut the extremists and break up the country's entrenched oligarchy controlling most of the country's resources and wealth. Thus, the New Society would ensure a more equitable distribution of income and eliminate a major cause of unrest among the population.

This in turn would weaken the left's critique of a ruling dispensation favoring the privileged few over the masses. Nevertheless, the underground left would keep hammering at the state and therefore, the threat of a Communist takeover had to be met firmly, through an increase in the military's strength; the suspension of civil liberties (that the New Society portrayed as being routinely abused by anti-government activists); a crackdown on groups that regularly challenged the establishment, such as labor unions, student activists, peasant organizations, and even journalists; and the confiscation of unregistered firearms along with the dissolution of private armies.

A curfew was imposed and military and police checkpoints set up in many parts of the country, especially in and around Metro Manila. In its drive to restore an atmosphere of peace and order, the government claimed to have confiscated half a million firearms. At the outset, civil society grudgingly accepted limits on its liberties. Traffic rules were obeyed, garbage collected, street crime was down, and petty government bureaucrats, mirabile dictu, seemed more conscientious in the performance of their duties and not so eager to solicit bribes.

To formulate the theoretical and operative principles along which the New Society would be constructed, Marcos relied heavily on tech-nocrats, more so than any previous administration. It was also a public relations ploy, as the jargon of the technocracy imparted to government policies a veneer of professionalism and legitimacy. Yet, in one respect, Marcos was exactly like most other dictators: he and his wife eagerly sought to portray themselves as saviors of an embattled country. They had a predilection for casting themselves in Philippine mythological terms: He was *Malakas* (Strength) and she was *Maganda* (Beauty), alluding to the Philippine creation myth, in which the first man and woman emerged simultaneously from a grove of bamboo as equal part-ners, fully formed and perfect. In one painting, Ferdinand, Imelda, and their children are portrayed as though they were a royal family. In addi-tion, Ferdinand authored several ghostwritten books, among them *Progress and Martial Law* and *The New Philippine Republic: A Third World Approach to Democracy*. As early as 1965 he commissioned the film biography *Iginuhit ng Tadhana* (*Destined by Fate*), before commis-sioning *Maharlika*, which starred the ill-fated Dovie Beams. As dictator, he ordered a gigantic bust of himself to be set up on a mountainside, à la Mt. Rushmore, in northern Luzon's Cordilleras, on land forcibly taken from an indigenous tribe.

He also relied on an increasingly compliant Constitutional Convention, which was convened in 1971 but whose proceedings were interrupted by martial law. The Con-Con, as it was known, was meant to draft a new law of the land that would replace the colonial-era 1935 constitution. When it resumed its deliberations after the imposition of martial law, the convention—through being bullied and manipulated by Marcos partisans—was transformed into a rubber stamp for Marcos's legislative agenda, a principal objective being to convert the current system of government into a parliamentary one, thus allowing him to stay in power beyond 1973, when his second and last term was to end. At his behest, his followers in the convention manipulated the drafting of the constitution so it extended martial law, authorized rule by decree, and theoretically allowed him to be both prime minister and president. The 1973 constitution was ratified through spurious citi-zens' assemblies, dominated by Marcos loyalists, rather than through a national referendum. It was a constitution created, in short, to serve the needs of one man rather than the nation.

Uncle Sam's Blessing

In the Philippine political world, how far one rises nationally is often linked to how well one cultivates, or is seen to cultivate, ties with Washington—a perception founded on colonial-era realities. It was automatically assumed that something as momentous as martial law had the support, albeit indirect, of the United States. True enough: hardly the type to raise a fuss over ethical conduct, embroiled as it was in the beginnings of the Watergate scandal that would ultimately force President Nixon to resign in 1974 in order to avoid impeachment, the U.S. government continued to support Marcos. Besides, with the war in Vietnam proving to be disastrous for the United States, resulting in its withdrawal in 1975, having a staunch anti-Communist ally, one that moreover hosted two of the largest U.S. bases in the world, assumed even more importance.

Given that Henry Kissinger—Nixon's national security adviser and later secretary of state and therefore the prime architect of Nixon's foreign policy—was a firm believer in realpolitik, Marcos was pretty confident of U.S. support. For Marcos too was a master at playing the game of realpolitik, and he knew that as long as the United States's economic and military interests—its bases and investments in the archipelago—were left untouched, then it would be business as usual. Following a predictable script, Marcos could, and did, sound all the right nationalist notes and still act as a subaltern of the United States. The wily strongman even committed a contingent of Philippine troops to Vietnam, the Philippine Civic Action Group, or PHILCAG, early in his first term. Consisting of an engineering battalion and medical and rural development teams, the 1,350-strong outfit worked on non-combat missions, mainly civic projects.

For all its rhetoric about democracy and the rule of law, the United States had almost always supported dictatorial regimes that were allied with U.S. strategic interests. The 1970s proved to be a golden decade for U.S.-backed strongman rule. The 1973 coup by General Augusto Pinochet that toppled the democratically elected government of left-leaning Salvador Allende in Chile had the blessings of Washington. So did General Park Chung-hee in South Korea, Suharto in Indonesia, the military junta in Argentina, and the Shah in Iran.

With Kissinger and Nixon in control of American foreign policy, America's support for dictators increased, in direct proportion to diminishing concern for democracy.

American businessmen in the Philippines were more effusive in their support of constitutional authoritarianism. The American Chamber of Commerce of the Philippines, headed by a William Mitchell, sent the president a congratulatory telegram on September 27, 1972, just five days after the state of emergency had been declared: "The American Chamber of Commerce wishes you every success in your endeavors to restore peace and order, business confidence, economic growth and the well being of the Filipino people and nation. We assure you of our confidence and cooperation in achieving these objectives. We are communicating these feelings to our associates and affiliates in the United States."

A 1973 study conducted by the National Council of Churches of Christ in the U.S. and meant for its investors who were concerned with U.S. corporate responsibility abroad, made it clear why the American Chamber of Commerce was so effusive. In 1971, the year preceding the declaration of martial law, 47 U.S. corporations were among the top 200 Philippine corporations and accounted for close to 32 percent average in total sales, income, assets, and equity, a percentage that increased to approximately 40 percent when considering only the top thirty-five. Among the 47 were the multinationals Caltex, Exxon, Procter & Gamble, PepsiCo, Ford, Union Carbide, Goodyear Tire & Rubber, and Del Monte Corporation. (The Del Monte pineapple plantation in Mindanao coincidentally occupies 20,000 hectares, or 44,000 acres, of prime agricultural land that has never been subject to land reform.)

One immediate result of Marcos's grab for power was the substantial increase in military aid from the Pentagon. Under the U.S. Military Assistance Program, in place since 1947, aid increased dramatically, from $80.8 million in the four years prior to martial law, to more than twice that—$166.3 million in the succeeding four years. Clearly not coincidental, this increase signaled to the Marcos regime that the Pentagon was willing to help in countering the Communist threat that martial law was supposed to address. Too, the aid bolstered the case for keeping U.S. bases on Philippine soil.

But the U.S. State Department's own assessment of Marcos and martial law was decidedly more somber, with a report stating "that martial law was not necessary to deal with the country's problems, which have in fact been considerably aggravated by Marcos's corrupt political style; that based on his record of ruthless self-aggrandizement he cannot necessarily be counted on to implement significant reforms."

Marcos's dictatorial rule exposed the darkness at the heart of U.S. foreign policy: as had been shown repeatedly in the past, in spite of the rhetoric, democracy was hardly the most important issue for the U.S. government when it came to its client states. Paramount were its economic and security interests. Marcos played the role of nationalist very well, but he was still "America's boy." The United States embassy seemed to have no doubts about Marcos, as it did about his opponents. It went along with martial law, convinced that Marcos would protect American interests. If martial law meant taking liberties with the people's own liberties, so be it.

Even as economic conditions and the state of human rights deteriorated over the course of twenty years of Ferdinand and Imelda Marcos's rule—and Imelda was as much a ruler as her husband the longer they remained in power, hence the reference to the partnership as a "conjugal dictatorship"—five successive U.S. presidents supported the Marcoses with little to no restraint exercised: Johnson, Nixon, Ford, Carter, and Reagan. Even when President Carter (1977-1980) emphasized human rights, it was more lip service than anything substantial when it came to the Philippines. U.S. aid flowed as before, and beyond some cosmetic changes, the Marcos regime knew it could continue on its repressive course.

Under President Ronald Reagan (1981-88), who had as governor of California and with Nancy at his side attended the inauguration of the Cultural Center of the Philippines in 1969, personal relations between the White House and Malacañang dramatically improved, to the dismay of critics of the Marcoses both domestically and abroad. Marcos's brand of constitutional authoritarianism fit perfectly with the foreign policy principles enunciated by Jeane Kirkpatrick, Reagan's neoconservative foreign-policy adviser and ambassador to the United Nations, who was fiercely anti-communist and who believed in supporting repressive regimes as long these regimes went along with U.S. policies. Kirkpatrick's views dismayed U.S. liberals who were shocked, shocked, that their government would endorse another government's routine violations of its citizens' most fundamental rights. Reagan's support for the Marcoses was demonstrated most vividly when, on the occasion of his visit to Manila in 1981, Vice President George Herbert Walker Bush toasted Marcos by saying with a straight face, "We love your adherence to democratic principles and to the democratic process." The ordinary Filipino would have been bewildered by such a compliment.

Bush may have been referring indirectly to Marcos's having lifted martial law on January 17, 1981, but by then Marcos had the mechanisms in place to maintain all the control he needed. His powers were as broad as ever: Amendment Six to the 1973 Constitution institutionalized one-man rule over the nation. With at least 1,000 decrees issued, the dictator could shape the different facets of Philippine society, whether this was the economy or the military, however he saw fit. And in the elections held in June of 1981, which marked a return to the presidential system (but this time a system that included the post of prime minister), Marcos won with 86 percent of the vote. With mainstream opposition parties boycotting the elections and with the regime controlling the electoral machinery as well as the press, the elections simply furnished Marcos's prolonged stay in office with a legal veneer.

Imelda: Holding Up Half of Heaven

In 1954, she started out as the naïve wife of a brilliant politician, but by the time of martial law, Imelda had, through conscious determination and psychiatric help in New York City, remade herself into a powerful national figure. With martial law she metamorphosed into more than just a ceremonial First Lady. She had emerged a steel butterfly, as many called her simultaneously in awe and derision. Thus, the commonplace reference to His and Hers governments was right on target.

She was no longer the darling of the masses who beat up the Beatles for turning down her invitation to lunch at Malacañang. That hostility was made manifest on December 7, 1972, less than three months after martial law had been declared, when an assailant tried to stab her at a public event. The First Lady sustained cuts to her arms but survived the attempt. The would-be assassin, Carlito Dimahilig, of whom nothing seems to be known, was shot to death by her security detail.

In his Presidential Decree 731, on June 7, 1975, Ferdinand Marcos made Imelda head of the commission that would exercise power in the event of his death or incapacitation. He also appointed her governor of the newly created Metropolitan Manila District, a merger of four cities—including the country's two largest, Manila and Quezon City—and seven towns. In 1978, not surprisingly, she won a seat in the *Batasan Pambansa*, or National Assembly. And that same year, she was named Minister of Human Settlements, a mega-agency with practically unlimited resources, endowing her with even more power as a dispenser of pork.

She also served as the regime's roving ambassador, moving easily from Egypt and Bolivia to China and Cuba. Imelda traveled with a large entourage, consisting mainly of women who came to be known as the Blue Ladies, usually the wives of influential men in military, economic, and political circles, and who themselves became influential and wealthy. She acquired a reputation for world-class shopping, for which the term "Imeldific" was coined. Tiffany, Saks Fifth Avenue, and other tony establishments not just in New York City but in other capitals like Paris and Rome loved her, for she thought nothing of dropping hundreds of thousands of dollars on one visit. Her extravagant taste included choice real estate as well, and in the 1980s she snapped up choice Manhattan properties, including the prestigious Crown Building in midtown ($51 million) and the Herald Shopping Center ($60 million), catty corner from Macy's department store. Her choice of residence while visiting Manhattan was a suite at the Waldorf Astoria.

Like Ferdinand, Imelda was consumed by the pathological desire to remake herself, which meant reinventing her past to conform to a grander self-image. No telling or more extravagant monument testifies to this obsession than the *Santo Niño* (Holy Infant) shrine in the city in which she grew up, Tacloban—the very same capital where, in 1944, General Douglas MacArthur first announced to Filipinos that he had, as promised, returned. Built at a reputed $23 million in 1980, the huge two-story affair—part antebellum Southern mansion and part Spanish grandee's home with Moorish arches—sits on a lot once occupied by a rather more modest dwelling that was young Imelda's residence. The statue of the Holy Infant Jesus is ensconced in a ground floor chapel, flanked incongruously by guest bedrooms, each with a different motif. On the grand stairway leading to the second floor is a huge portrait of a gossamer-like Imelda, rising from the misty waters, an unmistakable reference to Botticelli's *Birth of Venus*. Upstairs are cavernous master bedrooms, with a reception hall complete with two thrones at one end.

On the occasion of Pope John Paul's 1981 six-day visit to the Philippines, the only predominantly Roman Catholic nation in Asia, Imelda ordered that fences be erected and whitewashed, to hide the innumerable festering slums of Manila the Pope would otherwise see. She had also planned the construction of an extravagant basilica, at a cost of a reported $100 million, with a 48-foot statue of the Holy Infant. Drawing heavy criticism even from the conservative Catholic hierarchy, the plan was abandoned. The First Lady had wanted the pontiff to stay at the Coconut Palace, a massive residence situated on the grounds of the Cultural Center, which had gold-plated bathroom fixtures and was built largely with materials derived from the coconut tree. John Paul turned down the invitation, opting to stay at the Papal Nuncio's official residence.

With Imelda leading the charge and despite other pressing and chronic needs, such as low-cost housing, the government built luxury hotels in an effort to promote tourism; added to the Cultural Center complex a gigantic 10,000-seat Folk Arts Theater to stage the 1974 Miss Universe beauty pageant; and constructed the Heart Center, in a country where malnutrition, rather than heart disease, is the most pressing health concern. But it was in the hasty construction of the Film Palace—again, on the Cultural Center grounds—and the resulting deaths, which scandalized the public already inured to the First Lady's mania for oversized, unnecessary projects.

The Film Palace was to be the primary venue for what Imelda had hoped would be in 1982 an internationally known film festival, one that would compete with Cannes and Tokyo. To make it in time for the festival opening, construction proceeded twenty-four hours seven days a week. As a result, a top floor collapsed when its cement foundation gave way, having not fully dried. Though the government has never said how many workers died, many accounts put the number at 169. The government tried to hush up the accident, but the tragedy was simply too large to escape unnoticed. It cast a pall over the festival proceedings, as rumors spread that the building was being haunted by the restless spirits of the dead workers. Exorcism rites were thus performed, to placate them.

THE COSTS OF THE NEW SOCIETY

Human Rights

The Marcos regime stifled opposition, whether violent or not. From student activists to community organizers, from human rights advocates to academics, the sweep at the outset of martial law was broad and indiscriminate, with approximately 30,000 people arrested. Most were citizens who had peacefully expressed their democratic right of dissent. The regime also cracked down on radio and television stations and shut down the independent press. One of its first moves was to confiscate the giant media conglomerate ABS-CBN, owned by the López family, a pillar of the old oligarchy. Fernando López had been Ferdinand's vice president during his first term but had since fallen out of favor. The Lópezes' media empire was too irresistible a target for the Marcoses and the new oligarchs.

The suspension of civil liberties and the broad powers granted the military and the Philippine Constabulary led to systematic abuse, especially on the part of the constabulary, reprising its role as the main enforcer of American colonial rule. Amnesty International issued a report that stated four years after the declaration of martial law, the regime held at least 6,000 political prisoners, with torture a routine method of interrogating political dissidents. Female detainees were often sexually molested or raped. The most famous political prisoner was, of course, Senator Aquino, kept in solitary confinement.

In Latin America the term *desaparecidos*, or "disappeared," came to refer to unexplained, sudden disappearances and subsequent deaths at the hands of the authorities. In the Philippines, the equivalent term for extrajudicial killings was "salvaging," paradoxically referring to a meaning opposite that of being saved or rescued. In the grisly parlance of the Marcos years, a person who was "salvaged" was someone summarily executed, without any judicial proceedings whatsoever, the security and military forces acting as judge, jury, and executioner. The body would be dumped usually where it was sure to be found, sending an unmistakable signal of how the regime treated dissidents. From 1973 to 1985, a human rights group, Task Force Detainees Philippines (TFDP), documented a total of 2,255 cases of such killings, with 334 disappearances between 1977 and 1983, where no corpse was ever found.

One of the most notorious cases of salvaging was that of Macliing Dulag, a Kalinga tribal chief from the mountainous Cordillera region in northern Luzon. Dulag led a vigorous opposition to a proposed World Bank-funded Chico river dam that would have flooded ancient and sacred ancestral lands. Dulag was gunned down at this house on April 24, 1980—a date now commemorated as Cordillera Day. His death was not in vain, as the project was cancelled.

In the countryside, the government created armed militias known as the Civilian Home Defense Forces (CHDFs), which worked closely with the constabulary and army units. The CHDFs turned increasingly violent, as well as corrupt. Adding to this volatile mix were fanatically anti-communist paramilitary cults, backed by the local military commands. These terrorized rural hamlets where insurgents, or their sympathizers, were thought to be hiding. To be seen as a collaborator with the NPA was in their eyes tantamount to a death sentence. Ironically, such cults had their roots in indigenous resistance to Spanish rule in the previous century, reacting both to state oppression and religious tyranny. In their twentieth-century incarnation, they now acted as unofficial agents of the state. With names like Pulajanes and Tad-Tad—a name that translates chillingly as "chop-chop" and suggests this particular group's favored modus operandi—the cults appealed to disenfranchised and unemployed men in rural areas, men with little or no future.

With the change to the more human rights-oriented Carter administration, pro-democracy activists believed a window of opportunity had opened. It had, but, disappointingly, only by a crack. Nothing of substance changed. When Carter's vice president, Walter Mondale, paid a visit to Manila, he was expected to reiterate unambiguously Washington's emphasis on human rights. He met with Marcos and separately with the opposition as well as with the hugely influential Manila archbishop Jaime Cardinal Sin. While pro-democracy activists were hopeful these meetings would be publicized, they were in fact low-key sessions, and no press photographers were allowed, for fear of offending Marcos. The conference with Cardinal Sin was particularly disappointing since Sin and the other top Catholic prelates were untouchable, but Sin would not take the occasion to oppose one-man rule. He characterized his stance as one of critical collaboration with the Marcos regime. Observers felt, however, that the good cardinal was in fact more of a collaborator than a critic. As the *Far Eastern Economic*

Review put it, "With rare exceptions, Sin has pretty much toed the line of the regime."

"Some Are Smarter Than Others"

The first years of martial law saw a surge in economic growth, with an average annual rate of 7 percent, due mainly to an increase in government revenue, international lending, and tourism. New public schools were built, and massive infrastructure projects were undertaken that did improve highways and bridges. In particular, the Pan-Philippine Highway and the San Juanico Bridge—the longest bridge in the archipelago and spanning the straits between the islands of Samar and Leyte, Imelda's home province—were held up as examples of the New Society constructively engaged in modernizing the country.

Nevertheless, while immense wealth was being created, very little of it trickled down to the masses. By the end of the 1970s, economic indicators belied the rosy picture projected by government technocrats. Average monthly wages declined by 20 percent, with a 30 percent decline in agriculture and 40 percent in commerce. Prices for basic commodities such as cooking oil, rice, sugar and salt tripled. In 1971, the income of the lowest 40 percent of families was barely 12 percent of the total; in 1981, this declined to 9 percent. In contrast, the top 10 percent earned close to 40 percent of the total in 1971; this rose to 42 percent in 1981. Dictatorial rule did nothing to narrow the gap between the haves and the have-nots; on the contrary, martial law only made it worse. The percentage of people living below the poverty line increased to 50 percent of the population by the time the Marcoses fled the country. Hence, the proliferation of slums in Metro Manila and other major urban areas, as the jobless and the homeless flocked to the big cities seeking work.

It wasn't only members of the low-end of the wage spectrum that moved abroad, seeking greener pastures. Professionals, such as doctors, nurses, and engineers, did too. There was a demand for contract labor in the Middle East due to petro-dollar-financed construction projects, while in the United States, medical personnel from abroad were recruited avidly, the domestic ranks of doctors and nurses being depleted by the demands of the Vietnam War. Thus began what is more commonly known as the "brain drain." Increasingly, as a kind of mirror image of Japanese men going on sex tours of the Philippines—a trade that was implicitly encouraged by the Department of Tourism—young women sought work as dancers and entertainers in the dimly lit yakuza-controlled bars and clubs of such cities as Tokyo and Osaka. (Both types of exodus continue to this day.)

One major cause for the continuing slide into poverty for a majority of Filipinos was crony capitalism, where government projects became a cash cow not only for the Marcoses but also for their friends and relatives. While the regime had to a large degree broken up the old oligarchy and disbanded their private militias, it simply replaced the former with one of its own making, with its members forming their own private militias. It was indeed a New Society—a society of new oligarchs drawn from the Marcoses' respective clans and circle of friends. In 1979, Ricardo Manapat, a philosophy professor at a leading Philippine university, wrote a pamphlet that examined crony capitalism under the Marcos regime. The title Manapat gave it, "Some Are Smarter Than Others," was based on a remark Imelda made when asked about the sudden wealth of certain relatives: "Sometimes, you have smart relatives who can make it. . . . My dear, there are always people who are just a little faster, more brilliant, more aggressive."

One of the most egregious examples of crony capitalism was the deal to build a nuclear power plant on the Bataan Peninsula, northwest of Manila. The construction of the plant, began in 1976, was envisioned partly in response to the oil crisis of the decade. But it was hardly a project a poor country could afford; nevertheless the regime went ahead with its plans. The site of the power plant raised alarming prospects of a nuclear meltdown, being situated near three earthquake fault lines and a then dormant volcano Mt. Pinatubo that would in fact erupt fiercely in 1991. The facility was also at risk from possible tsunamis from the nearby South China Sea.

General Electric would have won the contract to build two reactors, with its bid of $700 million. However, Westinghouse managed to convince Herminio Disini—kin to Imelda by marriage, friend and golfing partner of Ferdinand—to intercede on its behalf. Disini was persuasive and the contract was awarded to Westinghouse instead. By then, the cost had escalated to $1.2 billion, the most expensive nuclear plant project in the world at that time. Though completed, it never got to operate and was shut down in the immediate aftermath of the Marcoses' forced departure in 1986. The Filipino taxpayer was, as usual, left holding the bag.

Crony capitalism also reared its head in agribusiness, with the two most profitable cash crops—sugar and coconuts—coming to be monopolized by Marcos confidants and business associates. The enormous profits generated by consolidated control bankrolled the regional domination—political, judicial, social, and military—by these new oligarchs. In sugar, Roberto Benedicto, a fraternity brother of Marcos when both were law students at the University of the Philippines, called the shots, while in the coconut industry, it was Defense Secretary Enrile and businessman Eduardo "Danding" Cojuangco (first cousin to Senator Aquino's wife, Corazon Cojuangco).

Through a tax on coconut production known as the coconut levy, the enormous amounts of money generated were then deposited in a bank specifically set up for this purpose, the United Coconut Planters Bank, or UCPB. Theoretically the bank and its assets were meant to serve the vast majority of coconut farmers who had small landholdings. Instead, the UCPB at the behest of its crony-dominated board set about acquiring a near-monopoly on coconut mills, thereby controlling prices for the processing of the nuts, which it set at below-market rates, and thus generating huge profits. Cojuangco used his position as Marcos crony and president of the bank—which had by the start of the 1980s over $1 billion in levies—to not only amass personal wealth in the hundreds of millions of dollars but also buy controlling shares in the country's largest food-and-beverage corporation, San Miguel, makers of the world-famous San Miguel beer.

For those who benefited from crony capitalism, the days under the Marcoses were happy ones. They had tons of cash, all the luxuries they wanted, and power, as well as access to the ultimate dispenser of power: Marcos. He was the godfather, and his cronies (as well as Imelda's) were the capos, who made sure that the godfather (and the godmother) received their share. They could operate with special dispensation from the government and were relatively immune from competition. Nevertheless, except in a few cases, crony businesses were inefficient in the long run, forcing the administration to bail out these compadre-run companies, increasing deficit spending and, of course, foreign debt. The losses that resulted from corporations that closed were borne not by the cronies but by the laid-off workers, who had no assets stowed away in various banks, and ultimately by the average taxpayer.

Rice Production and Land Reform

Land has always been central to the lives of the rural folk, who for most of the country's history have constituted the majority of the populace. Previous attempts to reform the system so there would be land for the landless tiller failed, despite the high-flown rhetoric and the dramatic photo opportunities occasioned by public officials presenting land titles to a few lucky recipients. Marcos promised to be different. Shortly after the proclamation of martial law, he declared in no uncertain terms, "If land reform fails, there is no New Society."

His program did fail. There was no *real* New Society. Rather than challenging the prevailing class system through the New Society or eliminating the entrenched oligarchy, Marcos simply changed the main cast of characters but not the play. His land reform program was bound to fail because no sustained attempt was made to implement it. More to the point, it left two-thirds of the country's agricultural lands untouched—huge estates dedicated to cash crops, such as sugar, coconuts, and pineapple. A mere 1,500 tenants—0.5 percent of the supposed beneficiaries—had, by 1979, gotten titles to 0.3 percent of the land reform area. Moreover, coverage did not include such sectors as landless rural workers and tenant farmers working crops other than rice or corn. Other loopholes existed that provided the savvy landowner with ways of evading land reform legally.

Small landowners and tenants were reluctant to participate. The former feared that they would not be fairly compensated. The latter knew that even if they were given land, they still had to shoulder new financial burdens, for farm tools, fertilizer, seeds, etc. Government credit that was supposedly available was more often than not insufficient. And of course borrowing from loan sharks simply increased the chances of defaulting on their debts. In the end, the rural poor gained nothing from the supposed reform.

One facet of the Marcos regime's agricultural program was its emphasis on the increased production of rice through the so-called Green Revolution. Through work at the International Rice Research Institute (IRRI) in nearby Los Baños—established in 1960 and funded by the Rockefeller and Ford foundations—hybrid, high-yield varieties of rice were cultivated. The idea was that increased production would lead to larger market sales and thus help alleviate poverty in the countryside. Marcos heralded the Green Revolution as a way of developing export agriculture and thereby increasing foreign exchange reserves.

In the early stages of martial law, due to increased borrowing on the part of the government, exports from the agricultural sector increased (as did the national debt). But the rather enormous fly in the ointment was that these high-yield strains of so-called miracle rice required large doses of chemical pesticides and oil-based fertilizers. These were not only expensive but harmful to the soil, adversely affecting the fragile ecology of soil nutrients and crop diversity. These strains only benefited already wealthy landowners and agribusinesses, and they forced the small farmer to incur loans that often, due to bad harvests, they would be unable to repay. As a consequence, many lost their lands they had originally mortgaged to secure loans. Total land area devoted to rice declined by the beginning of the 1980s. By 1985, the country needed to import 538,000 tons of rice. Rather than help resolve the land reform dilemma, the Green Revolution seemed to have exacerbated it.

Additionally, the income derived from export agriculture, while seemingly boosting GNP, was mostly kept by those of the elite who were close to the Marcos administration. Traditional moneymakers like sugar and coconut were controlled by powerful cronies such as Eduardo Cojuangco and Juan Ponce Enrile in coconut, and Roberto Benedicto in sugar, so that very little of those profits were ever seen by the small farmers. Other cash crops such as bananas and pineapple and forestry products proved to be hugely profitable as well, with the latter leading to an increase in deforestation. With the overriding emphasis on monoculture, huge plantations reduced the availability of land for other crops. Sadly, workers laboring over fruit rarely if ever tasted the fruit of their labors.

THE INSURGENCIES GROW

The New People's Army

Rather than discouraging the rebellious to lay down their arms, martial law bolstered the numbers of those taking to the hills to join the New People's Army. The NPA had succeeded the Hukbalahap, having been co-founded by the disaffected young Huk fighter Bernabe Buscayno and by José Maria Sison, the most prominent dissident member of the PKP, the Huks' parent organization. Both the Huks and the NPA emerged from the same region, Central Luzon, and both focused initially on land issues: from tenancy and sharecropping to profit-sharing and the aimed-for breakup of the huge estates for their redistribution to peasants. The larger context—of having a more active say in how they were to be governed, principally—linked the NPA to prior movements fueled by agrarian unrest, such as the Sakdalistas, and most significantly, to the older revolutionary tradition of the Bonifacio-led Kataastasan Kagalagalangan Katipunan, or KKK. This time, however, a well-defined ideology—Mao's interpretation of Marxist-Leninist thought—shaped the direction and internal policies of the CPP and, of course, the NPA.

Marcos proved to be the NPA's most effective recruiter, albeit unwittingly. The crackdown on civil liberties and media; the roundup of student activists, organizers, and left-leaning urban professionals; the use of torture; and the senseless salvagings forced a generation of young men and women to go underground, whether this was within the cities or to the hills. The infusion of a radicalized, educated, sophisticated middle-class segment, with networks all over the country, into the ranks of the CPP-NPA invigorated the insurgency, hastening its emergence as a nationwide movement. In 1973, the National Democratic Front (NDF) sprang into being, as a number of left-leaning groups, such as the Christians for National Liberation (CNL) and the Cordillera People's Democratic Front, saw the need for a coalition that would bring together similarly minded organizations and provide a channel through which progressive ideas about change could be disseminated. Due to its size and strength, the CPP/NPA dominated the NDF, rendering the latter in the view of the establishment a surrogate for the Communists.

Even with Buscayno's capture in 1976, and Sison's in 1977, the NPA continued to expand. By the mid 1980s, on the eve of the Marcos regime's collapse, the NPA had guerrilla fronts in 63 of 72 provinces, and by 1986, when the conjugal dictators fled, its armed strength was estimated by the Philippine military at 26,000 regular guerrillas, a larger force of part-time irregulars, and a mass base of 2 million.

Far more than the Huks, the NPA constituted a serious threat to the stability of the government. The Huks had been concentrated in Central Luzon and focused primarily on land redistribution. In contrast, the NPA operated nationally and sought to address a broader array of issues, from economic inequality and government corruption to the snail's pace of justice. Able to fight on many fronts, the NPA had the capacity at times to field company-strength units of 200 to 300 men and women (unlike the MNLF, the NPA included women fighters, and wholeheartedly believed in Mao's dictum that women hold up half of heaven).

According to a 1985 report issued by the U.S. Senate Select Committee on Intelligence, the "NPA in conjunction with the Communist Party of the Philippines (CPP) controls or is contesting control of settlements inhabited by at least 10 million people. The military initiative clearly rests with the NPA." The report went on to state, "NPA units nationwide now routinely attack Government forces. . . . Many NPA attacks on military outposts are intended to acquire weapons. By the end of 1983 the NPA claimed to have obtained 20,000 weapons, including machine guns and grenade launchers." Often, the CPP/NPA was the only government in the countryside in what were called "liberated zones." The NPA had units that worked with local communities to build schools, and help peasant farmers. It also dispensed justice rather swiftly, if not always impartially—in contrast to the many local grievances that languished in the courts.

Ideology may have shaped the thinking of top CPP and NPA leaders, but it was rarely, if ever, a factor in what motivated the rank and file. The bitter experiences of having suffered injustices too long at the hands of an indifferent, even callous, landlord-dominated system—the rape of a daughter, say, or the murder of a father—and the desire to see their children lead much better lives prompted them to take up arms or serve the guerrillas in some other way. Until the government in Manila dealt seriously with the underlying causes, there would always be willing recruits for the underground struggle.

The Moro National Liberation Front

If the intent of martial law was to tamp down the fires of rebellion, it failed miserably not just with the leftist insurgency of the New People's Army but with the Moro National Liberation Front, or MNLF. Founded in 1972 by Moro activists prior to the declaration of martial law from a relatively quiescent organization known as the Bangsa Moro Movement, the MNLF aimed to create a separate state (the Bangsa Moro)

248 A HISTORY OF THE PHILIPPINES

consisting of Mindanao, the Sulu Archipelago, and the island of Palawan. The MNLF was headed by University of the Philippines professor Nur Misuari, a member of the Taosug tribe of Jolo. The struggle for independence and now secession had of course deep historical roots, going all the way back to the struggle with the Spanish colonizers. During the American colonial era the Muslim elite were wary of being part of an independent, Christian Philippines, and they expressed the desire to be some sort of U.S. protectorate. This sentiment was ignored, and in 1946 an independent Philippine Republic emerged that was constituted of Luzon, the Visayas, and all of Mindanao.

One catalyst for the rapid rise in armed militancy among Filipino Muslims was the Jabidah Massacre of 1968. Young, able-bodied Moros in southern Mindanao had been recruited by the military and brought to Corregidor Island for training. There the recruits found out the real reason for their recruitment: as part of a secret elite unit, they were meant to foment disturbances among ethnic Tausug and Sama in the island of Sabah. Once British control of the island ended in 1963, it had become part of Malaysia. The Macapagal administration protested, saying that Sabah had been historically and was still part of the Sultanate of Sulu, and thus a part of the Republic of the Philippines. Marcos continued the suit but secretly planned the small-scale guerrilla war to strengthen his case.

The Moro recruits, not desiring to fight fellow Muslims who furthermore hailed from the same ethnic groups, expressed their intent to quit and return to southern Mindanao. Instead, on March 18, they were taken to a remote location on the island in small groups and machine-gunned. (The number of Moros massacred ranged from the government's low estimate of twenty-eight, to the Moro National Liberation Front's 200.) A survivor managed to escape to the mainland and tell his story, which outraged the Muslim communities and provoked a diplomatic firestorm with Malaysia that recalled its ambassador. The Jabidah massacre further radicalized Moro activists, one of whom was Nur Misuari.

Compared to their Christian compatriots, Moros were poorer, less educated, with their areas suffering from inadequate infrastructure. Concentrated in Basilan, Zamboanga, the Sulu archipelago, and southern Mindanao, along with animist tribes, Moros—only 5 percent of the population then—generally were treated as second-class citizens and routinely discriminated against. Their few political representatives acted as traditional warlords and often were allied with powerful Christian politicians. To top it all, the wholesale migration of Visayan and Luzon homesteaders to Mindanao—billed as "The Land of Promise"—had been encouraged early on by the United States and in the 1950s by Ramón Magsaysay. Christian settlers moving in and claiming Muslim communal and ancestral lands ironically replicated the process of land seizure their own forebears had suffered at the hands of the Spanish and the principalia. Predictably, such resettlement engendered land and power disputes that inevitably led to violence.

The Muslims had legitimate long-standing grievances, as the government, whether the legislature, the judiciary, or the military, was controlled by Christians. And Christians had started to form the majority population in many traditional Muslim areas—a clear threat to the Muslim political establishment. Animosity between the two groups led to both Muslim and Christian politicians forming private armies. Those of the Christians were known as the *Ilagas* (a Visayan word meaning "rats") while their Moro counterparts were called the Black Shirts, and, in one case, the Barracudas. Fighting between the two groups reached its height in the 1970s, when the MNLF and the Philippine state were at war.

The declaration of martial law in 1972 not only intensified their struggle for power but was the spark that ignited the deadly conflict all across southern Mindanao, one that conflated a religious war with a civil one, albeit not on a national scale. Not only did the decree further consolidate power in Manila, a bastion of Catholicism, it delegitimized any anti-establishment activity. Above all, the Marcos regime's attempt to confiscate firearms from the private sector was further interpreted as a move to leave the Muslims defenseless against the use of Christian-directed military force.

The MNLF was led by educated young men like Misuari who had studied either at Philippine universities or in the Middle East. They viewed themselves through the prism of their faith rather than as Maranao, Maguindanao, or Tausug. Committed to changing the traditional patterns of wealth and power, they dissociated themselves from the old-guard Moro politicians, most of whom they regarded as allied with Marcos. The MNLF leadership established contacts with Malaysian leaders and with Libya's Muammar Qaddafi. Once martial law was declared and the attempt made to seize firearms from Muslims, the armed phase of what had been a peaceful movement began. Malaysia, wanting to pay back Marcos for his botched 1968 attempt, provided training for a select group of MNLF commanders on Sabah itself, the territory contested by both the Philippines and Malaysia. And, along with Libya, Malaysia provided arms and supplies, with Libya doing so through Malaysia. From late 1972 to the first half of 1975, the MNLF held its own against the AFP and even scored victories in conventional battlefield encounters. In the meantime, Misuari had gone into exile in the Middle East, where he continued to lobby oil- and cash-rich Arab states for material support. Both the Organization of Petroleum Exporting Countries (OPEC) and the Organization of the Islamic Conference (OIC) were sympathetic to the MNLF's cause, which received widespread international coverage, fueling nationalist pride among Mindanao's Moros. According to government estimates, at its peak, the MNLF had from 50,000 to 60,000 fighters, though more realistic estimates placed the figure at closer to 30,000. The insurgency in Mindanao cost the public treasury immensely while tying down more than half of the military's combat units.

By late 1975, the MNLF began to experience setbacks in the field. Battle fatigue had set in, and there were significant numbers of rebel surrenderees. Sabah's titular politician and a strong supporter of the MNLF, Tun Mustapha, fell from power. By then, Marcos's tactics of cooptation—offering money and positions to local Muslim leaders—had had some success. Many Muslim politicians began to portray themselves as moderates—nationalist and pragmatic at the same time. Too, Imelda used her diplomatic charms on key Arab leaders, especially Qaddafi, who had threatened the Philippines with an oil embargo. In negotiations in Tripoli with four member states of the OIC—Saudi Arabia, Somalia, Senegal, and Libya—in late December of 1976, the Marcos regime negotiated a ceasefire with the MNLF. The ceasefire provided both sides room to breathe and regroup, while negotiations were undertaken to work out the details of what would later be known as the Tripoli Agreement.

The Tripoli Agreement represented a compromise between the Philippine republic and the MNLF. The latter now sought autonomy rather than independence while the Marcos government had to cede power to a region that it had long sought to dominate. Instead of the original twenty-one provinces the MNLF had wanted to include, it had to settle for thirteen, eight of which had Christian majorities. The agreement stipulated that within the autonomous areas Muslims had the right to form their own schools, establish courts based on *shariah* or Islamic law, and create administrative systems, including a legislative assembly, executive council, and its own security forces. However, at an unspecified date, the MNLF men-under-arms would be integrated with the Armed Forces of the Philippines.

While it seemed to hard-liners within the Marcos administration that he had given too many concessions to the Moro rebels, in fact, Marcos reduced pressure from the OIC and effectively took Libya, the MNLF's strongest supporter, out of the equation. Most significantly a key provision in the agreement left its implementation to the Marcos regime. Despite objections from Misuari and the MNLF, Marcos determined that a plebiscite was needed to approve the creation of an autonomous region. The results? Ten of the thirteen provinces opted for autonomy. The Marcos regime then divided the ten provinces into two regions, making it easier to rule these areas even if grouped as one autonomous entity. In the meantime, Misuari's leadership was challenged by his deputy Hashim Salamat, who resigned and formed a breakaway group, the Moro Islamic Liberation Front, or MILF. Educated at Cairo University and connected with Muslim reformers in the Philippines, Salamat was a more orthodox Muslim than the secular-minded Misuari and other MNLF leaders. Complicating the situation further was the emergence of the obscure Bangsa Moro Liberation Organization (BMLO), which claimed to represent traditional Moro society. Its leaders were old-school politicians, one of whom, Macapanton Abbas, had once served with the Marcos regime as government liaison to Moro districts. There were credible reports that in fact the regime was secretly funding the BMLO. The existence of three rival groups of course worked to the regime's advantage, as it now began to negotiate with the MILF, pointedly ignoring the MNLF. The MNLF, snubbed, took up arms once again, and the deadly conflict resumed, though on a lesser scale.

THE ASSASSINATION OF NINOY AQUINO: ENDGAME

In March of 1980, Senator Aquino had suffered a heart attack and in May was allowed to depart for the United States with his family. After a successful heart operation and three years of quiet exile with his family in Boston, which included teaching at Harvard University, in 1983, he decided to fly back to Manila to try and engage the dictator in a constructive dialogue in which he hoped Marcos would agree to a peaceful transfer of power. By now the strongman's deteriorating health was an open secret: he was suffering from lupus erythematosus, an autoimmune disorder that affected his kidneys, requiring regular dialysis. It meant there were times when he was not in charge. Aquino feared a bloody struggle of succession would tear the country apart when Marcos died. Despite warnings from friends and from insiders within the Marcos regime, and a rendezvous with Imelda in New York City where she tried to persuade him to stay put, he flew via a circuitous route and under an assumed name, Marcial Bonifacio (a play on martial law, and the name of the military camp he had been detained in), to Manila and arrived on August 21, 1983. His attempt at anonymity failed, nor did the bulletproof vest he wore protect him from a shot to the back of the head, killing him instantly as he was being escorted off the plane by a government security detail, part of the Aviation Security Command. Ironically, had Aquino been allowed to deliver a speech upon disembarking, part of what he would have read stated that "the willing sacrifice of the innocent is the most powerful answer to insolent tyranny that has yet been conceived by God or man." Earlier, before he flew to Manila, he had said prophetically, "The Filipino is worth dying for."

A lone gunman and small-time gangster by the name of Rolando Galman, with no history of radical association with either the Left or the Right, was blamed by the government for Aquino's assassination; conveniently, Galman was himself shot dead right after Aquino fell lifeless on the airport tarmac. No one believed this trumped-up story. Facts unearthed after the assassination revealed that the hapless Galman had been abducted by government security forces to play the role, literally, of fall guy. Thousands of mourners lined up to see Ninoy's "salvaged" body, displayed in an open casket, the bloodied face left untouched by the funeral parlor, upon instructions from his bereaved family who wanted to show the world the regime's calculated brutality. At least two million people lined the streets to watch the funeral cortege—an impressive and historic display of public grief, as well as an eloquent protest against the Marcoses, though the government-controlled media paid scant attention.

Ninoy's martyrdom energized Philippine society and heralded the beginning of the regime's end. While opposition from the poor and the left had always been a constant, what was new was the now active participation of the middle and upper classes in opposing the Marcoses. There was among them the growing feeling that if a member of the privileged class could be gunned down in broad daylight, no one was safe. Instead of passively holding, the center—whether in business, politics, or religion—moved actively into the ranks of the opposition. Massive street demonstrations became a regular feature of the urban landscape in Metro Manila. Revealing the depth of disenchantment with the Marcoses, the staid and normally apolitical businessmen and -women and white-collar workers of Makati—the country's Wall Street—enthusiastically showered the marchers on the broad boulevards below with confetti and shouted anti-government slogans.

The insistent question was, "Who killed Ninoy?" It didn't require a stretch of the imagination to see the hand of the military, if not the Marcoses, behind the foul deed. Under intense domestic and international pressure for an impartial investigation, Marcos dismissed the first inquiry commission, headed by a known Marcos partisan, and appointed one headed by Judge Corazon Agrava, respected for her independence. The Agrava Commission quickly threw out the lone-gunman theory and, in late 1984, concluded what the public instinctively believed, that the military escort had shot Aquino, and then shot and killed Galman. The Agrava Commission also determined that high-ranking military officers led by General Fabian Ver, Marcos's relative and chief of staff of the Armed Forces of the Philippines, had planned Aquino's murder. Ver was famous for his unswerving loyalty to the dictator. The standard joke in Manila about the devoted Ver was that if Marcos asked him to jump from a building, Ver's only question would be, "Sir, from which floor?" Marcos reluctantly suspended Ver prior to the forthcoming trial. In its Epilogue, the Agrava Commission indicted the regime as well when it stated:

> . . . the killing of the late former Senator Aquino has brought into sharper focus the ills pervading Philippine society. It was this concretization of the horror that has been haunting this country for decades, routinely manifested by the breakdown of peace and order, economic instability, graft and corruption, and an increasing number of abusive elements in what are otherwise noble institutions in our country—the military and law enforcement agencies.

254 A HISTORY OF THE PHILIPPINES

But after a sham trial before a special court, General Ver and twenty-four other high-ranking officials, and one civilian, were acquitted. Ver was quickly reinstated as chief of staff. Military support was absolutely essential if the Marcos regime were to weather the storm. In the end, only low-ranking soldiers received prison sentences.

The predictable outcome of course further inflamed the public and triggered even more demonstrations. With the credibility of Marcos's rule in shambles, and capital flight intensifying due to the threat of a precipitous descent into chaos, the economy was in a tailspin. It was the deepest crisis in the history of the dictatorship, one that would bring it to its knees ultimately. The crisis had other effects. For one thing, it spurred the rise of reformist elements in the military, notably the Reform the Armed Forces Movement, or RAM, a group of colonels, graduates of the Philippine Military Academy, that wished to rid the AFP of corruption, reinstill a sense of professionalism in the ranks, enforce a merit system of promotion—Marcos was notorious for his nepotism—and work for peaceful and legal change. Marcos's intransigence further enlarged the ranks of the NPA and deepened U.S. domestic opposition to the Reagan government's support of the dictatorship.

U.S. policies towards the regime began to change. What had been uncritical support now came under intense scrutiny. Congressman Stephen Solarz, influential chair of the Asian and Pacific Affairs Subcommittee of the House Foreign Affairs Committee, who had attended Ninoy Aquino's funeral, urged the Reagan administration to distance itself from the Marcoses. Adding his voice to the growing chorus of dissatisfaction was Senator Richard Lugar, head of the Senate Foreign Affairs Committee. Filipino anti-Marcos groups in the U.S., from all across the ideological spectrum, grew more stringent in their criticism both of the Marcos dictatorship and the Reagan government. In public, the White House held on tight to the regime, but at the same time the State Department and the Pentagon made it clear that reforms were needed in the AFP, and that the U.S. needed to approach the legal opposition to canvass for a suitable replacement for the ailing dictator, a liberal who would also protect U.S. interests. Marcos resisted the pressure to reform the military, as the leaders he had installed formed his main and, increasingly, sole support.

Nevertheless, in a bold and desperate ploy, on November 3, 1985, Marcos announced on the U.S. network television program, "This Week with David Brinkley," that he would hold early presidential elections in January of 1986. It was an experienced lawyer's calculated gamble, to cloak the retention of power in legality, somewhat mollifying U.S. critics but holding the very real threat of an upset win by the opposition. Because of the short notice, Filipinos referred to this as the "snap" election, later postponed to February.

THE SNAP ELECTIONS

Corazon Cojuangco Aquino would be David against Goliath.

A month after the strongman's announcement on U.S. television, and presented with 1.2 million signatures, the widow of the slain senator agreed reluctantly to run against the aging dictator and the ruling Kilusan Bagong Lipunan (KBL). Salvador Laurel, heretofore also a presidential candidate, was persuaded to be her running mate, thus presenting a unified opposition field under the banner of the political party formed by Ninoy Aquino in 1978, the Lakas ng Bayan, its acronym being *Laban*, a Tagalog word which means "Fight." (Ninoy had while in detention formed the party to oppose Marcos's KBL in the 1978 National Assembly's regional elections. All its 21 candidates lost in elections completely dominated by the ruling party.)

During the campaign, Marcos confidently projected a landslide victory for himself and his running mate, Arturo Tolentine, questioning how a convent-educated housewife (an image both campaigns utilized for diametrically opposed reasons) could possibly cope with the numerous and complicated economic and security problems facing the nation. He contrasted his skills with Aquino's lack of political experience, to which Aquino riposted that indeed, she lacked experience, especially in stealing and cheating. Hoping to placate the voters, Marcos dangled several carrots before them, such as reduced housing and utility costs, an increase in government salaries, more schools, and tax breaks.

A comic element was introduced when Imelda belittled the widow's lack of fashion sense and her preference for simple yellow dresses. (Yellow had become the opposition color, due to the yellow ribbons Filipinos displayed when her husband Ninoy was assassinated.) Part of the underlying tension between the two women, apart from the suspicion that Imelda had a hand in the plot to kill her husband, was due to class. Educated in exclusive schools at home and abroad, Cory

Cojuangco Aquino was born with the proverbial silver spoon in her mouth, being a member of the immensely wealthy Cojuangco clan that owned Hacienda Luisita. Imelda Romualdez, on the other hand, had grown up in genteel poverty in the sticks and had clawed her way to the top while attempting to erase the facts of her childhood.

The fact that the snap elections pitted an aging tyrant and wily master politician against a saintly political ingénue who happened to be the widow of Ninoy Aquino, a martyr for his country, presented a spectacle fraught with symbols in a country with a fetish for symbols. The elections were a morality play, and a moro-moro, where good and evil were clearly delineated. It was a good old-fashioned cinematic melodrama, an eminently hissable villain with a harridan for a wife plotting against a betrayed mother—Cory doing triple-duty as the mother herself, the grieving widow, and stand-in for the mother country long suffering from abuse heaped on her by a wayward son and daughter.

In Philippine iconography there are no more sacrosanct figures than a mother and a martyr's widow: beneath the jock veneer laid down by the Spanish and the Americans, Filipino society is strongly matriarchal—one reason the most revered Catholic figures are representations of mother and child: the Virgin Mary and the Holy Infant Jesus. During the campaign, the Marcoses vilified her gender, unwittingly galvanizing the women voters and betraying an ignorance of the Filipino psyche they claimed to know so well. In order to protect their aggrieved mother, the people had no choice but to rise up against a brutal regime. Part of the opposition strategy was to urge the public to boycott the goods and services of companies owned and operated by Marcos cronies.

Still, the Marcoses and the KBL held all the aces, and no one expected the elections to be a walk in the park for Cory. But a major revelation that seriously undermined whatever credibility Marcos had left was the fact that the twenty-seven medals supposedly awarded to him for his World War II heroics were fake. He was reputedly the most-decorated combat veteran of that war, second only to Audie Murphy, who went on to become a Hollywood star. (Marcos was also rumored to have an *anting-anting*, or amulet, embedded in his back that rendered him and his guerrilla unit impervious to harm.) During his tenure as chair of the Philippine Senate Appropriations Committee, for instance, Marcos received no fewer than ten medals in 1963. But research by war veteran Colonel Bonifacio Gillego and investigative pieces in *The New York Times* and *The Washington Post*, based on archival research done by the historian Alfred McCoy, debunked Marcos's claims to a storied war-time career. The guerrilla unit that he supposedly led, Maharlika, was of little value. Predictably, Marcos labeled the revelations part of a "smear campaign."

He claimed that Maharlika had 8,300 members and had performed valiantly under his leadership. In reality most of the exploits were figments of his imagination, and the guerrilla unit had approximately one hundred members, with no major feats accomplished. As early as 1948, after a thorough investigation, the U.S. military dismissed Marcos's claims that he and his outfit had helped hasten the end of the war and concluded that Marcos's false war claims amounted to a criminal act. Additionally, the records showed that Marcos had been arrested during the war for financial fraud. He was held but a short while before being released, an indication that the young politician-on-the-make was already well-connected.

In anticipation of the fact that the Marcoses would pull out all the stops to cling to power, the National Movement for Free Elections, or NAMFREL, was revived. NAMFREL had its origins in the early 1950s, created with CIA funds for the campaign of Ramón Magsaysay. In limbo during the martial law years, it was resurrected in 1983 and headed by an anti-Marcos entrepreneur, José Concepción Jr. It would compete with the government's Commission on Elections (COMELEC) and provide a quick count of the ballots, to preempt the shady practice of most Philippine elections, *dagdag-bawas* ("add and subtract"), wherein tabulation is rigged to favor one party (usually the one with the most resources) over the other. In fact, the administration did attempt to manipulate the overall tallies at the main COMELEC tabulation center, prompting a walk-out by COMELEC operators to protest such blatant cheating. Most of NAMFREL's funds for the 1986 election came from such U.S. sources as the Agency for International Development, the National Endowment for Democracy, as well as from the Japanese government and American businessmen living in the Philippines. NAMFREL also helped support the Reform the Armed Forces Movement, and Radio Veritas, the church-owned radio station that would play a key role in the February 1986 People Power uprising.

The Left Is Left Behind

The fast-moving developments caught the radical left unprepared. Before Marcos sprung the idea of a snap election on the nation, a coalition of various left-wing opposition groups had formed in early 1985, calling itself Bagong Alyansang Makabayan, the New Nationalist Alliance, or BAYAN, for short, an acronym that means "nation" in Tagalog. Taken together, its constituent organizations provided a base of two and half million people. While affirming the need to depose the Marcos regime, and after much internal debate, in January of 1986 BAYAN opted to boycott the elections, a decision it would later rue. It issued a statement that read in part:

> There is no sense believing, therefore, that the snap election shall lead to the ouster of Marcos from power. In truth, it shall only fortify the U.S.-backed Marcos dictatorship. . . . The snap election does not promise meaningful changes in Philippine society . . . unless the electoral campaign can be transformed into a militant forum for advancing the anti-dictatorship struggle, the snap election shall be entirely meaningless. . . . In view of the foregoing, the Bagong Alyansang Makabayan deems that the people are left with no other principled option but to boycott the snap election.

Some of BAYAN's leaders felt they were missing an unprecedented opportunity to move their agenda forward, and took a leave of absence from the organization, campaigning for Aquino. Other left-wing groups not allied with BAYAN also supported the elections and Aquino, arguing that she had spoken out against the retention of the U.S. bases; had promised the release of political prisoners if elected as well as amnesty for all those charged with political offenses by the regime; and would draft a new constitution to replace the Marcos-era one.

PEOPLE POWER

After ballots were cast on February 7, 1986—a day marked by the killings of at least thirty people and numerous instances of fraud by KBL, the ruling party—Marcos and Aquino issued competing declarations of victory. Aquino then proposed meeting with the ailing dictator to effect a smooth transition of power, a proposal speedily turned down.

For his part, trying to project a more neutral tone, President Reagan encouraged Marcos to work with his opponents to transform the political system—as though dictatorial rule since 1972 could so easily be changed. The U.S. president seemed to be in denial, however, when at a press conference shortly after the Marcos camp had officially declared its man the winner, he expressed his concern "about the violence that was evident there and the possibility of fraud, although it could have been that all of that was occurring on both sides." His loyalty to the Marcoses couldn't have been clearer. At the same time it infuriated the Filipino voters. U.S. Congressman Stephen Solarz sarcastically noted that the Reagan response was "evidence that the White House has been transformed into an opium den . . . [T]hey've clearly lost touch with reality."

To the Reagan administration Marcos was a known entity, America's Boy, whom different U.S. administrations had supported for twenty years. It found it difficult to envision a transition that would actually involve the mass participation of Filipinos taking to the streets to oust the dictatorship—democracy in its rawest form. And that is precisely what occurred between February 22 and February 25, when a military coup about to fall flat on its face succeeded when the aroused citizenry of Metro Manila rallied around the rebels and forced the Marcoses to flee.

Marcos's security forces had gotten wind of a coup being planned by the RAM leaders, who were close to Enrile and Fidel Ramos, head of the Philippine Constabulary (and a relative of Marcos to boot). The RAM group in turn learned of orders being issued for their arrest on February 22, prompting them, with Enrile and Ramos, to move to two military camps, Aguinaldo and Crame, that same day, with their followers. Abandoning his largely ineffective stance of so-called "critical collaboration" with the regime, two days before the elections, Cardinal Sin had declared that Catholics could practice civil disobedience if they believed the elections to be fraudulent. No one doubted that it was an endorsement of Aquino. And it was Sin who, through Radio Veritas, exhorted listeners to come out onto the streets surrounding the two camps where the anti-Marcos forces had holed up, and which faced each other across the broad lanes of Epifanio de los Santos Avenue, or EDSA, in Quezon City.

People Power, as it came to be known, was nothing short of a fairy tale come true. Unfolding over a period of four days, from February 22 to 25, at least a million citizens from all walks of life formed a human shield around the camps, an unprecedented display of the unarmed and the unnamed facing down the armed and dangerous. Beggar, priest, nun, matron, businessman, student, market vendor stood in the path of pro-Marcos tanks and assault troops, offering them flowers and food, and exorcising the helicopter gunships overhead with their rosaries, crucifixes, and cheers. It was awe-inspiring, a modern-day Cecil B. DeMille spectacle and a hippie dream come true: a bloodless revolution, a war of the roses sans thorns, and a miracle all rolled into one, which would inspire similar miracles in Berlin, Moscow, Tiananmen, and Prague. At one point, against her handlers' advice, Cory Aquino proceeded to one of the camps and told the cheering throngs there that "for the first time in the history of the world, a civilian population has been called to defend the military." That it would also herald, albeit unknowingly, the restoration of the ancien régime was at the moment scarcely evident. The urban populace, and the country—for similar outpourings occurred in other cities—had succeeded in forcing the Marcoses to seek refuge in Uncle Sam's arms.

On Tuesday, February 25, at 10:46 a.m., Corazon C. Aquino was sworn in as President of the Philippines at the Club Filipino in the upper-class enclave of Greenhills, the first woman to lead the nation. Addressing Filipinos as her "beloved brothers and sisters," she declared: "It is fitting and proper that, if rights and liberties of our people were taken away at midnight fourteen years ago, the people should recover those lost rights and liberties in the full light of day. . . . It took the brutal murder of Ninoy to bring about a unity so strong and the phenomenon of people power. We became exiles in our own land—we Filipinos who are at home only in freedom—when Marcos destroyed the Republic fourteen years ago."

Not to be outdone, Marcos also proclaimed himself president on the same day, from a balcony in Malacañang, surrounded by his family and a coterie of faithful "loyalists," as these die-hard Marcos followers came to be known. By then he had already been persuaded by U.S. Senator Paul Laxalt to resign. Laxalt, when asked by the dictator what he should do, had replied: "I think you should cut and cut cleanly. The time has come." Offered asylum in the U.S., later that same day, he,

Imelda, their family, and a few close friends were flown by helicopter to Clark Air Force Base, thence transferred to a plane that took them to Honolulu. Among the conjugal dictators' luggage were $200,000 in gold bullion, $1 million in pesos, and Pampers boxes crammed with jewelry that included a gold crown and three tiaras of precious gems.

Those heady February days not only signaled a new level of political consciousness—however temporary that may have been in hindsight—but resurrected and extended the collective stirrings of nationalism generated by the 1896 revolution against Spain—Asia's first against a colonial power. Ferdinand and Imelda Marcos desired more than anything else to be seen as great historical figures but wound up being, sadly, merely hysterical and much-ridiculed characters.

The Deluge

The night of the 25th, anti-Marcos crowds that had gathered by the gates of the palace burst through, overwhelming the loyalists who had stood guard. Long denied access to the palace, they ran through the corridors of power, partly in glee and partly in astonishment that they had even been able to penetrate the inner sanctum. They could have easily plundered and like Visigoths ransacked Malacañang but, perhaps mindful of history, did relatively little damage, except for some paintings of the couple that were defaced, furniture damaged, and various knick-knacks taken as souvenirs.

That the president was seriously ill was evident in the mini-clinic that had been set up with sophisticated medical equipment, cabinets full of vitamins and medications, disposable diapers, and a dialysis machine. In the basement two hospital rooms had been set up, one of them clearly meant for surgery. Imelda's quarters bore quantifiable evidence of her mania for expensive items—a never-ending attempt to fill the needs of a deprived childhood. Her mirrored dressing room was filled with hundreds of costly silk dresses, baskets crammed with soaps from around the world, and row upon row of expensive French perfumes. Elsewhere were a half-dozen wide-screen television sets, stereo units, and a double freezer full of frozen steaks. In her bedroom stood a ten-foot high closet packed with her nightgowns. Underneath her twelve-foot-wide bed, according to the late journalist and National Artist for Literature Nick Joaquin, were bundles "of gold-chain necklaces and a receipt for over two million dollars from the jewelers Van Cleef and Arpels. . . . Mrs.

Marcos's private bathroom was equipped with a 15-foot-square sunken bathtub, mirrored ceilings, gallon bottles of a custom-made French perfume called *First Lady*. And no fewer than five Italian bathrobes. . . . A tally would reveal that Imelda left behind three thousand panties, three thousand pairs of shoes, hundreds of black bras [one of which was bulletproof], and five fur coats, including minks."

SHE REIGNS BUT DOES NOT RULE

Corazon C. Aquino, or Cory to the public, was an unlikely president, with no experience of holding or even running for political office. She was, in short, not a *trapo*, an acronym for *tra*ditional *po*litician and a pun on the Tagalog word that means "rag." Her non-trapo status was a major reason for her immense popularity at the outset of her term. A conservative Catholic and a member of one of the richest Chinese-mestizo clans of the country, the Cojuangcos, she had been educated in the United States, studying mathematics and obtaining a degree in French at the private College of Mount Saint Vincent in New York City.

Her presidency began auspiciously enough, with a repudiation of the 1973 Constitution and the abolition of the legislature. By claiming legislative powers for her office, she had de facto established a revolutionary government. In effect, Aquino could rule by decree, just as Marcos had. Unlike the Marcos regime, however, President Aquino and her administration encouraged the creation of what the media referred to as "democratic space" by taking several measures, such as the restoration of the writ of habeas corpus; leaving the courts free to operate once more without executive or any political interference; the repeal of repressive Marcos-era labor laws; the establishment of a commission, headed by respected former senator and political prisoner José Diokno, to investigate those responsible for human rights abuses under the Marcos dictatorship; and the convening of a constitutional convention to replace the 1973 document with another constitution.

The long-suppressed frustrations, aspirations, and exuberance of the public found release when more than twenty dailies sprung up, including the revival of the two venerable English-language newspapers, *The Manila Times* and the Lopez-owned *The Manila Chronicle*. What had begun as an anti-Marcos tabloid, *Mr. & Mrs.*, incorporated with the weekly *Philippine Inquirer* to become the *Philippine Daily Inquirer* two months before the toppling of the Marcos regime. It soon became the largest-circulation English-language daily in the nation.

To deal with local officials that had come to power during the Marcos era, the Aquino administration simply replaced them with temporary office-holders, known as Officers-in-Charge, or OICs. It was a sweeping act, perhaps too sweeping, resulting often in throwing out the baby with the bath. Critics pointed out that, while it was true there were many who had been mere mouthpieces of the Marcos KBL machine, not all were political hacks or incompetent; many had won legitimately and enjoyed popular support. The removal of previous office holders didn't mean their dropping out of the political scene. They had an opportunity to reclaim their lost posts during the nation-wide elections for all political offices, from governorships to the revived bicameral legislature, from barangay councilor to mayor, held in May 1987 and many, in fact, did.

For a while, democratic space resulted in a détente, albeit uneasy, between the military and both the Communist New People's Army, and the secular Moro National Liberation Front. In recognition of their struggle against Marcos, political prisoners were released, the most prominent being the NPA head, Bernabe Buscayno, and the CPP founder, José Maria Sison, much to the dismay of hard-liners within Aquino's Cabinet and the military. Sison, who had spent nine years in prison and had endured torture, was a much-sought-after speaker by various civic and university groups, before leaving on a speaking tour of Europe. He decided to seek asylum in the Netherlands in 1987, after being warned by friends that returning to the islands would be detrimental to his health.

Buscayno and several other members of the left organized a political party Partido ng Bayan (PnB, Party of the Nation) to campaign for congressional seats in the 1987 elections. Forming a coalition with other cause-oriented groups that called itself Alliance for a New Politics, PnB disdained the traditional *palabas* for its election rallies and appealed to the electorate on the strength of their progressive platform. Hampered by a shoestring budget, the PnB slate of senatorial candidates, including an ex-beauty queen turned guerrilla, fared poorly. And in a sign that democratic space was viewed as a charade by extremist right-wing groups, Buscayno survived an assassination attempt, though two companions were killed and shrapnel permanently lodged in his back. Buscayno credited his instincts as a guerrilla, which he said enabled him to instinctively get down on the floor of the automobile he was in when shots rang out. Two other well-known PnB candidates led less charmed lives and were assassinated: Lean Alejandro, a young, charismatic former student activist at the University of the Philippines and Rolando Olalia, an important left-wing labor leader and organizer.

Nevertheless, the left viewed the post-Marcos democratic space as an opportunity to test new ideas and approaches. The NPA negotiated with the government for a sixty-day cease-fire while the CPP allowed for more vigorous internal debate, mindful of its costly blunder during the snap elections. Undertaking self-criticism of its boycott position, in its publication of May 1986, *Ang Bayan*, the leadership was contrite: "Where the people saw in the February 7 snap presidential election a chance to deliver a crippling blow on the Marcos regime . . . the Executive Committee of the Party Central Committee saw it merely as 'a noisy and empty political battle' among factions in the ruling classes. And when the aroused and militant people moved spontaneously but resolutely to oust the hated regime last February 22-25, the party and its forces were not there to lead them. . . . A recent assessment conducted by the Political Bureau (Politburo) of the Central Committee characterized the boycott policy as a major political blunder."

The debates within provoked internecine struggles, as the leadership attempted to define its policies and chart new directions in the post-Marcos era. The underground left's image of solidarity was further undermined by revelations that in the waning years of the Marcos dictatorship, the NPA conducted bloody purges of its ranks in Mindanao. Seized by a vengeful paranoia, and with reports of government agents having infiltrated their ranks, NPA commands executed a number of their own, suspecting them to be, in their parlance, "deep penetration agents." The movement was further shaken with arrests of top CPP figures in 1988, the result of much-improved military intelligence, aided undoubtedly by dissent within the CPP/NPA.

Extending the same olive branch to the MNLF, the Aquino government allowed exiled MNLF leader Nur Misuari to return. The military and many impartial observers viewed this as a tactical mistake, for the MNLF was moribund and Misuari's return revived it; the former university professor was hailed practically as a conquering hero when he went on tour of southern Mindanao, with a large and impressive heavily armed entourage. Casting aside the arrangement made during the Marcos era, another plebiscite was held in 1989, with the aim of creating an autonomous region for Filipino Muslims, as originally envisioned by the Tripoli Agreement. This time around, only Basilan, Maguindanao, Lanao del Sur, Sulu, and Tawi-Tawi out of thirteen provinces voted to be part of what was to be called the Autonomous Region of Muslim Mindanao (ARMM), to be governed by Misuari. That Misuari accepted the holding of a plebiscite and the resulting geographical area that was much smaller reflected both the fact that the MNLF was not as potent as before and that the years in exile had made him more realistic in his and his organization's aspirations.

Recovering the Loot

As early as 1969, the CIA determined that Marcos had already stolen several hundred million dollars, and, by 1972, other American officials had become aware that Marcos was raiding the national treasury. Nothing was said, however, to avoid embarrassing an ally. Estimates of how much the Marcoses had stolen from the government ranged from $5 billion to $10 billion. Due to the unwelcome spotlight placed on its secretive banking practices, the Swiss government promised to freeze all Marcos accounts even as the Aquino government, using documents seized that linked the Marcoses to numerous bank accounts and major expenditures, determined to recover at least $6 billion in assets it accused the Marcoses of unlawfully amassing. To take charge of the recovery efforts, the Aquino administration set up the Presidential Commission on Good Government (PCGG). The PCGG itself however became mired in charges of corruption and of individual officers turning sequestered corporations into their private fiefdoms.

The most publicized attempt to recover the ill-gotten wealth of the Marcoses was the trial of Imelda in New York's federal district court in May of 1990. (Ferdinand had died in 1989, so his widow had to undergo the humiliation of a public trial alone, a trial monitored closely by the PCGG.) She had been indicted the year before, with the government charging her and Adnan Khashoggi, the Saudi arms dealer alleged to have helped the Marcoses in their financial shenanigans. The four-count racketeering indictment centered on the purchase of four choice

Manhattan buildings with cash illicitly acquired—a crime under the Racketeer Influenced and Corrupt Organizations (RICO) Act, the scope of which includes pursuing criminal enterprises that operate outside the jurisdiction of the United States when part of the ill-gotten profits are then invested or otherwise used within the U.S. The act was originally meant as a key legislative bill aimed at organized crime syndicates such as the Mafia.

The trial lasted three months, the government prosecutors portraying the complexities of the case that included 95 witnesses, 5,700 pages of testimony, and 300,000 documents offered to the court as possible evidence. Prosecution witnesses painted a damaging portrait of money laundering of huge sums from the Philippines, cronyism, kickbacks from local and foreign businesses, as well as extravagant purchases that included jewelry and artworks. In the end, however, the jury acquitted Imelda and Khashoggi on all counts—on July 3rd, her 60th birthday, no less—testament to Imelda's lawyers' persuasive use of the blame-the-dead-man defense, and to the prosecution's inability to present a coherent and convincing picture of sustained criminal activity. To celebrate her acquittal, Imelda, throughout the proceedings the very picture of the demure and retiring widow, proceeded immediately to St. Patrick's Cathedral on Fifth Avenue, not far from the Crown Building, one of the four properties her family was believed to have owned. Surrounded by photographers and a coterie of loyalists, she made her way on padded knees to the altar and offered thanks to the Almighty and, presumably, to Ferdinand for his intervention from beyond the grave.

Democratic Space versus Military Restlessness

Marcos may have fled the country, but thousands of his supporters remained visible and voluble, taking advantage of the restoration of civil liberties to constantly criticize the Aquino administration. Barely two months after the February uprising, on April 12, twenty thousand Marcos supporters gathered on the streets of Manila and demanded his return. Though pro-Cory supporters had turned out as well, it was a peaceful if raucous demonstration, with the two sides kept apart by the police. The loyalists would stage such scenes sporadically during Aquino's tenure, but they were never a serious threat to her government's stability.

The most pressing threat the Aquino government faced, with its unlikely coalition of centrists, left-wingers and right-wingers, was from the military, now rechristened New Armed Forces of the Philippines, a public-relations ploy meant to indicate that men in uniform were now more attuned to a democratic society. It was a new military, not in the sense of having a renewed dedication to professionalism and respect for civilian rule but in the fact that the AFP was now disturbingly aware of its ability to take an active role in governance. Marcos often rewarded officers by assigning them to head non-military government agencies. With military expenditures becoming the biggest item of the national budget, the top brass had acquired a taste for the material benefits brought about by corruption, thanks to Marcos's coddling of the generals he needed to prop his regime up. The discipline and professionalism that Magsaysay had instilled in the ranks when he was dealing with the Huk rebellion had all but disappeared. Politicized, the military had grown from a pre-martial strength of 50,000 to 250,000 at its peak during the Marcos era and was no longer content to confine itself to the barracks. Henceforth, it would be impossible to put the genie back into the bottle.

The two leaders of the aborted 1986 coup against Marcos that led ultimately to People Power, Juan Ponce Enrile and General Fidel V. Ramos, held powerful posts in the Aquino Cabinet. Enrile was kept on as defense secretary while Ramos was appointed chief of staff of the AFP: Insiders in the Marcos regime, they were now insiders in the Aquino government. Neither Enrile nor Ramos had any love for the Communists or the Moro rebels or any group that professed similar ideals. Additionally, RAM officers were lobbying for more of a say in running the government, through both Enrile and Ramos and their demands on how President Aquino was to govern. The military hardliners felt passionately that without their support Cory would not have attained the presidency, and they often reminded her of her debt of gratitude, her *utang na loob*, to them.

They viewed with contempt and increasing alarm the Aquino government's efforts to reach out to both the Communist insurgency and the Moro rebellion. A general amnesty was proclaimed for NPA guerrillas, and many did come down from the hills, giving up their arms and attempting to take up the civilian life once more. On

November 24, 1986, a sixty-day ceasefire was agreed to by the government and the CPP/NPA. The day prior, Enrile had been sacked by Aquino; the defense secretary had made no secret of his dissatisfaction with Aquino's policies and openly voiced his sympathy with military malcontents. In early 1990, the government had him arrested on charges of rebellion and murder but the former defense secretary easily beat the charges.

Enrile's inability to accept Aquino's leadership proved symptomatic of the unusual restiveness afflicting the military. One military officer likened Aquino's conciliatory efforts to "castration." In all there were seven attempts to topple her government, all ending in failure, primarily due to Ramos's fidelity to Aquino. Nothing showed the influence of the hardliners within the administration more than the way the first coup attempt was dealt with. On July 6, 1986, civilian loyalists and about 300 soldiers, including some generals, took over the historic Manila Hotel. Arturo Tolentino, who had been Marcos's last vice president, stood on the hotel driveway and declared himself acting president. That it was a farce more than anything else was perhaps indicated by a quip uttered by Manuel Collantes, Tolentino's ersatz minister of foreign affairs: "For me, the revolution ended as soon as room service stopped." Assured by Defense Secretary Enrile that "we are not out to humiliate, punish, or embarrass any of you," the soldiers gave up and the loyalists, most of them from Manila's rougher neighborhoods, left the premises. So as not to be seen as letting them off too lightly, Ramos ordered the military miscreants to do thirty push-ups—with him joining in.

A telling indicator that the military seemed to be operating beyond Aquino's control was in January of 1987. Government security forces fired into the ranks of farmers, student activists, and laborers, who were marching on Malacañang to demand genuine land reform. Thirteen protesters lost their lives and thirty-nine were wounded. The bloody incident came to be known as the "Mendiola Massacre," referring to the nearby bridge that had also been the contested site of the 1971 First Quarter Storm. In protest, the head of the Commission on Human Rights, ex-Senator José Diokno, and his deputy resigned the day after. The killings further undermined popular support for Cory—and ate away at the space her government had been granted by the underground left. The cease-fire with the NPA ended the month after the massacre, in early February 1987, when the CPP ruled out any extension. In turn, adopting a harder line and bowing to pressure from the army, Aquino called for a "total war" and declared that only victory, not compromise, would end the insurgency.

Six more coup attempts followed. One, staged on August 28, 1987, was led by Colonel Gregorio "Gringo" Honasan, a handsome and charismatic leader of RAM and a veteran of the counterinsurgency wars in Mindanao. The coup failed, and Honasan was arrested. But because of the widespread sympathy he had in the military, as well as with a large segment of the public that viewed him as a romantic freedom fighter, he escaped easily and continued to plague the Aquino government. Indeed, his hand, and that of RAM, could be seen in the most serious coup attempt yet, on December 1, 1989, when 3,000 troops, spearheaded by elite units such as the Scout Rangers and the Marines, targeted Makati, the prime financial district of the country, and the site of exclusive gated communities and high-rise luxury hotels. The rebels forced the closing of the airport (now named the Ninoy Aquino International Airport), commandeered two TV stations, and occupied military outposts through the metropolitan area. Aquino's government survived after President George H.W. Bush ordered U.S. jets to fly over the city and signaled to the rebels that the United States would shoot down any rebel aircraft. The nearly successful week-long grab for power resulted in 190 dead and close to 600 wounded. It cost the economy an estimated $1.2 billion and dampened foreign-investor confidence that had been rising steadily since 1986.

With Aquino in power and perceived to be sympathetic after all to U.S. concerns, Washington stuck to the same goals it had had for nearly a century: the preservation of U.S. military and economic interests for which it was willing to oppose any popular movement that might undermine those interests. It continued to encourage Aquino to deal with the insurgency through military means, reduce or eliminate the leftists in her government, allow for the retention of the bases, and further encourage free enterprise.

One more sign that the Aquino government was reverting to Marcos-era policy when it came to the seemingly intractable insurgency was its approval of the military-created, Orwellian-sounding Citizen Armed Force Geographical Units (CAFGUs). It was simply the CHDF of the Marcos regime being given a new name, with essentially the same responsibility: to augment regular army units in counterinsurgency work in areas where the NPA was believed to be operating. Fidel Ramos, now the defense secretary, oversaw their creation. Not surprisingly, the CAFGUs proved to be as problematic as the CHDFs had been, with complaints about their abusive behavior being filed with disturbing regularity with the Commission on Human Rights.

The Aquino government's increasing emphasis on military solutions to the insurgency and away from economic and social reform meant a resumption of the army's dirty war, whose victims were mainly civilians. According to the human rights group, Task Force Detainees of the Philippines (TFDP), by 1988, the army was responsible for 54.7 percent of human rights violations, and that in Aquino's first 1,000 days, 11,911 persons were arrested for political reasons, mainly in slum areas and rural communities, by the police or the military; 1,676 individuals were subjected to torture; and 705 people were salvaged. In 1987, according to Amnesty International, more than 100 left-wing political activists, trade unionists, and peasant organizers were assassinated either by the military, paramilitary units, or vigilante groups supported by the military.

Old Lamps for the New

In May of 1986, President Aquino decreed the establishment of a constitutional convention, the third in a little more than half a century, to replace the martial-law-era 1973 Constitution. Those appointed to draft the new constitution were mainly from the upper class, including former legislators, judges, and politicians. One convenor was the internationally known film director Lino Brocka, who was from a working class family and known for his landmark social-realist melodramas that had bedeviled Imelda Marcos, whose vision of cinema was largely defined by works such as *The Sound of Music*, one of her favorite films. She believed Filipino cinema should be a repository of the "good, the beautiful, and the true" and that it should make people elsewhere want to be Filipinos. In this light, social realist films were a no-no. But precisely due to repressive policies, the 1970s and early 1980s were a golden age for Filipino films, when a whole slew of filmmakers—including Brocka, Ishmael Bernal, Marilou Diaz, Eddie Romero, Mike de Leon, Peque Gallaga, and Tikoy Aguiluz—created works that challenged government control and were insightful critiques of contemporary Philippine society. Brocka resigned before the final version of the constitution was drafted, charging that the convention seemed intent on restoring the old guard, one that had been displaced by the Marcoses, rather than incorporating much-needed reforms. He felt that the working-class and the peasantry were hardly represented, if at all. To him, it was the Malolos Congress once again, dominated by society's elite.

And indeed, the proposed constitution—ratified in February of 1987—adhered closely in many respects to the 1935 model, with the switch back to a presidential system (but this time, with only a single six-year term) and a bicameral legislature. Voters could once again elect a president and a vice president from different parties. A human rights commission was created, a bill of rights incorporated, and checks placed on authoritarian rule. There were however at least three significant differences. The first had the Constitution providing for party-list representation, a concession to those who, like Brocka, had criticized the convention for excluding the less fortunate from its framers.

The party-list feature allows for legislative representation for under-represented segments of society, such as the urban poor, women, labor, peasants, and indigenous communities. Voters in each Congressional district can cast two votes: one for a district representative who will represent the constituents, and the other for a party-list organization, which has a national platform rather than a local one. If a party-list group obtains at least 2 percent of the total votes cast nation-wide, it then lands a seat in Congress, with a maximum of three seats. This system first went into effect with the 1998 national elections, when thirteen party-list organizations won seats.

The new constitution also mandated making the country nuclear-free, as long as this was "consistent with national interest." But the most significant difference relative to Philippines-U.S. relationship now elevated any agreement between the United States and the Philippines regarding the fate of U.S. bases to treaty status, which meant it was subject to ratification by the Philippine Senate. During her presidential campaign, Aquino had been in favor of terminating the bases' lease. It was one way of establishing her nationalist credentials and distinguishing herself from Marcos. Once she had ascended to the presidency, however, and faced with constant pressure from the U.S., hard-liners within her cabinet, and the military, she changed her tune, saying merely that she wanted keep her options open.

An interim bases agreement was drawn up in late 1988 after seven months of negotiations, with Secretary of State George Shultz and Philippine Foreign Secretary Raul Manglapus signing for their respective governments. The United States agreed to pay $481 million for the bases over two years. At the end of this interim agreement, the Senate would then decide the fate of the bases. And on September 16, 1991, with nationalist solons, particularly those with the Liberal Party, carrying the day, the Senate rejected the treaty. It was a momentous occasion, a cause for celebration among all those who believed that the presence of U.S. soldiers on Philippine soil, begun in 1898, demeaned the country's sovereignty. The practical effect would only be on Subic Bay Naval Base, for earlier that year, Mt. Pinatubo had erupted spectacularly, after six hundred years of dormancy, effectively shutting down Clark Air Force Base.

The Economy

The Marcos government's programs, which relied heavily on international lending agencies, had increased the country's external debt to $28.5 billion, giving the country the dubious distinction of being among the ten most indebted countries in the world. Overspending on the elections, crony capitalism, bureaucratic corruption, and the flight of capital that intensified after Senator Aquino was assassinated left the state coffers drained. In the last five years of the Marcos regime, per capita income fell by close to 20 percent, and the prices of basic commodities had risen in an inflationary spiral that threatened to go out of control. As a result, poverty levels rose, with close to 60 percent of the rural population living below the poverty line. In Metropolitan Manila alone, 1.5 million families were similarly afflicted. With an average population growth rate of nearly 3 percent, poverty levels were sure to increase even more, straining barely adequate government resources and services.

This rendered the dilemma facing the Aquino government—how to service its external debt—an acute one. As elsewhere in other Third World countries facing enormous debt, some segments of Philippine society argued that the debts incurred under the Marcos regime should be repudiated, as these benefited his cronies more than the country, and financed projects that should never have been undertaken. Aquino's minister of economic planning, Solita Monsod, made a strong case for this, within the larger context of achieving social justice and reducing the yawning inequities between the haves and the have-nots. Cardinal Sin argued as well for selective debt repudiation; to do otherwise would be "morally wrong," given the penury of the people and the country. A case in point was the Bataan Nuclear Plan, which had been mothballed. Daily interest payments alone amounted to $300,000.

But the neoliberals within her cabinet, primarily Jaime Ongpin, her influential and respected finance minister, and Central Bank Governor Jobo Fernandez insisted that the nation meet all its external obligations. Default was not an option, they argued, if the country wished to remain a credible part of the global financial market. This meant payments of $3.5 billion a year, or 10 percent of the GDP. At the end of the day, Ongpin, Fernandez, and their allies convinced the Aquino administration to borrow even further, thus allowing international lending agencies such as the International Monetary fund, the World Bank, and the Asian Development Bank to help shape the government's economic policies. The strategy in essence was that through increased borrowing the economy would be stimulated, which would in turn increase revenues that would then drive down the debt. It was also a precondition to approval of the $10 billion Multilateral Aid Initiative (MAI), primarily backed by the United States, as well as Japan and other creditor nations. It was a precondition similar to the strings-attached aid that the U.S. extended to the spectacularly ruined country right after World War II.

Combining payments on both foreign and domestic debt during Aquino's tenure ate up almost 50 percent of government revenues—leaving little for infrastructure, poverty alleviation and other social programs, and education. Poverty levels did decline somewhat, from close to 50 percent down to 46.5 percent, but this was nowhere close to significant. Beginning with the Marcos years, when the export of labor overseas was actively promoted, remittances from the expanding Filipino diaspora helped soften the blows of a stagnant economy. During Aquino's six-year term, remittances averaged $4 billion a year.

That figure has risen in the first decade of the twenty-first century to close to $16 billion.

The Failure of Land Reform

A major cause of the insurgency has always been the inequitable distribution of agricultural land. More than a quarter of arable land was owned by less than four percent of land-owning families. The desired end was simple—to break up huge, landed estates—but the means to that end were not. Making land transfers work meant fair compensation for the owners and setting up a whole government network of financing and farm-production distribution. Where was the money to come from? More importantly, would the landed families, long a part of the historical ruling elites, agree?

While the 1987 constitution recognized the need for "an agrarian reform program," the specific provision was less than compelling:

> To this end, the State shall encourage and undertake the just distribution of all agricultural lands, subject to such priorities and reasonable retention limits as the Congress may prescribe, taking into account ecological, developmental or equity considerations, and subject to payment of just compensation. In determining retention limits, the State shall respect the rights of small landowners. The State shall further provide incentives for voluntary land sharing.

Instead of using her emergency powers to interpret the constitution and apply far-reaching changes with regards to land reform, Aquino deferred to the newly elected Congress. By allowing its members to set the "priorities and reasonable retention limits," she essentially left it to a landlord-dominated body to legislate against its own interests. It wouldn't and didn't. The clearest and most eloquent instance of the failure of Aquino's land reform program lay in the fact that Hacienda Luisita, her family's huge 6,000-plus hectare hacienda, where the family's racehorses received better care than the tenant laborers, remained intact. She had promised in her campaign that the hacienda would be affected. There was a nominal attempt to incorporate the hacienda so that it became the Hacienda Luisita Incorporated, with 33 percent of the stock to be turned over to the tenant farmers, but over a period of thirty years. The Cojuangco family would retain the rest of the stock. In the end, Cory was unable, or unwilling, to act against the interests of her clan.

By the time her Comprehensive Agrarian Reform Program had metamorphosed into the Comprehensive Agrarian Reform Law of 1988, it had lost much of its bite. Instead of more than 27 million acres being subject, only 9.4 million acres would be affected. There was a corresponding decline from 3 million farmer-beneficiaries to fewer than 2 million. And most significantly, no sugar and coconut lands were to be subject to land reform, essentially leaving most of the major agribusiness plantations untouched. Land-owning lawmakers, and lawmakers beholden to wealthy landowners in their districts, heaved a sigh of relief in private even as they publicly praised the law as a landmark. Such emasculation made it possible for Congresswoman Hortensia Starke, a wealthy, prominent sugar planter from Negros Occidental and outspoken opponent of land reform, to walk dramatically through the Congress session hall in July of 1988, clad in an expensive ball gown and twirling a parasol—a clear "I don't give a damn" in the face of the popular clamor for land.

What She Hath Wrought

The problems facing Corazon C. Aquino when she took office were seemingly innumerable, intractable, and multilayered. Viewed as a manager and administrator, she seemed helpless, nowhere more so than in the energy sector. With no coherent and sustained policy, regular blackouts plagued residential and industrial areas, driving up the cost of doing business in the country and discouraging potential investors. Infrastructure was left to deteriorate. And the economy, after rebounding in the first two years of her term, started to decline. Poverty levels thus remained substantially high.

A major factor in the continuing high levels of poverty was her administration's commitment to paying in full the country's foreign debt, essentially continuing Marcos's policy of automatically appropriating from the national budget the full amount to service the debt due each year. As a result, from 1986 to 1993, according to economist Walden Bello in a 2009 article for the *Philippine Daily Inquirer* examining her economic legacy shortly after her death that year, "some 8 to

10 percent of the Philippines GDP left the country in debt-service payments adding up to a total of nearly $30 billion—an appalling sum, especially considering that the Philippines' external debt was only $21.5 billion."

In contrast, Bello pointed to Argentina's President Norberto Kirchner who, in 2002, confronted with bankruptcy caused in the main by debt repayments, decided to repay only 25 cents out of every dollar owed. In spite of initial resistance from the creditors, they eventually agreed, and Argentina, able to reduce capital outflow, "grew by an average of 10 percent between 2003 and 2008."

While the more insidious forms of crony capitalism were discontinued, as were the monopolistic mechanisms for sugar and coconut, Aquino's government didn't quite know what to do with all the corporations the Marcos regime had controlled, either through heavy subsidies or outright ownership. Through the Assets Privatization Trust under the management of the PCGG, attempts were made to sell off these assets, attempts complicated by legal wrangling, internal disputes, and allegations that the PCGG itself was becoming corrupt.

Complicating and rendering the process of governance even more difficult was a military that always seemed on the verge of taking over— a threat that kept the Aquino administration off balance throughout and discouraged foreign investment. And there was the old guard, the pre-martial law oligarchy, slowly reinserting itself into power, and reviving their fortunes (both political and financial) that had been put on hold by the Marcos regime. What began seemingly as a revolution wound up as a restoration.

Be that as it may, Cory Aquino did mediate a peaceful transition to a post-Marcos era, a housewife turned midwife. Free speech, an often licentious press, courts liberated from the yoke of executive interference: all were hallmarks of the democratic processes she had revived, along with the centrality of the ballot box. That she refused to entertain a second term (which she could have done as the limitation of one six-year term took effect after the 1987 constitution had been ratified), had survived the many failed coup attempts with a calm that bordered on the unnatural, and resisted the many temptations to profit from high office (though the same could not be said of some of her relatives) were key to the orderly succession that occurred with the elections of May 11, 1992, and that imparted to her a saintly aura. It was an extraordinary election, for not only was every elective office up for grabs—more than 17,000—but close to 80 percent out of 32 million eligible voters exercised their right of suffrage. Too, fraud and violence were at a minimum.

The man she had picked to be her successor, Fidel V. Ramos, who had shielded her from his brothers in arms, won, and on June 30, 1992, took over the presidency.

7. QUO VADIS, PHILIPPINES

"The AFP remains in a state of almost total denial . . . of its need to respond effectively and authentically to the significant number of killings which have been convincingly attributed to them. The President needs to persuade the military that its reputation and effectiveness will be enhanced rather than undermined by acknowledging the facts and taking genuine steps to investigate. When the Chief of the AFP contents himself with telephoning Maj-Gen Palparan three times in order to satisfy himself that the persistent and extensive allegations against the General were entirely unfounded, rather than launching a thorough internal investigation, it is clear that there is still a very long way to go."

—From a press statement by Philip Alston, Special Rapporteur of the United Nations Human Rights Council on extrajudicial, summary, or arbitrary executions; Manila, February 21, 2007

STEADY EDDIE

A GRADUATE OF WEST POINT AND A CAREER MILITARY MAN, President Fidel V. Ramos (1992-98) had seen combat as a platoon leader during the Korean War and from 1966 to 1968 headed the non-combat Philippine Civic Action Group in Vietnam. Steady Eddie, as he was called by many for his seemingly unflappable disposition particularly during the tumultuous years of his predecessor as president, was from Pangasinan Province in northern Luzon and was on his mother's side second cousin to Marcos.

In 1972, Marcos appointed Ramos to head the Philippine Constabulary, the agency primarily entrusted with enforcing martial law and many of whose units were blamed for the profligate abuse of human rights committed while Marcos ruled as a dictator. Though Ramos must have at the very least known of such abuses, he somehow avoided the taint of criminalization. Whatever taint there may have been was washed away by his helping to lead (along with Enrile and the Reform the Armed Forces Movement) the successful People Power uprising against the regime. In his capacity as Corazon Aquino's chief of staff of the Armed Forces of the Philippines, and later on, as the secretary of national defense, he helped save her administration from seven coup attempts. No one was surprised then that she endorsed him to succeed her as president.

Aquino herself had steadfastly refused to run and continue on as president, even though the one-term limit set by the 1987 constitution did not apply to her since she ascended to power in 1986. Whatever the shortcomings of her administration, and there were many, she herself was held in high public regard. A political ingénue at the outset and a reluctant ruler, Aquino possessed an innate decency and modesty, shunning the extravagance that had been the signature of the Marcoses, especially Imelda, choosing, for instance, to live in the presidential guest house rather than Malacañang proper, to symbolize the difference between her and her immediate predecessors. She had a calm demeanor, underneath which lay a steely resolve that stood her well during the tumultuous years of her presidency. With no allegations of personal corruption—though the same could not be said of her family—she was a saint in the eyes of the public. Her endorsement of Ramos thus carried considerable weight.

Not only were there presidential elections in 1992, there were elections for every government position in the country, including municipal councilors. Congress had decided the previous year that both local and national elections were to be held at the same time, on the same day. An astonishing eighty thousand candidates vied for more than 17,000 seats. Twenty-three years after the last freely held presidential elections, Filipinos trooped to the polls. Ramos, a Protestant, won, in spite of the Catholic Church hierarchy coming out against him, and with barely a quarter of the vote but enough to edge out the six other candidates, including Eduardo "Danding" Cojuangco, one of Marcos's closest cronies and Cory Aquino's estranged cousin, who had returned quietly in 1989. Senator Joseph Estrada, from another party, former movie action star and an unabashed Marcos loyalist, secured the vice-presidency by a wide margin, positioning himself as likely the next president once Ramos's term was up.

The 1992 elections reflected the rather stark fact that the glory days of the two-party system were over. Before martial law, one belonged either to the Nacionalistas or the Liberals, with affiliation based more on political convenience than on party platforms. True, the Nacionalistas and the Liberals participated in these elections—Vice President Salvador Laurel for the former and Senator Jovito Salonga for the latter—but they fared poorly. There were other parties now, such as Marcos's Kilusan Bagong Lipunan (New Society Movement), Lakas ng Tao (People Power), Laban ng Demokratikong Pilipino (Hope for a Democratic Philippines), National Union of Christian Democrats (NUCD), and the People's Reformed Party. Ramos had formed Lakas ng Tao, and allied it with the NUCD as well as with an obscure party, the United Muslim Democrats of the Philippines. These post-Marcos political parties were however no more distinct from each other as the Liberals had been from the Nacionalistas, the original Tweedledum and Tweedledee of Philippine politics.

Philippines 2000

As all presidents before him, Ramos promised change. Marcos had his New Society; Ramos came up with "Philippines 2000." By the millennium, he wanted the country to join the ranks of the newly industrialized countries and thus be an Asian tiger as well or, at the very least, a cub. He envisioned a strong state, as he put it in his 1993 State of the Nation speech, "that can assert our country's strategic interests because it has relative autonomy over the influence of oligarchic groups. . . . We have had a political system that has been too responsive to groups possessing wealth and power enough to bend the State to their will. Such a political system has distorted our economy and rendered government ineffectual."

Under Ramos, the manufacturing of export goods was accelerated and the economy further deregulated to attract more foreign capital. Civil aviation, shipping, telecommunications, and the oil industry, for example, were subjected to deregulation. Export-processing zones were established in designated strategic areas, where foreign firms could set up shop with less stringent government controls, create thousands of new jobs, and stimulate the local economies of the region they were located in, whether in Metro Manila, Baguio City in northern Luzon, or Cebu—the latter the business hub of the Visayas, where the surge in the economy, accompanied by an accelerated real estate development, came to be known as "Ceboom."

The Ramos administration continued the dismantling began by the Aquino government of both state-owned enterprises and monopolies. One of its biggest success stories was in facilitating the availability of telephone lines to consumers. Telecommunications had long been dominated by the Cojuangco-owned Philippine Long Distance Telephone Company. It wasn't uncommon for a family to wait years before a line could be had, and even then it might be shared with another family—referred to commonly as "party line"—leading either to frostiness on both ends or a live-and-let-live accommodation. With deregulation, competition markedly increased so that, by 1996, at least thirteen companies provided service and at favorable rates. Ramos also hastened decentralization began under Aquino, decreasing state bureaucratic power in favor of stronger local governments, with a corresponding increase in their share of government revenues.

But Ramos's Philippines 2000 was conditioned on economic development models largely used by the affluent West but that would not necessarily translate well in a developing Third World country. In a sense, it was a one-size-fits-all plan that came at the expense of agriculture—the traditional base of the economy and source of livelihood for millions of Filipinos—and burgeoning industries that concentrated on self-sufficiency, one that disregarded indigenous culture and traditions. The free-market export-oriented approach was encouraged by international lending institutions such as the World Bank, the International Monetary Fund, and the Asian Development Bank—and opposed by nationalists, hard-line Marxists, and various nongovernmental organizations, especially those that provided social services to the poor in lieu of failed or nonexistent government programs. Too, the Western model favored by technocrats had arisen ironically due to historical factors such as colonialism and the corresponding systematic exploitation by the colonizers of the colonies' natural wealth and resources. The native comprador class and the elites benefited hugely, the concentration of wealth among their ranks a major reason why a vigorous middle class never emerged. To follow such a model blindly then would in effect make the country a party to its own continuing exploitation.

Government corruption however proved to be as deeply rooted and as intractable as before. As much as 45 percent of pork-barrel funds for lawmakers wound up in their personal accounts. President Ramos himself conceded that at least twenty percent of the government budget was siphoned off due to corruption. This was, for instance, glaringly evident in the shoddy state of infrastructure in many provinces, where stretches of paved road alternated with barely passable ones and where bridges damaged by typhoons often took an inordinate amount of time to repair. Age-old hurdles remained the same: too many people lived at poverty level, and lacked access to safe water, basic health care, and decent housing. Government economic policies were conditioned on the classic trickle-down premise, the idea that a rising tide lifted all boats. Unfortunately, the rising tide often swamped smaller, rickety boats.

Triggered by speculation, a severe economic crisis afflicted Asia in 1997 and threatened to lead to a global one. Sudden devaluations undermined several Asian currencies, particularly those of Thailand,

Malaysia, South Korea, and Indonesia, and led to a subsequent increase in foreign-debt ratio to GDP. While the Philippine economy was hurt—growth in 1998 was near zero—it wasn't as hard hit as its neighbors, being that the country still hadn't been that well integrated into global financial markets. Efforts by the Ramos government to stabilize the peso by unloading as much as $4.5 billion depleted foreign reserves but did prevent the peso from a drastic free fall. Domestic enterprises that relied on imports cut back and laid off workers, causing a surge in unemployment. On the other hand, depreciation of the peso helped boost exports, which narrowed the trade deficit. And the remittances of the overseas workers, amounting to almost $6 billion, provided a much-needed financial cushion. Thus, the country emerged from the 1997 crisis a bit bloody but unbowed. In 1999, the economy rebounded and grew by more than 3 percent.

Contributing to President Ramos's growing reputation as a capable manager was his handling of the energy crisis and the inefficient water supply system that had long plagued Metro Manila. Power outages, known as brownouts and sometimes lasting as long as twelve hours in smaller cities, were so regular during Aquino's term that they were a national embarrassment. Energy shortfalls averaged 1,000 megawatts daily. Demand had far outstripped supply; the nation's power plants were too few and antiquated. The need for businesses to purchase generators added considerable expense to their overhead. Such deficiencies in the power infrastructure discouraged potential foreign investors. In response, the Ramos government, granted emergency powers by Congress, issued licenses to independent contractors to construct power plants, with the proviso that these were to be up and running within 24 months. By 1994, the power crisis had been almost completely resolved. Only one problem remained: power was available but the rates were the second highest in the region, with Japan taking the lead. Japan, however, was the world's second-largest economy.

Similarly, Ramos moved to deregulate the Metropolitan Waterworks and Sewage System, the government body charged with providing potable water to Metro Manila's ever-expanding population. By 1992, the National Capital Region (Metro Manila's official designation) had close to 10 million residents. The system in place had been built during the American colonial era, suffered extensive damage during World War II, and had never really been repaired fully, let alone upgraded.

Through financing arranged through the World Bank, four firms—two foreign and two local—committed $7 billion to improving and modernizing the system.

The New Heroes

Despite improvements in the economy, the exodus of workers for employment overseas continued unabated. In 1996, for example, over a six-month period, according to the Philippine government's National Statistics Office, the number of registered workers going abroad for employment, or Overseas Filipino Workers, was 900,000. By 1999, that figure had reached 1,043,000. According to a 2007 cover story by Jason DeParle in *The New York Times Magazine*, in 2006 the exodus was enough to fill six 747 planes daily. Of the population of 92 million, approximately 10 percent live abroad, with Filipino workers scattered throughout 170 countries. The article noted, "There are a million O.F.W.s in Saudi Arabia alone, followed by Japan, Hong Kong, the United Arab Emirates, and Taiwan." The largest segment of the diaspora was and continues to be in the United States, where close to 4 million Filipinos live. Abuse of overseas Filipino workers, especially of domestic workers, has been a recurring problem. Two cases made the front pages and dramatically illustrated how life abroad for these women (for most if not all domestic workers were women) was fraught with not only alienation and loneliness, but physical danger as well. Later, the stories were to form the basis of two critically acclaimed Philippine feature films.

The first case involved Flor Contemplacion, a middle-aged domestic worker in Singapore who was accused of murdering another Filipina domestic and drowning the child in the victim's care in 1991. Contemplacion was eventually convicted of the murders in 1995 and sentenced to die by hanging. However, two Filipina witnesses came forward with evidence purporting to show that Contemplacion had been framed for the murders. According to them, the child had inadvertently drowned in a bathtub and the father had been so incensed by his son's death that he killed the nanny and then framed Contemplacion. The Singapore courts considered the evidence proffered but decided to let the conviction stand. Contemplacion was hanged despite President Ramos's plea for clemency. Her death became a cause célèbre, with the city-state's punitive act sparking numerous demonstrations against Singapore in Manila and other Philippine cities. The Philippine foreign Secretary resigned and the ambassador to Singapore was recalled, with Ramos suspending diplomatic relations between the two countries.

Ramos had referred to Contemplacion as a *Bagong Bayani*, or a "New Hero," an unambiguous recognition that the monies sent to the Philippines by OFWs were essential in keeping the economy afloat. The term became part of standard government rhetoric when referring to overseas workers. Such rhetoric aimed to defuse public wrath at Malacañang's perceived ineptitude and powerlesness when it came to protecting its own citizens abroad. (From time to time, the government honors the returning overseas workers with a red-carpet reception at the Ninoy Aquino International Airport and a chance to win cash prizes.) The Contemplacion case speeded up the enactment later that year of the Migrant Workers Act by Congress, intended to recognize overseas workers' rights and outlining specific steps to protect these rights.

A few months after the hanging of Contemplacion, in September 1995, another Filipina domestic worker, this time in the United Arab Emirates, was convicted of stabbing her employer thirty-four times and killing him. Sarah Balabagan, a fifteen-year-old Muslim Filipina, claimed self-defense as the man, having raped her once, was attempting to do so again. After two trials, she was found guilty of premeditated murder, with the second court ruling that there was no evidence of rape. After a plea from the UAE's ruling sheikh, the late employer's family agreed to accept payment of blood money—donated by a wealthy Filipino businessman—a year's imprisonment, and one hundred strokes of a cane. According to Balabagan, the dead man's family cheered at each stroke of the cane. In 1996, the young woman was deported to the Philippines. That year alone saw 14,000 complaints of abuse filed with the government's Overseas Workers Welfare Administration.

Contributing to the ever-pressing need for jobs, with the resultant unceasing exodus for greener pastures overseas, was the high rate of population growth. One major reason top Catholic prelates in the country had stood against Ramos was not simply because he was a Protestant, but that he might promulgate government policies aimed at lowering the country's birth rate. In contrast, the convent-bred President Cory Aquino, known informally as a *Catolica cerrada* (literally, a closed Catholic), devout and deeply conservative, had essentially ignored the population problem. During her term, annual population increase was 2.35 percent. (It had declined to 2.04 percent by 2007—still one of the highest growth rates globally. By 2050 the population is expected to exceed 150 million.) Aquino's conservatism reflected the local Catholic hierarchy's own. In 2003, Cardinal Sin's responded flippantly when queried by *The New York Times* about the fast-growing population: "The more the merrier." The church steadfastly opposed curbing the population growth through condoms and other artificial contraceptives, which it condemned as immoral, favoring instead the rhythm method or abstinence.

To show that he was serious about family planning, Ramos appointed Dr. Juan Flavier, also a Protestant, as secretary of health. The doctor had been the president of the International Institute of Rural Reconstruction as well as the Philippine Rural Reconstruction Movement and had acquired a no-nonsense reputation when he worked as a doctor among the poor barrios of Cavite and Nueva Ecija provinces, witnessing the difficulties of a subsistence life, compounded by the lack of family planning. He proved to be a colorful, plain-speaking physician who had no qualms about shaking up the Catholic hierarchy's obstinate refusal to consider contraceptives as morally legitimate tools for dealing with unwanted pregnancies. Flavier would himself often distribute condoms to popularize the need for reducing the country's population growth. At the end of Ramos's term, the annual population increase of 2.35 percent under Aquino was lowered closer to 2 percent.

The Post-U.S. Bases Era

The bases treaty had been rejected in the last year of Cory Aquino's term. Five months after Ramos took office, on November 24, 1992, Subic Bay Naval Base ceased to be American territory. (Clark Air Force Base, as noted in the previous chapter, had been effectively shut down even before the Senate vote, due to Mt. Pinatubo's cataclysmic eruption and the subsequent heavy damage Clark suffered.) A contingent of U.S. Marines prepared to depart as the Stars and Stripes was lowered, permanently drawing the curtains on U.S. occupation of the base that began in 1899. As President Ramos remarked, "There has been no day that foreign troops were not based on our soil," with foreign military presence finally ending after more than four hundred years.

Part of the Ramos administration's ambitious plan for modernization involved converting the former Subic Bay Naval Base into a free
port, a regional hub where foreign corporations could take advantage
of the facilities left behind by the United States. These included industrial warehouses, power plants, residential housing, a 9,000-foot run-
way, and even a golf course. Within the vast complex were a 5,000-acre
watershed area and a 10,000-acre rain forest, whose resident indigenous
tribe had for decades taught jungle survival skills to U.S. soldiers. The
Subic Bay Metropolitan Authority (SBMA) was created in 1992, after
the U.S. withdrawal, to oversee development and to make sure that the
looting, often in collusion with local military units, that had stripped
Clark Air Base bare would not be repeated.

President Ramos appointed the mayor of Olongapo, Richard
Gordon, as the SBMA head. The withdrawal of the U.S. troops had
adversely affected the region's economy; Gordon had actively campaigned for the retention of the bases. Now he proved up to the challenge of recasting the baselands as the major component of a revitalized
economy. Security was tightened, volunteers from Olongapo City were
initially recruited to help maintain the site, and the rain forest and
watershed areas protected from poachers and illegal logging. The
centerpiece of the redevelopment was the Subic Special Economic and
Free Zone, slated to include industrial parks, a ship and maritime
center, tourism, a financial center, and private businesses. By 1996,
Gordon and his staff were able to convince more than 200 companies
to invest over $1.2 billion in Subic. Among these companies were
Federal Express, Enron, Acer (a Taiwanese computer firm), and Hutch-
inson Whampoa, a Hong Kong shipping company. Gordon would later
parlay his success and win a Senate seat in 2004, thereby positioning
himself for a future presidential run.

One thing the SBMA and the United States military did little or
nothing about was the environmental pollution at Subic. Over the
decades, the United States military personnel produced tons of hazardous and toxic wastes, absorbed into the ground, dumped into the
bay, dispersed through the air, and buried within landfills. These toxic
wastes posed very real dangers to base workers and the mostly poor villagers who lived along the base's perimeter—dangers that included
exposure to asbestos, low-level radiation in the waters due to nuclear-
powered vessels (a threat to marine ecosystems), and unexploded

ordnance—this last has caused some deaths and severe injuries among scrap metal scavengers. Of five million gallons of wastewater emptied into Subic Bay daily, only a quarter was treated, with lead and other heavy metals drained from ship-repair facilities directly into the bay.

A 1992 U.S. General Accounting Office study of environmental problems at Subic listed three major health hazards: PCB contamination, toxic lead and other hazardous substances, and fuel and chemical leakage into the soil and groundwater. The report also mentioned the presence of the lethal poison pentachlorophenol and the toxic metal lithium. The GAO report noted that "at the time of our review, the Air Force and the Navy had no plans to clean up at these sites." Nor did the 1988 Memorandum of Agreement (MOA) between the two countries offer any legal recourse. On the contrary, it absolved the United States of any responsibility. It stated: "The United States is not obligated to turn over the bases to the Philippines at the expiration of this agreement or the earlier relinquishment of any bases in the condition in which they were at the time of their occupation."

There were social costs as well. Olongapo and Angeles cities were well-known rest-and-recreation havens, particularly during the Vietnam War, when approximately a million servicemen passed through. The brothels, bars, massage parlors, and other related businesses took in $135 million a year. Out of the countless liaisons between the men and the bar girls, an estimated 50,000 mixed-race childen were born. Most were abandoned by the fathers, their care and upbringing left to their impoverished mothers and a few social agencies.

Dealing with the Army

During Ramos's six years in power, the military was quiescent. Its restive elements, such as RAM, could hardly complain now that one of their own was at the helm. Ramos was a career officer, a veteran, and one of the principals behind the ouster of Marcos. Though he stood firmly by Aquino's side while his brothers in uniform tried to oust her, he never came down unduly hard on the miscreants. To further demonstrate his fraternal solidarity, in 1995 Ramos granted blanket amnesty to military rebels involved in various coup attempts. (The amnesty may have backfired. One of those pardoned was Gregorio "Gringo" Honasan, one of the founders of RAM, who was involved in the various coup attempts against Aquino. In 2003, Honasan, already a senator—he had won in 1995 and 2001—was once again a prime suspect in a failed coup attempt on July 27 against the presidency of Gloria Macapagal Arroyo. Implicated by the mutineers, the senator vowed to clear his name. He was implicated yet again in another attempt in 2006, for which he was arrested and held at a military camp. In early 2007, a regional trial court cleared him of any involvement with these failed coups. He ran for reelection in May of 2007 and won.)

But if military malcontents ceased to plot against civil government under Ramos, nevertheless the army and the Philippine National Police (the result of a merger between the Philippine Constabulary and the Integrated National Police in 1991), along with the auxiliarly militia Citizen Armed Force Geographic Units (CAFGU), continued to be accused of perpetrating human-rights abuses against labor activists, religious personnel, journalists, community organizers, and their supporters in both city and countryside. Often, those arrested were framed for crimes they did not commit; being in jail as a common criminal rather than a political detainee posed considerable difficulties for human rights organizations working on their behalf.

One type of genuine criminal activity that did see an upsurge between 1993 and 1997 was kidnapping, with wealthy Chinese Filipinos the favored target. The abductions were usually carried out with military precision. Not surprising, as the perpetrators were more often than not former and active military personnel, crooked cops, guerrillas from both the Communist and Moro insurgencies; in short, professionals with and trained in the use of guns. Wealthy families responded by sending their children to study abroad and beefing up their own private security details. The lure of illicit lucre even led to bizarre cases of preemptive kidnappings that targeted middle-income professionals. A potential victim would be forewarned by a kidnap gang to pay a stated amount of cash, on threat of carrying out the kidnapping. To combat the crime wave, Ramos appointed Vice President Estrada to be his anti-crime czar. Unfortunately, Estrada's silver-screen macho prowess as a crime fighter did little to discourage criminals. And his seeming preference for frontier-style justice led to charges by human-rights organizations that the government anti-crime units were too quick on the draw, with suspects often killed before any judicial proceedings could begin.

The most brazen outfit to engage in kidnappings was the Mindanao-based Abu Sayyaf Group (ASG), supposedly a militant

Islamic renegade branch of the MNLF and founded in 1991 by Abdurajak Janjalani, who had trained and fought as a mujahideen in Afghanistan against the Russians. The ASG's formal name is Al Harakatul al Islamiya, or the United Islamic Movement. Abu Sayyaf (meaning, in Arabic, "Father of the Sword") was said to be one of many "lost command" groups—a term that refers to a smaller break-away faction that supposedly had cut off ties with its former parent group but in reality still worked clandestinely with the larger outfit. This tactic enabled, for instance, both the MNLF and the MILF to dis-avow the ASG while benefiting from the fact that the latter was tying down military units hot on their pursuit. A thorn in the military's side since the early 1990s, with bombings and attacks on poor Christian villages, the ASG purported to be fighting for an independent Islamic homeland in the southern Philippines and was believed to obtain some funding from Al Qaeda, through one of Osama bin Laden's brothers-in-law, Mustapha Jammal Khalifa, who had married a Muslim Filipina and set up a charity in Mindanao. Upon the death of Janjalani in 1998, and under the leadership of his twenty-three-year-old brother Khaddafy Janjalani—who would himself be killed in a 2006 gunbattle with the police—the ASG reverted to kidnappings and assassinations that seemed motivated by financial gain rather than any ideological or religious motives—the main reason why its support among local Muslim populations was low. In one year alone, the ASG was reported to have received more than $10 million in ransom monies. The ASG used some of its loot to buy off both local politicians, so they would turn a blind eye to their presence, and army commanders to not pur-sue the gang so earnestly.

In its modus operandi, the ASG was nothing if not bold. Among the many criminal acts it carried out was the abducting of 21 tourists and workers from a Sipadan, Malaysia, resort in 2000, and twenty vacationers from a Palawan resort in late 2001. In 2002, of the twen-ty vacationers, three hostages remained in the hands of the ASG (the others having been ransomed or killed earlier, with one victim, Guillermo Sobero from California, beheaded): a missionary couple, Martin and Gracia Burnham, and Ediborah Yap, a Filipina nurse. A rescue operation mounted by U.S.-trained Philippine Rangers that same year resulted in the deaths of Martin and Ediborah and the res-cue of Gracia.

The Insurgencies Continue

In 1996, the Ramos administration concluded an agreement with Nur Misuari and the Moro National Liberation Front. The five provinces that had voted for autonomy—Basilan, Tawi-Tawi, Sulu, Lanao del Sur, and Maguindanao—would make up the Autonomous Region of Muslim Mindanao (ARMM), to be governed by a Misuari-led administration. A precedent, somewhat, had been set when President Aquino in 1987 had by executive fiat authorized the creation of the land-locked Cordillera Administrative Region (CAR), in northern Luzon—home to the Igorot indigenous peoples—consisting of six provinces and the city of Baguio. The designation was to be a step towards an autonomous region but in a plebiscite in 1998, the regional inhabitants rejected the idea, preferring instead the current setup, which provided for instance for more local consultation with towns and villages, but not as much authority as would have been legislated under an autonomous framework.

The agreement may have meant the end of hostilities between Manila and the MNLF, by then a pale version of its 1970s self, but not the cessation of armed conflict in Mindanao. The Moro Islamic Liberation Front (MILF), the breakaway faction led by Hashim Salamat (noted in an earlier chapter), was still at violent odds with the central government and theoretically with the MNLF, though the two groups steered clear of each other. Neither side wanted to fight brother Muslims. And if the MILF could gain concessions from the Ramos government, then the MNLF conceivably would benefit as well.

Islamic fundamentalism, hinted at by the MILF's more orthodox views on Islam, first reared its ugly head in the country in 1995, when a plot to assassinate Pope John Paul VI, due to visit Manila once more (the first visit had been in 1981) was discovered inadvertently. The plotters were a Middle Eastern group led by a Pakistani militant Abdul Hakim Murad and Kuwait-born Ramzi Youssef. The apartment the men had rented was in Ermita, a tourist district of Manila, only 200 yards away from the Vatican embassy. The place caught fire and in the subsequent search of the place the police discovered papers and computer disks that revealed not just the plot to kill the pope but to plant bombs on U.S. airlines flying out of Manila and other Asian cities and have them detonate in mid-flight. Youssef, it turned out, had been one of the planners of the 1993 bombing of the World Trade Center in New York City, when a van packed with explosives detonated in one of the towers' underground parking lots. In 1995, he was arrested in Islamabad in Pakistan, tried and convicted in Manhattan's federal courts, and sentenced to 240 years in prison.

The plot, code-named Project Bojinka (which means "loud explosion" in Arabic) included hijacking airliners and crashing them into key structures in the U.S. Among those identified were the World Trade Center, the White House, the Pentagon, the CIA headquarters in Langley, Virginia, and the Sears Tower in Chicago. A trial run had in fact been conducted when Youssef boarded a 1994 Tokyo-bound Philippine Airlines flight out of Manila, hid a small bomb underneath a passenger seat, then deplaned at a stopover in Cebu. En route to Tokyo, the bomb exploded, killing a Japanese tourist, and forcing the plane to land in Okinawa.

Murad, subsequent investigations determined, had taken flying lessons in aviation schools in the United States, earning a commercial pilot certificate in 1992. He was convicted for his part in Operation Bojinka. Philippine authorities passed this information on to the U.S. Embassy in Manila and to the U.S. Joint Task force on Terrorism. Instead of envisioning a similar scenario playing out at domestic U.S. airports and tightening security that might conceivably have foiled the September 11, 2001 tragedy, U.S. authorities instead demanded extra security precautions at Asian cities where U.S.-bound flights originated. On that grim morning, four passenger jets on U.S. domestic flights were hijacked by terrorists from the Islamic fundamentalist group, Al Qaeda: kamikaze-style, two were crashed into the World Trade Center towers, collapsing them and taking close to 3,000 lives; one jet was flown into the Pentagon, seriously damaging it; and the fourth airliner crashed into a field in Pennsylvania after the passengers put up a fight.

As for the CPP and its armed wing, the New People's Army, though the guerrilla force had dwindled to approximately 6,000 fighters by the time Aquino's term had ended, it experienced a resurgence in the mid 1990s, the ranks estimated to have grown to 12,000 fighters by the beginning of the second millennium. Patricio Abinales and Donna Amoroso in *State and Society in the Philippines* attribute the resurgence to "deepening rural poverty and increased migration of poor lowlanders to mountainous areas." They point out another reason: the Philippine military assigning a majority of its fighting units to Mindanao, to engage the MILF and the Abu Sayyaf Group, thus leaving fewer troops to deal with the NPA. Undoubtedly, the U.S. emphasis on combating Islamic fundamentalism, combined with its traditional role as patron, influenced the overall strategy.

Dancing the Cha-Cha

Energized by his supporters and by a business community that viewed approvingly the political stability and sustained economic recovery, with the inevitable comparison with Singapore's Lee Kuan Yew, towards the end of his six-year term, Ramos sought to change the one-term limit as mandated by the Constitution. A movement was quickly created, the People's Initiative for Reform, Modernization, and Action, or PIRMA, its acronym a clever play on the Tagalog word meaning "to sign." The aim was to get enough signatures for a referendum on a constitutional convention. Ramos's move for charter change through such a convention was quickly dubbed "Cha-Cha." Powerful elements reacted quickly. Top Catholic bishops came out with a pastoral letter voicing their opposition. And ex-president Cory Aquino spoke impassionedly to a crowd of 200,000 at a rally meant to signal Ramos that the public wouldn't stand for any extension of his or anyone's term.

With the memory of Marcos's disastrous attempts to perpetuate himself in power still fresh in the collective memory, the move by Ramos supporters for constitutional change fizzled out. Chastened, President Ramos pledged not to endeavor amending the constitution and to ensure a peaceful transfer of power in 1998, when the next round of national elections were to be held. Ramos and the governing party Lakas ng Tao, or People Power, backed House Speaker José de Venecia for the presidency and Gloria Macapagal Arroyo, the daughter of the former president Diosdado Macapagal, for the vice presidency. The opposition candidates were Ramos's vice president Joseph Estrada; Senator Raul Roco; Secretary of Defense Renato de Villa; Juan Ponce Enrile; Senator Miriam Defensor Santiago; and Imelda Marcos. (In 1993, given permission by the Ramos government, the dictator's widow had flown back from Honolulu with the body of her late husband, who had finally succumbed to the ravages of his long-term illness in September of 1989. To prevent a loyalist mob scene in Manila, the government ordered the plane to fly directly to Laoag City, in the heavily pro-Marcos Ilocos region in northern Luzon.)

Once again, elections were held for all 17,200 elective positions in May of 1998. This time, the number of candidates exceeded 100,000—an average of almost six people competing for every position. For the highest office in the land, eighty-three individuals initially filed for certification from the Commission on Elections (COMELEC), including a certain Mario Legazpi, who declared that he had descended from heaven to assume the presidency. The Commission weeded out all those unqualified, reducing the presidential field to seven candidates, including Vice President Estrada and Imelda Marcos. Presumably, Legazpi ascended to his ethereal home, sorely disappointed at the less than worshipful reception he had gotten on Earth.

But Ferdinand's widow was forced to drop out due to a conviction on charges of graft, which she was appealing, and which was subsequently overturned in 1998, after the elections.* Her loyalist bloc swung their votes in favor of Estrada, and Marcos-era cronies such as Eduardo Cojuangco and the tobacco tycoon Lucio Tan, both of whom had deep pockets, endorsed him. Estrada managed to garner limited support from the left, as he had voted against the ratification of the bases' treaty in 1991—and had even produced and starred in an anti-bases film. He won with forty percent of the vote, with his nearest rival de Venecia garnering only 15 percent—the largest margin of victory in free Philippine elections. Estrada had been propelled to office by the urban poor and the disenfranchised, whose imagination he had captured by picturing himself as their savior.

THE BIGGEST ROLE OF HIS CAREER

He was—and is—known to the public as Erap (from the Tagalog word *pare*, or buddy, spelled backwards). *"Erap para sa Mahirap"* ("Erap for the Poor") was the catchy slogan President Joseph Estrada (1998-2000) used during his successful campaign, building on the cinematic portrait of himself as a death-defying proletarian action-star who always won in

---

*Close to a thousand civil and criminal cases had been filed against the Marcoses, but a majority of the cases were dismissed for lack of evidence. In 2007, sixty remained to be resolved. The Steel Butterfly has never spent a day in prison and no one bets she will anytime soon.

his crusade against evildoers, the main reason President Ramos had appointed him his crime czar. His campaign brilliantly capitalized on his well-known tendency to fracture English and commit linguistic malapropisms to stress his common-man qualities, releasing a collection of his unintentionally humorous use of English, *Eraptions: How to Speak English Without Really Trial*. (Sample: annoyed on one occasion by the fact that his listener couldn't understand his English, Estrada was said to have remarked: "From now on, I will speak in the binocular!")

It made it easier for the common *tao* to identify with him; he was the sort of fellow folks would love to have a beer with. The fact that he had been a movie star gave him a tremendous advantage at the innumerable de rigueur campaign rallies all over the archipelago. Not only did he speak the earthy language of the *masa* (or masses), he could attract top-drawer names from the entertainment world to wow the crowds. None had more star power than a close friend of his, Fernando Poe, Jr., the king of action cinema and an even bigger star than Estrada. As expected, he endorsed Estrada. He himself would run unsuccessfully for the presidency in 2004.

In fact, Estrada may have had pedestrian tastes but was decidedly un-proletarian, being from a solidly bourgeois family from San Juan, a relatively affluent municipality that was part of Metro Manila and where the shots that ignited the brutal 1899 Philippine-American War had been fired. He had attended private schools, including the exclusive all-male Ateneo de Manila High School, from which he was expelled for fighting. Later, he dropped out from the college where he had enrolled for an engineering degree, to pursue a career in film and quickly became a star, one who combined the derring-do of James Bond with a social conscience. Once he retired from the movies, he served as mayor of his hometown for seventeen years, before winning a Senate seat in 1987, and the vice-presidency in 1992.

New Political Groupings

By 1998, the political landscape had changed significantly. Along with Estrada, for the first time, following the mandate of the 1987 Constitution, 13 party-list representatives were elected, out of a potential 52. As briefly discussed in the previous chapter, the idea behind this new elective category, the party-list—a direct outcome of the 1986 People Power uprising—was to allow nongovernmental organizations to formally represent the sectors that they worked with, such as the urban poor, women, and workers, traditionally with little input in governance.

In addition, there had arisen evangelical movements with popular followings among the working class and urban poor: El Shaddai and Jesus Is Lord. Both groups were capable of organizing huge rallies and, through endorsements, mobilizing their respective followers to back a particular candidate. These popular movements were well within the grassroots tradition of folk Christianity dating back to the Spanish colonial era—reminiscent of, for instance, the populist Christianity espoused in mid nineteenth century by Apolinario de la Cruz (discussed in Chapter Three) and his Cofradía, who felt the Church hierarchy was too devoted to the Spanish and pro-Spanish native elite, thereby ignoring the particular circumstances of folk Catholicism as practiced by the majority of Filipinos in less circumscribed and institutionalized procedures. The gap between the social elites and the masses were in some ways reflected in the gap between the church hierarchs and affluent congregations on one hand and grassroots clerics and their poorer flocks, on the other hand.

Nevertheless, as to be expected, the Catholic Church retained its considerable political clout, as did the Iglesia ni Kristo (INK, or Church of Christ) whose voters among its more than 2 million members vote as a bloc according to guidelines laid down by the church leadership. Hence, the INK, dominated by the Manalo family since its founding in 1914 by family patriarch Felix Manalo, was always courted by the political establishment. In contrast is the older nationalist Independiente Filipina Iglesia (IFI), the Independent Philippine Church, better known as the Aglipayan church, discussed in chapter four. With a majority of its congregation based in the Ilocos region, the IFI retains its nationalist, anti-imperialist leanings, and is in communion with the Episcopalian church as well as with the Old Catholics. Aglipayans are often viewed as troublesome anti-government activists. Its Chief Bishop, Alberto Ramento, a vocal critic of the Arroyo government, was killed in 2007 by, it was suspected, a pro-government death squad.

Other clear indications of deep-seated voter dissatisfaction with the *trapos*, or traditional politicians, were made evident when a number of celebrities from the entertainment, sports, and media worlds, undoubtedly encouraged by Estrada's success, ran for political office, with many winning. Thus, for example, Robert Jaworski, a hugely popular professional basketball star; Ramon Revilla, a silver-screen action hero in the same mold as Estrada though not as popular; and Tito Sotto, a well-known television personality, gained seats in the Senate. (A beloved comedian Dolphy was encouraged to run but refused. Asked why, he replied with a straight face, "I might win.") Grown disenchanted, the voters sought fresh faces. At the same time, the faces had to be familiar ones, of figures who had risen to prominence outside the conventional political processes that had churned out society's leaders. There were more than enough stars in the movies, sports, and media who met this criterion and only too willing to meet this need.

The MILF

The Ramos government and the 12,000-strong MNLF having reached an agreement in 1996 to set up ARMM, the AFP turned its attention to the MILF. The Ramos administration had agreed to a truce with the MILF in 1997, and had set up peace talks. But encounters still took place between the rebels and the army. In early 2000, with President Estrada's blessing, the army rejected the truce and launched what it termed an "all-out war" on thirteen MILF camps in Mindanao, renewing armed conflict on the island. At the same time, it took over the island of Jolo in its pursuit of the ASG, leading to more encounters. In an event that made newspaper headlines, Estrada flew to the stronghold of the MILF in central Mindanao, Camp Abu Bakar, once it had been overran by the army, and celebrated with the troops by eating roast pig—a deliberate, provocative act that was seen as an insult to all Muslims. The MILF head Hashim Salamat fled to Malaysia and declared a jihad against the Philippine government. Warrants for his arrest were issued, and a reward for his capture offered.

A ceasefire was agreed to under the new government of Gloria Macapagal Arroyo and talks were once again resumed in 2001. The warrants were suspended, and Salamat returned to Mindanao. Not surprisingly, the talks stalled the same year. A key demand of the government was for the MILF to renounce terrorism, which Salamat did in mid 2003. Shortly after, the founder of the MILF died in Lanao del Sur Province, with its military commander Al Haj Murad emerging as the new chair.

In a move that once again drew the U.S. military into this complicated picture, in 1998, the Estrada government and the United States had drawn up the Visiting Forces Agreement (VFA), which the Senate ratified in 1999. For the first time since the termination of the bases treaty in 1992, U.S. troops were allowed into the country along with vessels and aircraft. Like the old bases treaty, the VFA reserved the right of jurisdiction over U.S military personnel to U.S. military authorities for purported crimes, unless such crimes were deemed to be of special significance to the Philippines. What that meant in practice was that it would still be difficult to prosecute a U.S. serviceman under Philippine law. The VFA provided an opening which would widen considerably in the immediate aftermath of September 11, 2001, when Gloria Macapagal Arroyo had already succeeded Estrada as president.

ERAP'S DOWNFALL

Erap proved to be less than assiduous in his devotion to the *mahirap*. For the electorate, it was déjà vu, since corruption during his brief tenure stemmed largely, à la Marcos, from vulnerability to his family and cronies. Relying on friendships built over the years, over nights of carousing and drinking, his friends easily got presidential approval for loans, lucrative deals and government contracts. These friends got to be known as Estrada's Midnight Cabinet—in truth a reprise of the *barkada* system, a *barkada* being a tightly knit circle of close friends who knew each other from their salad days and whose loyalty to one another was almost as strong as family ties. One never said No to either the barkada or the family. Estrada was thus as easily influenced by his close-knit barkada as by his kin.

Was he in fact the second coming of Marcos? While Estrada used public office for enrichment for himself, his family, and his barkada, the cronyism was not as devastating to the economy as it had been under Marcos, when the individuals involved were experienced players in business and international finance, and the sums much larger. Too, Estrada's time in office was short, two and a half years, compared to the two decades that the Marcoses had been in power.

No doubt encouraged by her friendship with Estrada and by his style of personal governance—something she could relate to—Imelda Marcos announced to the world that she was determined to recover $12 billion in assets her late husband and she owned. She had dropped this bombshell in response to the ongoing struggle—began during

Aquino's term—over who actually owned and controlled San Miguel Corporation, the country's largest business enterprise and responsible for 4 percent of GDP, and 6 percent of tax revenues. She was miffed by supposedly ungrateful cronies who she claimed were given large amounts of money by her late husband to acquire companies on his behalf. Imelda declared, "This was in the 1970s. Now they want to hold on to wealth they did not own in the first place." She defiantly told the press, "We own practically everything in the country." This was indeed a dramatic turnaround from when her defense lawyer proclaimed during her 1990 New York trial that she was really a poor girl who relied on the kindness of strangers. (The 1990 trial was the first time she had publicly and reluctantly allowed that her upbringing was less than privileged.)

Knowing that President Estrada was sympathetic to the Marcoses, Imelda also sought to have Ferdinand interred at the Libingan ng Mga Bayani, or National Heroes Cemetery, the Philippine equivalent of the Arlington National Cemetery. Estrada indicated that he was of a mind to approve her request but the firestorm of protest that erupted forced him to back down. Imelda and the Marcos loyalists had to content themselves with the display of the late dictator's embalmed corpse in a mausoleum located in Batac, Ilocos Norte, open to the public.

But what proved to be fatally damaging to his presidency were revelations made in mid-October 2000 by the governor of Ilocos Sur, Luis "Chavit" Singson, a friend and fellow gambler. Governor Singson had collected more than $20 million in bribes from illegal gambling syndicates that operated a numbers game, popular throughout the country, known as *jueteng*, bribes that he then claimed to have passed on to the president. Singson said he had made these revelations to protect himself, alleging that the president (or the president's men) had made not just threats on his life but that in the wee hours of October 9, 2000, policemen had surrounded him and his bodyguards in his bulletproof Chevrolet Suburban. Nothing came of the confrontation and Singson lived to tell tales out of school. Other sordid revelations followed: siphoning money from national lottery funds intended for charities, and from tobacco taxes. Newspaper accounts provided details of how the money was spent to support the lifestyles of Estrada's different mistresses and their offspring, including the construction of expensive residences and the purchase of luxury vehicles.

Estrada himself seemed unapologetic for his penchant for high living. During his campaign for the presidency he made no secret of his amorous life; it may even have boosted his popularity. Media reports revealed that the president had at least three known mistresses, with each getting a mansion, and only in wealthy neighborhoods such as Forbes Park, the most exclusive enclave in the country. One home cost the equivalent of $4 million. Another palatial residence, a 7,400-square-meter property, was nicknamed "Boracay," after an island in the south famed for its sugary white beaches. Some of the island's fine sand had been flown in to create a mini-beach by the residence's gargantuan swimming pool that came with a wave-making device.

The obvious question of course was, where did all the money come from? Investigative reports, principally from the Philippine Center for Investigative Journalism, portrayed a sordid network of kickbacks, commissions from jueteng, and the use of government funds (principally from Social Security and the Government Service Insurance System) to purchase shares in or acquire private corporations. Impeachment proceedings against President Estrada began on November 13, 2000, when the House of Representatives approved and passed a motion on to the Senate for Estrada's removal. Less than a month later, on December 7, the Senate opened impeachment hearings against the president, citing a long list of bribery and corruption charges. A turning point was reached on December 20, when an investigation began into a particular bank account with the Philippines third-largest bank, Equitable PCI. Apparently, a check for $2.8 million had been issued in the name of José Velarde. Prosecutors alleged that Velarde was a nom de plume of Estrada's. A bank clerk came forward to testify that she saw the president sign the check. The bank—itself the merger of two banks orchestrated by Estrada cronies—was believed to be the repository where at least $2.2 billion was alleged by government prosecutors to have been deposited between August 1999 (when the Velarde account was opened) and January 2000.

But Estrada partisans had the majority in the Senate. By early January 2001, the televised impeachment trial was stopped in its tracks when the senators voted 11 to 10 not to open bank records that would have allegedly provided the smoking gun and thus incriminate the president. One pro-Estrada senator, Teresa Aquino Oreta (the sister of the slain Ninoy Aquino), was caught on camera doing an impromptu jig, an image that helped to inflame anti-Estrada protests in Metro Manila. The citizenry took to the streets in a reprise of People Power, quickly nicknamed "EDSA Dos," or EDSA Two, demanding Estrada's resignation. (EDSA stands for Epifanio de los Santos Avenue, Metro Manila's major thoroughfare, and the site for the People Power uprising of 1986.) The number of protesters swelled to a million, and on January 19, a chorus of military and church leaders declared their support for Vice President Arroyo to take over as president. The embattled Estrada called out his own followers (a large number of whom were Marcos loyalists) in a counter-rally, "EDSA Tres" (EDSA Three), but to no effect. On January 20, 2001, the Armed Forces of the Philippines formally withdrew its backing for Erap. The Supreme Court ruled that the presidency was now vacant, and Macapagal Arroyo was sworn in as president that same day. Charging that it was a coup since he had been constitutionally elected, Estrada and his family were forced to abandon Malacañang.

Arrested and formally accused of plunder in April of 2001, Estrada was in detention for six years, for most of that period not at any common jail or military stockade but at his rather luxurious vacation home—complete with theater, gym, and library—in a hilly suburb of Manila. After innumerable procedural delays, and testimony by a variety of witnesses, on September 12, 2007, the former president was found guilty of the crime of plunder by an anti-corruption court in Manila, and sentenced to forty years in prison. Estrada was ordered to pay the government $15.6 million and forfeit a home he had built for a mistress—presumably funded by ill-gotten money. Prosecutors had charged him with being paid $85 million in kickbacks from tobacco taxes, commissions from both the illegal purchase of shares in private firms with government insurance funds and from jueteng—the various payoffs being deposited at the bank that figured prominently in the failed impeachment trial. A little more than a month after his conviction, on October 25, 2007, President Gloria Macapagal Arroyo pardoned the disgraced former president on condition that he not run again for national office.

GOVERNANCE IN THE AGE OF TERRORISM

Educated at private schools, including two years of undergraduate study at Georgetown University in Washington, D.C., and with a doctorate from the University of the Philippines, President Gloria Macapagal Arroyo (2001-10), married to José Miguel Arroyo, is the daughter of the late president Diosdado Macapagal. A professor of economics at the Ateneo de Manila University, she was tapped by President Aquino to serve as undersecretary of trade and industry in 1987. She decided to run for a Senate seat and won in 1992. In the presidential elections of 1998, as mentioned earlier, she was chosen as José de Venecia's vice presidental mate in his run for the presidency, under the aegis of the Lakas ng Tao Party. De Venecia lost but Macapagal Arroyo won. Estrada appointed her secretary of social welfare and development.

Since she hadn't been elected to the presidency, the constitutional one-term limit did not apply to her. Nevertheless, in 2002, Macapagal Arroyo stated that she wouldn't seek a second term as president, causing a dramatic surge in her approval ratings. Pressured by her advisers and family and friends, it wasn't too long, however, before she reneged on her word and declared that she would indeed seek a second term come the 2004 elections. Her main rival was Fernando Poe Jr. a close friend of Estrada whom he had endorsed in the last elections, and, as noted, was an even bigger star. It didn't hurt that his wife was Susan Roces, a former movie star herself, the reigning celluloid queen in the late 1950s and early 1960s. While the iconic film hero's immense popularity meant an early lead in the polls, Poe lacked the campaign machinery, the political experience, and media know-how that Macapagal Arroyo had. Amidst protestations of poll irregularities, the incumbent was declared winner of the 2004 elections.

Hello Garci, Goodbye, Gloria—Almost

Allegations that GMA had had the electoral tally rigged—or in popular slang, subjected to *dagdag, bawas,* or additions and subtractions surreptitiously done to influence the outcome—gained traction when wiretapped conversations surfaced in mid 2005, between a woman widely presumed to be the president and a man widely believed to be COMELEC Commissioner Virgilio Garcilano. Between May 26, 2004 and

June 10, 2004, there were fifteen phone calls altogether. The subject was the electoral count. The exchanges had taken place after the voting was over but before a winner had been declared, and reflected two concerns: one, that the margin of victory be more than 1 million; and two, that the electoral tallies from the official certificates of canvass (a summary of votes from each region) and from the statements of votes from each of a region's precincts, when added up, would not match as they were supposed to. The conversations were promptly dubbed the "Hello Garci" tapes" by the media, and the ring tone that could be heard on the tapes became commercially popular. The caller expressed particular concern about the tallies from southern Mindanao, given that there were reports in the media of irregularities there. A Hadji Abdullah Dalidig, head of NAMFREL in the province of Lanao del Sur, declared, for instance, that the 2004 elections were "the worst and dirtiest" of the five elections he had monitored in the province. "What was done to the votes at the presidential level, even grade one schoolchildren would know the votes of the other candidates were sabotaged."

In the nearby province of Maguindanao, the governor Andal Ampatuan, patriarch of the entrenched political clan, the Ampatuans, and a close political ally of President Macapagal Arroyo, guaranteed that his bailiwick would go for her. He was so good at keeping his word that in two towns there were zero votes for the movie superstar turned presidential candidate, Fernando Poe, Jr.

Both the House and Senate demanded an investigation; there were calls for Arroyo's resignation. A motion for impeachment was filed but got nowhere. The president refused to step down, though she did admit talking to a COMELEC official during the canvassing period. She conceded that it was a "lapse in judgment." However, she emphasized that the conversations occurred after the votes had been counted. Nor did she name the official involved. Once the scandal broke, Garcillano dropped from public view; there were sightings of him in various places, even abroad. More than five months later, he surfaced and admitted that he had conversed with President Arroyo during the canvassing period, and, as she had stated, after the votes had been tallied. He denied that the president had asked him to rig the count in her favor. The calls were unseemly, and the probability that Arroyo had interfered with the 2004 elections led to the resignation in July 2005 of eight cabinet members and two bureau heads—dubbed "the Hyatt 10" for having announced their decision at the Manila Hyatt hotel. The group asked the president to resign, pointing out in a prepared statement that "resignation is a legitimate constitutional option for effecting leadership change." That call was renewed in 2009, on the fourth anniversary of the group's mass resignation, with its members now adding the charge that the president was seeking to stay in power beyond the constitutional limit, either by declaring a state of emergency or through charter change—the same possibility that President Ramos had tentatively explored—and that was once again being proposed.

Other scandals mainly involving corruption plagued Arroyo's administration, with one in particular eroding its credibility further. In April 2007, the Philippine government and a Chinese firm, ZTE, agreed on a $329.5 million contract for a national broadband network. Soon after, allegations were made about kickbacks from ZTE involving Benjamin Abalos, the new chair of COMELEC, and the president's husband, Mike Arroyo. The allegations were credible enough for the Supreme Court in September 2007 to issue a temporary restraining order, freezing the deal. Due to the political brouhaha and threatened investigations by Congress, President Arroyo cancelled the contract in October of the same year. Complicating the entire matter was the claim of a mid-level government official, Rodolfo Lozada, who declared in different public fora that indeed the president's husband and the COMELEC chair were behind the kickback scheme—charges both parties were quick to deny. By early 2008, calls for the president's resignation intensifed, with charges of her having cheated in the 2004 elections—never actually resolved—being revived. Among those demanding her ouster were former presidents Aquino and Estrada; in the latter's case, it was clearly payback for his peremptory removal from office, even though Arroyo had pardoned him. People called for the president to step down at public rallies; there were hopes for another massive outpouring of citizens onto the streets—a reprise of the 1986 People Power phenomenon— to force her resignation. None materialized, however. One reason was that Arroyo's vice president Noli de Castro, formerly a well-known broadcast anchor, was on no one's list as a plausible alternative. For another, the flamboyant theater of the streets had ultimately proved to be disappointing as a way of effecting fundamental change—the current president herself being proof of this axiom—and the population had become understandably wary of going this route once more.

QUO VADIS, PHILIPPINES?

The Global War on Terror

Since 2001, the administration of Gloria Macapagal Arroyo's record on human rights has led critics to compare her government to that of Ferdinand Marcos. A major reason for the deterioration of the state of human rights that had been restored so dramatically during Cory Aquino's tenure came from the alignment, in the immediate aftermath of September 11, 2001, of Philippine government policies with those of U.S. President George W. Bush that came to be labeled the "Global War on Terror. "

Eight days after the collapse of the World Trade Center towers, President Gloria Macapagal Arroyo became the first Asian leader to endorse the Bush administration's global war on terrorism. By doing so, she internationalized her country's two insurgencies, recasting these as terrorist threats to an ill-defined world order. None of the insurgencies, past or present, that the AFP had faced since the country regained its independence in 1946, were ever viewed by Manila as more than internal, albeit serious, threats. However, as detailed in previous chapters, any serious domestic challenge to the Philippine government, such as the Huk insurgency in the 1950s, was invariably seen by the U.S. as a threat to its own interests, mainly to its bases in the country, for which Washington extended economic and military aid to Manila and guaranteed U.S. interference in Philippine affairs. Through the war on terror, the country was thus once again able to tap into U.S. aid, reduced substantially since the closing of the bases in 1992, and facilitated the revival of U.S. proprietary aims on the archipelago.

By February 2002, U.S. troops had been deployed in the islands for a series of joint exercises with the Armed Forces of the Philippines (AFP), dubbed *Balikatan,* or Shoulder-to-Shoulder—apparently in violation of the Philippine Constitution, which prohibits the presence of foreign troops in the country but which the government contended was allowed by the Visiting Forces Agreement of 1998. At the outset of these joint exercises, the Bush government promised the Philippines $100 million in mostly military aid. For the peace talks between Manila and the

MILF, U.S. Congress earmarked $30 million in 2003, while USAID promised $20 million for the following year.

Arroyo's enthusiastic support for Bush's war, while embarrassing to nationalists, was unsurprising, and was in keeping with how Philippine leaders have traditionally used the country's strategic location in Southeast Asia as a bargaining chip, extracting economic and military aid from the United States, which has always viewed the Philippines as crucial to maintaining both its regional and global hegemony—and of containing China, a prize sought during the heyday of empire, but now a superpower rival.

Two other factors increased the Philippines' strategic value: a possible U.S. confrontation with North Korea as it sought to develop nuclear weapons, and the Philippines' claim to the Spratly Islands in the South China Sea. Halfway between Vietnam and the Philippines, surrounded by rich fishing grounds, and thought to contain enormous reserves of oil and gas, this desolate stretch of tiny isles and coral reefs is being claimed as well by China, Taiwan, Vietnam, Borneo, and Malaysia, either in part or in its entirety. Dispersed over 410,000 square kilometers, this patch of ocean may yet be a flashpoint between China and the U.S., with the Philippines as an American surrogate. For now, there is an uneasy détente, with the rival claimants forswearing the use of force to resolve disputes.

U.S. troop presence in Mindanao was of course an iffy proposition, since memories of the campaign to pacify Mindanao during the 1899 Philippine-American War remained vivid, particularly of atrocities committed by American troops, such as the 1906 massacre of 600 largely defenseless Muslim men, women, and children in Bud Dajo. And unlike their Christian counterparts elsewhere in Mindanao and in the country, Moros identified more with the Middle East than with the United States. Nevertheless, its troops were welcomed to the island of Basilan, which had a fairly large Christian community, since the initial target of this Balikatan exercise was the Abu Sayyaf, and Basilan was a stronghold of the gang. For the U.S., fighting the ASG bolstered its claim to be waging and winning the war against terrorism. It was widely believed that the local military units in pursuit of the Abu Sayyaf were on the gang's payroll—enabling the ASG to conveniently elude the military just when they were about to close in. If it took U.S. involvement to rid the island of the ASG scourge, so be it. People were simply sick and tired of the gang.

The tragedy of 9/11 allowed both governments a way of exploiting other ends—one regional and global, the other, local—seeming to play the role of avenging angels while reprising their roles as colonizer and colonized. Under the 2002 Mutual Logistics Supply Agreement (MLSA) between the two governments, the Pentagon could once again use the archipelago as a springboard for intervention—euphemistically termed "stability operations." The MLSA granted U.S. forces access to Philippine military facilities throughout the country, converting the whole archipelago into a virtual base for the Pentagon, without being tied down to fixed sites, as had been the case with Clark and Subic, that would otherwise leave the U.S. open once again to charges of permanent tenure. The 2002 agreement also allowed storage and stockpiling facilities for U.S. troops, as well as the construction of "temporary" buildings, all of which critics charged was a violation of the 1987 constitution, which requires that the building of "foreign military facilities" in addition to "foreign military troops and bases" be ratified by the Senate.

The 1999 VFA and the 2002 MLSA allowed the United States military to broaden the scope of its activities, including U.S. troops accompanying Filipino soldiers into combat or conflict areas. A U.S. embassy spokesman in Manila explained that the troops were "not involved in any combat roles but will fire back if fired upon. ... Our role is to advise and assist the Philippine military." The danger, of course, was that these advisers could be drawn into combat, and wind up in a Vietnam-style quagmire.

The Mindanao Conflict

With the establishment in 1996 of ARMM, and Misuari as ARMM governor, the MNLF ceased for the most part to be a threat. But that peace between the AFP and MNLF was disrupted when in November 2001, Misuari engineered an armed uprising against the former. Elections to replace him as governor of ARMM were scheduled for later in the month. His followers attacked the army headquarters in Jolo, the largest of the Sulu islands. The attack failed, however, and Misuari with some of his aides fled to Malaysia. There, much to his unpleasant surprise and in contrast with the sanctuary he was accorded in the 1970s during the Marcos regime, he was arrested, extradited to Manila, and imprisoned in a military stockade. In February 2005, supporters loyal to Misuari launched a series of assaults on army troops in Jolo. The trigger for the violence was thought to be the start of a huge military operation against the Abu Sayyaf. While the assaults were repulsed, they sent an unmistakable signal that the deposed ARMM governor and ex-head of the MNLF still had a significant following.

Today, the AFP continues to face the NPA nation-wide, and the Moro Islamic Liberation Front (MILF) in Mindanao—and to a lesser extent the Abu Sayyaf Group. Reliable estimates put the strength of each guerrilla army at between 12,000 to 15,000 men under arms, while the ASG is believed to number no more than 400 armed men. The MILF, with more emphasis on its Islamic roots than the MNLF and based in central Mindanao, has broad popular support in rural areas where the historic lack of economic development has encouraged armed dissent. In 2000, as mentioned earlier in this chapter, the army under then-president Joseph Estrada launched a crackdown on the MILF, leading to a renewal of armed conflict. The two sides signed a peace deal in 2001, but violent interludes seem to alternate with periods of relative peace. In February 2003, the Philippine military accused the MILF of harboring members of the small but militant Pentagon kidnap gang, yet another "lost command" group accused of abducting foreigners for ransom, and launched a new offensive. The MILF denied providing sanctuary to Pentagon members. It also denied being behind a bomb blast at Davao City Airport in March 2003, that killed 21 people.

Both the U.S. and the Philippine governments also suspected the MILF of having ties with fundamentalist groups such as Jemah Islamiyah in Indonesia, held responsible for deadly bombings on Bali in 2002 and 2005, links the MILF denied having. Still, neither the U.S. nor the Philippine government had branded the group as terrorist—allowing the Philippine government to hold talks with the group in Malaysia, with tacit U.S. support. (In contrast, in 2002, the Bush administration designated the NPA a terrorist group even though everyone acknowledged that it had no ties to any foreign terrorist organization.) The truth was somewhere between: given the history shared by MILF and other Southeast Asian mujahideen in fighting the Soviets in Afghanistan, and porous southern sea borders between Indonesia, Malaysia, and the Philippines, ad hoc ties but no formal arrangements probably existed between the different groups.

Shortly before his death from a heart attack in July 2003, MILF head Salamat Hashim issued a statement renouncing terrorism and underlining the MILF's commitment to achieving a peace settlement. A ceasefire was agreed upon, and both sides returned to the bargaining table. In mid 2008, the Philippine government and the MILF drafted a potentially significant Memorandum of Agreement concerning the so-called ancestral domain of the Muslims. The lands alluded to were to be made up of the ARMM provinces, plus specified towns and geographic areas in three other Mindanao provinces. The effect would be to add 712 towns to the existing Autonomous Region of Muslim Mindanao. Subject to a plebiscite, the designated territory, the Bangsamoro Homeland, would not be under the jurisdiction of the central government but would instead be ruled by the Bangsamoro Juridical Entity.

The proposed expansion led to protests among predominantly Christian villages that would have become part of ARMM, resulting in a legal challenge to the proposed agreement. Prior to the formal signing between the MILF and Philippine government officials in Malaysia, the Philippine Supreme Court issued a temporary restraining order that froze the agreement and led to the cancellation of the signing ceremony. As feared, the setback led to a violent backlash, with MILF and army units clashing in central Mindanao in August 2008, with at least thirty fatalities. Accused of political insensitivity, the central government stepped back from the proposed deal and said that it would seek a way to accommodate MILF demands through another mechanism. What that mechanism might be was never specified. Nevertheless, another ceasefire was agreed to in late July of 2009, leading to a revival of peace talks.

The NPA Rebounds

The focus on the MILF obscured the ongoing, by 2009, forty-year-old conflict with the NPA, even as the guerrilla army stepped up its attacks on army and police units. From its peak of at least 25,000 armed regulars in the waning years of the Marcos regime, the NPA, as stated previously, had declined by 1994 to 6,000, and at the beginning of the second millennium, had climbed back to more than 12,000 strong. It remained a palpable presence in rural areas, where poverty seemed to be, as it had always been, a permanent feature of the landscape. Too, it and its political base, the Communist Party of the Philippines, were no longer plagued by the internecine and bloody struggles of the late 1980s.

Like those with the Muslim insurgents, talks with the National Democratic Front (NDF)—representing the CPP (whose founder, José Maria Sison, has lived in exile at The Hague in the Netherlands since 1987) and the NPA—have occurred in fits and starts since the late 1980s. Complicating matters was the fact that in August 2002, the U.S. labeled the NPA a terrorist organization, with the European Union following suit in 2004, even though Washington never linked the NPA to any foreign group. The NDF broke off the talks and demanded that the label be withdrawn. Sison was put on the terrorist list as well, arrested by Dutch police in August 2007, and charged with ordering three assassinations in the Philippines. He was then ordered released by the Dutch courts while investigations into the allegations were being pursued. The Arroyo government, for its part, has not labeled the NPA a terrorist group, and even though formal talks had stalled, engaged the NDF in informal sessions. Up until the resumption of formal talks in the Norwegian capital of Oslo in 2009, the two sides in principle had agreed to certain steps that would move towards a formal peace deal. These steps would include setting up a joint commission to examine human rights abuses on both sides, and working together for the removal of the NPA, and of Sison, from the U.S. and the EU's list of terrorist organizations. In late September of 2009, Sison's name was struck from the list of terrorists, paving the way for the resumption of peace talks.

Keeping the AFP in Line

Playing subaltern to the United States in the war on terrorism also enables the Philippine military to push its own agenda to the forefront. Under Marcos, the size of the AFP had increased dramatically, from 50,000 to 274,000 (including a paramilitary force of 65,000). With the ouster of the dictator and his shoe-loving wife Imelda in 1986, and with the corresponding decline in U.S. military aid once the bases treaty had been rejected by the Philippine Senate in 1992, the AFP's size was whittled down to 127,000. In 2004 its budget for its army, air force, and navy was less than $1 billion, hardly adequate given the decrepit state of much of its equipment, from aging M-14 and M-16 rifles to outmoded fighter planes. Wages were raised but not nearly enough. Grunts and lower-level officers had a litany of complaints, ranging from meager meal allowances to inadequate clothing and faulty weaponry.

It seems that it isn't tactical intelligence or foreign advisers the AFP needs but sweeping reforms. One factor that saps morale above all is that of financial hijinks at the top. A 2001 study of military corruption conducted by the nonprofit Philippine Center for Investigative Journalism, found that as much as 30 to 50 percent of military funds goes to kickbacks. Widespread malfeasance in high places was in fact one of the major charges leveled against the government by the group of 350 mutinous soldiers, led by junior-grade officers, in the earlier-mentioned failed coup attempt of July 27, 2003. Having failed to inspire mass defections from the ranks and an outpouring of civilians onto the streets to protect them, as was the case in the 1986 "people power" uprising against Marcos, the attempt fizzled, and the officers arrested.

The officers accused their superiors of making money at the expense of the rank and file, by selling government weapons to their enemies and of orchestrating bombings in Mindanao—acts which had been blamed on the MILF but which the MILF refuted—in order to receive anti-terrorist funds from the U.S. While the putsch was universally condemned, the officers' allegations drew widespread sympathy. Even AFP officials admitted to corruption in their ranks. In perhaps the most publicized instance of corruption in the military, former AFP comptroller General Carlos Garcia was found guilty in February of 2009 by a Manila court of perjury in misdeclaring his assets in 2000, which the prosecution contended amounted to more than P300 million, or approximately $6 million, a princely sum for an officer in a service that notoriously underpays its men. In addition, two of his sons were indicted in the U.S. for smuggling $100,00 in cash into the country in 2003. As one local journalist put it, waging war and getting money from the U.S. "is an industry."

In the post-Marcos era, a politicized and demoralized AFP represents a greater threat to the government than either the MILF or the NPA, as shown by the number of coup attempts since 1986, the last two being the July 2003 coup attempt and another one in February of 2006, which shook Arroyo, especially as she had assiduously cultivated her relationship with the military—and which led her to declare a weeklong state of emergency. There was a popular outcry against the decree, with critics denouncing it as a Marcos-era ploy, since the last coup attempt fizzled out apparently even before it could be launched.

The War on Terrorism Terrorizes

The war on terrorism is as much one of words, centered on the label "terrorist." It means, as a character in *Alice in Wonderland* would have it, anything its user chooses it to mean. Marcos always paired "communist" with "subversive," to tar anyone who opposed his regime. Both the U.S. government and Arroyo, by their wholesale labeling blur the distinction between ideologically driven groups like the NPA and the MILF, with their military targets, and a criminal gang like the Abu Sayyaf, to whom Islam and its alleged association with Al Qaeda is simply a cover for mayhem.

What have been the effects of war on terrorism in the Philippines? Rather than improve the lives of those directly affected, it has made them worse. The war itself, especially in Mindanao, with its roots in the Spanish colonial-era conflicts, can be regarded as terroristic. The number of internal refugees ebbs and flows, depending on the state of the ongoing war. Most military encampments lie in civilian areas, putting these residents in danger every time hostilities resume. And the economic costs to both the government and the farmers, workers, and small entrepreneurs have been staggering—from 1975 to 2002, P5 billion to P10 billion (roughly $100 to $200 million) were spent annually on the conflict, monies that could have gone towards social services and infrastructure development in the country's poorest provinces.

A horrifying corollary of Philippine participation in the war on terrorism has been the rise of politically motivated killings in the country since 2001. According to Karapatan, an umbrella group for various Philippine human rights organizations, towards the end of 2009, 1,118 men and women had been summarily executed—"salvaged"—under Gloria Macapagal Arroyo's government. There were 204 cases of desaparecidos, where no body was ever found, and 1,026 cases of torture. Supposedly in compliance with Bush's global war on terror, President Arroyo ratcheted up her government's pressure on the Philippine left, reviving memories of the Marcos dictatorship and its dirty war against the opposition. Human rights groups such as Amnesty International and Human Rights First have criticized the Arroyo government for failing to prevent—and even abetting—such killings. A

2007 report to the UN General Assembly by Special Rapporteur Phillip Alston, based on a fact-finding visit in February of that same year, echoed such criticism.* Alston pointed to two underlying causes for the unchecked murders: the indiscriminate labeling of left-wing groups as "front organizations" for "armed groups whose aim is to destroy democracy," and a government "counter-insurgency strategy" that encourages "the extrajudicial killings of activists and other 'enemies' in certain circumstances." Even the 2006 government-appointed Melo Commission, created precisely to investigate the unexplained killings of activists and journalists, blamed rogue elements in the military for these salvagings, or extrajudicial murders. The Commission took pains to mention Major General Jovito Palparan, whom a number of human-rights organizations accused of orchestrating the extrajudicial killings of anti-government activists wherever he was stationed. Noted the Melo Commission: "There is certainly evidence pointing the finger of suspicion at some elements and personalities in the armed forces, in particular General Palparan, as responsible for an undetermined number of killings, by allowing, tolerating, and even encouraging the killings." Palparan denied being directly responsible for the killings, though he did state "I just inspired the [triggermen]. We're not admitting responsibility here, what I'm saying is these are necessary incidents."

Those assassinated have included pastors, labor leaders, student activists, farmers, workers, and journalists—at least fifty-nine of the latter were killed between 2001 and 2009, because of reasons directly related to their work, according to the Committee to Protect Journalists, which ranks the Philippines as one of the most dangerous places for its profession. As a veteran Manila columnist Luis Teodoro wrote, "The killings are an integral part of the policy to dismantle whatever else remains of the democratic and populist legacies" brought about by the 1986 overthrow of the Marcoses.

On November 23, 2009, the worst case of a political massacre in the recent history of the country took place on the dusty roads of Maguindanao Province, turf of the Ampatuan clan, close political allies of President Macapagal Arroyo—the very same clan whose patriarch, governor Andal Ampatuan, had guaranteed her 2004 electoral victory

---

* See the excerpt from his press release that begins this chapter.

in his province. Close to sixty people were slain by gunmen who had stopped the convoy they were traveling in, and the two or three vehicles that happened to be passing by as well. All the occupants—men, women, and children—were forced to get out of their vehicles and marched to a nearby hilltop, where they were shot. None survived. The bodies were buried in a mass grave, dug up earlier, a backhoe still on the scene, one that apparently belonged to the provincial government. The murdered included thirty journalists—the most killed in one incident in the country, and the worst such case in recent press history globally, according to the Committee to Protect Journalists. They were accompanying the convoy headed to the provincial capital, where the candidacy papers of a potential gubernatorial rival was to be filed, for the 2010 elections. A majority of the victims were women, most of them Muslims. The rival clan, the Mangudadatus, believed that if the party were made up mainly of women, they would not be harmed, as the Koran teaches that they and children should be respected, even in times of conflict.

Certainly contributing to the continuing threat of more human rights abuses was the passage by the Philippine Congress in July of 2007, of the Human Security Act (HSA)—a virtual copy of the U.S. Homeland Security Act. By broadening the government's arrest-and-detention powers, the law seriously undermined civil liberties. With its vague definition of what constitutes "terrorism," HSA in effect criminalized political dissent, e.g., burning an effigy could be seen as a terrorist act. In August of that year, in one of the first instances of the law's application, three visiting women's-rights activists and members of the U.S.-based Gabriela Network, an affiliate of Gabriela Philippines, the nation's largest feminist militant group with party-list representation in Congress, were initially prevented from leaving Manila. Having attended the 10th Women's International Solidarity Affair in the Philippines, the three found themselves on a government watch list due to suspected ties to the Taliban—a nonsensical charge that was later dropped, and the women allowed to depart. It was a chilling exercise in arbitrary detention.

The Cancer of Endemic Corruption

The fact that the worldwide financial meltdown of 2008 didn't affect the Philippines too much was, as it was in 1997, not so much due to the strength of the economy but rather to the relative lack of integration into global financial markets. Philippine banks, having taken steps to strengthen themselves during the 1997 Asian financial crisis and conservative in their lending policies, were not as reliant as U.S. and European banks had been on financial products that turned out to be toxic. Nevertheless, since the United States plays a major part in the economy of the country—in 2007, it was the source of 33 percent of direct foreign investment—the pinch was bound to be felt. While negative growth was avoided, there were layoffs by foreign corporations such as Intel Philippines, and Goodyear Tire & Rubber Company shut down its plant first established in 1950. Additionally, remittances from OFWs, which make up 10 percent of GDP and without which the Philippine economy would be in mortal danger (in 2009, these totaled $17.3 billion), lessened as the recession in such countries as the U.S. and the UK led to the layoffs of foreign workers. And with a global weakening of consumption, exports were expected to decline.

The Philippines spends one-third of its budget just servicing its $54 billion foreign debt (as of the beginning of 2009), monies that could otherwise stimulate the economy and reduce the high levels of poverty—still the best single recruiter of angry young militants—with 44 percent of the population subsisting on $2 a day. Hunger is a daily companion to at least 20 percent of the population. Workers see their purchasing power weaken. In 2009, out of 73 cities globally, Manila ranked 70th in terms of what the ordinary worker's wages could buy. Another factor that bleeds the economy, as noted, has been the policy of militarization to combat insurgency, which has not worked. If it seemed effective during the Huk insurgency of the 1950s, that was due to civil programs such as land resettlement for peasant Huk fighters and the speedy resolution of judicial cases.

But the illness that vitiates the body politic above all is that of corruption. The tremendous amounts of illicit lucre to be gained in elective office and in many of the government-sector jobs has created a culture of impunity, with the result that the term "public service" too often becomes an oxymoron. Manila's most pressing need is to root out corruption in government, a cancer that in the long run not only encourages but wreaks havoc more than any insurgency, and makes junior military officers harbor thoughts of coup d'etat. From the underpaid policeman susceptible to bribes from a motorist who commits a traffic violation to a desk-bound government bureaucrat who discreetly wangles for a commission or kickback to expedite the processing of a contract, corruption is a deeply entrenched fact of government. Ranked by Transparency International in terms of corruptibility, in 2008 the Philippines was 141st out of 180 nations. In contrast, the country's Southeast Asian neighbors, Malaysia, Thailand, and Indonesia, were ranked 47th, 80th, and 126th, respectively.

Two government departments long notorious as places to earn quick and easy money are the Bureau of Internal Revenue (BIR) and the Customs Bureau. According to a World Bank study quoted in a 2003 Philippine Center for Investigative Journalism report into how certain officials at the BIR amassed considerable wealth, half of every tax peso that can be collected is lost to corruption. The government's Department of Finance says that total average annual tax leakage is 240 billion in pesos, or roughly $5.1 billion. The PCIJ report went on to say, "BIR postings are so lucrative and BIR officials so used to tampering [with] official records that they try to delay retirement by 'correcting'— pushing forward—their dates of birth. . . . From 1989 to the first quarter of 2001 alone, 24 BIR personnel have petitioned the Civil Service Commission to change their birth records." Civil service requirements decree enforced retirement at the age of 65.

The losses of revenue from the corruption at Customs are another example of how pervasive this culture of payoffs and kickbacks is, and demonstrate how the burden of taxation falls disproportionately on the average Filipino taxpayer. According to a study made of the trade between the Philippines and China, between 1994 and 2007, every year revealed substantial discrepancies between the value of what China exported to the Philippines and the value declared by the Bureau of Customs of those goods or imports. In 1994, the difference was $181.4 million, or 38.1 percent less than the Chinese valuation. In 2007, the difference was $3.470 billion, or almost 50 percent of what the Chinese declared.

The differences when it comes to Philippine exports to China are even greater. Thus, for 2007, according to export and import manifest forms supplied by Customs and compiled by the government's own National Statistics Office, Philippine exports were valued at $5.715 billion while the Chinese valued the very same goods at $23.12 billion—a whopping difference of $17.405 billion, thrice more than the official Philippine figure. The study concludes that "the value of Philippine exports to China for 1994-2007 were understated by an annual average of 137 percent, while the value of imports of the Philippines were under-stated by an annual average of 46.6 percent." Clearly, when business-men underreport both exports and imports, they save hugely on taxes and tariffs. The undervaluation of foreign products in turn hurts the domestic industry that manufactures the same kind of goods. The footwear, textile, garment and the nascent petrochemical industries are instances where the combination of low tariffs, and smuggling has had a huge negative impact. Nor is the trade with China the largest source of revenue losses. In an analysis of data made under the auspices of the Manila-based University of Asia and the Pacific and conducted by Dr. Victor Abola, an economist, the results indicated that between 1999 and 2001, "the largest trade leakages came from trade with Japan, the United States, Singapore, Korea, Hong Kong, and China," with discrep-ancies ranging from 24.4 percent to 35.9 percent.

Should the revenue losses due to corruption be stemmed consider-ably, the effects on the economy would be obvious: the principal on the country's foreign debt could be paid off in a few years, expenditures on social services could be increased, and incentives for joining the guerril-las in the hills would be diminished.

Food Production

The reliance on agricultural exports, or cash crops, has meant that pro-duction for local consumption and self-sufficiency in food has suffered. Instead, due to trade liberalization, there is an over-reliance on food imports. If the country is to improve its capacity to feed an ever-increasing population, the government must pay attention as well to more efficient agricultural production. According to a 2008 study, once the Philippines became a member of the World Trade Organization in 1995, "the con-tribution of local agriculture to the GDP . . . declined from 20.3 percent in 1995 to 14.9 percent in the first quarter of 2008. Of the 14.2 million hectares alienable and disposable lands, 93 percent or 13 million hectares are classified as agricultural lands and yet agricultural mechanization remains at the tail-end of our neighboring countries. Less than one per-cent of farmers use tractors and power tillers. Only five bags of fertilizer from the recommended eight per hectare is [*sic*] being used." In terms of mechanization and rice production per hectare the Philippines ranked eight and sixth respectively out of eleven Asian countries. The result is one of the lowest productivity rates in Southeast Asia.

By 2009, the country had attained the dubious distinction of being the world's largest importer of rice, with a total of 2.2 metric tons, mostly from Vietnam, Thailand, and the United States, with some shipments from China and Pakistan. The obvious irony in this is that the Philippines used to be an exporter of rice. Moreover, Vietnam and Thailand (the world's largest exporter of rice) learned rice cultivation methods from the Philippine-based International Rice Research Institute (IRRI), which has developed high-yield varieties of rice. It was with some urgency that the Arroyo administration announced plans, also in 2009, to attain self-sufficiency in rice by 2010—though how that would be attained was left unclear.

Creating and aggravating the insufficiencies of domestic food production particularly in the case of rice is the lack of systematic and comprehensive government programs to provide, for instance, credit to small farmers, develop infrastructure such as irrigation, increase government purchase of rice (and thus lessen the importation of rice), and institute a genuine land-reform program to address landlessness.

Changing the Game to Suit the Players

By the end of her term in mid 2010, Gloria Macapagal Arroyo will have been in power as president longer than any other Philippine president, with the notable exception of Ferdinand Marcos, who had defeated her father, President Diosdado Mapacagal, when the latter ran for reelection in 1964. Like Ramos, President Arroyo signaled her desire to continue on as president or chief executive, through a change from the presidential to the parliamentary system of government. The speaker of the House of Representatives, dominated by her supporters, pushed in 2009 for a resolution that the House convene itself—and itself alone—as a Constituent Assembly that would then consider amendments to the 1987 Constitution, ostensibly to override provisions that stand in the way of fast-track economic development, and to switch to the parliamentary system.

There are arguments to be made for a switch to a system that its advocates say is more responsive to Philippine political realities. Under a parliamentary system, for instance, it would have been easier to force Macapagal Arroyo to step down if she had been prime minister rather than president. But political analysts, and public sentiment seems to agree, insist that the Constituent Assembly, or Con-Ass, as it is referred to disparagingly in the media, really aims to convert the current presidential system to a parliamentary one, so that President Arroyo can then serve as prime minister and sidestep the current constitutional ban on a second-term presidency that would require her to vacate the presidency after the May 2010 national elections. The Senate has warned the lower House of its unwavering opposition were the congressmen to push on ahead without the Senate.

And there will most certainly be opposition in the streets were the 1987 Freedom Constitution altered to suit the ambitions of one person. This was made abundantly clear when former President Corazon Aquino, at the age of 76, died from colon cancer on August 1, 2009. The outpouring of grief was overwhelming. People stood in line for three to four hours for a quick glimpse of the late president. It took the funeral procession, attended by an honor guard from the different military branches, nine hours to reach the memorial park where she was buried alongside her late husband Ninoy Aquino, due to the throngs that lined the streets six deep, many bearing her portrait or likeness and signs that attested to the love people bore for her.

The national mourning and the praise heaped on her as she lay in her bier, reminded anyone who needed reminding that the country had not forgotten the pivotal role that their *Tita* Cory (Aunt Cory) had played in replacing the twenty-year regime of Ferdinand and Imelda Marcos with a freewheeling, raucous democracy, however flawed. The public comparison between the recently deceased former president who never wished to extend her stay in Malacañang even by one day, and the sitting president who has made it clear that she does, rendered crystal clear the dismay with which Macapagal Arroyo's tenure, and stature, have been viewed.

That dismay was reflected in the sudden ascent of Cory and Ninoy's son, Noynoy, elected to the Senate in 2004, to being the presidential candidate of the Liberal Party, when Senator Mar Roxas (grandson of Manuel, first president of the Republic), withdrew in his favor and agreed to run for vice president instead. Noynoy is the sentimental favorite to win, and it will be very difficult for any other presidential candidate to match his popularity.

Like Fidel Ramos, realizing that changing the current presidential system to a parliamentary one would be an uphill battle, in late November of 2009, President Macapagal Arroyo filed her candidacy papers, to run for election as congresswoman from her home province of Pampanga—the first president in Philippine history to seek lower office. She would be replacing her son, Congressman Mike Arroyo Jr. This move has triggered intense speculation that she has done so in order to head off any attempt on the part of the next Congress to hold her to account for alleged high crimes and misdemeanors while president, and to spearhead a renewed drive to institute a parliamentary system, so she can then seek the post of prime minister.

Whether the next president and a new Congress will listen to the persistent voices of the electorate for substantial changes in the mode of governance to resemble more faithfully a much more democratic society remains to be seen. Serious, reform-minded legislators would have to go against the grain of special-interest clan politics—in essence, against their own families—no mean feat in a society long accustomed to the transference of power and privilege along blood lines. Many of these elected mandarins are more in tune with Louis XIV's dictum, "L'etat, c'est moi," than with the democratic notion of a government by the people, for the people, and of the people. President Aquino's heart, her *corazon*, was undoubtedly in the right place, but family pressure as much as anything else doomed her land reform program since it left the family's vast Hacienda Luisita untouched.

Nowhere is the hold of clan politics more evident than in Congress, the nation's preeminent legislative body. Ever since the Malolos Congress of 1898, lawmakers have consistently been drawn from the ranks of the Philippine elite. A groundbreaking study conducted by the nonprofit, nonpartisan Philippine Center for Investigative Journalism and published in 2004, *The Rulemakers,* describes the modern Filipino legislator as predominantly male, someone who "has previously held a local government post and is a member of a political family with a sibling, father, or grandfather who has been voted into public office in the past."

A perfect illustration of how political power, once attained, breeds a sense of entitlement is the Cojuangco family, which has had nine members elected to Congress since 1907, with President Cory Cojuangco Aquino representing the zenith of clan power. Her and Ninoy Aquino's son, Noynoy, may yet reclaim that position. (Through him of course are linked two powerful political families, with the Aquinos, as of 2004, having had eight members elected to Congress.) Cory's main rival, Ferdinand Marcos, with his own father having been a local politician, established the Marcoses as a political dynasty, serving as a congressman, then senator, and going on to rule the state for twenty-one years, with Imelda beside him. In a series of musical-chair moves, his heirs are making sure the family remains a prominent player on the political scene. His son, Ferdinand Jr., has served as governor of Ilocos Norte—Marcos's home province, where the late dictator is viewed almost as a deity—and will be running for the Senate in 2010. His sister Imee, having served in Congress, will now run for the governorship vacated by her sibling. And the ruling matriarch Imelda, resilient as ever even at the age of 80, having represented her home district of Leyte as a congresswoman, has filed her candidacy papers for the congressional seat Imee is leaving behind.

There have been positive changes to the almost monopolistic nature of the power structure. The party-list feature, introduced by the 1987 Constitution, has produced cracks in the façade; while party-list representatives are a minority bloc, still, they do bring viewpoints that represent the left as well as segments of society—workers, women, the youth—normally underrepresented in Congress. The party-list solons eschew the trappings of their more conventional colleagues, portraying themselves as non-traditional politicians. Another pressure block is that of the overseas Filipino workers who have registered for the May 2010 elections, numbering approximately 600,000—almost twice the number that registered for the 2004 elections. With a perspective gained from living abroad, they are not as subject to the intense politicking that goes on in the islands in the run-up to the elections and are therefore less likely to feel bound by parochial interests. Candidates who can tap into their discontent would have quite an advantage at the polls.

In the continuing dance between former colonizer and former colony, the United States remains the country's most dominant foreign partner. While the U.S. no longer touts the Philippines as a showcase of democracy, it often invokes what it terms the "special relationship" between the two countries. This is echoed in how Manila reliably follows the lead of Washington when it comes to foreign policy. In both its regional and international involvement, whether through the Association of Southeast Asian Nations (ASEAN) and the Asian Pacific Economic Cooperative (APEC), or the United Nations, the Philippines rarely deviates, if at all, from any given United States position. It was not surprising therefore that in 2002, President Arroyo stepped forward as the first Asian president to endorse the U.S.-initiated Global War on Terror, for which the U.S. designated the Philippines as a major non-NATO ally in 2003. In economic terms, this "special relationship" translates into the U.S. being the Philippines' largest trading partner, with $17 billion worth of trade in 2008, and $6 billion in direct investments. The country is the U.S.'s 31st largest export market and its 37th largest supplier. Starkly put, the challenge is for the Philippine government to forge a more independent foreign policy while maintaining its trading ties with the United States.

One way to do that is to develop wisely and efficiently the natural resources with which the country, like its Southeast Asian neighbors and so many other developing countries, is abundantly blessed. While afflicted, for instance, by deforestation, destruction of its coral reefs, and depletion of rich fishing grounds, the country sits on enormous mineral reserves—gold, copper, nickel, silver, gypsum, among them—said to be one of the world's largest and estimated to be worth at least $840 billion. In addition, off the coast of Palawan Island are believed to lie tremendous natural gas reserves. Given these treasures, there is every reason the country should manage to lift itself out of poverty that has crippled it for so long and that propels millions of its citizens to seek a better life outside its borders. To do that, there has to be a consistent, long-term, and transparent government-funded anti-corruption drive, accompanied by more efficient revenue collection to provide for much-needed government services and to regularly upgrade the country's perennially creaky infrastructure. And the narrow, personalized politics of clan rule—with its roots in the datu system abetted by a procession of colonial rulers—must give way to the rule of the majority rather than the few. Somewhat like its mineral wealth, the country's democratic spirit may at times appear to be buried but it is vast and powerful. That democratic spirit has been tapped into before, most notably in 1896 and in 1986. To harness it on an ongoing basis and transform the nation fundamentally and for the better has always been the challenge faced by the Philippine Republic since its inception.

REFERENCES

CHAPTER 1.

Abu-Lughod, Janet. *Before European Hegemony: The World System A.D. 1250-1350*. New York: Oxford University Press, 1989.

Bergreen, Laurence. *Over the Edge of the World*. New York: William Morrow, 2003.

Blair, Helen Emma, and Robertson, James Alexander. *The Philippine Islands, 1493-1898*. With additional historical notes by Edward Gaylord Bourne. Volume III, 1569-1576; Volume XII, 1601-1604; Volume XIII, 1604-1605; and Volume XXXIII, 1519-1522. Cleveland, Ohio: The Arthur H. Clark Company, 1903-1905.

Constantino, Renato. *A Past Revisited*. Volume 1. Quezon City: Foundation for Nationalist Studies, 1978.

Corpuz, Onofre D. *The Roots of the Filipino Nation*. Volume 1. Quezon City: AKLAHI Foundation, 1989.

———. *The Philippines*. Englewood Cliffs, NJ: Prentice-Hall, Inc., 1966.

Feleo, Anita, ed. *KASAYSAY: The Story of the Filipino People*. Revised edition. Manila: University of Santo Tomás, National Historical Institute, and the Philippine Historical Association, 2001.

Junker, Laura Lee. *Raiding, Trading, and Feasting: The Political Economy of Philippine Chiefdoms*. Honolulu: University of Hawaii Press, 1999.

Patanñe, E.P. *The Philippines in the Sixth to Sixteenth Centuries*. Manila: LSA Press, 1996.

Rafael, Vicente. *Contracting Colonialism: Translation and Christian Conversion in Tagalog Society Under Early Spanish Rule*. Quezon City: Ateneo de Manila University Press, 1988.

Reyes, Pedrito; Grau-Santa Maria, Mercedes; Beyer, Otley H.; De Veyra, Jaime. *Pictorial History of the Philippines*. Quezon City: Capitol Publishing House, 1952.

Scott, William Henry. *Barangay: Sixteenth Century Philippine Culture and Society*. Quezon City: Ateneo de Manila University Press, 1994.

Solheim, Wilhelm G. II. *Archaeology and Culture in Southeast Asia: Unraveling the Nusantao*. Quezon City: University of the Philippines Press, 2006.

Zafra, Nicolas. *Philippine History Through Selected Sources*. Quezon City: Alemar-Phoenix Publishing House, 1967.

CHAPTER 2.

Arcilla, Jose S., S.J. *An Introduction to Philippine History*. Fourth edition. Quezon City: Ateneo de Manila University Press, 1994.

Bergreen, Laurence. *Over the Edge of the World*. New York: William Morrow, 2003.

Blair, Helen Emma, and Robertson, James Alexander. *The Philippine Islands 1493-1898*. With additional notes by Edward Gaylord Bourne. Volume III, 1569-1576; Volume XII, 1602-1604; Volume XXXIII, 1519-1522.

Constantino, Renato. *A Past Revisited*. Volume 1. Quezon City: Foundation for Nationalist Studies, 1978.

Corpuz, Onofre D. *The Roots of the Filipino Nation*. Volume 1. Quezon City: AKLAHI Foundation, 1989.

——. *The Philippines*. Englewood Cliffs, NJ: Prentice-Hall, Inc. 1966.

Junker, Laura Lee. *Raiding, Trading, and Feasting: The Political Economy of Philippine Chiefdoms*. Honolulu: University of Hawai'i Press, 1999.

Reyes, Pedrito; Grau-Santa Maria, Mercedes; Beyer, Otley H.; De Veyra, Jaime. *Pictorial History of the Philippines*. Quezon City: Capitol Publishing House, 1952.

Schumacher, John N. *The Propaganda Movement: 1880-1895*. Manila: Solidaridad Publishing House, 1973.

Scott, James C. *Seeing Like a State: How Certain Schemes to Improve the Human Condition Have Failed*. New Haven: Yale University Press, 1998.

Warren, James Francis. *The Sulu Zone: 1768-1898*. Second edition. Singapore: National University of Singapore Press, 2007.

Zafra, Nicolas. *Philippine History Through Selected Sources*. Quezon City: Alemar-Phoenix Publishing House, 1967.

ARTICLES

Churchill, Malcolm H. "Louisiana History and Early Filipino Settlement: Searching for the Story." No. 2, 27, *Bulletin of the American Historical Collection*, 1999.

Hearn, Lafcadio. "St. Malo Story." *Harper's Weekly*, March 31, 1883.

Roces, Alejandro R. "Roses and Thorns." *The Philippine Star*, January 9, 2010.

CHAPTER 3.

Agoncillo, Teodoro A. *The Revolt of the Masses*. Quezon City: University of the Philippines Press, 1956.

Anderson, Benedict. *Under Three Flags: Anachronism and the Anti-Colonial Imagination*. London and New York: Verso Books, 2005.

Arcilla, Jose S., S.J. *An Introduction to Philippine History*. Fourth edition. Quezon City: Ateneo de Manila University Press, 1994.

Constantino, Renato. *A Past Revisited*. Vol. 1. Quezon City: Foundation for Nationalist Studies, 1978.

Corpuz, Onofre D. *The Roots of the Filipino Nation*. Vols. 1 & 2. Quezon City: AKLAHI Foundation, 1989.

Feleo, Anita, ed. *KASAYSAY: The Story of the Filipino People*. Manila: University of Santo Tomas, National Historical Institute, and the Philippine Historical Association, 2001. Rev. ed.

Guardiola, Juan, ed. *Filipinas. Arte, identitad y discurso postcolonial*. Madrid: Ministerio de Cultura, 2008.

Ileto, Reynaldo. *Filipinos and Their Revolution: Event, Discourse, and Historiography*. Quezon City: Ateneo de Manila University Press, 1998.

Joaquin, Nick. *A Question of Heroes*. Pasig City: Anvil Publishing, 2005.

Kalaw-Tirol, Lorna, ed. *The World of 1896*. Makati City and Quezon City: Bookmark, Inc. and Ateneo de Manila University, 1998.

Martinez-Sicat, MA. Teresa & Naida V. Rivera, eds. *Affirming the Filipino: An Anthology of Philippine Literature*. Quezon City: University of the Philippines, Department of English and Comparative Literature, 2004.

Ocampo, Ambeth. *Meaning and History: The Rizal Lectures*. Manila: Anvil Publishing, 2001.

Pomeroy, William J. *The Philippines: Colonialism, Collaboration, and Resistance!* New York: International Publishers, 1992.

Rizal, José. *Noli Me Tangere.* Translated by Harold Augenbraum. New York and London: Penguin Classics, 2006.

Schumacher, John N. *The Propaganda Movement: 1880-1895.* Manila: Solidaridad Publishing House, 1973.

Scott, James C. *Seeing Like a State: How Certain Schemes to Improve the Human Condition Have Failed.* New Haven: Yale University Press, 1998.

Zafra, Nicolas. *Philippine History Through Selected Sources.* Quezon City: Alemar-Phoenix Publishing House, 1967.

CHAPTER 4.

Arcilla, Jose S., S.J. *An Introduction to Philippine History.* Fourth edition. Quezon City: Ateneo de Manila University Press, 1994.

Bulosan, Carlos. *America Is in the Heart.* Introduction by Carey McWilliams. Seattle and London: University of Washington Press, 2003.

Connaughton, Richard. *MacArthur and Defeat in the Philippines.* New York: The Overlook Press, 2001.

Constantino, Renato. *The Miseducation of the Filipino.* Quezon City: Foundation for Nationalist Studies, 1982.

———. *The Philippines: The Continuing Past.* Vol. II. Quezon City: Foundation for Nationalist Studies, 1978.

Friend, Theodore. *Between Two Empires.* New Haven and London: Yale University Press, 1965.

Go, Julian. *American Empire and the Politics of Meaning.* Durham, North Carolina: Duke University Press, 2008.

Graff, Henry, ed. *American Imperialism and the Philippine Insurrection.* Boston: Little, Brown and Company, 1969.

Ileto, Reynaldo. *Filipinos and Their Revolution: Event, Discourse, and Historiography.* Quezon City: Ateneo de Manila University Press, 1998.

———. *Pasyon and Revolution: Popular Movements in the Philippines, 1840-1910.* Quezon City: Ateneo de Manila University press, 1979.

Kramer, Paul A. *The Blood of Government: Race, Empire, the United States, and the Philippines.* Chapel Hill, NC: University of North Carolina Press, 2008.

Pabico, Rufino. *The Exiled Government: The Philippine Commonwealth in the United States During the Second World War*. Amherst, New York: Humanities Books, 2006.

Pomeroy, William J. *The Philippines: Colonialism, Collaboration, and Resistance!* New York: International Publishers, 1992.

Schirmer, Daniel Boone. *Republic or Empire: American Resistance to the Philippine War*. Cambridge, Mass.: Schenkman Publishing Co., 1972.

———— & Shalom, Stephen, eds. *The Philippines Reader*. Boston: South End Press, 1987.

Shaw, Angel Velasco & Francia, Luis H., eds. *Vestiges of War: The Philippine-American War and the Aftermath of an Imperial Dream, 1899-1999*. New York: New York University Press, 2002.

Takaki, Ronald. *Strangers from a Different Shore: A History of Asian Americans*. Boston: Little, Brown, 1998.

Wolff, Leon. *Little Brown Brother: How the United States Purchased and Pacified the Philippines*. New York: Oxford University Press, 1991.

Yu-Jose, Lydia. *Japan Views the Philippines*. Quezon City: Ateneo de Manila University Press, 1999.

Zafra, Nicolas. *Philippine History Through Selected Sources*. Quezon City: Alemar-Phoenix Publishing House, 1967.

Zwick, Jim. *Mark Twain's Weapons of Satire: Anti-Imperialist Writings on the Philippine-American War*. Syracuse, New York: Syracuse University Press, 1992.

CHAPTER 5.

Abaya, Hernando. *Betrayal in the Philippines*. New York, A.A. Wyn, Inc., 1946.

Abinales, Patricio N. & Amoroso, Donna J. *State and Society in the Philippines*. New York: Rowman & Littlefield, 2005.

Bonner, Raymond. *Waltzing with a Dictator: The Marcoses and the Making of American Policy*. New York: Times Books, 1987.

Bresnan, John, ed. *Crisis in the Philippines: The Marcos Era and Beyond*. Princeton, NJ: Princeton University Press, 1986.

Constantino, Renato. *The Miseducation of the Filipino*. Quezon City: Foundation for Nationalist Studies, 1982.

————. *The Philippines: The Continuing Past*. Vol. II. Quezon City: Foundation for Nationalist Studies, 1978.

Corpuz, Onofre D. *The Roots of the Filipino Nation.* Volume II. Quezon City: AKLAHI Foundation, Inc. 1989.

Hamilton-Paterson, James. *America's Boy: The Marcoses and the Philippines.* London and Manila: Granta Books and Anvil Publishing, 1998.

Lacaba, José F. *Days of Disquiet, Nights of Rage: The First Quarter Storm and Related Events.* Manila: Anvil Publishing, 2003.

Pomeroy, William J. *The Philippines: Colonialism, Collaboration, and Resistance!* New York: International Publishers, 1992.

Schirmer, Daniel Boone & Shalom, Stephen, eds. *The Philippines Reader.* Boston: South End Press, 1987.

Zafra, Nicolas. *Philippine History Through Selected Sources.* Quezon City: Alemar-Phoenix Publishing House, 1967.

CHAPTER 6.

Abinales, Patricio N. & Amoroso, Donna J. *State and Society in the Philippines.* New York: Rowman & Littlefield, 2005.

Bonner, Raymond. *Waltzing with a Dictator: The Marcoses and the Making of American Policy.* New York: Times Books, 1987.

Bresnan, John, ed. *Crisis in the Philippines: The Marcos Era and Beyond.* Princeton, NJ: Princeton University Press, 1986.

Coronel, Sheila S.; Chua, Yvonne T.; Rimban, Luz; & Cruz, Booma B. *The Rulemakers: How the Wealthy and the Well-Born Dominate Congress.* Quezon City: Philippine Center for Investigative Journalism, 2004.

Francia, Luis H. *Memories of Overdevelopment: Reviews and Essays of Two Decades.* Pasig City, Metro Manila: Anvil Publishing, 1998.

Hamilton-Paterson, James. *America's Boy: The Marcoses and the Philippines.* London and Manila: Granta Books and Anvil Publishing, 1998.

Joaquin, Nick. *A Question of Heroes.* Pasig City: Anvil Publishing, 2005.

———. *Quartet of the Tiger Moon: Scenes from the People Power Apocalypse.* Manila: Book Stop, 1986.

Nadeau, Kathleen. *The History of the Philippines.* Histories of Modern Nations series. Westport, Connecticut and London: Greenwood Press, 2008.

Pomeroy, William J. *The Philippines: Colonialism, Collaboration, and Resistance!* New York: International Publishers, 1992.

Schirmer, Daniel Boone & Shalom, Stephen, eds. *The Philippines Reader.* Boston: South End Press, 1987.

Steinberg, David Joel. *The Philippines: A Singular and a Plural Place.* Boulder, Colorado: Westview Press, 2000.

ARTICLES

Bello, Walden. "Afterthoughts: Cory and her Creditors." Inquirer.net, of the *Philippine Daily Inquirer*, August 12, 2009.

CHAPTER 7.

Abinales, Patricio N. & Amoroso, Donna J. *State and Society in the Philippines.* Lanham, MD: Rowman and Littlefield Publishers, 2005.

Coronel, Sheila S.; Chua, Yvonne T.; Rimban, Luz; & Cruz, Booma B. *The Rulemakers: How the Wealthy and the Well-Born Dominate Congress.* Quezon City: Philippine Center for Investigative Journalism, 2004.

Francia, Luis H. *Memories of Overdevelopment: Reviews and Essays of Two Decades.* Pasig City, Metro Manila: Anvil Publishing, 1998.

Karapatan: Alliance for the Advancement of People's Rights. *2009 Year-end Report on the Human Rights Situation in the Philippines.* Quezon City: Karapatan, 2009.

Lance, Peter. *Triple Cross.* New York and Los Angeles: Regan, HarperCollins, 2006.

McCoy, Alfred W. *An Anarchy of Families: State and Family in the Philippines.* Quezon City: Ateneo de Manila University Press, 1994.

Nadeau, Kathleen. *The History of the Philippines.* Histories of Modern Nations series. Westport, Connecticut and London: Greenfield Press, 2008.

Steinberg, David Joel. *The Philippines: A Singular and a Plural Place.* Boulder, CO: Westview Press, 2000.

ARTICLES

Abola, Victor A. "Source of Leakages in BOC Collections." Paper, March 2004. Manila: Center for Research and Communications, University of Asia and the Pacific.

Bacalla, Tess. "BIR Officials Amass Unexplained Wealth." May 12-14, 2003. Manila: Philippine Center for Investigative Journalism, *http://www.pcij.org/stories/2003/bir.html*

Burgonio, T. J. "Hyatt 10 Marks 4th, Prays for Last Anniversary." *The Philippine Daily Inquirer*, July 7, 2009.

Conde, Carlos. "Toll Rises to 46 in Philippine Election Unrest." *The New York Times*, November 25, 2009.

———. "Marcos Seeks Seat in Philippine Congress." *The New York Times*, December 3, 2009.

Cosico, Finesa. "Prometheus Bound: Modernizing Agriculture." *The Manila Times*, June 5, 2008.

Cruz, Booma B. "Did Mike Arroyo Fund Postelection 'Special Operations' in Lanao?" October 10, 2005. Manila: Philippine Center for Investigative Journalism, *http://www.pcij.org/stories /2005/lanao.html*

DeParle, Jason. "A Good Provider Is One Who Leaves." *The New York Times Magazine*, April 22, 2007.

Francia, Luis H. "Local Is Global: Bomb Plots in Manila, Mayhem in Manhattan." *The Village Voice*, September 25, 2001.

———. "U.S. Troops in the Philippines: War on Terrorism or Retaking a Choice Outpost?" *The Village Voice*, February 19, 2002.

———. "Meanwhile, in Manila . . ." *The Nation*, October 27, 2003.

———. "Global War on Terror: The Philippines." *The Nation*, December 31, 2007.

Hu, Pei. "Philippines Considers General Jovito Palparan for Dangerous Drug Board." Impunity Watch Asia, February 5, 2009. *www.impunitywatch.com/impunity_watch_asia/2009/02*

Mydans, Seth. "Resisting Birth Control, the Philippines Grows Crowded." *The New York Times*, March 21, 2003.

Pagaduan-Araullo, Carol. "The Crux of the Moro Problem." *Business World*, August 17-18, 2007.

WEBSITES

Karapatan: Alliance for the Advancement of People's Rights, *http://www.karapatan.org*

Philippine Center for Investigative Journalism: *http://www.pcij.org*

Philippine government statistics: *http://www.census.gov.ph/data*

Impunity Watch Asia: *www.impunitywatch.com/impunity_watch_asia*

GLOSSARY

FILIPINO TERMS

Aeta. Also known as *Agta*, *Ita*, *Ati*, and to the Spanish as *Negritos*, characterized by short stature, dark pigmentation, and curly or kinky hair, these indigenous groups are descended from the Australoids, one of two discrete movements of people that over time dispersed through Southeast Asia, the other movement being that of the Austronesians.

Alipin. In pre-colonial Philippines, these were slaves occupying the bottom rung of the social structure, either as *namamahay*, house-owning slaves, or *sagigilid*, slaves who lived at the periphery of their master's household.

Ambahan. A form of poetry of the Hanunoo Mangyan tribe of Mindoro Island inscribed on bamboo in *baybayin*, the pre-Hispanic script.

Anito. An idol to which pre-colonial shrines were often dedicated.

Anting-anting. Amulets used to ward off misfortune, the evil eye, and demonic spirits.

Aswang. In folklore, a malevolent inhabitant of the netherworld that can assume different forms to terrorize humans and believed to eat their flesh.

Babaylan. In the Visayas, a shaman and seer who could be male or female and was believed to have otherworldly connections; known as *katolonan* in the Tagalog region and *mumbaki* to the highlanders of Luzon.

Balangay/balanghai. Seafaring vessels outfitted with innovative bamboo outriggers, devised about 4000 B.C.E., that balance the shallow-draft vessel to navigate smoothly and speedily over water, enabling major outmigrations by water.

Balikatan. Literally "shoulder-to-shoulder"; joint exercises between U.S. and Philippine troops that have taken place since 2002 as part of the Global War on Terror.

Barangay. Village or settlement, named after the *balangay*, the outriggered seafaring vessels of the pre-colonial Philippines, on which a family or clan traveled; the smallest politico-social unit, consisting usually of thirty to one hundred houses, with from one hundred to five hundred persons.

Barkada. A tightly knit circle of friends whose loyalty to one another can be as strong as family ties.

Batasan Pambansa. National Assembly that replaced the bicameral Congress under the martial law regime of Ferdinand and Imelda Marcos.

Bathala May Kapal. The supreme deity for the Tagalogs; from the Sanskrit word *Batthara*, meaning noble lord; comparable to Laon for the Visayans and Kabunian for the Igorots.

Bayan. Country or nation or town.

Bayani. Hero or heroine.

Bayanihan. Communal solidarity; the tradition of shared labor.

Baybayin. The native script, influenced by Sanskrit and Arabic, in use in pre-colonial Philippines; essentially consisting, with variations in alphabet according to the region, of twenty letters.

Bolo. A local machete.

Bulul. To the Ifugao, an Igorot tribe, a guardian deity, represented by carved wooden icons, that watched over rice granaries and were thought to increase the supply of stored grain.

Dagdag, bawas. Addition and subtraction surreptitiously done, after ballots have been cast, to influence election outcomes.

Dap-ay. An open-air community space where Igorot elders gather to discuss pressing community issues.

Datu. Chief; the head of the *barangay*.

Diwata. Muse, nymph, fairy, or deity; from the Sanskrit *deva*.

Duwende. A mischievous being, similar to a leprechaun or hobgoblin; from the Spanish *duende*.

Gugu. An earlier version of gook, and a corruption of the *Tagalog gago*, meaning idiot or simpleton; used by U.S. soldiers during the 1899 Philippine-American War to denigrate Filipinos.

Hukbo ng Bayan Laban sa Hapon. The Anti-Japanese People's Army, otherwise known as the Huks, organized in March of 1942 to constitute the military arm of the Partidong Komunista ng Pilipinas (Philippine Communist Party); after the war, renamed to *Hukbo Magpalaya ng Bayan* (HMB), or People's Liberation Army.

Igorot. The collective term for the different mountain tribes of the Cordillera region in northern Luzon.

Ilagas. A Visayan word meaning "rats," referring to private armies formed by Christian politicians in Mindanao in the 1970s to counter those of the Muslims, or *Moros*, called the Black Shirts, and, in one case, the Barracudas.

Jueteng. A very popular and illegal numbers game controlled by criminal syndicates, often with ties to the local political establishment.

Kabataan Makabayan (KM). Nationalist Youth, a radical student group founded by José Maria Sison in 1964, who went on to found in 1968 the Communist Party of the Philippines (CPP), and in 1969, co-founded with Bernabe Buscayno the New People's Army (NPA), the CPP's military arm.

Karakoas. Or *prahus*, war *balangays* outfitted with sails and platforms above the outriggers upon which as many as a hundred warriors could stand.

Kasamas. Sharecroppers that worked for landowners in exchange for a share in the harvest; companions; comrades.

Katipunan. "Society" or "Association," often used as shorthand for the 19th-century revolutionary organization, the *KKK,* or *Kataastasang Kagalagalangan Katipunan ng Mga Anak ng Bayan* (the Highest, Most Honorable Society of the Sons and Daughters of the Nation).

Katolonan. The Tagalog equivalent of the *babaylan.*

Kilusan Bagong Lipunan (KBL). The New Society Movement, a political party established by Ferdinand Marcos to spearhead his remaking of Philippine society under martial law.

Laban. A Tagalog word meaning "fight"; the political party formed by Senator Benigno Aquino Jr. in 1978 while a political prisoner of the Marcos regime.

Lakas ng Tao. The People Power Party, founded by Fidel Ramos, to capitalize on the success of the 1986 People Power uprising that forced the Marcoses into exile.

Lantaka. In pre-colonial Philippines, a bronze cannon that was often mounted on swivels.

Maganda. Beautiful; the first woman in the Tagalog creation myth, emerging fully formed and at the same time as *Malakas,* or Strength, the first male.

Magdalo. A faction of the Katipunan that was pro-Emilio Aguinaldo.

Magdiwang. A faction of the Katipunan that was pro-Andrés Bonifacio.

Maginoo. Gentleman; in pre-Hispanic times, connoted nobility and was the class to which the *datu* belonged.

Maharlika. Noble, aristocratic followers of the *datu* who functioned roughly as knights did for a king.

Mahirap. The poor; also means difficult.

Malakas. See *Maganda.*

Manananggal. A fly-by-night ghoul that hides its lower body in a secret place while the other half searches for a victim, preferably a pregnant woman whose fetus it craves.

Manong. Older brother, from the Spanish *hermano;* refers to the male Filipino immigrants who formed mostly bachelor societies in the U.S. until the end of World War II; provided labor for farms and canneries in Hawai'i and the West Coast starting in 1906.

Ma-Yi. The Chinese name for the island of Mindoro and by extension for the Philippines.

Mumbaki. Shaman; the Igorot counterpart of the Visayan *babaylan* and the Tagalog *Katolonan.*

Namamahay. "One who keeps house"; a type of *alipin,* or slave, who had his or her own house but could be called upon to serve the master to pay off a debt.

Nayon. Barrio or hamlet, outside town; during the Spanish colonial era, referred to small groups of inhabitants who lived in a spirit of cooperation and harmony (*bayanihan*), and usually had a village elder to shape communal policies and adjudicate conflicts; life in the *nayon* often combined traditional and Hispanic mores.

Nono. Or *nuno.* Animist spirit.

Palabas. During political campaigns, spectacles that in addition to campaign speeches include glitzy entertainment for the crowd.

Partido ng Bayan (PnB). Party of the Nation, a short-lived coalition of various left-wing groups that fielded candidates in the post-Marcos 1987 elections.

Partidong Komunista ng Pilipinas (PKP). Philippine Communist Party, founded in 1930.

Prahus. See *karakoas.*

Sagigilid. "On the edge or periphery"; a type of *alipin,* or slave, who formed part of the master's household and was expected to render service on a daily basis.

Sakdal. "Accusation" or "indictment"; the name of a movement and later political party formed by Benigno Ramos in 1930 that was anti-colonial and accused the native leaders of betraying the nationalist cause.

Salakot. A conical shaped hat made of natural fiber.

Sandugo. "One blood"; a rite that simulated blood ties and established an alliance between two *datus* of different *barangays,* or between the Spanish and the datus.

Shariah. Islamic law.

Tagalog. "Of the river"; the ethnic group predominant in metropolitan Manila, parts of Central and Southern Luzon and whose language is a branch of the Austronesian language tree, the dominant source of the Philippine's seven other major tongues—Cebuano, Hiligaynon, Waray, Ilocano, Pangasinan, Bicolano, and Kapampangan. (Austronesians were one of two discrete movements of people that over time dispersed through Southeast Asia.) Tagalog is the principal basis of the national tongue, Pilipino.

Tao. Person.

Timawa. Freemen; followers of the *datu* who rendered service primarily in non-military ways.

Trapo. Rag; a pejorative term for politicians, a rough acronym of TRAditional and POlitician.

Ulama. A Muslim community.

Utang na loob. Debt of the inner self; a social virtue, whereby someone who has benefited significantly from someone's beneficence or intervention is in that person's debt and must acknowledge it in tangible ways.

Spanish Terms

Abajo de las campanas. "Under the bells"; the new settlement pattern under Spanish rule was partly determined by the idea that every resident should live within hearing distance of the church bells so that they could attend Mass regularly and respond to a call to arms when necessary.

Alcalde mayor. Provincial governor; held by a Spaniard answerable only to Manila.

Alguacil. Judge, in charge of peace and order of the *ayuntamientos*, or metropolitan districts.

Ayuntamientos. In modern parlance, these would be metropolitan districts, governed by two *alcaldes en ordinario*, or magistrates, elected by Spanish residents; a city council; an *alguacil*, or judge, in charge of peace and order; and a scrivener or record-keeper.

Azucareras. Large-scale sugar refineries that in the late nineteenth-century caused agrarian upheaval and created a class of seasonal farm laborers called *sacadas*.

Barrio. Small habitation outside of town.

Cabecerias de barangay. An agglomeration of barangays, each consisting approximately of forty to fifty families and headed by a *cabeza de barangay*.

Cabeza de barangay. Barangay chief and head of the *cabeceria de barangay* or barangays that constituted a municipality; traditionally drawn from pre-Hispanic *datu* families but over time appointed by the municipal government.

Catolica cerrada. Literally, a closed Catholic; a devout and deeply conservative Catholic; a term used to refer to President Corazon Aquino

Consejo de Administración. Administration Council, an advisory body to the Governor General.

Cortes. The Spanish parliament, representation in which was a key demand of Filipino reformers.

Creoles. See *Insulares*.

Desaparecidos. "The disappeared," first used in Latin America to refer to victims of extrajudicial killings.

Doctrina. Mission station or area in which a friar was responsible for the religious indoctrination of its inhabitants.

Encomendero. From *encomendar*, meaning "to entrust"; the Spanish head of an *encomienda* who was responsible for its inhabitants and had the power to collect tribute and to expect unpaid labor from them.

Encomienda. A system adopted in the Spanish colonies in which an *encomendero* was entrusted a number of natives living within a specific geographic area; it was usually the reward for military men who had participated in the conquest of a colony.

Filibustero. One who filibusters; a subversive working to emancipate the colony from Spanish rule.

Gobernadorcillo. The town mayor and the highest position open to the Filipino; he served the colonial state, collecting tributes and mobilizing labor for government projects.

Guardia Civil. Civil Guard; notorious for abuse of power and for manhandling villagers who did not display the proper attitude of obedience.

Ilustrados. "Enlightened Ones"; Filipinos who were members of the rising haute bourgeoisie and had the means to go abroad for education or political exile.

Indio. Indian, the Spanish term for the indigenous populations they colonized.

Inquilinos. Natives who had the means to sublet their land leases to tenant farmers.

Insulares. Philippine-born Spaniards, distinguished from the *peninsulares*, or those born in Spain; also referred to as *Creoles*.

Isla de Ladrones. Island of Thieves, the name given by Magellan to what later was renamed to the Marianas and is now present-day Guam.

Junta de Autoridades. Board of Authorities, an advisory body to the Governor General.

Leyes de Indias. Laws and decrees to govern the colonies, enacted by the Council of the Indies on behalf of the throne.

Moro. Muslim or Moor.

Moro-moros. Highly popular costume dramas with predictable endings, where the Moros are archetypal villains and the Christians are virtuous heroes.

Municipio. Municipality; town hall.

Obras pias. Charitable organizations that also functioned as commercial banks.

Patronato Real. An agreement between the pope and the Spanish crown that gave the Spanish monarch and colonial authorities power over the clergy and churches in Spanish colonies.

Pensionados. Pensioners; Filipino scholars drawn mostly from middle- to upper-middle-class families sent to earn university degrees in the United States under a program set up in 1903. The pensionados in turn were required to return and work as civil servants for the colonial government.

Peninsulares. Spaniards living in the Philippines who were born in Spain, as distinguished from the *Insulares,* or Philippine-born Spaniards.

Pintados. Painted ones; tattooed warriors from the Visayas, the central Philippine islands; the number and intricacy of a man's tattoos signaled his strength and abilities as a fighter.

Polos y servicios. The labor required for forty days each year of men between the ages of 16 and 60, later reduced to 15 days in the nineteenth century; services included servant work, the supply of foodstuffs, shipbuilding, and military service.

Principalia. Power-holders; officials that were drawn at the outset from the ranks of the pre-Hispanic ruling families and who mediated between the colonizer and the native population.

Real Audiencia. The Spanish colonial legislative-judicial body that sought to enforce royal decrees and to oversee the office of the Governor General.

Reconcentrado. The policy of resettling and hamletting used by the Spanish as a counterinsurgency tactic during the Cuban Revolution of 1895, and adopted by the American army during the 1899 Philippine-American War.

Reconquista. Reconquest; period during which the Catholic kingdoms of Spain united under Ferdinand and Isabella to drive out the Moors from the Iberian peninsula, finally succeeding in 1492.

Reducción. A resettlement program initiated by the Spanish wherein a large number of *barangays* were consolidated to form *pueblos* and facilitate administrative control.

Sacadas. Extractors, or seasonal laborers that migrated to different plantations during the harvest season; created with the development in the late nineteenth-century of *azucareras,* large-scale sugar refineries.

Sangley. From the Chinese "to trade"; used as a generic term for the Chinese residing in the Philippines during the Spanish era.

Santo Niño. The Holy Infant Jesus, a statue of which Magellan gave the queen of Cebu in 1521.

Sitios. Small communities outside of town centers; similar, on a smaller scale, to the barrio.

Visita. Periodic visits by the parish priest to *barrios* and *sitios,* communities outside of towns, to say mass and teach catechism.

INDEX

Liga Filipina, La, 120–22
Liga, La, 125
Limahong, 60
line of demarcation, 51
Little Brown Brother, 165
Loarca, Miguel de *(Relación de las Islas Filipinas)*, 57
Loaysa, Francisco García Jofre de, 55
López family, 216, 239
López, Fernando, 220
Low Intensity Conflict (LIC), 197
Lozada, Rodolfo, 306
Lugar, Richard, 254
Luna, Antonio, founder and editor of *La Independencia*,140; as general, 147–68
Luna, Juan, 118
Luzones, 29

Mabini, Apolinario, 159, 162; as Aguinaldo's political advisor, 140; member of Rizal's La Liga Filipina, 140; opposition to constitution, 142; guerilla warfare, 147; exile, 150; death, 151
Macapagal Arroyo, Gloria, 291, 304; ceasefire agreement with MILF, 299–300; pre-president years, swearing in, 303; election rigging, 304–7; endorses Bush Admin. war on terror, 307; changing Philippine governmental system, 320–24; corruption scandals, 306; run for congresswoman, 322
Macapagal, Diosdado, 211, 216–18, 304
MacArthur, Douglas, 175, 196, 237; resignation, 157; money from Philippines, 180; return to Philippines, 184; ties to pre-war Philippine elite, 193, 201; Manila Hotel, 201
Maganda, 232
Magellan, Ferdinand, 29, 51, 54–55; description of first voyage, 52
maginoo, 32, 33
Magsaysay men, loss in 1959 elections, 215
Magsaysay, Ramón, 206–7, 249, 257; and CIA backing, 208; death, 211
maharlika, 10, 32, 33, 224, 257
mahirap, 300

Makabayang Katipunan ng Mga Pilipino (MaKaPili), 183
Malakas, 232
Malayan National Liberation Army (MNLA), 197
Malolos Congress, 142–43, 144, 150, 159, 271
Malvar, General, 153, 154, 157
Manalo, Felix, 298
Manapat, Ricardo, 242
Manchuria Province, 178
Manglapus, Raul, 272
Manila, engine of early trade, 74–82; free and open port in 1789 and onwards, 78–79; population growth, 78; invasion of by British East India Company, 85–86; fall to Japan, 180; declared open city, 179; 1941 bombing of by Japan, 179; devastation of, 185. *See also* Maynila
Manila Chronicle, 229
Manila Electric Company, or Meralco, 215
Manila Hotel, 268
Manilamen, 76
manong, 170
Manunggul Cave, 38. *See also* Tabon Cave
Manunggul Jar, 38. *See also* Tabon Cave
Mao Tse-tung, 9
Marcos, declaration of martial law, 226
Marcos, Ferdinand Jr., 323
Marcos, Ferdinand, renaming of Philippines, 10; birth, 219; early years, 219; rule before martial law, 219–226; martial law, 229–39; film biography, *Iginuhit ng Tadhana*(Destined by Fate), 232; writings, 232; increase military aid from Pentagon, 234; costs of martial law, 239–45; authenticity of war medals, 256; coup against, 259; fleeing, 259; storming palace of, 261; recovering loot from, 265–66; Kilusan Bagong Lipunan (New Society Movement), 282; burial request by Imelda, 301; mausoleum, 301
Marcos, Imee, 323
Marcos, Imelda Romualdez, 219, 236,